Baseball on Maryland's
Eastern Shore, 1866–1950

Baseball on Maryland's Eastern Shore, 1866–1950

Marty Payne

McFarland & Company, Inc., Publishers
Jefferson, North Carolina

ISBN (print) 978-1-4766-9218-0
ISBN (ebook) 978-1-4766-5033-3

LIBRARY OF CONGRESS AND BRITISH LIBRARY
CATALOGUING DATA ARE AVAILABLE

Library of Congress Control Number 2023040502

© 2023 Marty Payne. All rights reserved

No part of this book may be reproduced or transmitted in any form or by any means, electronic or mechanical, including photocopying or recording, or by any information storage and retrieval system, without permission in writing from the publisher.

On the cover: "The Hero" (Nabb Research Center/Wicomico Historical Society); background map of Maryland, 1900 (Jim Pruitt/Shutterstock)

Printed in the United States of America

*McFarland & Company, Inc., Publishers
Box 611, Jefferson, North Carolina 28640
www.mcfarlandpub.com*

Table of Contents

Acknowledgments	vii
Preface	1
Introduction	3

Part I—Frost Out of the Hands

1. Before the Shore	7
2. The First Pitch	11
3. Baseball Prevails	22
4. Grass in the Springtime	33
5. The Bushes Blossom	44
6. For the Almighty Dollar	59
7. End of an Era	77

Part II—The Baby Loop

8. No Town Too Small	93
9. The Eyes of Landis	104
10. Umpire Uprising	118
11. Chaos	124
12. Promise Kept	131
13. Transition	134

Part III—Heyday

14. Another League	145
15. Wonder Club	148
16. Secret Deal	158
17. Fog, Tomatoes, and Rabbits	166
18. Be Careful What You Wish For	171

Part IV—G.I. Jitters

19. Will Greenville Yield?	179
20. Watermelon, Skunks, and More Tomatoes	191
21. And Take Your Batboy with You	198
Afterword	207
Appendix A: Selected Biographical Sketches	209
Appendix B: Players and Umpires	222
Appendix C: Eastern Shore League Standings, 1922–1949	226
Chapter Notes	229
Bibliography	243
Index	247

Acknowledgments

Many have done their part to preserve the history of baseball on the Eastern Shore of Maryland. Ed Nichols of the *Salisbury Times* did much to chronicle the minor leagues, as has Dan Tabler. Hurtt Dehringer focused on the Chestertown area and Washington College, and included the 19th century in his research. Bill Perry and Barry Sparks wrote often over the years of their own or others' memories of the 1930s and 1940s. Bill Mowbray did the same and contributed the pioneering *Eastern Shore Baseball League*. Mike Lambert has contributed his photo and artifact book, *Eastern Shore League*.

The Eastern Shore Baseball Hall of Fame in Salisbury, Maryland, is dedicated to the preservation of the history of Eastern Shore baseball through their exhibits and outreach. Curators Charlie and Debbie Silcott and the board helped in piecing together and understanding the minor league era in particular. Private collectors Donnie Davidson and Mike Lambert have absorbed their knowledge through decades of collecting artifacts and documents. From Donnie I learned not to underestimate what knowledge you might glean from an old ticket stub, program, or seat cushion. Ralph Deaton and Dr. Kirkland Hall are preserving African American baseball on the Shore and contemporary articles have been written in local newspapers on the subject.

Melinda McPeek, formerly of the Nabb Research Center of Salisbury University, was another invaluable source of assistance. The center's efforts to collect and preserve the history of baseball in the region brought photos, documents and articles out into the public eye, and provided a clearer picture of activities on the southern peninsula. Melinda also provided a thorough and formative reading of the manuscript. Peggy Morey and the Talbot County Historical Society provided a file instrumental to understanding the Eastern Shore League in the 1930s. The Federalsburg Historical Society has a permanent baseball display, and Dickie Wheatley delivered a file that provided needed insight on the operations of independent and Class D town teams. And a word of acknowledgment to Ann Phillips, formerly of the Dorchester Historical Society, for providing events and displays that allowed a forum for local baseball historians and enthusiasts. Loretta Walls of the Jimmie Foxx Museum has always been an enthusiastic supporter of Eastern Shore baseball history over the years, and thanks to Jim Gates and Cassidy Lent of the National Baseball Hall of Fame for their assistance. Jim's father was from Princess Anne and was inducted into the Eastern Shore Baseball Hall of Fame.

Acknowledgments

There have been so many from the Society for American Baseball Research (SABR) who have helped me over the years that I cannot name them all. Larry McCray got me involved in broader and varied baseball projects and is particularly adept at bending a provincial mind to new ways of thinking and perspectives. Jan Finkel, without knowing it, and in a single sentence, provided a piece of encouragement not forgotten. And thanks to the many other SABR members who have helped and encouraged me, particularly those enthusiastic and spirited souls who gather at the Frederick Ivor-Campbell 19th Century Base Ball Conference.

And a special thanks to the many kindred spirits over the years, some whose names I have forgotten, with whom I bought, exchanged, or was gifted many images and artifacts of Eastern Shore baseball, and the knowledge that came with them.

If there were a driving tour for Eastern Shore baseball it might start in the north with the statue of Bill "Swish" Nicholson in Chestertown. From there it is not far to Sudlersville with the statue of Jimmie Foxx and the Sudlersville Train Station Museum exhibit. And while you are at it, take a moment to stop in Centreville, Baseball Town U.S.A. Then it is a slightly longer excursion to the Federalsburg Historical Society and its baseball display and files. The Eastern Shore Hall of Fame is further south in Salisbury, where one can take in a Shorebirds game and the museum. Then on to Snow Hill, where there is a monument for Negro League star Judy Johnson. And since you've gone that far, keep heading south to Parksley, and see if you can find the town of a few hundred that hoisted three organized baseball pennants in six years.

And a nod to Peter Mancuso, who likes to remind us that baseball history is more than baseball history.

Thanks to all.

Preface

This book has allowed me to write about two things I love dearly: baseball and the Eastern Shore of Maryland. It began with reading Bill Mowbray's *The Eastern Shore Baseball League*, which led me to wonder what the baseball environment was prior to the Class D minor leagues in 1922. After all, the minor leagues did not just rise up from nothing. Once I had traced the beginnings of baseball on the Eastern Shore to 1866–67, I was compelled to continue my survey, eventually through the minor league era. While secondary sources, documents, artifacts, and oral histories were used in the research, newspapers were the primary source of information for this account. One of the advantages of newspapers is that one is ever seeing historical events through the fresh eyes of those living the events. They participate, complain, rejoice, and opine about something 140 years ago, and one is reading it as if it were the first time it ever happened. Through all these many different eyes, over time, a story gradually emerged. It is a story that brought a new appreciation of baseball's relationship with rural American culture.

Sources indicated a shift in contemporary perception of the game by 1922. Baseball was once a fad, then excitingly evolving. There were exhilarating trips, hot air and hubris. Then, gradually, baseball becomes everyday. Not everyday as in drab or boring, but something deeply ingrained and intense, central to daily life. This subtle change suggested distinct periods that encouraged me to approach the work in parts. These components are different from each other, yet they are a piece of the whole.

It is my intention to portray the impact of baseball in a rural area, and illustrate the symbiotic relationship between the two. I also hope to put this connection in perspective of the national game, show the high quality of baseball played on the Eastern Shore of Maryland, and demonstrate the pervading role it came to play in community life. In attempting this, I hope to provide a distinct perspective of the history of baseball and rural life on Maryland's Eastern Shore.

This book is not the end of a story as much as a beginning. Many gaps remain within its pages. A book is out on the 1937 Salisbury Indians. The Delaware and Virginia towns of the peninsula were included in this manuscript as members of the later minor leagues, but little has been done on the independent years in those regions. A more thorough treatment of those areas is needed and a more general baseball history of the entire Delmarva Peninsula may be revealing. A collection of biographical sketches of selected players and participants would be a different path and provide perspective on baseball and a distinct rural culture. Certainly, more can be done on black rural baseball and its role in these communities. It is something that needs to be further explored, documented, placed in context, and given its due. And a closer look at the founding White Cloud of Salisbury and their players could provide a unique perception of the Eastern Shore's commercial and community life. These are just a few of many topics arising from the manuscript that could be developed into autonomous pieces. Many more stories remain to be told.

Introduction

Most histories of the Eastern Shore pay scant attention to sports and their importance in rural culture. The focus is usually on business and commerce, life on the Chesapeake Bay, politics, and the landed elite. But the same history seen through the lens of baseball provides a distinct perspective of everyday life on the Eastern Shore.

Maryland's Eastern Shore would appear, at least historically, as geographically isolated, and by assumption, economically challenged. It was neither. For most of the time period addressed in this book, the region was accessible and prosperous. There was an apparent relationship that developed between baseball and these rural towns, socially, culturally, and economically. Certain factors led to a high quality of baseball on the Eastern Shore so that by the early 1900s the region was nationally acknowledged as a hotbed of activity for the national pastime. Woven through these historical factors are the people who participated, whether we see them in fleeting incidents or as enduring contributors, not only in baseball, but also in their communities. In many ways baseball on the Eastern Shore is representative of what happened in other rural areas throughout the country, but in many other ways it was singular.

Mostly, this is really about the people of the Eastern Shore. It is about the men, women, and children who simply loved baseball. These fans did far more than just watch. They subscribed their dollars, opened their homes in hospitality, chased and pummeled umpires, and bought players ice-cream sundaes. They fought blue laws, sat in sizzling summer suns and hot muggy nights. They gambled, swore, drank, harassed, threw fists. They showered their heartfelt and monetary gratitude on their heroes. They hurled tomatoes and pop bottles, and looked out for those young players so far from home for the first time. Businessmen organized fundraisers, closed up shop on game day, and held torchlit parades. Ladies held dances and bake sales, and sold raffle tickets and may have played to some extent. Boys followed on the heels of their favorite players, sat fences, peeped through knotholes, climbed trees and poles, fished balls out of rivers and ran them down in cornfields. When it came to baseball on the Eastern Shore of Maryland, "there were hot times ... shore's yer born."

Part I

Frost Out of the Hands

1

Before the Shore

Most baseball historians now acknowledge the evolutionary nature of the game's early years, yet it is human nature to seek a flash point or a big bang for a definitive beginning to all things. So on Monday, October 1, 1888, the *Baltimore Daily News* confidently announced that Sunday marked the 43rd anniversary of baseball in America. This was a direct reference to the New York Knickerbocker Base Ball Club and the adoption of the New York rules. This 19th-century citation is not isolated in attributing a beginning of the pastime, and indicates that there was little doubt in the minds of early baseball fans as to the who, when, and where of the game of baseball. Modern baseball came directly from what was known as the New York game and the Knickerbocker Base Ball Club which embodied it.[1]

Rudimentary ball and stick games are described in writings and gleamed from artifacts of a considerable number of civilizations, societies, and cultures, many dating to ancient times. The first known European-derived North American ball game was played at Jamestown in 1609. A couple of Polish tradesmen recruited to the colony found time from toil, disease, privation, and warfare for the simple diversion. The Puritans were less tolerant a decade or so later. Within a year of landing at Plymouth Rock, Governor William Bradford was admonishing some of the heathen that had accompanied the Dissenters for playing ball on the village green during town meetings and holidays. Those heathens and their ball games may have been responsible for our first blue laws that prevented playing baseball on Sundays. In 1797 the commissioners of Fayetteville, North Carolina, directed town constables to hand out 15 lashes to "negros" found playing ball on the Sabbath. These loosely structured rural and recreational bat and ball games would eventually undergo a transformation.[2]

By the early 1800s the United States followed England and Europe into the Industrial Revolution. Young men were drawn to urban areas with the lure of wages in factories, or sedentary positions with banks, brokerages, and other commercial enterprises. Stifled inside most of the week, these young men found recreation, exercise, and release in ball and stick games. The Industrial Revolution put an emphasis on organization, efficiency, and teamwork that influenced the physical activity of these young men. In many urban areas the ball and stick games began to take on some semblance of organization with rules and limitations, leading to skills and strategies. By the time the Knickerbockers wrote down the prevailing New York rules in the 1840s, other urban areas had already developed their own versions of ball and stick games. In New England, the Massachusetts game grew and spread out of the Boston area. In Philadelphia they played town ball. The British import of cricket was also popular up and down the East Coast. But it was the New York game that would spread out of its region to the rest of the country. This version began to form by the 1830s and the clubs were organized by upwardly mobile young men seeking, not only physical exercise, but the social and economic opportunities these clubs provided to their members. The Knickerbockers emerged as the prominent team by the middle 1840s. At the center of baseball's first proliferation, and considered the epitome of what a team should be, they have garnered much of the credit for its inception.[3]

In the late 1850s, in what is sometimes referred to as the second diffusion of baseball, the New York game spread, with significant help from railroads and steamboats, to distant regional metropolitan centers. By 1860 baseball clubs playing by the New York rules were formed and active in most of the major cities. Boston, Philadelphia, Baltimore, Washington, Cleveland, Rochester, Milwaukee, Chicago, Portland (Maine), Detroit, Denver and San Francisco fielded clubs. Much of this was due to the migration of baseball participants heading westward in search of opportunity. They took with them their love of the game, and a desire to keep playing it. Yet, the playing of the New York game, and the other codified versions of baseball, were primarily a metropolitan occurrence up to this point. There was some activity in rural areas proximate to these cities, and in remote western outposts and mining towns where they clung to every expression of culture.

Some refer to the 1850s as when the world first became truly global. The steam engine had revolutionized travel, whether local or international. Not only did steam drastically reduce travel times but it helped make transportation safer, and more efficient in commerce. The telegraph was now stretching its wires across the country, particularly as a management tool for the ever-expanding railroads. For the first time in recorded history, communication hundreds of miles away could be instantaneous. Events from around the world once took months to circulate, but now a combination of telegraph and mail carriers made world events in many parts of the globe reportable in weeks, usually days, in some instances, minutes. Added to this expanding technology came mass media. Printed periodicals began to spring up throughout the country, first as monthly, later as weekly publications. This was spurred on by improvements in printing technology. The periodicals were distributed nationally by the vast and still growing network of rail and waterborne steam transportation. They looked to fill their pages with whatever interested the American reader. The world was speeding up and baseball was one of those things that fit the emerging American technology and culture.[4]

What happened in Baltimore may give some insight into the dynamics of the early diffusion of baseball. Henry B. Polhemus was the Brooklyn representative for the Baltimore Woodberry Mills and played outfield for the vaunted Brooklyn Excelsior. George Beam was a Baltimore grocer whose New York business associate was Excelsior catcher Joseph Leggett. The Excelsior were one of the best teams of the period. It was while on one of his business trips north that Beam was invited to witness an Excelsior game. Excited by what he saw, Beam was determined that Baltimore would adopt the New York game over cricket, town ball, and the many other informal versions of stick and ball games.[5]

In 1858 Beam found enough young fellow enthusiasts to form a team that named themselves the Excelsior in emulation of their mentors. Beam was named captain and would pitch. Polhemus and other Brooklyn players were brought down to teach the Baltimore neophytes the rules, skills and tactics needed to play the New York game. It was decided the new Baltimore club would meet and choose up sides to play games twice a week. From this humble beginning baseball would soon spread throughout the region.

The Waverly Club and the Maryland Club of Baltimore were formed in 1860, and in 1861 the Baltimore Base Ball Convention was formed, with 38 teams joining from the metropolitan area. The convention was not a league but simply a registration of your club for "standing." Further south the baseball fever had made it to Washington, D.C. In 1860 the Washington Nationals invited the Baltimore Excelsior to play on the "white lot," which some described as a cow pasture just south of the president's mansion. The game was played June 6, 1860, and the Excelsior of Baltimore prevailed 40–24.

This early intercity contest would be overshadowed by a tour soon taken by the Brooklyn Excelsior. Starting in upstate New York, they then ventured south, and after dispatching all comers with relative ease, eventually reached Philadelphia and Baltimore. To be competitive, Beam padded his lineup with players from the Waverly Club and the Continentals, also of Baltimore. On September 22, 1860, some 5,000 enthusiasts turned out to watch the Brooklyn squad handily defeat their Baltimore namesakes 51–6.[6]

In 1861 the Excelsior of Baltimore merged with the rival Waverly to form the Pastime. The onset of the Civil War may have slowed baseball activities, but the game did continue. Maryland being a border state, many teams were composed of both Northern and Southern sympathizers, yet according to William Ridgely Griffith, in his *History of Base Ball in Maryland, 1858–1871*, political rivalries were not carried onto the playing field. While the war may have impeded immediate baseball activity, it can be argued that it did prepare the way for baseball's subsequent growth after the event, whether directly or indirectly as part of the technology surge.

Conventional wisdom has always been that the New York game went from the cities to army camps where this improved version of the game was passed on to the rubes in the ranks and subsequently to rural America. Direct transmission of the New York game's rules or skills was one of many ways baseball disseminated. There are numerous citations of baseball in Civil War military settings, and the New York game is their game of choice. Writing in 1911, Will Irwin quoted one of his pieces from a 1909 *Collier's Magazine* in a typical vignette: "A volunteer private returned invalided to Rockford, Illinois, in 1863. He saw the boys batting up some flies, and he told them he knew a better game. He had learned it in the army. One tall, wiry boy took a special interest. It was Al Spalding." The war certainly provided a vehicle that helped spread this more formal version of ball and stick games, and it became the preferred form.[7]

The American Civil War's contribution to the diffusion of baseball may have just as much to do with infrastructure as anything else. It was one of the first conflicts in which the strategic and tactical deliveries of supplies and troops by railroads and steamboats so heavily influenced the outcome of the hostilities. Railroads were expanded during the conflict, and new ones built. The value of standardized gauge and stock were now appreciated, while management and scheduling were refined. It is here that the Civil War had its greatest impact. Where the rails went, so followed the telegraph, improving communications not only amongst cities but now into smaller towns as well. Baseball had spread through New York City, in part, with the help of the new trolley and ferry lines being built, and then to other metropolitan centers via the railroads and steamboats prior to the war. After the conflict, both the railroad and the game spread to every city, town, village, and district they could reach. As important as driving the golden spike in Provo, Utah, to connect the two coasts, the railroads and telegraph wires were reaching into every cow town, commercial center, and farming hamlet in the country.

2

The First Pitch

> The base ball fever now so prevalent in cities, seems to have spread somewhat to our Eastern Shore towns.
> —*Dorchester Democrat-News*, May 25, 1872

The Eastern Shore of Maryland lies on that appendage of land known as the Delmarva Peninsula. The part that is Maryland is bounded on the west by the Chesapeake Bay, and to the east partly by the state of Delaware, and partly by the Atlantic Ocean. The northern part of the peninsula begins just south of the Philadelphia and Wilmington area where the boundary of the peninsula is geographically defined as east of the head of the Elk River. To the south, below the Maryland towns of Princess Anne and Pocomoke City, Virginia takes over the lower part of the peninsula to Cape Charles, hence the designation as the Delmarva Peninsula. Geographically isolated in its early years, the people of this rural area developed a distinct, iconic, taciturn, if xenophobic, culture based on farming and the fisheries. The natives of the area have always been noticeably reluctant to concede their local ethos of exclusivity in the face of broader values brought on by subsequent waves of immigration.

The Shore, as the Eastern Shore of Maryland is familiarly known, was first settled in the later part of the 1600s, although Virginia traders came up the bay from their initial settlement at Jamestown and were well established in the region on Kent Island by 1631. Deep tidal rivers and coves along the bay provided the immediate portage that allowed large tobacco plantations to prosper, some of those original patents still exist in portion today. Tobacco was originally the cash crop requiring a large labor force. This brought in slaves to the Eastern Shore. While some people tended to be Southern in their sympathies during the Civil War, significant numbers from the Eastern Shore also fought for or sided with the North, and most counties were evenly split.

In 1860 the population of Maryland was just over 687,000, with 87,000 listed as slaves. It is estimated that there were another 70,000 African Americans living in Maryland as freedmen. This put the black population in the state at nearly 25 percent, nearly half of them freedmen. Eastern Shore slave owners faced a common predicament for those in border states.

Slavery had found a home on the Shore with the cultivation of tobacco, but by the middle 1800s other cash crops had emerged as more suitable to the soil and gained favor. Most of these crops required less intensive labor than tobacco. Some large plantations remained, but most slaves were owned by those with smaller holdings. Slaves worked these smaller properties and were often hired out as laborers and tradesman, many into the maritime industry. Sometimes they hired out for their masters, and at other times they were allowed to hire out for themselves. Slaves and freed persons often married and families could be a combination of free and slave. It was a rigid yet complex system. The slave owner's problem in this commercial setup was location. Many slaves could take the risky trek through fields, dismal swamps and thick woods to Delaware, where they were greeted by abolitionist societies and individuals who helped them on the first leg of the Underground Railroad up to Philadelphia. Others followed the Chesapeake Bay north to the Susquehanna River and Pennsylvania, where they received the same reception as in Delaware. Escape may have not been easy, but it was not the formidable task faced by slaves living deep in the South, imprisoned in the stark, harsh, and brutal plantation culture. The risk in getting caught was sale to the southern plantations, considered a death sentence by most.

Slave owners of the Chesapeake sought to mitigate this constant threat of escape by offering manumission for either financial compensation or for years of services rendered as with indentured servants. When slaves were allowed to hire out independently of the owner for cash payment, it was as an incentive to keep them home, or allow them to buy their freedom so owners could recoup on their investment. This tepid attempt at a quasi-indentured servant arrangement did not work for slaves. Not all agreements for manumission were honored by owners, and the law did not favor a slave pressing suit in the courts. Harriet Tubman escaped from Dorchester County and would become renowned as a leader on the Underground Railroad, guiding and exhorting her charges through the swamps, fields and woods of the Eastern Shore into Delaware and then north. Frederick Douglass was born in 1817 or 1818 just a few miles north of Tubman in Talbot County. In 1839, Douglass, like Tubman, escaped north, where he became a famous writer, lecturer, and abolitionist who befriended a president.[1]

Many freedmen left the Shore the first chance they had, but many stayed for a variety of reasons and they formed their own enclaves. Some were freestanding communities, others parts of existing towns and villages. With emancipation, many former slaves and soldiers abandoned their former residences and some formed new independent communities as freedmen had done prior to the war. The Eastern Shore, as part of a border state, underwent its own process of Reconstruction and Jim Crow.

Most baseball historians agree that African Americans' pursuit of the national pastime paralleled that of whites, but was a bit slower due to what were described as "obstacles and difficulties." There may have been a long informal tradition of ball games in black communities as in white, as the Fayetteville, North Carolina, ordinance might indicate. There is evidence of black teams in the Northeast prior to the Civil War, but organized teams seemed to have come mostly during baseball's third diffusion after the war. Much of this activity was in the Northeast and some Midwestern cities that were nurturing an aspiring black middle class with money to spend. Like their fellow white enthusiasts on the Eastern Shore, teams formed along the Knickerbocker social club model, eventually to yield to competition and professionalism.[2]

Two things are notable in the newspapers of the Eastern Shore at the end of the Civil War. The first was that weekly rural newspapers were beginning to carry the scores of the metropolitan baseball teams throughout the country. There seemed to be a sudden enthusiasm for this New York game. Staid newspapers had previously focused on announcements, and advertisements, but the Civil War had filled their pages with sensational battlefield reports. Baseball, in what might be called its third diffusion, with its uniforms and contesting of forces and skills, seemed a natural and safe replacement for those grown accustomed to the sensational.

The other noticeable feature in these papers was the amount of coverage given to local railroad ventures. Every week there were reports of their progress. Enthusiastic investors pleaded with banks, the people, and whoever would listen for more capital to complete the local spur lines. The New York–Norfolk Railroad was completed down the spine of Delaware in 1866 to the newly built port town of Crisfield, Maryland. In a few years, the New York–Norfolk would become the Delaware Railroad and span the last length of the peninsula through Virginia to the port in Cape Charles, Virginia.

The railroads getting all the attention in these newspapers were those locally and independently owned and connected the New York–Norfolk with port towns on the eastern side of the Chesapeake Bay. Between 1865 and 1866 five railroads opened for commercial and passenger use on the Eastern Shore of Maryland. Chestertown connected to Clayton, Delaware, with the Kent County Railroad. The Queen Anne–Kent Railroad stretched east from Centreville, again to Clayton. To the south the Maryland–Delaware was working out of Easton Point while the Seaford Railroad in Delaware laid the six miles of track to link up with the Dorchester Railroad and the Maryland towns of Federalsburg, Hurlock, and Cambridge. Further south the local lines of the Wicomico and Pocomoke, destined for Salisbury, were nearing completion. All these railroads connected with the local and cross-bay steamboat lines. By 1870, an Easton businessman could have breakfast at home, leave town on the 6:00 a.m. train, be in New York at 4:54 p.m., and dining in a posh Gotham restaurant by 6:00 p.m. No one had to be alerted to the commercial possibilities presented. The Eastern Shore became a breadbasket of the East Coast. Bumper crops of peaches and wheat and catches from the rich fisheries of the bay teeming with oysters, crabs, and fish had traditionally gravitated to the Baltimore market and then westward. Canning, along with steam transportation, turned once distant cities into available markets. Now, Philadelphia, New York, and even Boston consumers were accessible. To the south, it was the port city of Norfolk, Virginia, and inland to Richmond and beyond.[3]

In 1865 the four largest towns on the Eastern Shore of Maryland were Chestertown, Easton, Cambridge, and Salisbury. The population of each barely exceeded 2,000. A couple of other towns numbered 1,000 to 1,500 but most communities were mere villages and hamlets. All of this was about to change with the advent of steam transportation, Reconstruction, and a postwar regional economic upswing. A later writer would observe of the peninsula's distinct rural culture, and the changes that came to it, "Until the railroad was built in modern times, nobody ever passed through the Eastern Shore…. This makes a great difference in the development of a community. Few strangers came among them. They nourished, ripened, and handed down their own notions undisturbed." Another observed that at the time it was "ground never trodden by a tourist."[4]

Baseball had continued in Baltimore during the Civil War, albeit on a reduced basis. After the hostilities, baseball seemed to proliferate beyond anyone's anticipations. Membership in the Baltimore Base Ball Convention not only attained previous levels of participation, but soon surpassed those numbers, and expanded in geographic scope. When the convention accepted memberships for the 1867 season, it for the first time included clubs from outside the immediate Baltimore area. From the western shore of Maryland were clubs from Frederick, Hagerstown, and as far west as Cumberland. From the Eastern Shore there were the Avalanche of Cecil, the Chesterfield of Queen Anne, the Dorchester of Milton, and the Excelsior of Sudlersville.

A few early baseball players realized the money to be made by selling uniforms and equipment to the growing number of clubs being formed. Al Spalding and Al Reach are two examples of early-19th-century star players who seized that opportunity. Their counterpart in Baltimore was George Gratton. While not a star player like Reach and Spalding, the English immigrant was trained as a plumber and was associated with the Syracuse Club before moving to Baltimore, where he opened a book and gift store and also conducted auctions and estate sales. He did realize the financial potential of baseball when he opened the Baltimore Baseball Emporium in 1866 to serve the members of the Baltimore Base Ball Convention, and he later served as its treasurer. Not satisfied with that limited market, Gratton sent out his salesmen "the length and breadth of Maryland" in the fall of 1866 on the railroads to sell the game of baseball and the merchandise people needed to play it. It may have been one of Gratton's salesmen who entered this into the *Easton Gazette*, September 29, 1866:

"The young men of Easton and its vicinity favorable to the organization of a Base Ball Club in this place will please meet at the Court House on Saturday, the 29th inst. At 10 o'clock a.m. The object of the formation of this club will be to improve physically its members and to give social standing and representation in the Base Ball Association of Baltimore." A similar advertisement in Chestertown drew a favorable response, noting, "We mean to substitute this manly game for the cock fighting, card gambling, and other deviltry which disgraced this place in the past."[5]

The Easton blades did not appear to react right away. Others were not so tardy to the latest fashion. To the north, the advertisement that appeared in Chestertown drew immediate response. Earlier that summer of 1866, the New York game had already started on the northern fringes of the peninsula. In the town of Elkton in Cecil County and its surrounding villages, games were already taking place. Elkton was near the metropolitan centers of Philadelphia and Wilmington and situated on the Baltimore–Ohio Railroad that connected this urban region with Baltimore and points west. Due to its location, the town was the first to be hit with the postwar baseball experience. The Eclipse of Elkton faced off against St. Georges of Delaware on July 14, 1866, in front of a large crowd. A detailed account of the almost six-hour game and an explanation of the sport were provided. Afterwards a sumptuous dinner and champagne were served at the "social game" played in the Knickerbocker tradition. In September, an appeal to form baseball teams in the area appeared in the *Chestertown Transcript*, which included a detailed account as to how the New York game was played. Despite such early descriptions of the New York game, the fact that most subsequent game accounts consist only of rudimentary box scores, with little or no narrative, may indicate a prior familiarity with the game by many or most readers.[6]

A county history ascribed 1865 as the year that baseball began in Chestertown in Kent County, Maryland, with the Ozenies, but the writer may have been a little foggy in his memory. He may have had the team right but not the year. Newspapers indicate that the Ozenies were among the first to form in Chestertown, in the fall of 1866, but not necessarily the first in the area to play. The first club to make it to print was the team that formed at the Head of the Sassafras reported on September 15. This was not even a town or village, but a geographic district near a tidal river. The Ozenies formed in Chestertown by September 25 but the first box score reported was of neither. On September 22, the Kent of Galena, Maryland, played the Undaunted of Cecil County. The account and box score had no description of the game but did mention that two new teams were formed in the county seat of Chestertown.[7]

Baseball seemed to creep down from the north from Elkton, to Galena, to Chestertown. There, after a last December flurry, it appears to have taken a break for the winter. With the spring thaw came baseball like a freshet with nothing to stop it. South of Chestertown calls went out again in Easton newspapers in the spring to form a baseball club. In April, the young men of Easton came together to form the Fair Play, and like the Baltimore Excelsior a few years earlier, met two days a week to play in a field behind a Dr. Earle's house. Easton would play these isolated social events for five months before venturing against another club. Teams from Cecil, Queen Anne, and Dorchester Counties had already joined and gained standing in the Baltimore Base Ball Convention. The Kent and Cecil County clubs picked up where they had left off in December. Teams were also forming in the towns and communities of Caroline, Talbot, Dorchester, and Wicomico Counties, and other points south on the peninsula. These teams were too late or had little concern with gaining standing in the Baltimore Base Ball Convention.

In Salisbury, on the southern part of the peninsula, another former participant was a little vague when he recalled in a 1903 trip down memory lane that baseball began "not long after the unpleasantness between the states," and replaced the o'cat games played there. A group from Chestertown seemed to be equally foggy with its long-term memory. At a 25th reunion in 1893, H. Rickey was adamant that 1867 started it all when Chestertown abandoned cricket and adopted the New York game as its prominent sport. In a room with a score or more of fellow participants, it is odd that someone did not remind him of the fall of 1866. Perhaps there was something about 1867 that separated it from the rushed, late-season activities of the previous year. Baseball took the entire peninsula by storm in 1867. An observer from Baltimore would refer to 1867 as "A Great Year in Base Ball."[8]

The White Cloud was the founding club in Salisbury, Maryland. It was named for a respected Native American chief from Minnesota. Back row, left to right: Ned Gillis, lf; E. Stanley (Ned) Toadvine, captain and p.; George W. Truitt, ss; Joseph (Jack) Graham, cf. Center row: Howard Humphries, rf; Harvey Todd, 2b. Front row: Gid Jordan, c.; L.W. Gunby, 3b; Samuel Smith, 1b. The *Salisbury Times*, April 19, 1946, ran the photograph with an additional list of White Cloud players that included Samuel Gordy, 2b; George Todd, ss; Lacey Thoroughgood, rf; Charles Duffy, p.; Dave Farlow, cf; George Bell, manager (Nabb Research Center/Wicomico Historical Society).

Technology may help us understand how baseball physically proliferated into rural areas, but not why it appealed to so many so quickly. Industrial urbanization trapped many young men in factories and offices through most of the week. Baseball was perceived as a means of activity to work off physical and mental stresses of an emerging, and increasingly fast-paced, complex society. Whether through this intrinsic need, or spurred by the more tangible excitement of gambling, the game was quickly becoming more competitive. Games were designated as social or match events. Social games were played for fun and afterwards included dinner, toasts, speeches, and dances. Match games usually played for a trumped-up championship or some physical token of conquest, which could be a silver ball, or a loving cup, or simply the loser's bat and ball.

The uniform may have represented another driving force. A man in uniform, strutting around in a field, sweating, showing his physical prowess in front of the ladies, had to have been appealing and on the cutting edge of their Victorian Age sensibilities. The New York game seemed more structured, orderly, and to fit in with these sensibilities than the less structured versions that arose in Massachusetts and Philadelphia. While the degree of impact of direct teaching and diffusion of baseball during the Civil War is important, there was also an intrinsic psychological influence. This may be best represented by a bit of doggerel widely printed in newspapers throughout the country after the war. Part of one verse goes,

Base Ball on The Brain

At length the war cry's hushed and still,
And peaceful are the signs
The cannon roar affrights us not—
"All quiet on the lines!"
No more the fearful charge we brave—
For raids we look in vain,
But still excitement we must have,
And we've base ball on the brain!
Base ball, base ball
Base ball on the brain;
But still excitement we must have,
And we've base ball on the brain.[9]

As clubs formed and played on the Eastern Shore in 1867, the Fair Play of Easton dawdled amongst themselves those two days a week in Dr. Earle's field. In other places clubs were hopping onto steamboats and trains to play clubs from other communities. It was not until September that the sluggish Fair Play caught on to what was called a "fever season," They finally played a social game with the Choptank of Trappe, Maryland. A celebrity umpire, A.N. Sutton of the Philadelphia Athletic Club, was brought in for the event. "After the game the players retired to the Talbot House and partook of a supper given for the occasion by the Fair Play." Speeches were delivered by J.F. Turner esq. of the Fair Play and Mr. Valliant of the Choptank Club. "Although someone was beaten, as is generally the case at such times, all were delighted." The rematch, with a crowd described as "ladies and gentlemen," was captioned with the declaration, "We are not totally behind the times in Talbot in this particular." In what would prove to be an early and fleeting exhibition of sportsmanship, the Choptank cheered the victorious Fair Play when they finally won the third of their social games. It was not until October 17 that the Fair Play finally entered a match game with the Claiborne of St. Michaels, adopting the concept of charging admission to see a rural baseball game. The Fair Play charged 10 cents for the benefit of the club to offset expenses.[10]

Other clubs pushed towards the excitement of competitive match play earlier in the season. On May 25 two Kent County teams that had formed the previous fall met in a match game that had all the fervor and fanfare of a championship game, and offers some indication that baseball was heading away from the concept of baseball as a genteel physical and social event. The Kent of Galena, Maryland, and the Wissahickon Club of Washington College in Chestertown met on the Kent grounds. It was noted that the players were "animated" in their skill and vigor, from a large and "respectable" audience. It appeared that the younger Wissahickon Club of Washington College began to show signs of fatigue, while the more mature Kent Club remained strong.

"At the expiration of the seventh inning the Wissahicon Club called the game and as there was a difference of only one run in their favor, they were declared the victors. Surprise and regret could easily be discerned among all who witnessed the game, and watched it with much interest, particularly the ladies, who graced the occasion with their cheering presence. A sense of disappointment was at once expressed." It was implied that the college lads feared a Waterloo-type defeat, but "all are agreed that the rules of the game entitle a party to demand a decision after the fifth inning." While the decision to terminate play may have been justified in a technical sense, the spectators questioned the integrity of the action, "A definite principle of *right* will enable a man to do many silly things, but a nice sense of social, generous rivalry will not be controlled by the naked duty of right." Once the correspondent got past the controversy, he noted the innovative tactics of the players, and thanked the owner of the playing field.

"Where all played well it would be invidious to praise individuals.... Anthony and Dyre (Kent) made bases when they were hopeless by the ingenious mode of slipping into them *in the teeth* of the base men. The umpire has the confidence and esteem of all parties.... The match was played upon the field of Dr. T.N. Taymine, near his residence, he having liberally consented to its use for that purpose."[11]

Other match games were also being reported on the peninsula. This dichotomy of social and match games, the genteel versus the zealous, would last only a short time. Gratton's salesmen had sold the game on the Knickerbocker style of physical exercise, social standing, and an excuse for a party. But the game really prospered on the concept of competition. Some game accounts focused primarily on the social aspects of the event while others concentrated solely on the game events.

Even with the steam network that now connected the Shore to cities of the East Coast, travel from town to town was still long and costly, which made early baseball contests all-day, sometimes two-day events. For this reason, even as baseball became more competitive, the rural baseball experience retained certain expectations associated with social games, as a matter of courtesy to the visitors. Any shortcomings in these rituals were roundly criticized in the newspapers. The trip Easton took to play in Cambridge in 1869 on the slow and small steamer the Highland Light serves as an example of an early baseball excursion:

> Starting from the Point before daybreak and arriving at Cambridge at 8 a.m.
> Some of the "Scorers" met us at the wharf and escorted us to Bradshaw's Hotel where we fixed a little and then proceeded to the grounds about 1½ miles out of town.... After the loss, Easton dined with the "Scorers" at Bradshaw's Hotel, and after walking about and viewing the "mud machine" {steam dredge} and other celebrities of our rival for the "first position," embarked on the Highland Light about 5:00 p.m. and reached our destination about 10:00 p.m.... Our return trip we whiled away the hours by making the echoes of the Choptank and Tred Avon (rivers) "vive la company" and other many old songs—the verses composed on the spot for the occasion, and in them remembered the "Scorers," the steamer, ourselves, and those we left behind.[12]

"After the loss" was the only reference to the game itself. It would have been quicker for the Easton contingent to get to New York City than travel the 12 miles by river to play at Cambridge and return home. The railroads were blocked direct access between these two towns by the broad Choptank River, making the pokey Highland Light the choice of transportation. There was a three- to four-hour game, two meals and a tour of the town, yet it was a significant investment of time and money for Easton, and these social amenities were expected. Within this bucolic account lie the seeds of rural competition. The mud machine was being used to widen and deepen the Cambridge harbor and the "first position" the teams vied for was nothing less than commercial dominance of the Eastern Shore of Maryland. Both sought shipping ties west to Baltimore, and connection east by rail to the New York–Norfolk RR to points north and south.

Three things may have contributed to this move towards the competitive version of baseball. Metropolitan teams had been going in that direction for several years with compensation to players. The extended city tours of the Brooklyn Excelsior in 1860 and the openly professional road trip of the Cincinnati Red Stockings in 1869 were both intended to show the superiority of those clubs. The Civil War also contributed to this element in baseball. Uniforms, victory, physical tests of skill, and young ladies in attendance helped draw young men to the game. Added to this was local commercial competition. Several towns were vying for economic position, and what better way to reflect and promote those gains than with the quality of a town's baseball team. Teams quickly transitioned from private clubs to representatives of the community. Soon, rule changes would contribute to this competitive environment. All social amenities, though important, would take a back seat to the new bearing of aggression being assumed by baseball. This antagonistic demeanor became more commonplace, as was reflected in this boastful account:

> Never was vain ostentation more arrogantly displayed than by the *Rustic Nine.* For a week they were continually vaunting of their superior playing, especially the Captain, until

the time rolled round for a practical illustration. Arriving on the college ground[s] the game commenced. The *Rustic* countenances wore a beaming aspect until the third inning when lo! what an amazing transmutation! How quickly their merry laughter and happy exchange of congratulations changed to gloomy and dejected mutterings. When we, the Chester, next to bat last inning, the Captain walked to the pitcher's stand and uttered this terrible mandate to his ambitious pitcher, "Go to the third base, sir." He went with some reluctance, for 'twas a great fall of his feathers and aspiration[s]. There stood their crest-fallen Captain, witnessing the fall of what he once thought *mighty*.

—B[13]

Young boys were immediately drawn to the New York game—with or without supervision, and there rested the future of baseball. In June of 1867, the Chester of Denton squared off against the Senora of Greensboro, the teams described as clubs composed of juveniles "desirous of displaying their proficiency in this game." Most teams appeared to have played under some degree of supervision, but adults were not always around to contain the unbridled enthusiasm of the boys:

> The interest which has revived in this game, has brought with it the renewal of the dangerous practice of playing in the streets of our town, and neither broken noses or broken hands seem to abate it.
> A few days since, a gentleman and his wife with an infant in her arms, were walking down the main street, and the ball, driven by a heavy bat, came very near the infant.
> The votaries of this game practice it openly and daily in our streets, utterly regardless of the ordinances of their town and the safety and comfort of the passersby. During the session of Court they threw their heavy balls about the Court Yard crowded with people.[14]

Most early clubs featured a second nine that served as source of replacement players for the first nine, and a chance for younger players to gain experience. During the 1880s independent juvenile teams emerged, taking to the rails and steamboats to display their prowess in neighboring towns. In peak seasons a town might field the town team, with one or more secondary adult teams, and several youth teams of varying ages. In 1884 Easton proclaimed that they would be as well represented as the year before, and further represented by several local clubs, the youngest's members being nine to 10 years old. In Chestertown in the 1880s the Printer's Athletic Club was composed of boys who worked the presses for the town newspapers.

There was no set standard for players' ages from town to town and no known leagues or schedules. When competition could not be found within town, the young teams took to the road like the adult teams. Cambridge featured a team of 14- to 16-year-olds, affectionately called the Muffers. Although this was the contemporary nomenclature for an error or bad play, they bore their name proudly. They then represented Cambridge as 16- to 18-year-olds until they soundly beat the fading adult town team, the Resolute, and the Taylor's Island Pastimes. Based on these victories, they assumed the role as the main town adult team for several years, and many players went on to direct and finance future clubs. A team of youngsters from the small town of East New Market caught everyone's attention one year for their proficiency even though it was said they were "barely high enough to see over a good dinner table."[15]

There is little evidence as to how they were financed. Some money may have trickled down from the town team as a feeder system, but youth teams became more independent of the town teams as professionalism took over. Youth teams might be sponsored by businesses, organizations, or enthusiastic adults. It appears that most youth teams had local adult supervision, but no centralized organizational oversight. They were just as jealously independent as the big team.

While George Gratton and his salesmen were instrumental in spreading baseball throughout Maryland, his contributions were fleeting. In 1866 he offered a silver ball and a silk flag for separate match games in Baltimore. He was in the upper echelons of the Baltimore baseball community. But by 1868, Gratton had filed for bankruptcy and faced several pending lawsuits. He moved to Omaha, Nebraska, where he speculated some in real estate and was mostly engaged as a ticket agent for the railroads. Ticket agents traveled east to recruit "colonies" to be established on railroad lands and right of ways. It was not unusual to take a menagerie of flora and fauna east in order to show to prospective colonists the blessings of the wilds of 1870s Nebraska. He also worked as a gas inspector and died in 1881 at the age of 53 following an extended illness. No record has been found that Gratton was involved in baseball in the West.[16]

3

Baseball Prevails

> As soon as the Spring sun[] draws the frost out of the hands of the idle boys and half-grown men who loaf about our streets, the nuisance of throwing base-balls about our thoroughfares—to the terror of ladies and small children—commences.
> —*Chestertown Transcript*, April 13, 1872

Within a few short years baseball changed radically in the minds of its participants, spectators, and detractors. Gratton had relied on the Knickerbocker image of healthy, hardworking, upwardly mobile, intelligent men of moral values and integrity to sell baseball, but many rural editors were already denouncing a game that was becoming increasingly competitive, violent, ugly in behavior, and overrun with those folks with a little less concern for social standing than before. It was not unusual for a county to have five or six weekly newspapers, and a town of 2,000 might have three. Some editors promoted baseball, while others ignored it completely. Some blew hot and cold, depending on the year. A few expressed preference for the old bucolic versions of the game.

In rural areas the transition from private club to town team was an important one and well in process during the 1870s. As the emphasis on baseball as a social event and all the ballyhoo that went with it gravitated to a competition of one town being better than another, money became more of an issue on many fronts. From uniforms to equipment to transportation, paying for the social events for fans and foes, money was needed. And where were they going to play? The men playing this game were young and did not always have the financial means to keep up with the expenses. Admissions were being charged in the first full year of baseball on the Shore. Soon older advocates of the game were solicited for help in defraying costs. They first appeared in the guise of "honorary members." This was simply expanding membership to the club to generate funds to cover expenses. It was in the tradition set by the New York teams. Some of the rural participants resented the infusion of money outside of the players, as Easton's rival from Cambridge noted,

> We noticed those (names) of ex-governor Thomas, Hon. Samuel Hambleton, the entire medical fraternity, the bar, the merchants, undertakers, editors, and in fact nearly every prominent man in Easton is connected with the club.... If honorary membership can add prominence to it, it will occupy the first rank. But we think a nine can be raised in Cambridge--minus the honorary members that could repeat the campaign of '69 and administer a second defeat to the Easton nines.

But the Cambridge Star was merely behind the times. Eventually, Cambridge, like everyone else, acknowledged their financial arrangements, revealing that "the active members of the Star, exclusive of the aid derived from a half dozen honorary members, shoulder the expenses of the club."[1]

Because most towns rarely played more than a dozen games a year at this point, even match and championship games could be gala social events with a balloon ascension and other novelties. In Dorchester County two teams squared off in what was termed a championship of the county:

"We understand that on Saturday afternoon next the first match game of base ball for the Championship of the county will take place on the grounds of Dr. John Neville between the Resolute of our town and the Excelsior of Salem, and should the weather prove favorable, Dr. Baisel will send up his large Balloon 'Cambridge' for the pleasure of those persons present."

A week later Dr. Baisel's balloon, eight to 10 feet in length and bearing the inscription "Champion Base Ball Club of Cambridge," was found across the Choptank River in the Trappe district of Talbot County.[2]

Playing teams from the western shore of the bay was rare at first, but became more frequent as improvements to transportation connections continued to progress. How far the team was coming, the length of the games, and expected social amenities turned most of these excursions into extended events. The first game between an Eastern Shore team and one from the western shore came in 1874 when the Druids of Baltimore took on the Star of St. Michaels on Canton Field in St. Michaels. What was referred to as a "friendly" game drew enough attention to be reported in the *Baltimore Sun* and communicated from the *St. Michaels Comet* to the *Easton Journal*. The contest was four hours and 30 minutes long, attended by what was described as an "immense crowd" and won by the St. Michaels Star. The visitors were privately entertained in the homes of the members of the Star before returning that night on the steamer the *Massachusetts*.[3]

All baseball teams played on what they referred to as the "grounds." Many clubs were offered playing areas on properties of influential citizens, just outside of town, often near railroad depots or steamboat terminals. The Fair Play used a field behind Dr. Earle's lot, and the Kent of Galena, a Dr. Taymine's. Later, in Easton, the club would play at Commodore Feiberger's property on Point Road, near the Easton harbor, or, as with the Cambridge balloon ascension, Dr. Neville's near Cambridge. Washington College in Chestertown typically offered its college grounds for community use. In St. Michaels, the grounds were located at Canton Field, on a narrow neck of land close to both the railroad and the harbor. But most of the early grounds were vaguely described in location and condition. Evidence suggests that benefactors helped these young clubs and early town teams with a place to play by providing the grounds or renting them. Denoting a baseball field as the "grounds" would last well into the 20th century. Salisbury described its facility in the 1870s:

> The ground is well shaded by magnificent Oak trees under which seats will be placed for the accommodation of the ladies. On account of the heavy expenses attending the renting of the ground, and the many little things too numerous to mention, it has been thought

advisable to charge an admission fee of ten cents. The entrance will be at the lower gate. Perfect order will be kept during the progress of the game. The Salisbury Brass band have kindly tendered their services for the occasion.[4]

While the White Cloud of Salisbury were proud of these grounds, not all their opponents were quite so impressed. The Snow Hill team, after a protracted dispute over whether a game was social or match, complained in the *Snow Hill Messenger* of the rough condition of the grounds and that they were not much more than a half-acre in size.

Evidence that the game was diverting from the Knickerbocker demeanor continued to creep into the papers. In a match game reported as a presumptuous championship of the Eastern Shore, Easton played well the first five or six innings, and then things fell apart. When the Easton fans asked what the matter was, the Cambridge players were quick to point out, "They are sick." At the time, this was often a euphemism for a player being under the influence. The reporter half tactfully explained the insult:

> Mr. Trippe was taken sick in the seventh inning. The next news we expect to hear from Easton is that the Star man has been whipped or sued by Mr. Trippe for publishing such an insult. We won't wrong the Easton club by believing the slanderous insinuation contained in the Star that the Easton Club can't play nine innings without it making them sick.... The Star reporter is a brave man. We would not dare say that a Resolute hadn't nerve or muscle enough to play the game without being made sick unless we wanted to hand in our checks, have our will written and bargain completed with the undertaker. We are uneasy about the Star writer, for the Easton Club must be wanting in the nerve necessary to the Knights of the ball and bat if they do not revenge themselves upon the man by using his head or some other part of him for a foot-ball.[5]

Specifying a team, much less a player, as being unwell was an accusation aired to the folks of two entire communities that the team was, if not inebriated, lacking in fortitude, quitters. But the *Star* man had only casually mentioned Trippe was unwell, and that may have been all it was. The Dorchester paper was the one who made much more of the incident. Yet baseball was getting uglier in ways other than a vitriolic pen. Physical violence was also taking a foothold in the new pastime. In a game played in Cambridge the players from the district of Tobaccostick were described as "deficient," which may explain the incident.

> A game of baseball was played near town on Saturday last between the Cambridge and Tobaccostick clubs, resulting in a victory for the former by the score of 44 to 25. During the game Mr. Ed Maguire, of Tobaccostick was seriously hurt by a blow upon the head from one of the Cambridge players, he having run before the bat as the batter struck at the ball. He was knocked senseless.
>
> P.S. we have since learned that Mr. Maguire has been seriously affected by the severe contusion, and apprehensions are felt as to the result.[6]

A report three days later however, reported, "Mr. Maguire being out of position, received a terrible blow from the bat ... and fears were entertained at first of his recovery; but we are glad to hear that he is now considered out of danger."[7]

One of the best illustrations of the divergence from the genteel to the rough coming to rural baseball is contained in a lengthy but telling account of a game between Cambridge and Seaford, Delaware, in 1873 under the headline "Base Ball, Cambridge vs. Seaford—A Warm Reception and Hearty Welcome."

The Cambridge Club was fresh off a victory over Denton on a Monday. It was rare for town teams to play on consecutive days at this time, but on arriving home that night, "in the exuberance of their mirth," the Cambridge team went straight to the telegraph office to send a midnight wire to the Delaware Club of Seaford. In it they challenged the Seaford team to a game the following day at noon. Since all unsolicited challenges at the time were accepted as a matter of civic and chauvinistic pride, this was a blatant attempt to catch their opponents without their full complement of players. As the Cambridge Club and their fans rode the train the next morning, "the cars rang with the merry laughter of the pleasure party." But when they arrived at the station, they did not find the customary welcoming committee and they impatiently waited.

At last, they were told to be ready by three o'clock. This would give the Delaware Club time to collect its "imported players," an early allusion to the use of professional players in these small towns. The usual welcoming committee never did show up, but a "rough" appeared and told all the Seaford players who had arrived at the station to get in the wagon while the Cambridge contingent "rode shank's mare. We walked for some time around vacant lots, leaping mud puddles, until we were brought to a dead halt upon a pile of sand surrounded by cockles and prickly pears."

The first two pitches from the Cambridge pitcher brought a protest from Seaford and the *Base-Ball Player* of 1873 was consulted. The new pitching rules were read and the umpire ruled in favor of Cambridge. The response was "Go ahead, we can beat them anyhow." But as Cambridge forged a lead, their opponents took on the countenance of the "heathen chinee, very peculiar … oaths and vulgarity filled the air. The presence of young ladies was no restraint upon them, but only seemed to stimulate them to give full reign to their ungentlemanlike instincts." The account ends with the disparagement of the Seaford team for their lack of baseball etiquette, and was punctuated with a parting shot, "Adieu, Seaford Base Ball Club. The pitcher sends his love."[8]

There were two methods of arranging games in the early years. The first, and the slowest, was to place a challenge in one of your opponents' weekly newspapers and await the response. The other option, an innovative technology, and new to many rural areas, was the telegraph. The details of a match could be arranged much more quickly and efficiently, then placed in the local paper to advertise the game for fans. The telegraph became the preferred method to coordinate games. Cambridge certainly took advantage of this method. Sending the wire in the evening of the night before, they simply announce their pending arrival at noon. It is a likely assumption that Seaford used the same method to notify their "imported players" or professionals to report to the station before proceeding with the match. There was another reason for games to be arranged at a club's convenience. With the pitching rule changes in 1873 came an increase in velocity. Now the condition of the catcher's hands was paramount. Two willing and capable catchers were rare on rural teams. The use of gloves and rudimentary chest protectors came about in the early 1880s and became widespread by 1884. Until then, a player's hands or fingers on a rural town team could be an excuse, or a valid reason, to avoid a challenge. By the middle of the 1880s all rural references to split hands, fingers, noses and lips subsided, and challenges were not refused for those reasons. As in the major leagues, there were a few old-school players who would eschew this new equipment, but rural players quickly adapted new innovations and protections as they were devised and became available on the market.

Where once losing teams lustily cheered the victors as if they had won themselves, that was not likely to happen in 1873. The rule book was pulled out to validate a delivery that promoted the competitive ugliness encroaching the game. The fast delivery from 45 feet was an increased danger. The rule was that a batter had to attempt first base on the third strike, which forced the catcher closer to the plate so he could gather the ball and record the out. With the game being played more aggressively, base runners were giving catchers another reason to be closer to the plate in order to throw them out. Catchers realized they had to field more pitches on the fly rather than on a bounce as they had previously done. Twenty-five years after the fact an old-timer of the White Cloud of Salisbury recalled what it was like: "Duffy pitched the first five innings, during which no other player touched the ball except Jordan and himself. Jordan, with bursted hands and blood trickling down his arms, caught like a fiend, having the game well in hand Dave Farlow was put in to finish it." Farlow was the second catcher and would later take the battered Jordan's spot in the batting order.[9]

Another emerging feature was the rudeness and animosity shown by the home team to the visitors. The Seaford players felt justified in their behavior toward Cambridge after they tried to pull a fast one with the short notice challenge, but such instances of hostility were on the increase. Drinking, cursing, and gambling, particularly in front of the ladies who frequented these games, was turning away many with Victorian sensibilities.

The pitcher was also becoming more hazardous to the batter. The pitcher worked from a box that varied in size through the 19th century. The pitch had to be delivered 45 feet, later 50 feet, from the batter. Until 1887 the pitcher could run, hop, or skip, to add impetus to his release. Pitchers were free to roam the box, gain forward momentum from sharp angles to the batter. Encroaching the front of the box with the pitch was hard to detect from a flat surface by an umpire. The height of the arm at delivery of the pitch was laxly enforced with subsequent rule changes that allowed the eventual rising of the arm to an overhand motion. Such deliveries could gain speeds of over a hundred miles per hour, and there was no rule allowing for hit batters to take their base when struck. Pitchers went about their business with impunity. It would take two decades of groping rule changes for baseball to find balance between pitching and hitting. Until then, even in doggerel, baseball's transformation was evident:

Struck Out

The boy stood squarely on the base—
Already two were out—
The grin that lighted up his face
Shone round about his snout.
The boy he raised his ash aloft,
And called for one hip high,
The pitcher put it in red hot.
It hit him in the eye.
Again the gallant youth stood up,
Determined he would score;
The next one hit him in the paunch—
He playeth ball no more.[10]

Under the bold notice "Base Ball and Murder," it was reported that in Clarke County, near Atlanta, Georgia, in what was described as a "quarrel," a player named Pink Price had turned and struck another named Luther Thrasher over the head with his bat, killing him instantly. The violence was also within the game itself. Closer to home in the village of Rising Sun in Maryland, a young man was called from the stands as a substitute when a team was shorthanded. He was struck in the chest by the pitcher's delivery, walked a few steps away from the plate and collapsed. A doctor was called from the spectators, but he could not save him. The young man left a wife and young son.[11]

If there was a time for baseball to fail, it was the 1870s. Along with the violence came arguing and bickering. Known as "kicking," it became prevalent at all levels of competition. This was the 19th-century term for arguing with opposing players, umpires, and fans and became such an accepted practice that it was an encouraged and an expected strategy by the 1880s. Kicking came to include the many on-field tactics to obstruct or distract to your team's advantage. Among the tactics employed might be for players to simply argue with umpires, or coaches' positioning themselves to harass the opponent's catcher and the umpire from close range. Another ploy was for the coach to break down the third base line as if he were the runner on third base in order to distract the pitcher or draw a wild throw. And an ardent fan usually considered it his duty to storm the field with a mob of his brethren to protest calls and further the cause of his team.

On top of the unsavory field antics, off-the-field activities were also giving the game a bad name as well. Dissipation, or the use of alcohol and other substances, sometimes during games, was becoming more common, but it was not the problem that gambling became. Wagering by fans started early. It was one explanation for baseball's appeal as a spectator sport. Metropolitan newspapers were reporting these activities by the 1860s with the rise of professional players. By the 1870s rumors abounded that games were being fixed. Regulatory bodies were looking for ways to protect the integrity of the game. The Lord Baltimores were one of the better teams in the first major league, the National Association, and managed two third-place finishes in 1872 and '73. After a strong start in '74 they began to lose games with an alarming regularity and were chastised in the local papers and called "mosquitos," a term usually applied to young boys' teams.

At the end of the season a committee met and threw out Baltimore's record. When the new National League formed in 1876, it inherited the gambling problem. In 1877, what became known as the Louisville Four were banished for life for throwing games. The league went on to create a blacklist for those who gambled, dissipated, jumped contracts, and committed any discernable offense to the integrity of the game.[12]

Within 10 years of baseball's beginning on the peninsula, it appeared that the game had become the very deviltry it was intended to replace. Many were turning against the sport:

> We are glad to learn that there will not be any organization of a base ball club (white) in Salisbury this spring. This is cheering news, as much, very much, valuable time has been wasted in this country by persons engaged in this worse than game of folly. It is not needed for exercise given in a game and is of so violent a character as to be injurious to the health of those engaged. If half the time which has been lost by lookers on of this game in the state had been usefully employed by the same number of persons at some productive employment, the benefits would have been incalculable, or, had the same time been spent in the pursuit of knowledge, how much better would it? have been for the intelligence of the people. Then we say to the young men who heretofore engaged in this game, let it pass into the hands of those who have no desire to better their prospects in life, or to benefit their fellow men.[13]

Yet there was always a base of enthusiastic support for the game. In 1876 a Cincinnati newspaper referred to baseball as the "National Lunacy." While the Salisbury editor lambasted ne'er-do-well baseball players, Wes from Easton encouraged lovers of the sport:

> A word to the people. Easton can never have a successful ball club unless more attention is paid to it than there is. More time should be given to practice and the people of Easton should encourage them to do better, not praise them when victor, and scoff at them when defeated, but encourage them to try again. Give them a chance to practice, and try not to keep them from it by refusing to let them play or oppose their having suitable grounds. Base ball is one of the healthiest games and gives better exercise than anything else. It is true there is some danger in it, but what is there no danger in? The report that the Easton's catcher had the bridge of his nose broken in a practice game is false, but only struck on the nose and bruised. The club has now procured a mask and there is no more danger in that quarter.
>
> Let Easton have some excitement if it is nothing more than base ball, and she will be none the worse for it; and players, practice! practice! *practice!*
>
> —Wes[14]

One of the best documented early black teams was the Pythian Base Ball Club of Philadelphia in 1867. Two years later, Charles Douglass took his Mutual of Washington, D.C., on an extended tour of the Northeast. Douglass was an avid baseball fanatic and the son of Frederick Douglass. He played and captained several early black teams. In 1871 the Unique of Chicago took the first continental tour. From there, professionalism was certain. Black teams were playing regularly in Baltimore by 1870 in a four-team league formed and played at Newington Park.[15]

According to baseball historian Japheth Knopp, "Baseball functioned as a critical component in the separate economy catering to black consumers in the

A rare rural baseball score book signed by Miss Bessie Collison. Early local box scores typically list men as scorekeepers. Miss Collison appears as an exception. Based on the method of scoring, this book dates from the late 1860s or early 1870s (Dorchester Historical Society; photograph from the author's collection).

urban centers of both North and South." That baseball was also an integral part of the rural black community is evidenced in the earliest mention of black baseball found on the Eastern Shore in an article carrying the title "The Colored Odd-Fellows":

> Of this town accompanied by friends to the number of about three hundred made an excursion to Seaford on Tuesday of this week. They filled eight cars and were met in Seaford by a deputation of odd-fellows of that town, who escorted the visiting lodge to Ross's Grove, where croquet-playing, dancing &c were freely indulged in. Large representations from Laurel, Bridgeville and "the country round about," swelled the crowd to a thousand. The Cambridge boys were defeated in a game of base ball and presented the Seaford Club with a large ball. The Citizen says the best of order prevailed. They reached Cambridge on the return about nine o'clock. The proceeds of the trip, which are said considerable, will go towards purchasing instruments for a brass band.[16]

Eighteen seventy-eight would prove to be another fever season. The Easton Club accepted a free ride from the railroad for the trip to Greensboro, Maryland, for a game. The *Easton Star* editor and an entourage were also invited. The newspaper man reported on the town's fine houses and public buildings and the hospitality of their hosts, with homes being open to the Easton contingent for refreshments. The game ended after seven innings, Easton having to catch the train home, where they arrived at 5:30 p.m. The railroad was profusely thanked by all for their generosity. He lastly reported that "challenges are flying between the Easton and other clubs." One of those challenges was with the Queenstown Club, played in the town of Centreville. Like the Cambridge team five years earlier, the Easton Club was required to sit around until 3 o'clock as the home team waited for its players to arrive at the station. Easton took their loss politely in the newspapers, complimenting their hosts for their hospitality, and the Queenstown Club players for their civility. The Queenstown Club then issued its big challenge for a match game to be played in July against any team on the Shore for the best silver ball money could buy in New York City. In the article one of the Queenstown players disparaged the Easton nine, "The presumption of these Eastonians makes me sick. The idea of such indifferent players undertaking to play with us. Umph." On July 6, the *St. Michaels Comet* conjectured Easton would decline the challenge. There was an exchange between Queenstown and Easton that each other's players were "some pumpkins." There is no record of a game played for a silver ball but there was plenty of baseball activity.[17]

In August Easton partook of a "friendly game" with the newly formed St. Michaels Club. The Easton lineup included some new names with Tucker pitching, Roche catching, and Grove at shortstop. A month later Easton again faced what was now the Bolingly Club of Queenstown in what was billed as the second of a series of match games. Again, Easton sent onto the field the battery of Tucker and Roche as they evened the series.

Gambling was also a part of rural town baseball, and, again, might be an explanation for the extreme behavior of many rural fans if large sums of money were involved. Incidents of gambling did not always reach the printed accounts of games but appear frequently enough to indicate it was commonplace.

The Wilmington Quicksteps of the late 1870s were a highly regarded professional team. Due to their location on the East Coast, they were a favorite exhibition stop for National Association and National League teams on road trips, and they won many of those contests. The Salisbury White Cloud claimed the baseball championship of the Eastern Shore from 1872 to 1875. Even so, to get the Quicksteps to the town of Salisbury took some enticing and that was, assuredly, money.

> During this regime the famous Quicksteps of Wilmington had become one of the stars of the baseball firmament. They had met and defeated some of the best teams of that day. Salisbury, ambitious and confident, "sighing for more worlds to conquer," deemed the Quicksteps fair fruit so arranged a series of games with them.... It was September when the Quicksteps "came down like wolves on the fold." Out on the Fair Grounds they met. The Quicksteps went out turning handsprings and throwing somersaults. They had padded their team with Lafferty, of the famous Athletics, and two or three other league players. They thought they had a picnic, and they had, but Salisbury had strengthened by getting Tucker, a curve pitcher, Roach, catcher, and Groves 2b., from Baltimore. In the presence of about 1,000 of our best citizens the battle began. If the Quicksteps had consulted the seer of Wilmington perhaps they would have heard the warning:
>
> > Quickstep, Quickstep, beware the day
> > When you meet Salisbury in battle array.

Salisbury won both matches, after which it was reported, "The Quicksteps, after the game, wanted to make a match for $500 a side, intending no doubt to pad their team. Their bluff was called by Col. Samuel A. Graham, who was a lover of the game and never missed one—offering to back the Salisbury bet, the same men to be played, game to be played at Dover. This did not suit the Quicksteps, so the game was never played."[18]

Wilmington newspapers indicated at least two games were played between the two teams. The first was delayed when "broken up" by fans and called for darkness in the eighth inning with Salisbury winning 9–8. The second game resulted in the White Cloud taking a lopsided 16–6 victory. On October 28, 1878, it was announced that a third game was to be played in the neutral town of Dover, but a letter from Colonel Graham in the same publication refused the match for $500 since Wilmington insisted on improving their roster with imported talent.[19]

There had even been a call to form a peninsula league that year, but it fell on deaf ears. After the fever season the inevitable happened. In their excitement, towns went after what were referred to as "imported players," or "foreign men." Most towns overspent for professional players in their enthusiasm, and with evidence of significant gambling, communities periodically opted for a more affordable caliber of baseball for a couple of years. In 1879 one alarmed fan decried, "What has become of our ballists?" Activity appears to have decreased throughout the peninsula. By September, the *Easton Star* editor, Thomas Robeson, confidently declared, "Base ball appears to be playing out in this country. Racing is the only sport bound to last. A good race is better than a play." At first Robeson appeared to have been justified. Easton and Trappe announced a best-of-three series for the championship of the county, and the first game was played. A second game was not played until a year later, and there is no record of the third. In 1880 Greensborough went to Denton and it was only "by dint of a good deal of hunting around, the home nine were enabled to get together the required number to play."[20]

Transportation on the Shore continued to improve. More track was laid, and steamboat companies coordinated their schedules with the rails. All of those independently owned and operated were being absorbed by larger entities that further improved their efficiency. By the late 1870s a Baltimore resident looking to escape the city's summer heat could catch a ferry to the port of Oxford on the Eastern Shore, grab the train, and be in the new beach resort of Ocean City, Maryland, in less than two hours. It was in the 1870s that the Atlantic Hotel was built in this sandy, sleepy, windswept ocean village. Ocean City was now promoting itself as a tourist destination with its cooling ocean breezes and waters. The docks in Claiborne and Cambridge would offer the same rail services for vacationers in a few years. Still a daylong trip from Baltimore for most, it demonstrated a new mobility and opportunity. But this trip from the western shore was not something everyone could afford, monetarily, or time-wise.

The Eastern Shore had undergone a migration of the population from 1820 to 1840, but now many anticipated and hoped to profit from the postwar growth brought on by the railroads of the 1860s and 1870s. William Halstean was one, but not the only one, of those visionaries and carpetbaggers. A real estate agent from New York state, he recognized the region's new direction. Halstean listed his Eastern Shore properties and large estates in promotional pamphlets that he distributed directly into wealthy urban markets. These pamphlets extolled the virtues of the peninsula, vast stands of timber, agriculture, fisheries, and commerce. He confidently predicted a mass immigration of labor and capital, saying the region was "destined to become one of the finest agricultural and manufacturing districts in the land." The town of Crisfield was literally built by the railroad on oyster shells and 3,000 people had moved to the new bustling port town by 1900.[21]

Others saw this potential as well. By the 1860s, railroad guides were published for professional travelers and adventurous tourists from the increasing middle class. These guides provided brief descriptions of different geographic areas, including the Eastern Shore. Monthly periodicals of the 1870s also featured the Eastern Shore and its attractions for their middle-class readers and potential tourists. It was described as a "Peninsular Canaan," and a "forgotten nook." One writer perceived the clash of this immigration and the distinct, isolated cultural ethos of the Eastern Shore:

"A tide of immigration has set in from the northern latitudes which has already produced a marked impression upon populations as the great attractions of the country become more widely known, it will undoubtedly swell the proportions which most revolutionize public sentiment ... especially when sentiment is the result of the hold maintained by old traditions and local ideas upon the affection of the people."[22]

4

Grass in the Springtime

> Baseball, like the famous ghost will not down. The noble, patriotic game, like grass in the springtime, comes creeping, creeping everywhere.
> —*Salisbury Advertiser*, June 8, 1895

While a significant amount of the attention focused on baseball in the 1870s may have tended to the negative, it was still the decided attraction of the rural summer season. A game in Salisbury between Seaford and the Salisbury White Cloud drew an estimated 2,000 people to their shaded grounds, where they took in $150 on 10-cent admissions. Salisbury excited these fans with a 21–20 win secured with a one-handed grab down the line by left fielder Gillis, after which "pandemonium broke loose! Shouts of victory, hats, bonnets, canes and umbrellas rent the air!" Salisbury's population barely exceeded 2,000 at the time. A game in the town of Federalsburg in 1884 charged the same 25-cent admission levied by the major league American Association, and still drew 1,000 enthusiasts. Federalsburg's population was no more than a thousand. Crowds equal to or exceeding a community's population were not everyday occurrences, but neither were they unusual, and significant crowds of around half the town's population were a regularity.[1]

The communities of the Eastern Shore located on the Chesapeake Bay had their westerly bay breezes and cooling waters. The bayside towns of Tolchester and Betterton in Kent County were located on the narrower northern neck of the bay and directly across from Baltimore. By the 1870s they were promoting themselves as a more convenient and affordable option to the long trip to the Atlantic Hotel and Ocean City. These two towns offered Baltimore and Philadelphia tourists the enticing alliterative combination of bay breezes, boardwalk, beaches, bathing beauties and baseball. Both towns were noted for the excellence of their baseball grounds, and the quality of the baseball teams that played in these towns was a top drawing card for the tourists. Tolchester sometimes fielded their own team, but usually rented their grounds to local and touring teams, sometimes filling the town to capacity. Betterton became known for the quality of their town team, printing and circulating their schedule so that the baseball fans of Baltimore and Philadelphia could plan their excursions around games of interest. All Eastern Shore towns encouraged day excursions from Baltimore, even if not to the same degree as these two resorts. Steamboats would drop off hundreds of people in the bayside communities, where they toured the towns and spent money. Baseball and tourism would form an important partnership in the Eastern Shore's economy. An idyllic example of one of these excursions came from Chestertown:

> The Chestertown base ball club went to Betterton on Saturday last and played an interesting game with the Betterton Club.... After the game the club and visitors were entertained at Spry's Hotel so noted for the excellence of its table, and thoroughly enjoyed a splendid supper of white perch, crabs in all styles, chickens, etc. Mirth provoking stories of the "champion eater" of Betterton who gets away with gingerbread, ice-cream and coconuts against time enhanced the meal and seemed to stir up the boys to gastronomic efforts little short of the "champion." It is reported that "the major" who was offered a free seat to Betterton and refused to go, wept on hearing of the supper.
>
> The club set out to return about 8 o'clock and songs and jests were the order of the evening. It was 10 o'clock when the club reached home after the most pleasant trip of the year.[2]

The gastronomic favor was returned two weeks later at Arminger and Spark's Hotel in Chestertown.

Typically, a visiting baseball contingent, whether from a Shore town, or from across the bay could include a couple hundred or more people. The visiting team, sometimes with a second nine, would include family, friends, fans, and the town brass band. Sometimes town teams used regularly scheduled trains or steamers, but often they chartered their passages. Clubs advertised passage to games for their fans, and the response would be so great that the steamboat company would hire a sloop for the excess of passengers and tow it to their destination. It was acknowledged practice that all games end in time for the visitors to make their connection home. When early departures cut a game short, the unwritten rural rule was for the game to be treated the same as a rainout, as it was when the railroad provided the excursion for the Easton Club to Greensboro in 1878.

Baseball's growth also benefited from the absence of direct competition for people's attention, at least on the Eastern Shore at this time. There were very few activities that could compete with baseball as a participatory, spectator, or social event. Horse racing also gained in popularity in the late 1860s. As with baseball, challenges were often printed in the newspapers, and certain roads outside of town became informal raceways. Also driven by gambling, harness racing became popular on the peninsula, and multiple oval tracks sprang up in rural locations in each county. These were built by equine and competitively minded farmers. Eventually most county seats would build a fairground for formal seasonal meets to augment informal matches at these smaller gathering places. The fairgrounds served as the site of the county fair, balloon ascensions, bicycle racing, shooting matches, horse racing, and included the baseball grounds. One county fair horse racing event in the 1890s reported a crowd of 4,000, but the fairs lasted only a week. The rest of the summer belonged to baseball.

The only event that could consistently compete with baseball for crowd appeal was the camp meeting. These were religious rallies held throughout the warmer months. Some were sponsored by local churches, others led by itinerant preachers. They were so popular that tent villages sprung up in the woods and clearings around the main canopy, and families might spend a week or more camped out in religious fervor. Some rural churches actually gave up and closed during the summer, yielding to the competition. Camp meetings drew crowds, sometimes in the thousands, as much for social opportunities as for any spiritual improvement or inspiration. It did not take long for town teams to realize the opportunity provided them. Players and managers went to the camp meetings in order to promote their team and upcoming games.

Competitive sailing also emerged on the bay as commercial watermen put their working skipjacks, bugeyes, and log canoes in races against each other. Sailboat racing likely emerged out of the Oyster Wars being waged on the bay. Since the Civil War the oyster was a favorite item on restaurant menus from Boston to Savannah, and the Chesapeake Bay oyster was the most prized. In many cities street vendors offered oysters for a penny each and were advertised as "fresh from the bed every day." Oyster pirates throve on both shores of the bay, the dredgers raiding unsanctioned areas, or oyster beds set aside for the tongers. The newly formed Maryland Oyster Police, or "navy," as it was sometimes called, were hard pressed to stop them. The competition and threat of danger led to the need for more speed out of their sailing work boats. The pirates were usually better armed and their boats built for speed to elude pursuit. But the racing that evolved out of this environment did not allow easy spectating.

By the 1880s the oyster industry was in full swing. There were over 20,000 people on the Eastern Shore working, shucking, packing and shipping the bivalve. Dorchester County alone had more than a hundred seafood packing houses of varying sizes. In one year Dorchester harvested a million bushels of oysters, over half going to market in Oxford or on buy boats that plied the bay to purchase the oysters before the boats put back in to harbor. This shortened the distance to the vendors and shippers of Baltimore. And that was just one out of the eight Eastern Shore counties that partook of the oyster trade. This boom in oysters created a severe labor shortage for farming, considered by many to be the mainstay of the peninsula economy. With the railroads, agriculture had quickly expanded. By 1876 Queen Anne County alone was producing nearly a million three-pound cans of peaches a year and another 33,000 pounds dried. One farm had over 135,000 peach trees and employed more than 700 workers in peak season. There were jobs to be had on the Eastern Shore for those willing to move there. Many came as migratory workers to the fields and canning houses from urban areas. They were often referred to as "Polish" regardless of their race or ethnicity, and usually lived in small, squalid quarters through the hot picking and canning seasons.

Metropolitan restaurants were clamoring for more than oysters, rockfish and terrapin. All types of wild waterfowl were considered a delicacy at discerning tables. A flourishing local and urban market developed for these birds that filled the rivers and skies of the Chesapeake. While some trapped their prey, most were harvested with the gun under dangerous conditions. Most hunting was done on cold winter nights on icy rivers and snowbound shores.

Several methods of hunting were devised. The sink box was popular in coves and shallow water. It allowed a man to lie down below water's level and pop up to shoot. The weakness of the method was that one floated at water level and was easily swamped. It was usually a long, cold walk to shore when that happened. Another method was the skiff. The narrow 12-foot skiff normally used was silently rowed to the prey, where the hunter stood in a crouch and blasted with his shotgun. Others arrayed a battery of up to seven 12-gauge shotguns across the bow of the little skiff to deadly affect. Some only mounted three barrels to the bow, but they might range from 0' to 4' gauge. But the prized weapon was the "big gun." These could range over 10 feet in length with stock and had a two-inch muzzle-loading bore. These cannons had a shoulder stock and were fired as a rifle from a standing or prone position in the skiff, and the discharge thundered down the dark rivers. An industry grew up around dressing and shipping the many species of birds. Though hard and dangerous, market hunting paid and appealed to the independent nature of many Eastern Shoremen. It was considered a respected profession.[3]

One of the things that helped grow the enthusiasm for baseball on the Eastern Shore was the major leagues. Baltimore had a franchise in the first major league, the National Association, from 1872 to 1874. Baltimore failed to gain entry to the new National League formed in 1876, and it was not until the American Association was formed in 1882 to compete with the National League that Baltimore got a second chance at a major league franchise. They were managed through most of their 10-year existence by Billie Barnie. At one time they were referred to as a "bunch of cast-off beer tanks," but Barnie did manage to scout up a handful of talented players and field a couple of respectable clubs, though they were mostly a second division team. Nevertheless, enthusiasm ran high as Eastern Shore towns could now receive the Baltimore newspapers within a day and many local baseball fanatics followed the Orioles religiously. A Cambridge newspaper took notice:

> Cambridge is full of base ball enthusiasts who never tire of discussing the subject. Each day the arrival of the newspaper is eagerly awaited, and the first piece of news looked for is the base ball score. There are several young men in town who know the names of every player in the American Association.... Politics, railroad disasters, conflagrations (sic), occupy a small part of popular attention here compared to the latest game of ball. Whenever a young man, or even an old one, is noticed to be unusually lively in speech or manner, you can safely put it down that he is describing or illustrating some ballists' accomplishments.[4]

While there were periodic American Association or National League franchises in Washington, D.C., at the time, Baltimore was Maryland's franchise. Eighteen eighty-seven was one of the better years for Barnie's Orioles and a big series with the American Association champion St. Louis Browns drew 15,000 people. It was reported,

> People who never took an interest in base ball were asking all sorts of questions and making all sorts of prophesies yesterday. Business was a matter of no consequence and, if necessary, stores were locked, for the clerk must go to the game. It is not too much to say that the city was raised to a frenzy in the matter, and everybody was crazy.... The excitement

was not confined to the city, by any means but throughout the state the greatest interest was manifested, and five hundred people came to town from points along the lines from Western Maryland, while the Eastern Shore boats brought great crowds in the morning. There were probably 2,000 in the city from out-of-town points. During the entire day the night telegrams inquiring the score were coming to the American offices from points in the counties, in Delaware and Virginia—one coming from Roanoke, and another coming all the way from North Carolina.[5]

Fever seasons swept the Shore again in 1883 and 1884. The change in ownership of the Baltimore Orioles, and the new hope that comes from such transitions, may have contributed to a degree, but other factors certainly played a role in the resurgence in enthusiasm and activity. Early in 1883 Salisbury admitted to a "weakness for the movements on the diamond," but a team did not form until June. In Chestertown it was reported that "several base ball nines at various points are distinguishing themselves in one way or the other," and in Dorchester County it was agreed that "base ball clubs are being organized throughout the county, and the games seems destined to become more popular."[6]

It was in Dorchester County that baseball enthusiasm reached its highest pitch. Teams emerged out of all the villages and hamlets, and now obscure crossroads and districts like Bucktown and Drawbridge. The Cyclones came out of Williamsburg, and the Red Stockings from Crotcher's Ferry. The Resolute of Cambridge had always been the power of the county, but they fell to the Pastime of Taylor's Island. Flush with victory the Pastime took on the Bayards, which developed into an inane dispute that drained the supply of ink at local newspapers. Under the militaristic headlines "Base Ball Battle," and "The Taylor's Island Base Ball Skirmish," the two teams became embroiled in a childish dispute as each tried to catch the other on short notice without their full complement of players. When difficulties were resolved it was presented in the newspaper as "A Truce."[7]

Baltimore teams coming across the bay were becoming more common. The Maryland Club of Towsontowne made a tour of the Shore during the fever season of 1883 as the Pastime of Taylor's Island had emerged as the front runner of Dorchester County. The Marylands were referred to as an amateur club but they brought several professionals to ensure a victory in a country town. A few rural players had seen the underhand curve of Toadvine of the White Cloud in the 1870s. But the players from the Shore had a tough time with the Marylands' pitcher's now overhand curves. Undaunted by their defeat, the Pastime challenged the Baltimore-area team to a second game, which was refused in order to catch the steamer home. Within a couple of weeks of their departure, Pastime pitcher Henry Lake unleashed his version of the overhand curve on the local nines.[8]

Teams folded and reorganized during the chaotic season. Throughout the summer the team from the railroad crossing of Linkwood had gone undefeated, and their open challenge was ignored by all. After finally beating a Cambridge nine, Linkwood claimed the county championship. None of this was satisfactory to baseball fans. There were exhortations in local papers for the formation of a peninsula association.

The main reasons town teams eschewed leagues and the schedules that went with them were health, strategy, and finances. The challenge method of arranging games allowed teams to accept or refuse depending on the availability of players. The Resolute of Cambridge refused challenges due to the condition of their players' fingers, a legitimate reason in a gloveless era. Catchers endured the most of bruised hands and broken fingers. A schedule would also eliminate the popular ploy of telegraphing late challenges. A league and a schedule also committed a town to specific dates requiring a regular and significant cash flow spurred by competition. When a team felt that they had failed to procure enough foreign men to ensure victory, they simply did not show up. Appearance bonds soon became part of the pregame negotiations, but these were unenforceable and uncollectable unless escrowed. While an association or league may have produced a clear-cut champion, dubious and unsubstantiated claims were more easily asserted. Independence was preferred more than anything else.

At the end of 1883 it was reported that Somerset County had boasted seven teams, while the town of Smyrna, Delaware, fielded nine. Easton ended their season with a "Fete Champêtre" with St. Michaels. To start the 1884 season the young Dr. J.H. Shepherd, one of the few respected umpires in the region, repeated the call for a peninsula association, commenting on the "unsatisfactory and irregular system" being used to determine championships. Shepherd called for a meeting. "The association would adopt rules and regulations of government, which ought to receive support and co-operation of its members. The effect ... would be that each team would have the opportunity at specified dates to play every other team in the association during the season for the county championship and whatever prize may be offered." Nobody was ready for that just yet.[9]

The fever continued into 1884. The team from the village of Sudlersville in Queen Anne's County was said to be the best team in three counties. The Bayards and the Clevelands, financed by the political coffers of presidential hopefuls, continued to bicker in Dorchester County without an association to govern them, while the youthful Muffers took over as the town team of Cambridge after they beat the Pastime and the Resolute for bragging rights of the county. The Muffers would remain the dominant team there and one of the best on the Shore for several years. Easton was determined to raise their standard as well, and rumored to be using an imported pitcher from Baltimore. Easton denied the accusation by saying the pitcher had lived in the county for some time and was engaged in farming.

The Maryland Club made a second tour of the Shore in 1884 and faced Easton. The Easton Club kept up with the Marylands until the eighth inning, when their catcher's hands gave out and he had to be replaced. The visitors then scored 11 runs in the last two innings for the win. It was an example that losing a starting catcher on a town team was as devastating as losing a pitcher. The catcher's glove and chest protector were just coming into wide use in the major leagues and the local players were quick to adopt all innovations as they became available. Easton then played the touring Madison Squares of New York City and their professional Baltimore battery of Taliaferro and Mills. A "miscommunication" by telegram caught Easton without their full complement of players, including their own professional pitcher, but they played anyhow for an inevitable loss. Easton raised their prices from 15 cents for general admission and 25 cents for box seats to a major league 25 cents general admission for all tickets for the event. When the Butchers of Baltimore arrived on the heels of the Madison Squares, Easton retained the Madison Square battery. Taliaferro was "taken ill" but no accusations were made of the itinerate pitcher.[10]

One notable, if frequent, sort of account does appear in the 1884 season. The up-and-coming Muffers took on the Federalsburg Redcaps at Todd's Park in Cambridge. The umpire, a Mr. Sullivan, was accused of being partial, and taken to task by a home crowd that he could not keep off the field.

> The game was made remarkable by the (to be moderate) odd and clearly incorrect decisions of the umpire, a Mr. Sulivane {sic} of Federalsburg. These decisions were unfortunately averse to the home nine every time, and the spectators expressed their disapproval very emphatically. The fact is probably that the umpire was not posted, besides being nervous and excitable.... We deprecate any interference of the spectators with the game; and the umpire being master of the field, as on Friday last it would have tried Job's patience to have witnessed the umpire's willful partiality without protesting.[11]

None of this was unusual. A week later the American Associations rules regarding an umpire's responsibility and powers to control spectator interference at games were printed, but mobs storming the field to protest umpires simply mirrored the national scene.

A headline had recently appeared in a *Baltimore American* newspaper, "Bad Row at Oriole Park—A Close Decision Raises an Ugly Spirit in the Crowd—A Run for Brennan—A Blow in the Jaw—An Exciting Game." During a game in Baltimore umpire John Brennan made a bad call in the third inning that rankled the home crowd. A second bad call in the 10th brought hundreds onto the field, one waving a huge revolver, threatening to shoot Brennan if he made another wrong decision. The police and both teams restored order. Brennan took abuse from the crowd for the remainder of the game. In the 13th inning, Brennan called the contest for darkness and the mob descended a second time. This time Brennan was punched to the ground, then spirited away by the Orioles players to the temporary safety of the clubhouse. He was later snuck to an Orioles player's house for his safety, and then put on the first train out of town. The man who punched Brennan was fined $1. No report was found of the man with the revolver being charged.[12]

Umpires would prove to be a particular problem for the typically raucous rural crowds of the Eastern Shore. The first few years they had not been an issue. Easton had their celebrity umpire in 1867, and most games were officiated by members of nearby clubs. They were knowledgeable of the game, and whether working a social or match game, they could count on a party afterward. Competition changed that. When fractious fans started to take to the field, neighboring club members no longer wanted anything to do with umpiring. No one wanted to be hounded by a mob.

Towns now appointed or solicited local umpires A visiting team and contingent now faced a home team, a hometown umpire, and hundreds or thousands of hometown fans who thought it their right to harass visiting fans and storm the field on the merest pretext. No matter how good the hospitality of town tours, brass bands, the fare of local restaurants or private homes, the game itself could be intimidating. In an attempt to mitigate these occurrences, clubs began to negotiate whose town's umpire would work the game. It made sense that a visiting umpire would not dare stretch the bounds of impartiality by overly favoring his team on foreign grounds, but that did not always work, as already noted. Over time, the umpires became associated directly with the team rather than the town. When the Ring Tail Rovers of Cambridge listed their opening season roster, it included their umpire. A team photo of the Sudlersville Club includes their umpire in the picture, as did the photo of the 1907 Cambridge team.

At times, certain umpires gained a name for themselves for their "impartiality," which was more common than it would seem. Complimenting the umpire for a job well done did happen with a modest frequency. Yet even those umpires with favorable reputations could sometimes skew things for a home team. In 1885 St. John's of Annapolis took on the Federalsburg Redcaps on neutral grounds in Cambridge. In the eighth inning with the score tied at 10, a dispute arose over a decision by respected umpire C.T. Parks, who had been brought in for the occasion. During the discussion St. John's had to leave in order to catch the steamer home. At first the game seems to have been concluded under the rainout provision. One newspaper did report it as a tie, but no lead was safe on the Shore, even after the game was over. With St. John's several days departed, and the width of the bay in between, Mr. Parks declared Federalsburg the winner, citing rule 39, section 2 of the *American Base Ball Guide*. This regulation stated that when a team refused to play the game, it was forfeited and not suspended. In the umpire's estimation, catching the last boat home constituted a refusal to play.[13]

As some umpires gained such a reputation and were brought in as neutral participants, there was the possibility they were being paid for their troubles. But the preferred umpire was always your own. The use of two umpires was also tried, but this usually just led to 10-man teams with each umpire working diligently for his own club. There was never a satisfactory solution during this era, but given the volatile nature of baseball fans of the times, the concept of a fairly called game was impossible for most fans to fathom.

Gambling also continued through the decade and may help explain the acrimonious crowds. In a game with the Muffers in 1885 the Taylor's Island Eclipse picked up a pitcher, R.T. Magennis of Baltimore, for the occasion. Expecting victory, the Taylor's Island fans were devastated as they watched their expensive hurler falter in the seventh inning. When the Muffers emerged the victors, Magennis' own team accused him of having thrown the game. The insinuation was that he had accepted money to pitch for the Dorchester Club, and then accepted more money from the other side for a more advantageous personal outcome. A bet on the game would have rendered yet an even more profitable day. In such situations a savvy and amoral player could significantly improve his already lucrative compensation for a day's work. Later, the Eclipse attempted a rematch and challenged the Cambridge Club for the championship of the county for anywhere from $50 to $500 a side. But the Muffers thought their opponents had "more money than confidence," and declined the offer.[14]

In the 1880s baseball asserted itself as an indelible part of the rural Eastern Shore culture. Prosperity and population were steadily rising after the Civil War. The larger towns were building fairgrounds, with baseball grounds provided. In Cambridge it was the Driving Park, and in Easton the Idlewild Fairgrounds, from which the town team took its name. Salisbury also had its Fair Grounds. The Muffers of Cambridge and the Idlewilds of Easton played an important series in 1887. The vaunted Muffers were surprised by the lopsided loss, but qualified it in their account, noting that "Easton had put up a trick," and used an imported pitcher and catcher. For the rematch played in Cambridge two weeks later, "The merchant left his counter, the carpenter dropped his tools, and the professional men forsook their offices for the base ball field." More than a thousand gathered for the 10:00 a.m. start but a bitter dispute ensued. Easton had brought too many imported players, and while the Muffers were willing to take on all of Talbot County, they were not willing to tackle the "whole country." A protracted discussion raged as to who and how many of each team's professionals would play. The Muffers were not caught shorthanded, running out to the pitcher's box the Baltimore semipro hurler familiar to local fans. But Taliaferro had little success on the Shore, giving up six runs in two innings before Cambridge replaced him with the curveballing Lake. The Muffers battled back and won the eight-inning contest before the Idlewild had to depart to catch the steamer.[15]

Even when baseball on the Eastern Shore transitioned from club vs. club to town vs. town, the unwritten rule was that a town's team be represented by the best young men that town had to offer. But this remaining vestige of the quaint custom of amateur superiority of character over professionalism hung on as long as it could. It was a competitive environment that transcended baseball to include everything from commercial dealings to who had the best town brass band. Towns did not routinely admit to the use of foreign men. Most references come from the losers and malcontents. Baseball increasingly became the means by which a town measured itself against its neighbor, and no expense was spared.

Black baseball seemed to prosper through the 1880s. Sol White, an early black baseball pioneer and historian, referred to it as the "money period." Professional teams were forming in all the cities on the East Coast and in the Midwest. A second professional opportunity came on what might be referred to as the resort circuit. Many of the better jobs available to African Americans came as service staff for posh restaurants, hotels, and the associated railroads. Baseball experience might be included on a man's job application. In 1886 the Southern League of Base Ballists was formed. A year later several clubs met at the Douglas Institute in Baltimore to attempt the National Colored Base Ball League. In 1888 there was a colored championship played for a silver ball. But make no mistake that the difficulties of Jim Crow were replacing Reconstruction, as was the case in Cambridge in 1887 when it was reported,

> Some white and colored boys had a little disagreement about ball playing on the new academy lot on Saturday evening last the colored lads becoming greatly offended. That night in town they organized a crowd to have revenge and armed themselves with clubs for the purpose. They became so insolent and boisterous that Bailiff Anderson took one to the lock up. The decided actions of some citizens dispersed what one time threatened to be a mob.[16]

The "decided actions" were not described.

At the end of the 1880s one can still see the dichotomy of the initial and continuing social expectations of a baseball event, and the more seedy competitive nature of the game. Two reports illustrate the good, the bad, and the ugly of baseball in rural towns:

> It was very warm last Friday when the baseball nine and their admirers left Secretary wharf to sail over to Jamaica Point to play the Trappe team. It was a jovial party of about twenty, bent on having a good time. Despite unfavorable wind we soon reached Jamaica Point, thanks to the excellent management of the boat by Mr. Charles Spence. The party was met at the Point by teams and we were soon enjoying our six-mile ride to Trappe, our driver pointing out the objects of interest along the way. We made note of one thing, and that is we saw no wheat to beat ours around New Market. We noticed fine stands of clover. We soon reached Trappe and received a cordial welcome. After taking a stroll through the interesting town we adjourned to the ball field. We found the Trappe nine to be as gentlemanly a club as we have ever crossed bats with and we were treated well by the spectators, though our boys were winning. After meeting the genial editor of the Talbot Times, admiring the nice looking girls and altogether enjoying ourselves immensely, we left, hoping we made on them half as good an "impression" as they made on us.[17]

Yet two months later an account indicates the other direction baseball could take in "Cambridge vs. Oxford-Tell the Truth." It was written as a defensive response to a scathing piece in another newspaper. The correspondent stated the crux of the problem:

"It is perhaps well to state that about the only items of truth contained in the communication from Oxford, appearing in the Easton Gazette of July 20th, are the score and the assertion that the umpire is a fair and square man. That the umpire did his best no one doubts, and we have no desire to criticize his work except to say that on several occasions his decisions were decidedly off, and though no partiality was intended, every decision was in favor of the Tred Avon club." But there was more, and the writer disparaged his opponents. The American Association fined the pitchers when they hit a batter starting in the 1880s, and later, they settled on awarding first base, but many umpires required the batter to be hit with "sufficient force." Not all were uniform in the interpretation of this rule or its enforcement. So the "pitcher of the Tred Avon was struck several times by Lake, but this became a topic of laughter to the crowd present, as all were convinced that he despaired of ever coming near the ball in any other manner. Lake is a fair man, and would scorn to injure an opponent in such a manner."

The correspondent then felt compelled to justify the third accusation imposed on the Cambridge squad: "We frankly admit that the crowd was heartily in sympathy with the home club, and we would like to see any home crowd show any other disposition. That the umpire was surrounded by an eager, excited crowd we also admit, and opposition was offered to many of his decisions. That violence was offered or intended, we deny." If violence was not intended, it was certainly felt by the visitors. Eastern Shore fans were used to intimidation at baseball games, and expected it, but the actions of the Cambridge fans must have transcended the accepted norm and the correspondent went on with his attempt at his version of events and continued with his we-are-only-human defense and a lame apology:

> We have no desire to defend the Cambridge crowd, and wish the game could have been played without any of the display of excited partisanship, which is always exhibited in local games, whether in Oxford or Cambridge. We have not reached the millennium yet, and until then, do not expect to see an amateur game without the usual display of excited feeling and interest ... it is evident that the Oxford boys were badly seated, and in fear of that terrible mob which would not have permitted them to win under any circumstances.

The correspondent acted incredulous, "as we thought our nine had won a well-played and hotly contested game of ball on its merits, and it is deeply mortifying to find what we considered to be a game fairly won was not won at all, but simply presented in order that the appetite of the Cambridge mob for gore might be satisfied."

In the end the Cambridge defender admits the accuracy of the Oxford account and asks for better treatment at the hands of Oxford if there was to be a rematch played there. "In conclusion, let us beg the Tred Avon club and the Oxford public to show the Cambridge nine, when the return game is played, that courtesy and fair treatment which they claim to have found lacking here; and if a game is played let it be decided on its merits, and not by the bull-dozing tactics of a blood thirsty negro, backed up by a crowd of 'white toughs.'"[18]

5

The Bushes Blossom

> The absorbing thing with young people now seems to be base ball. It is the talk day and night. The church, the young people's meeting and the Sunday school are mostly given the go-by, while the game on the field is never too hot, and the peculiar lingo that belongs to such exciting contests is readily absorbed by these young hopefuls. A simple game of ball for diversion is all right, but parents can hardly look upon the demoralizing association and bad language so prevalent in exciting contests as a good thing for boys of an impressionable age.
>
> —*Easton Gazette,* August 4, 1894

It was a hot summer day in 1897 when hundreds of fans of the Federalsburg Club gathered for a game. This small town of barely a thousand souls was proud of their team. Little did they know that three of the teenagers taking the field for them that day would make it to the major leagues. Jack "the Whirlwind" Townsend was from across the border in Delaware and as a boy walked around imitating the deliveries of star pitchers of the day. He developed a blazing fastball throwing rocks to knock apples from trees. It was his way of enlivening the otherwise mundane chore of feeding the pigs on his father's farm. Behind the plate was Bob Unglaub. Bob grew up two blocks from Oriole Park in Baltimore and worked his way from the knothole gang to batboy to mascot of the league champion Orioles. He learned the finer points of the game shagging flies and practicing with future Hall of Fame players like John McGraw, Hughie Jennings, Wee Willie Keeler, and Wilbert Robinson. Down on third base for Federalsburg was Chappy Charles. He left New Jersey as Charles Achenbach and turned up in Federalsburg as Chappy Charles. How and why did these three young men and future major league players end up on the baseball team of this small, rural community, supposedly so far off the beaten track?[1]

The previous, nominally clandestine, use of foreign men during the last 20 years became open and accepted during the 1890s. Any stigma attached gave way to competition, enthusiasm, and economics. One of the first to do so seems an unlikely candidate as professional innovator. Washington College in Chestertown, Maryland, lies on the banks of the Chester River. During this era, the college student body was composed of 70 to 80 young men. From 1866 to about 1880 they primarily played against local amateur nines. That changed with the formation of the Maryland Intercollegiate Athletic Association, established to determine Maryland college sports champions. Facing Western Maryland, Mt. St. Mary's, Maryland Agricultural College (University of Maryland), and St. John's College of Annapolis raised the level of play. In 1883 Washington College was accused of using an imported player, but they defended the action by saying he was from the class of '80 and therefore legitimate.

There were no restrictions on paying college players in the 1890s, and most seemed to do it. New Windsor College was one of the college's new foes and was described as having players from all over the country, backed by a hired battery. Few of the players on the Diechman School squad were said to be enrolled there. Washington College responded to the new level of competition the only way they knew how.[2]

In 1891, the college faced an important game with rival St. John's of Annapolis. A young Baltimore pitcher by the name of Dick Hawke was making the rounds as an arm for hire for semipro and town teams on both sides of the bay, so his services were secured for the game. Afterwards, the faculty, hoping to adhere to the ideal of pure amateurism, then imposed a rule that only college students could be used. Then, a week later, when their second baseman was injured, they conceded to let an outside player fill the position. All pretenses were then swept aside. Three years later Hawke, after pitching the first major league no-hitter from the modern pitching distance, was in a holdout with the Baltimore Orioles. It was fully expected that the college would sign him for the season. Unfortunately for the college, Hawke and Baltimore reached an agreement.

In 1892, the college signed local pitching sensation Al Burris, and brought in the twenty-five-year-old Dave Zearfoss as catcher and

Born in Sharptown, Maryland, Homer Smoot was the first Eastern Shore native to attain the major leagues after starting with local town teams and Washington College. Jack "Brewery" Taylor and Lou "Buttercup" Dickerson were born on Maryland's Eastern Shore, but moved at early ages (courtesy Eastern Shore Hall of Fame).

a coach. Both would see action in the major leagues. Burris got his chance in 1894 in a one-game shot with the Philadelphia Nationals after his junior year. On his return to the college he was made coach, athletic director, and a college instructor. As long as Burris was involved, he continued to use imported players. Preseason Chestertown newspapers speculated whether a player would be secured, or when another might arrive. Local talent and future major league players like Homer Smoot of Sharptown and Jack Townsend of Delaware were brought in. Burris found additional talent on the local semipro circuit with foreign men like Charles and Unglaub. When playing at the University of Maryland, Unglaub went under his middle name of Bob Alexander. When playing for Washington College, and the Eastern Shore town teams of Millington, Cambridge, Federalsburg, and Crisfield, he went by his real name.

Washington College was not the first to use foreign men, but they were early to openly report and admit it, rather than leave that to their disgruntled opponents. Others quickly followed suit and the Eastern Shore would soon gain a reputation for the quality of its baseball. One of the reasons for that was the peninsula was no commercial backwater. By now the Pennsylvania Railroad had bought up most of the independent railroads and coordinated their schedules. This was complemented by the increasing number and efficiency of the steamboat lines. While much of the country suffered through a recession in the 1890s, the Eastern Shore continued to produce crops of peaches and wheat, and the bay's fisheries of oysters, crabs, and fish were teeming. Better canning techniques further expanded national and international markets for those rich fisheries of the bay and new crops like tomatoes and potatoes. These commodities loaded the rails to Philadelphia and New York, and boats across the Chesapeake as products of the bay region extended in all directions. Quality baseball players from these nearby metropolitan areas reversed the routes of commerce to the towns of the Eastern Shore, where the money in these rural communities was flowing and the citizens were willing to spend it on baseball. In the words of one reporter, "The base ball contagion has seized upon our lads. Much practicing is done each week."[3]

Over the next few years the use of foreign men would become the rule rather than the exception. Burris, taking all his new titles at the college in stride, was not shy in his schedule. Opponents included Maryland and out-of-state colleges, Baltimore semipro teams, as well as the larger universities of Syracuse, Pennsylvania, and Villanova. When Zearfoss began his fourth and final season he was highly respected and had earned the affectionate nicknames "Old Reliable" and the "BB Slugger." After a game against a Baltimore squad, the 700 fans attending presented Zearfoss with a purse of $30 in gold, and unspecified gifts were handed out to other players.[4]

Later that summer, the Western Maryland Railroad brought its baseball team and 1,800 employees to the small but popular resort town of Tolchester in Kent County. It had rented the town's grounds for a game with a team from Hanover, Pennsylvania, who featured the future New York Giant Charlie Gettig on the mound. Both contingents must have overwhelmed the bayside community and taxed the capacity of the town's boardwalk and beaches. Certainly,

5. The Bushes Blossom   47

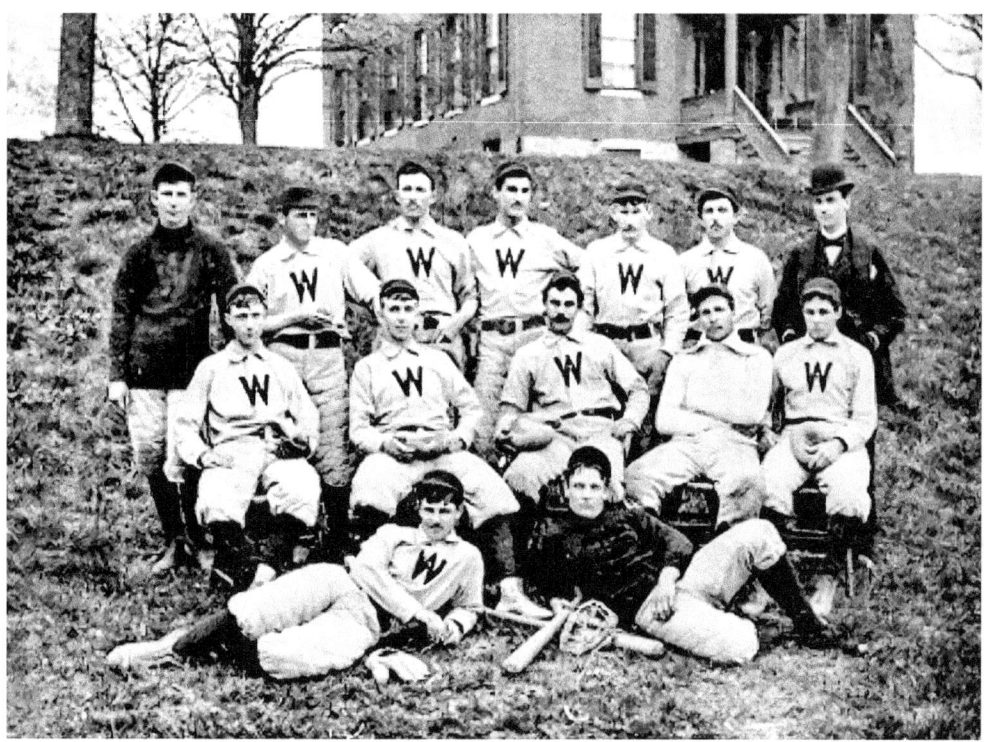

The Washington College Wissahickons of Chestertown, Maryland, 1895. The team recruited local and regional talent from the town teams of the peninsula and Baltimore. Al Burris had already seen major league action when this picture was taken. Dave Zearfoss soon would. Top row, from left: Brown, Burris, Davis, Holloway, Faithful, Boston, Perkins; middle row, from left: Deakyne, Stidham, Zearfoss, Brice, Massey, manager; bottom row, from left: Cameron, Patton (author's collection).

local baseball fans were drawn to this contest, but no actual attendance figure was given. Tolchester routinely offered to rent its grounds to touring professional teams. One year it offered a 60/40 split of the take, with dinner at the resort hotel thrown in. By 1900 Tolchester expected 5,000 people at the resort on the Fourth of July for a gala day that included beaches, breezes, swimming, boardwalk, shopping, baseball, and fireworks.[5]

When baseball began on the Eastern Shore of Maryland, Chestertown, Easton, Cambridge, and Salisbury were the major population centers. By 1890 the growing intricate tentacles of steam transportation had affected significant demographic shifts. Easton had been the second largest town in the region when baseball began with a population of 2,000. By 1880 it had reached 3,000 and leveled off there in the 1890s. Salisbury was becoming an important depot on the now named Delaware Railroad that ran south to the new port city of Cape Charles, Virginia, which ferried goods across the mouth of the Chesapeake Bay to the port of Norfolk. Because of this shift, Crisfield's rise from a pile of oyster shells was about to peak around 3,000 people as that town made the transition from a dynamic port to a lively watermen's town. When Claiborne, near St.

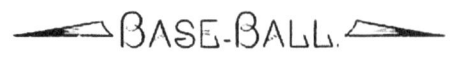

SEASON OF '95.

D. W. T. ZEARFOSS, c. and captain.

B. F. DEAKYNE, 2b.,	A. B. BURRIS, p.,
N. CAMERON, s. s.,	L. A. DAVIS, 1b.,
C. D. BOSTON, l. f.,	C. S. BROWN, c. f.,
J. G. C. STIDHAM, 3b.,	T. MASSEY, r. f.

SUBSTITUTES:

H. V. HOLLOWAY,   W. E. B. FAITHFUL,

M. PATTON.

GAMES PLAYED:

April 17,	Washington vs. Johns Hopkins,		7—6
" 20,	Washington vs. Baltimore City,		12—9
May 1,	Washington vs. Mt. St. Mary's,		(postponed)
" 4,	Washington vs. Peabody,		9—3
" 11,	Washington vs. Md. Agricultural,	(unfinished)	3—4
" 15,	Washington vs. Clinton A. C.,		8—12
" 18,	Washington vs. Johns Hopkins,		(postponed)

GAMES TO BE PLAYED:

May 25, Washington vs. W. M. C.,
June 1, Washington vs. New Windsor,
" 3, Washington vs. Pennsylvania University,
" 8, Washington vs. Clinton A. C.,
" 12, Washington vs. Mt. St. Joseph's,
Commencement Day, Washington vs. Monumentals.

Schedule and roster of the 1895 Washington College team (author's collection).

Michaels, became the primary point of embarkation for summer tourists heading to the alluring resort of Ocean City, the route passed through Salisbury. That town also became the distribution center for goods coming in and going out of the southern Shore, lower Delaware, and the Eastern Shore of Virginia. In a slow, steady increase the population went from 2,000 in 1870 to 2,700 in 1880, and continued to expand. Cambridge experienced the most profound increase in the first 25 years of baseball in the region, as its population jumped from 1,600 to 4,000. People were immigrating to the Eastern Shore. Mobility and growth translated into commercial prosperity and civic pride. These became the same, and people of the time thought there was no better way to display it than a town's baseball team. What was called a "fast" team was sure to attract quality opposition and notice from Baltimore and Philadelphia and other cities in the region. This was seen to promote and advertise the community and "put it on the map."[6]

In the words of historian Melvin Adleman, "At the heart of any meaningful analysis of athletics lies the question of sponsorship." Baseball on the rural Eastern Shore of Maryland became a total community effort. Each town had a baseball board of directors or committee. These were now usually composed of former players who later prospered and held positions of responsibility in the community. By the 1890s members of the old White Cloud assumed that role in Salisbury, as the Muffers did the same in Cambridge. All towns and villages had similar core support. Their initial responsibility was ensuring the finances necessary for uniforms and equipment, securing and maintaining the grounds, and procuring the talent needed to excel for the duration of the season. After their own contributions, they solicited money from the community through subscriptions. A subscription was a cross between owning stock and a season ticket that included a choice seat in the grandstand. Even Washington College sold subscriptions at $2 a season for gentlemen, 75 cents for ladies, and 25 cents for regular admission. But this was never enough. Local governments were expected to contribute, if not in cash, then in kind. By the late 1880s the larger communities provided playing facilities at the local fairgrounds . An Easton baller once complained of the town's tardiness in this regard saying that "suitable grounds ought at least be provided for them. There is hardly a town in the country that does not do that."[7]

All businesses were solicited for funds with the selling point that a good team advertised the town, bringing in excursionists from nearby metropolitan centers. The problem was that these contributions were not always a one-time occurrence. With each game of the season came increased competition and the need for better players, and business owners found themselves on the wrong side of something akin to a protection racket, with multiple solicitations as expectations increased. And there were also ladies' auxiliaries who raised funds for the baseball team throughout the year with bake sales, box lunches, and benefit dances. During the offseason, vaudeville and minstrel shows were advertised and brought to town to create additional revenue.

Barnstorming teams were another fundraising opportunity for local towns. In 1893 a women's team from New York described as "nine young and handsome ladies" came to the area. Five hundred fans turned out for the contest, but the game was interrupted in the fifth inning by a fight in the stands and the visitors' manager was compelled to remove the ladies for their own safety. Not everyone accepted this incursion into what was perceived by many as a man's domain. One newspaper observed, "The young ladies were well behaved and gentle and quiet, yet they seemed woefully out of their sphere.... But there is an almighty dollar in it, and that usually shadows all other questions." A competing paper shared the sentiment: "The game was very profitable for them. It is hoped they will soon make enough money to abandon the business." Such would not always be the case. Later, local fans also got a chance to see some "real Indians" with the Cherokee Nationals and the Nebraska Indians. Barnstormers like the Stricker All-Stars, the Kilduff All-Stars, the Bloomer Girls, and the Chinese Nationals were among the others that later came through the area and provided fundraising opportunities.[8]

This total town involvement of financing a team appears to have been a gradual, natural progression, assuming a coherent model by the 1890s. Individual sponsorship or ownership was the exception. The concept and the necessity of entire community commitment was clearly established by the early 1900s.

Starting in 1894 the Baltimore Orioles of the National League reeled off three straight years of first-place finishes followed by two of second-place finishes. Much excitement was generated by a team many still argue was one of the best of all time with seven future Hall of Fame players. One local pundit noticed, "In every hamlet and village of the land, there are young urchins, scarcely out of swaddling clothes, youths, and men, who's first inquiry on the receipt of the newspaper is as to the status of the professional clubs. Every town has its own club and grounds and gives the people a chance to witness the sport."[9]

Washington College opened the 1895 season with Burris coming off his one-game stint with the Philadelphia Nationals and veteran Zearfoss returning as his battery mate. The college team usually ended its campaign at graduation in June as many town teams on the peninsula did not usually form until then, sometimes waiting as late as the Fourth of July. Spring and early summer were for planting in these farming communities, and the shorter baseball season made for less expense as well. After early-season success, the college took on one of the best college nines in the country with the University of Pennsylvania. The loss did not dampen their enthusiasm. They avenged an earlier loss to the Clinton Club of Baltimore, after which Zearfoss and his teammates were presented with their hosts' tokens of appreciation. There was talk of forming a town team later in the summer to compete with the other Chestertown teams.

The Cambridge Sunshine prematurely claimed the championship of the Eastern Shore based on their early-season record, but this was the year that Salisbury, flaunting its commercial ascendency, became more ambitious with its baseball club. Some of the more successful former White Cloud players committed themselves to the best team their money could buy. They acquired players out of Wilmington, and Arthur Haddaway of Easton was one of the many impressed by the quality of the club. Under the headline "The Boys Got Licked," he observed of the Salisbury victors, "the games there are attended by the very best people. A battery is hired for the season and the expenses are vouched for by a dozen of the best men in town. As a result, their club plays good ball and every week has two or three of the leading clubs of the peninsula to play." Not everyone took Salisbury's nine in such good spirit.[10]

Salisbury and 275 supporters went to play in Laurel, Delaware, where they were met by the Laurel Guards and a brass band, but the amenities were short-lived. The *Laurel Gazette* would later accuse Salisbury of having bought the umpire. In a rematch, Laurel ignored pregame agreements and insisted an umpire with connections to their club be used and Salisbury conceded. But Salisbury brought in a former major league player for the game and the first pitch to him "received such a slap from Morlock's ash as to rise gracefully toward the cerulean and finally alight in a corn field some distance beyond and without the high board enclosure." In the sixth inning an argument erupted over a call by the

5. The Bushes Blossom 51

The new Salisbury White Cloud at Gordy Field in 1896. Easton conceded to these polished professionals. Cambridge brought in more players to compete (Nabb Research Center/Wicomico Historical Society).

Laurel umpire as he failed to yield to the vigorous protests of the Salisbury fans. The game was called with Salisbury leading, but the visitors refused to pay the $20 bet on the game.[11]

For a time in the 1890s the bicycle craze seemed to threaten baseball's hold on people's spectating fervor. Easton, Federalsburg, Chestertown, and Cambridge were among the teams that added cyclists to their rosters and were referred to as cycle or combination clubs. They offered spectators both for the price of admission, and fans were as likely to see professional cyclists as baseball players. People complained when Federalsburg hired cyclists for a race, but not about the imported players on the baseball team. But the allure of the bicycle craze equaled baseball's for a few short years before it settled into its own smaller niche.

The highlight of the Salisbury 1895 season was a three-game series with the reformed Cycle Club of Cambridge. The first match took place at the Driving Park in Cambridge. The Cycle Club came out on top in an exciting 14–13 come from behind win. The Salisbury Club was publicly admonished in the press that they could not be successful just by sitting around and talking baseball all day in front of Schenk's Hotel. The rematch that took place in Salisbury in July was just as exciting, if for different reasons. The score was tied 4–4 in the ninth inning with one out when Salisbury got a man on base. He promptly stole second. Then the

During the bicycle craze of the 1890s, many town teams formed and referred to themselves as Cycle or Combination clubs. They offered fans a chance to watch and bet on a bicycle race and a baseball game for a single admission. This appears to be the Avon Cycle and Base Ball Club of Easton, c. 1896 (courtesy Talbot Historical Society).

Cambridge umpire called the man out on a pickoff play. The runner jumped up in protest. The Cambridge umpire, named Percy, called the Salisbury player an "a__ hole" and the Salisbury crowd stormed the field and refused to let the game continue unless the call was reversed. Percy bravely declared the game a forfeit.[12]

The final game between the two clubs was played in Cambridge, and the reporter provides us the scene:

> Between 500 and 1000 people were present at the Cambridge Driving Park Tuesday afternoon to witness the third match game of baseball this season between the Salisbury and Cambridge clubs.... The visitors had a stronger team than before and it is said they (Salisbury) had on several men from Philadelphia obtained special for the occasion.... The last inning was the most exciting ever witnessed on the Cambridge diamond. When the home boys went to the bat for the last time the score stood 13 to 21, and they crawled up to 18 before a single hand was out. Then one man got out, but he brought in another run making the tally 19. Victory was in sight. There were three men on bases, only one hand out, and Gill was at the bat. Such yelling, whooping, and shouting, and "rooting" generally was never seen in Cambridge. Hats were flying in the air and men and boys were beside themselves with excitement. They were doomed to disappointment. Gill knocked a long ball but it went up in the air and fell into the hands of the centre (sic) fielder who quickly threw the ball to second base and put out the man who was on that base making a double play thereby winning the game.

Was this Cambridge or Mudville? Was it Gill at the bat or Casey? Thayer's poem may be steeped more in realistic settings than is normally presumed, or the people of the times saw themselves in Thayer's light. Yet, the poet's account did not include this aftermath:

"After the game was over some of the crowd, not players on the home club, who were incensed at what they deemed foul playing on the part of the Salisbury man, chased him around the grounds, and, we understand, struck him several times. Others interfered and saved the young man from further injury."[13]

According to Sol White, many of the black players of the period were young enough that their childhood memories were during the optimistic years of Reconstruction. It was during the 1880s that the brothers Weldy and Fleet Walker played major league baseball for Toledo of the American Association. A few African Americans played for high minor league clubs, while others played for black teams in white leagues associated with organized baseball. By the 1890s Jim Crow contributed to a decline in black professional baseball. According to White, from 1892 to 1894, there was only one black professional team left, and opportunities in white leagues were diminishing. After 1900 it became difficult for black players to even play for independent leagues or teams. It was a time of racial assaults and retaliations as blacks tried to defend their newly won freedom. As the lynching of African Americans escalated across the country, the segregated communities pressed on with their baseball. In 1890 the Hope Lodge of Baltimore came over to Cambridge on the steamer *Tolchester* with the Mt. Washington Club to take on the local team. In the words of one contemporary observer, "Negro is just as good as a white man and just as much right to play ball.... The Negro question on the diamond might as well be settled now as any time."[14]

When certain individual white players balked at playing with African Americans, no one stood up to protest, leading to the unspoken, systemic racism traditionally known as the "color line." While many whites acknowledged the quality of black baseball, not all were willing to give black players their due. The *Easton Gazette*'s "It Was a Great Game" was written in prejudice, yet seems to grudgingly recognize the ability of the participants.

> There was a great game of ball played between the colored champion teams of Easton on Thursday afternoon in the Hammondtown Park.
>
> Both teams might have been classed as Orioles, for black and yellow were the prevailing hues of the players.
>
> The Easton team had a handicap on the Trappe boys in that Prof. Walter Graham, artistic polisher of pedal extremities, was very much in evidence when there was work to be done and anything to say.
>
> One "Empire," as not a few called him, had the appearance at having just umpired a game and given an unpopular decision.
>
> The other umpire was kept alive dodging balls.
>
> It looked at one time as though there was going to be a "parrot and Monkey" time, but the clouds rolled by, and George Washington Pennington shook the hand of Napoleon Bonaparte Van Rensselaer—no other names could be grasped in the excitement of the minute—and the congealing of the atmosphere at once cleared.
>
> The catcher for Easton team got his thumb knocked out of place by a wicked ball, but he bore it with Christian resignation.

> There were happenings more or less of a base ball character, and it was "good ball" all around, orderly, and an interesting exhibition of what can be done-for fun.
> The score stood well in favor of Easton, as the following figures show, to the satisfaction of Prof. Graham, and his team of champions.
> Out of courtesy to strangers we put the Trappe team first, and result of the game carries out the adage: "the first shall be last."
> —Trappe 17; A. Johnson, Captain. Easton 21; Walter Graham, Captain.[15]

Burris returned to Washington College for the 1896 season, only he was without "Old Reliable." He had signed with the New York Giants. The New York Club president thought the twenty-eight-year-old Zearfoss the best catching prospect in spring training. He would go on to a career in organized baseball as a defensive specialist. The college enjoyed another successful year as Burris stepped down as pitcher and manager but continued to play in the field when needed. He would play as a faculty member off and on for a period of 10 years. Eighteen ninety-six also marked the first season that Chestertown formed a town team to compete with the larger local communities and touring Baltimore squads after the college let out in June.

Cambridge's initial intent of fielding an entirely local team was short-lived. Arthur Haddaway of Easton, who had praised Salisbury and their professionals a year earlier, had a different opinion when it was their rival in Cambridge,

> In reference to the many victories of the Cambridge Base Ball Club, it would be well to say for the benefit of the public that nearly half its men are hired professional players; also if our sister town would consent to send her team away from home, her victories would be less numerous. So far Cambridge has played two games off her home grounds, and one of these was a loss to Chestertown. Bring us a home talent team, but you cannot expect us to face the likes of Charles, Hillary and Seltzer, who have handled the ball for years and have given their whole attention to the sport.

Easton's Avon Cycle Club did more cycling than baseball that summer.[16]

Baltimore teams were coming over with increasing regularity, offering the Eastern Shore towns fresh competition, but they had difficulty matching up with the quality of Eastern Shore clubs. Again, it was Salisbury, Chestertown and Cambridge who dominated play. The Cambridge professionals appeared in box scores for other teams, but always returned for the Cambridge games, suggesting seasonal agreements with the club that allowed the players to pick up extra cash on game contracts with other towns. It was a common arrangement and attractive to players earning their living outside the salary restrictions of organized baseball. Cambridge proved their mettle in a July contest in Salisbury. Updates were relayed to the local train station by telegraph. The newspaper account focused on the response of the town of 4,000 to those reports:

"The game was witnessed by a large crowd and was extremely exciting…. Intelligence from the game was eagerly waited for in Cambridge, and the news that the score was 9 to 2 in favor of Salisbury made the boys at home feel bad." But at the end of seven innings the score was tied. Cambridge scored five more in the eighth, and Salisbury only one. With the final report came the news of the exciting comeback:

Sorrow was soon turned to joy, however, when the final message of victory was received from Dr. Mace, and posted at Brayly's Brick Hotel. Everybody was gratified at the result, and the more they talked about it, the more gratified they became, until it was decided to make a demonstration in honor of the ball-players when they returned on the 8:15 train. The brass band was procured, and a crowd of not less than 500 citizens went over to the train. As the train pulled into the depot a mighty yell was sent up. A line was formed, the ball players in the van, and mid the shouts of the multitude and the music of the band, the procession marched to Brayly's Hotel, which was brilliantly illuminated, and there gathered a thousand strong. Mr. P.L. Goldsborough was called for a speech, and he appropriately responded thanking the people for the demonstration. Dr. Mace, W. Irving Mace, and Thomas W. Simmons were called upon in the order mentioned and each had something fitting to say to the enthusiastic "rooters."

The boys were treated in the most hospitable manner while in Salisbury, and their visit in every respect was a pleasant one.[17]

The reason Cambridge did not venture far from their home grounds as Haddaway had pointed out, was the two experiences they had when they did. They arranged to play the solid Washington College squad. The Cambridge team and 50 rooters crammed aboard a small tug at 4:00 a.m. to take the usual six-hour water route up the bay to Chestertown. Due to weather it was nine hours before they made the docks. Following a short parade through the town strewn with bunting, and despite their professionals, they were summarily dispatched by a score of 21–2. Even with an obvious available excuse of travel conditions, they conceded that the college nine was too strong for them. Then, in a rare excursion across the bay to the western shore to the "ancient town" of Annapolis, Cambridge hired a schooner and were towed by a steamboat to their scheduled game. There they, "struck a hard crowd. The umpire had bet money on the Annapolis nine, notwithstanding he was a Sunday school teacher, and, of course, his decisions were a little off. The game was fussed through for seven innings, when darkness put an end to it. The score standing 5 to 4 against Cambridge. They got back at 4 o'clock Friday morning, feeling pretty badly used up, and utterly disgusted with the treatment they received."[18]

After the loss to Cambridge that had sent that team home to their torch-lit parade, the Salisbury directors sent out their "agents" to strengthen the team. Then someone saw an announcement from J.A. Mathison of the Starlight of Baltimore. They claimed the championship of Maryland based on having beaten the best teams in the city, including the National League champion Orioles in an exhibition. The Starlight had plenty of talent, including their young third baseman named Dunn, who drew the jeers of the boys in the bleachers when he "nearly killed" the Salisbury catcher with a flung bat. The Baltimore club was easily beaten, and their young skipper Mathison conceded that Salisbury was "hot stuff" and the best team in the state. Caught up in the heat of the moment Salisbury boasted they were not afraid of anyone, even the pennant-winning Orioles. On July 22 they issued their challenge to the National League club to play a game and take an excursion to the resort of Ocean City. Cambridge, as was their wont, took offense: "They say they have been beaten but once and have never said who it was that beat them. It was the Cambridge Club that did them up on their home ground, and the return game was to have been July 18th, but they desired rather to cancel the date than run the risk of another defeat." There is no record of the plans with the Orioles being accomplished.[19]

The Browns of Baltimore then took exception to the Starlight claim and embarked on a tour of the Shore to prove their mettle. Beaten by both Cambridge and Salisbury, they returned home. Many fans on the peninsula expressed that they had become "fairly disgusted" with the quality of Baltimore teams. The *Chestertown Transcript* reported Chestertown had formed their summer team and were planning an extended tour of the peninsula with stops in Smyrna and Dover, Delaware, before heading south to take on the best Maryland teams in Salisbury, Cambridge, and Pocomoke City. As these plans were being finalized, Chestertown lured Salisbury up to the northern neck of the bay. Instead of taking a laboring tug like Cambridge, they took the train in an uneventful trip. Losing to Chestertown with dispatch, Salisbury blamed it on the "light fare" provided by the Voshell House. Chestertown made no claim to any championship based on this one win, and their subsequent tour did not go as well as hoped. After a loss in Salisbury, F.G. Usilton wired his son and first baseman that he was by no means to proceed to Cambridge, and he was not to play Salisbury that day because it was so hot. Having used up all their funds staying at the Peninsula House, they lost a second game to Salisbury the next day and disbanded.

This led to Salisbury and Cambridge patching up their differences and arranging a best two out of three series. Where Salisbury had tried to get the entire Oriole team to come over, Cambridge was now determined to hire at least a couple of them for the series. Dr. Mace led a small delegation to Baltimore on behalf of his associates. He first approached pitcher Joe Corbett of the Orioles, brother of heavyweight boxing champion Gentleman Jim Corbett, but Corbett was scheduled to pitch in the coming series with the Clevelands. Mace then turned to journeyman Dad Clarkson, who quickly rebuffed the overture, stating he had no intention of risking his reputation in a country town. The best they could do was Owens out of Atlantic City. Salisbury easily won the first two games, which effectively put an end to the season.[20]

The entire Salisbury nine had been nonresidents while Cambridge had only a few outside professionals. It was estimated to cost Salisbury $150 a week to keep a team in the field, "too much to be expended for fun." It was hoped that a Peninsula League would be formed, composed entirely of home talent. That would not happen, yet.[21]

The Cambridge newspapers were accurate in their assessment of the state of baseball on the Eastern Shore. Salisbury failed to field a team capable of capturing the attention of their local scribes in 1897. The old White Cloud did not seem eager to foot the bill this time. Cambridge, following a fundraising game between the Merchants and the Professionals, made it known that plans for a paid club had been abandoned in favor of a purely local nine. This was a pattern that had emerged and was furthered by the consistent use of professional players. After a period of enthusiasm and overspending, most towns would take a hiatus from amateur ball until sponsors and fans were ready to return to the professionals and satisfy their addiction for baseball and ballyhoo. Towns still preferred this imperfect independent environment. Teams played games when they wanted, against whom they wanted, using what players they wanted. The only restriction was money and enthusiasm. When towns like Salisbury and Cambridge stepped aside for a year or two, there were always others to step up and fill the void.

Washington College printed and circulated a set 20-game schedule. Burris had come back for a sixth season and their competition had changed. Their schedule was stacked with colleges and Baltimore teams, although the club was far from a modern-day amateur college team. Preparing for a game against the Millington team that included Townsend, Unglaub, and Charles, Cambridge gave in to the temptation of using outside players, starting with Al Burris to pitch. Exactly 432 tickets were sold to the Cambridge victory at home. Cambridge then retained a pitcher from a touring Baltimore team for a doubleheader against the Walbrooks of Baltimore with ex-Oriole Otis Stocksdale on the mound. More than 1,000 fans showed up in Cambridge to watch the home team sweep the afternoon and emerge as one of the top teams on the Eastern Shore.

Chestertown again formed a summer team once the college let out. After making short work of the quality Millington squad, they announced a planned tour of the peninsula with stops in Dover, Seaford, and Laurel, all in Delaware, and then Federalsburg and Cambridge. They arranged for a special excursion to Cambridge on the sidewheeler the *Forest City* at the price of one dollar a head for an 80-mile, estimated six-and-a-half-hour trip down the bay. As with Cambridge the previous year, the journey extended to nine hours but the Chestertonians took it in stride. The folks from Chestertown were impressed with their reception at Long Wharf in Cambridge, which included "doctors, lawyers, ministers, men, women, and children.... The beautiful town on the Choptank [River] took a half a holiday in honor of the occasion." For the special event Cambridge had brought in Hughlett, a professional rooter from Baltimore, to whip up the crowd. The cheering seemed to have been a little more managed than was typical for the Eastern Shore. Rooting from the men was described as "vigorous" yet "courteous," as "there were hot times in Cambridge shore's (sic) yer born." White handkerchiefs of the ladies fluttered in the bleachers, the women's "sweet voices ... stole out of the applause for the visitors." Amid this Gilded Age setting, the two pitchers labored in the hot July sun for 12 innings before Chestertown prevailed. Cambridge resolved to strengthen their team.[22]

A rematch was set for a week later in Chestertown. No game had been as extensively advertised in that town. The day was declared a holiday. A "Welcome Cambridge" sign was stretched across the street and banners and bunting were strewn the way leading to the college grounds in anticipation of the 2:30 arrival. Cambridge packed 225 rooters and the Mechanics' Brass Band on the steamer for 6:45 a.m. departure. As before, they were two hours late in arriving. The journey was described as "tedious" and the boat "very slow." But the patient welcoming party of Chestertown was waiting with its brass band as hundreds formed a loosely organized parade through the town with both bands playing "El Capitan." Despite threatening weather, ladies and gentlemen came from all over the county.

A crowd of a thousand gathered, with outside the county contingents coming from Centreville and Sudlersville. Waiting for Cambridge at the college grounds were two surprises. The first was George Perkins, a professional rooter from Philadelphia brought in for the occasion. The other was Chestertown's new pitcher, Latimore, also known as the "Virginia Wizard." The Wizard allowed but three hits in a 10–0 win.

As was customary, a banquet was given for the teams and the Cambridge band at Shuster's Dining Parlor, where Cambridge's 400-pound manager Johnson took the seat of honor. During the festivities, the threatening weather finally took a turn for the worse as a series of thunderstorms rolled through, preventing the departure of the *Forest City*. Stam's Hall was then opened up, and the two brass bands provided music for an impromptu dance. The storms did not let up as many stayed at the hall until the wee hours of the morning, while many homes of the Chestertown hosts were offered to accommodate the large and sleepy group of visitors. Finally, at 5:00 a.m. it was called all clear, and they departed. Halfway home the weary excursionists ran into another series of squalls of lightning, heavy rains, and surging tide, further delaying the beleaguered passengers. It took 11 hours before the slow steamer made Long Wharf in Cambridge to the relief of all. Having suffered three consecutive defeats, the added expense of players and travel, a strong dose of excitement, and a harrowing journey home, Cambridge refrained from baseball for the rest of the summer.[23]

The two largest towns of Salisbury and Cambridge were not in it at this point but plenty of teams remained active, with Chestertown, Millington, Crisfield, and Federalsburg being the most prominent. With the continued services of the Virginia Wizard, Chestertown took on the Baltimore Yannigans. This was a team composed of the Orioles reserve players and a few choice Baltimore semipros. It appears the Yannigans had arranged an extended tour of the Shore as an advertisement has them playing a doubleheader in St. Michaels. On this occasion, "The Yannigans came over confident of victory, for with Horton, an Oriole pitcher in the box, and Dan McGann, who played with the league team last year … no thought of defeat by the countrymen entered the minds of the sturdy visitors." But they found themselves in a hotly contested game with Latimer holding his own against the Yannigans. Chestertown was down 6–5 going into the ninth inning when three Baltimore fielders converged on a pop fly and the umpire ruled that the ball had not been caught, which put two men on and nobody out. The Yannigans "demurred" the decision and refused to continue. When the visitors would not yield, Umpire Cannon finally forfeited the game. The local scribe pointed out that Elmer "Herkey Jerkey" Horton, a league pitcher, had expected a "cinch" and decided to end the game in a "kick" rather than go back to Baltimore defeated by a country town. The reporter went on to say that one of the Baltimore players involved in the pop up later admitted the ball had been trapped and not caught.[24]

6

For the Almighty Dollar

> It is of far greater honor to a town to have players who hail from home rather than scour the country for foreign men, many of whom are in it for the almighty dollar.
> —*Dorchester Democrat-News,* September 15, 1900

Complain as they might, they would not have it any other way. Contemporaries usually referred to it as "amateur" baseball, although their definition and our present-day interpretation may not be the same. Today we refer to it as semipro baseball, but often there was little semi about it. Usually it was simply independent, or more accurately, unorganized professional baseball where the degree of professionalism was in constant flux. You were as professional as you wanted to be. The region was economically prosperous and near urban sources of talent in Baltimore, Philadelphia, Washington, even New York. These metropolitan areas were known for their semipro activity, and the accessible peninsula was a logical place to begin or finish a career, and enhance one's earnings.

Young men in cities, particularly athletes on the lower economic scale, found baseball a path for upward mobility. By the 1890s metropolitan areas featured city semipro leagues with teams sponsored by political clubs, saloons, and other assorted businesses. A young man could earn some money and at the same time make community contacts to further his future while playing on these teams. A side hustle on the Eastern Shore exposed him to rural culture and new opportunities. Coming out of urban environments, a trip to the "land of pleasant living" was a broadening experience from the cramped and confining city streets. Definition and separation between amateur and professional was just now taking shape. Institutions of higher learning were still offering cash money, and a chance to attend classes. Attending classes was usually optional.

Parents, particularly immigrant parents of low economic status, supported and even encouraged the efforts of their children. Baseball was how they could make good in this country. Parents of the upper middle class and wealthy did not always share this high esteem for the game, since they had more traditional avenues to better themselves.[1]

Most towns insisted on having a top-notch team, not only for the local fans and civic pride, but for the people and attention it attracted to the town. Shipping lines now advertised excursions to all Eastern Shore waterfront communities in metropolitan newspapers. Steamboats came across the bay packed with excursionists, their money, and baseball teams. Always a boon to local merchants, the teams eventually drew complaints about the pickpockets, shoplifters, and other shady characters that came with them. What lured these excursionists were the same things that attracted baseball players from the nearby metropolitan areas.

Running an independent professional team at the town level was rarely a money-making proposition, and towns preferred their chaotic independence. The players preferred its flexibility even more. In a typical town team season, most players appeared for more than one team. Sometimes they might have a season contract with one team that allowed them to fill in open dates with other clubs. Some players just ignored previous agreements if the money was right. Sometimes there was no contract, often just a handshake. This only fed the fire of hot air and hubris.

These country towns from a few hundred to 4,000 sought out every resource for stocking their rosters. One of the main sources were the teenagers and young men looking to take that first step to the major leagues. Areas known for the quality of their town teams attracted the players' attention. These aspirants would send their resumes. From Sadie McMahon in 1886 to the likes of Nick Maddox, Buck Herzog and Sam Frock, in the early 1900s, to Eddie Rommel, Joe Boley and Jimmie Dykes in 1916, many such youngsters traveled to the peninsula to begin their professional careers. After claiming the championship of Maryland and Delaware in 1907, Cambridge received over a hundred such applications from throughout the country to sort through the following spring.[2]

Established independent players from the metropolitan areas were another significant source of talent. Pitchers Lefty High, Otis Stocksdale, and position players Jimmie Mathison and Buck Herzog were among the many city independent players and major league participants who also played on Eastern Shore teams. Major league teams often dipped into these local environs for quick-fix additions to their depleted rosters, whether at home or on the road. Many city semipro pitchers and town team players like Lefty High and Pete Loos got their proverbial cup of coffee in the major leagues fresh off of semipro grounds, only to return as quickly as they went.

Another source of talent were the nonroster reserve players from the major league clubs in the region. These players were not technically on the active major league roster but were kept close by if injury or poor play called for their services. Through the 1890s there were major league franchises in Baltimore, Washington, and by the early 1900s, two in Philadelphia. Sometimes these players would appear on a touring team sponsored by their own club like the Baltimore Yannigans, but nonroster major league reserve players were often allowed to play for independent teams to stay in shape and pick up extra money. Charlie Gettig and the non-roster Zeigler of the New York Giants are examples of those who appeared on the peninsula in this fashion.

Nor was organized baseball known for its generosity in paying its players at any level. Many realized they could make as much, if not more, playing outlaw baseball than in the minor leagues, or even the major leagues. Many of the outlaw leagues were of minor league caliber, but some players with major or minor league talent opted for independent town teams. Art Rooney, future owner of the Pittsburgh Steelers, turned down a major league contract because he could make more money playing independent baseball. Mike Cantwell pitched for Cambridge in the independent Peninsula League in 1915 and 1916 before going to the majors. He returned to pitch for Cambridge in 1921 and expressed a preference for independent ball. His three-year record of 1–6 and an ERA over six runs a game may have influenced his decision. Dickie Porter, a home-bred major league veteran of the 1930s, was of the opinion that many of the regional semi pro teams he saw around 1920 were as good as most later Class B minor league teams.[3]

Independent baseball was also an option for the disgruntled contract holdout. Some were of the minor league variety, but not all. In 1906 Bob Unglaub was paid less playing for the Boston Braves than he had made in the minor leagues, in violation of the rules. He signed a contract with the outlaw Tri-State League that nearly doubled his major league salary. Unfortunately for Unglaub, the Tri-State League reached an agreement with organized baseball before the season began and he had to return to the majors for far less money. (See Appendix A for a biographical sketch of Unglaub.)

Ty Cobb threatened to play for the independent professional team of a wealthy manufacturer if his major league salary demands were not met. His threat was taken seriously due to "Home Run" Baker's precedent. Baker was in a contract dispute with Connie Mack of the Philadelphia Athletics in 1915 and came home to Easton to play ball on their professional team.

There were times when active major league players were given permission to play independent ball. Buck Herzog played for Seaford, Delaware, against Cambridge in 1908 for the Maryland-Delaware Championship while playing in 64 games for the Giants. Cambridge's attempt to sign Orioles players in 1896 failed, but small towns were not intimidated in the asking when trying to secure the best talent for their fans.

If country ball was the first rung on the ladder for many young players, it was often the last stop of the professional journey for aging veterans. In 1904, it appears Steve Brodie of the old championship Orioles was brought in to play for Cambridge in the waning days of the failing Eastern Shore League. In 1907, the Hurlock town team was looking for a way to quiet the torrid hitting of the slugging Frank Baker. They found the answer with the crafty, soft-tossing, left-handed Frank Foreman of Baltimore. The "Waverly Wonder" had started his major league career in 1884 and appeared in four of the five major leagues that existed to that point.[4]

Through 30 years of independent quality country ball, the Eastern Shore of Maryland produced several homegrown talents for the major leagues. It started with the one-game stint of Al Burris in 1894, and was followed by Homer Smoot, Frank Baker, and the two-game stint of Jim Stevens of Williamsburg in the Dead Ball Era of the new century's first two decades. More were to follow.

Between 1886 and 1921, approximately 50 future, former, and contemporary major league players have been identified as having participated on the professional town teams on Maryland's Eastern Shore. This may be a conservative count, considering that many played under assumed names because they wanted to protect their amateur status, or they were double-dipping on a previous contract, or to protect their status in organized baseball. Some may have just lied to their parents about their summer job.

Simon Nichols was playing for the University of Maryland when he got a call to play for the Detroit Tigers at the end of 1903. His family was so embarrassed with their son playing professional baseball that they made him promise he would give up such notions. Not all parents of the era wanted their sons to grow up to be ballplayers. His teammate at Maryland was Buck Herzog, who brought Nichols with him when he came to Ridgely in 1904 and 1905. Nichols also played for other town teams in the area over the two-year span. Perhaps his parents did not see this as professional baseball, or he did not tell them what he was doing on the Eastern Shore for summer employment, just one year after his promise to give up the unsavory enterprise. Either way, Nichols did not keep his word to his parents. By 1907, he was playing shortstop for the Philadelphia Athletics.[5]

Through all of this, local players expected to be paid something, if not as much as the "foreign men." Completely amateur teams, even in the smallest of villages, were an exception. And local fans did not always know exactly what to expect when they bought a ticket to see a local game. Players could be from anywhere in the country. They might range in age from 14, like Chappy Charles or Jimmie Foxx, to those in their 40s, like Frank Foreman. Some had talent but no experience at all while others had played at the highest level, sometimes for a decade or more. There was one thing the small-town fans did expect, however, and that was the best baseball their money could buy. This was the baseball environment coming into being on the Eastern Shore at the beginning of the 20th century and it was reflected in its quality of play.

There was plenty of activity throughout the peninsula to start the 1900 season. Every town, village and hamlet put a team on the field. Cambridge was the first of the large towns to go professional, signing Johnnie Foreman (Frank's younger brother) out of Baltimore to pitch. As of mid–July Salisbury was yet fielding a local talent team with the expected results. Easton had bested "a few country scrub nines," but were "deserted" by 50 rooters when beaten by the Cambridge professionals. Salisbury then abandoned the home talent idea and signed Foreman away from their rivals. Early in August the management of Easton, Salisbury, and Cambridge met and agreed to play each other for the championship of the Eastern Shore of Maryland. It was sometimes referred to as the "Triplet" or "Tripartite" League. It was a league in name only. The *Salisbury Advertiser* was more accurate when the newspaper dubbed it the Tri City Series. The only agreement reached was that each team would play each other 10 games apiece, with the team with the best record being the champion. This was as close as the teams wanted to get to a league. When the series started, Cambridge fans had already pumped $800 through the turnstiles for their management. It was rumored that Easton had already spent $500 to put their club together and took more than 300 fans with them across the Choptank River for the first game at the Driving Park in Cambridge.

Salisbury lost its battery right from the start of the series with Foreman going to Easton, where he would remain financially faithful for the rest of the season. Other players jumped from one team to another as total confusion reigned. When the Easton players showed up in Salisbury for a game, they were surprised to find Skeeter Dent on the mound for their opponents. Easton put up a "baby act," claiming they had already secured Dent's services. The young medical student from Baltimore countered that his deal with Easton had fallen through, and he was free to pitch for Salisbury. Easton responded by signing Lefty High out of Baltimore. Easton won five of their last seven and claimed the championship based on their 6–4 record. Salisbury had declined the last game, conceding the superiority of their opponents, but also to avoid keeping the team on the payroll another week.

Crowds for the series ranged consistently in the upper hundreds to 1,200 for most of the games, but even those strong attendance figures were not enough to offset the teams' spendthrift management. Cambridge would complain that hundreds of dollars had been spent only for the team to end up in last place. There was a huge "indebtedness" of over $300 left to the principal sponsors of the club.

The Easton Club, winners of the Tri City Series of 1900. Semipro star pitchers and fringe major leaguers Johnnie Foreman (believed to be on the far right sitting with his knees under his chin, facing the rest of the team) and Lefty High proved the difference. Note the players' different uniforms, an indication of a fluid roster (courtesy Talbot Historical Society).

There was more talk of forming a peninsula league but the financial proceedings of the '00 season discouraged it.

There was no series forthcoming but communities continued the use of professional players. An Eastern Shore League was established on the lower Shore around this time, but it appears it was confined to the smaller towns south of Salisbury. By now it was evident that every village and hamlet on the Eastern Shore of Maryland could boast a quality product as unorganized baseball was beginning to reach its peak. Crumpton was a small farming village and a railway stop on the northern end of the Shore. Its baseball team in 1902 was described as a "catcher from Baltimore, a pitcher from Philadelphia, and a team from God knows where." One of its rivals was the slightly larger neighboring town of Sudlersville. For a handful of years Sudlersville was considered the best team on the peninsula. An exception to the general trend, it appeared to have had a single sponsor, Col. John E. George, a county commissioner of Queen Anne's County. A photo of the team shows the colonel, the biggest "sport" in the county, with his squad and umpire. One of the players sitting on those steps is Dell Foxx, father of future Hall of Fame player Jimmie Foxx. With only one man to answer to, the Sudlersville team's ties with the town were a little more tenuous than most. It was sometimes a team for hire. The Princess Anne squad failed in its previous games against Salisbury in the Eastern Shore League of the lower peninsula. Its answer was to bring in the "Johnny Georges" team from Sudlersville to play as Princess Anne in its next game. It worked.[6]

The Easton club hired Jimmie Green of Baltimore to manage the team for the 1902 season, and he brought with him several fellow Baltimore professionals: Lefty High, Jimmie Mathison, and Dan McGann. Cambridge, as they often said of others, "was not in it," their better players going to other teams on the peninsula. The women's team the Chicago Stars, "ably assisted" by three male players, toured the Shore. They brought their own fence with them to enclose the country grounds they might encounter. They made short work of the Cambridge High School team, and before they continued the tour, told the people of Cambridge they would not return if they could not put up stiffer competition. One game did catch the attention of a baseball-starved Cambridge reporter:

> A game of baseball was played in Cambridge Friday between the King Bees and a nine made up of young men visiting Cambridge. The King Bees were defeated in nine innings by a score of 16 to 5. The queer part about the game was the frequency of injuries. One man's finger was burst open; another was thrown on his face in the outfield; another ran into the first baseman and himself rolled over and over; another sprained two fingers running the bases; another was struck in the mouth by a pitched ball and his lip burst open; another fell over a man and landed on his chest, which was much bruised; another attempted to jump over a fence and when his foot caught in the top wire and threw him on his stomach in a bed of cow peas, and another was struck in the back. The game was called to prevent anyone from being killed.[7]

While Cambridge wallowed in the cowpeas for a couple of years, everybody else was on the baseball train. The quality of baseball being played on the peninsula prompted a horn-blowing yet accurate observation from one reporter:

Colonel John E. George and his Sudlersville Nine, c. 1902. As a rare private sponsor, George sometimes hired out his team out to other towns for big games. Top row, left to right: Colonel Bull, mascot; Seward Barwick, umpire. Second row: Bill Setley, 3b and utility field; McGlashey, 1b; Jack O'Brien, 3b; Dell Foxx, rf and c. Third Row: W.H. McGurley, c.; Vincent, p. Fourth row: William Seward, ss; John E. George, owner and manager; J. Walter Paynter, lf. Bottom: Hoffman, cf. (courtesy Sudlersville Train Museum).

The prospects are that there will be more baseball seen on the Delaware and Maryland peninsula than ever before in the history of the National game. The country papers give evidence that from Wilmington to Cape Charles clubs are being formed in every town and village where nine players can be gotten together ... many towns are making big preparations to put ball teams in the field, and some good sport can be expected. At some ... of the towns only local men will be used, but in others foreign talent will be employed.

Some of the people on the Eastern Shore are getting their baseball ideas well up in "G" and they are not satisfied with local material. They want good baseball and enthusiasts are willing to pay for it. It is safe to say no better baseball is seen anywhere than on this peninsula, in towns of similar size and this season will probably not be behind the former ones.[8]

Enthusiasm for baseball reached such a pitch that by 1904 the three towns again banded together to determine a championship. An organizational meeting was held in Salisbury in July and the Eastern Shore League was formed, minus the smaller lower Shore communities. Again, the larger Maryland peninsula towns of Easton, Salisbury and Cambridge would participate. For the first time, at least some of the baseball on the Eastern Shore was to have a predetermined schedule. The reason for this arrangement was that it had been agreed to hire a professional umpire. He was provided a place to live in the town of Hurlock, deemed to be centrally located to each of the participants. Each day he would venture by train to the town on the schedule. It was felt that being located at an isolated and neutral site would hinder the teams from bullying or tampering with the league's lone arbiter. It does not appear to have worked. The league would go through four umpires in their abbreviated season.

Whether this setup would meet the modern definition of a league is questionable. There is no mention of an independent administrative body governing the league. It would appear the management of the respective towns provided what little order there was. Box scores show stable rosters with position players, which may indicate some recognition of rival team contracts. Pitchers, however, came and went with frequency. There was an influx of imported position players when Cambridge began building a substantial lead. Box scores show Cambridge using four former and future major league players in league play. Many of these professionals were familiar to the Eastern Shore fan from past seasons; others were new to the fevered scene. One of the fan favorites was pitcher Nick Maddox of Baltimore. Maddox would pitch for all the big three peninsula teams over a five-year period. Only three years after appearing in the Eastern Shore League he won 24 games for the Pittsburgh Pirates, and a year after that won a game in the 1909 World Series.

The league was not the only game on the Shore in 1904. Ridgely, Centreville, St. Michaels, and the lively town of Crisfield were some of the communities with strong independent clubs. Pocomoke City was said to be "crazy over baseball." These clubs had no shortage of competition playing local teams, strong touring Baltimore squads, and Delaware clubs. Some would take on one of the league teams on open dates when the opportunity presented itself. But it was the Eastern Shore League that attracted the attention and the talent. Some of that talent was plucked from the rosters of these local teams and the Baltimore teams passing through.

Early September found Cambridge firmly entrenched in first place. The frequency of games did not allow for the excitement once associated with big matches as enthusiasm now ran in a steady stream through a scheduled season. The smallest crowd of the series was 375; 600–700 was normal, 900–1,000 not unusual. As customary, crowds were bolstered by large traveling contingents, sometimes in the hundreds. A 30-car train full of Cambridge day-trippers, returning from Ocean City convinced the railroad officials to allow their special excursion to lay over in Salisbury on their way home so they could catch the contest between those the Cambridge and Salisbury clubs.

Easton shook up their roster in late August, and Salisbury did the same the first of September. By now Easton was hopelessly out of the hunt and over $300 in debt so they "gave up the ghost." There was nothing else to gain for Cambridge to continue to play, so they called it quits. Salisbury was left all dressed up with no place to go. Even though the league failed to complete its schedule, it was considered a success.

> One of the happiest reflections of the now closed baseball season of 1904 is the fact that each town in the three cornered league preserved the best order at all the games. No disgraceful scenes, as are enacted took place.... Neither players or spectators in any instance indulged in what is known as "dirty ball" or "local squabbling" and very seldom did objections to umpiring reach a stage where umpire, players, and "bleachers" used the force of their wit or invective.... The contest was a sample of the game of baseball as it ought to be played.... The management of each club gave the people of the three towns the best sport possible, and went to great expense to obtain players to represent their towns and give the people the worth of admission price.[9]

The Eastern Shore League continued for a few years, but it reverted to a handful of teams in towns close to Salisbury. Circuit members usually came from the towns of Crisfield, Princess Anne, Snow Hill, Berlin, Pocomoke City, and Salisbury, which served as the hub of the "wheel." All of these communities were confined below the Wicomico River. With no team north of Salisbury, it wasn't truly a peninsula league.

Ridgely was another of those farming communities where the railroad had dropped in a depot to gather the crops of this sprawling flat expanse of woodlands and farms. Ridgely had ambitions. Stretching from the highway, the extra-wide Main Street that runs through the town ends abruptly into a back road to the hinterlands. But in the early 1900s the street was lined with retail stores and bustling with activity in what many thought would become the commercial center of the mid-Shore area. There was no better way to demonstrate that prosperity than with a good baseball team.

In 1904 the 19-year-old Buck Herzog of the University of Maryland was brought in to manage, or captain, the Ridgely squad. Herzog was following the norm. Getting paid to play and manage a baseball team was just a summer job and had no bearing on his collegiate status. He was getting paid there as well. Writing after Herzog had established himself in the major leagues, *Baltimore Sun* writer C. Starr Matthews talked of the player's Ridgely teams. Matthews asserts that little Ridgely had five future major league players on its roster, perhaps at the same time. Of the five he mentions are Herzog and his teammate at Maryland Si Nichols. The third player mentioned was Sam Frock, a pitcher and outfielder who four years later would appear with Maddox in the Pittsburgh ranks for their 1909 pennant run. The other imported player was Bill Kellogg, who appeared on a few

Shore town teams before he went to the minor leagues and starred for the Dallas Texans. In 1915, when Herzog was managing the Cincinnati Reds, he called on his old Ridgely first baseman to be a utility player on his major league club. The last player mentioned by Matthews was a local high school pitcher and outfielder. Languishing on the bench, this young prospect finally got a chance to fill in for the injured third baseman. His name was Frank Baker, future star of the 1911 World Series. Baker always credited Herzog as having discovered him and directing his switch to third base.[10]

All five playing together has not been verified. There have been no box scores or photos putting all five together. None of the local lore or newspaper accounts place Baker on Ridgely before 1905, but it is possible he appeared the year before. Frock, Nichols, Kellogg, and Herzog were together at Ridgely in '04, but by '05 Frock was with Concord of the New England League, and Nichols was with Piedmont in West Virginia. Nichols, however, also appears in a postcard photo of the independent Pocomoke City club on the southern Shore dated 1905. It shows the stalwart Burris in a bow tie. After 10 years of playing for Washington College, Burris now played and managed solely for the local independent teams. Also in the picture with Burris and Nichols is town team perennial Chappy Charles, and sitting on the far-right end is a tight-lipped Frank Baker. Obviously, the playing environment was fluid, with players appearing on multiple teams. It is tempting to believe all five were together in Ridgely, however briefly, but it can be no more than an assumption. Even so, that these two towns with populations of about a thousand apiece could put such talent on the field is to be noted.

The Pocomoke City Base Ball Club, 1905. A little town of a thousand people could field a surprisingly talented team. Burris, Nichols, Baker, and Charles played in the major leagues (author's collection).

6. For the Almighty Dollar

The Ridgely team, c. 1905. Ridgely was another small town with a big team. The University of Maryland's Buck Herzog captained the Ridgely club in the summer. Top row, from left: Hemmons, manager; Buck Herzog, shortstop; Stambaugh, right field; middle row, from left: Webster, pitcher; N. Baker, first base; F. Baker, third base; Pindell, second base; Somers, left field; bottom row, from left: Smith, captain; Nolan, center field; Benson, catcher. Local lore is that Norman Baker was the better ballplayer but didn't like to travel. Box scores and game accounts do not support the lore (author's collection).

Herzog, like many players coming from metropolitan areas, set his roots in the rural soil of the Eastern Shore. He met a girl while playing in Ridgely and was soon married. Once in the major leagues he bought a farm, and took to the country life. He was active in raising the unusual combination of chickens and thoroughbred horses, as well as crops for market. He loved horses and the gentrified sport of fox hunting and his car rarely came out of the garage when he was home.

Another exciting feature of independent baseball for its fans were barnstorming teams. The rubes of these small towns were the primary market for these novelties. Women's teams were only a part of these attractions. In 1906 the Nebraska Indians came to the peninsula for an extended tour. The "real Indians" were coming off a record of 164–27–1 for their 1905 campaign, and everyone was excited to see them. Managed by Guy Green, the team contained members of several tribes of American Indians, including Wyandotte and Yaquis. Green's favorite player was Nakomas, a Wyandotte from Indian Territory. In 1906 he was purported to be 55 years old and a "mass of scars of various ages and varieties. He was chipped so often." Green referred to him as a "a first class player," "the scrappiest player I ever had," and "a fighter all his life." Most of Green's players were younger, but all were talented.[11]

Anticipation exceeded reason with the arrival of this cast of characters coming down from the Pennsylvania leg of its tour. Chestertown planned a grand parade where it would to mount the Indians on horseback and have them war hoop their way to the grounds. There is no report that the game in Chestertown ever came off.

Green complained that he was often pulled aside by condescending hometown managers who hoped these wild Indians would put up a decent game. Their record spoke for itself. Games on the Eastern Shore are listed in the book Green wrote of his adventures, and it includes contests in Easton, Federalsburg, Princess Anne, and Seaford, Delaware, all lopsided wins for the Nebraskans. Another problem Green faced with his barnstorming team was hometown umpiring. He always insisted on using two, including one of his own. That way he was sure to get a "fair shake" half of the time.

Perhaps Green's biggest problem as manager of a barnstorming team was making sure he got his share of the gate, which was the reason some announced games did not get played. Hometown managers were not always on the square, so he had to keep a close eye on them. A big part of that problem were free passes and those who snuck into games, thus cutting into the profits. This is what might have happened to prevent the game from being played in Chestertown. A game had also been scheduled for Crisfield, and after an extended tour from Nebraska and Iowa in the west, to points east, and with 1,500 small-town games under their belts, Green had this to say about the Eastern Shore community,

> Crisfield, Maryland, is entitled to the premium "cheapest" town in the United States. I suppose the leading citizens of that end of the oyster commonwealth ruined a thousand dollars' worth of corn in a field adjacent to the park, and destroyed enough wardrobe to stock a big clothing store, in their crawlings, creepings and contrivings to see Indians perform without exchanging the proper amount of coin for the privilege. Of course I did not play in this village, and thereby did the natives a great wrong.[12]

Enthusiasm was in a fever heat in Cambridge in 1907. The new grounds were off Oakley Street, named after Annie Oakley, the star of Buffalo Bill's Wild West show. She and her husband had bought a home where they fit right in with the locals as she sat on her second story porch overlooking the broad Choptank River. There, with shooting in her blood, Annie was said to pick off the stray ducks that had the misfortune to venture in front of her house. At the grounds on the Oakley Street lot, the outfield was bordered by a cornfield up to its fence, with the backstop adjacent to the river, and "they are to have a boat brigade of boys to chase foul balls. The members of the brigade will attend games in bathing suits, and be on duty on the river shore." Cambridge claimed the championship for Maryland and Delaware in 1907 with the help of Frank Baker. Baker had returned home after a year playing for Sparrow's Point and a failed tryout with Jack Dunn of the high minor league Baltimore Orioles. Dunn felt Baker was yet too raw for that level of competition. Two years after leading Cambridge to the claimed championship, Baker played at an even higher level, starting at third base for Connie Mack's Athletics. It was one of the few times Dunn missed in his acquisition of prime talent. Ernie Shore, Babe Ruth, Lefty Grove, Fritz Maisel, and Dickie Porter were among

6. For the Almighty Dollar

the many to make the big leagues under Dunn's tutelage. When Cambridge set out to claim the two-state championship a second time, the importance of baseball to the community was clearly expressed:

> A ball team such as we have this year will be a credit to our town. Base ball does more towards advertising a town than most other medium, and the business men should give what assistance they possibly can so as to keep a good team in the field the entire season. While finances are in good shape this year, still it costs money to run a successful team, and the people should respond liberally with donations to help this time to make base ball a success in every respect.[13]

When they received their hundred applications that year, there were a lot of skillful players to choose from. While Annie Oakley continued to pluck off ducks from her porch, Cambridge finished the season with an unchallenged claim for their second consecutive two-state championship in 1908. In a season-ending fundraising doubleheader, they took on the storming "Cherokee Nationals." Cambridge boasted they were too "fast" for the Indians in their 6–0 win. Maud Nelson had pitched the first two innings for the Cherokee before being replaced. The second game was billed a "night frolic" as the Cherokee pitcher entertained the crowd with his wild and exaggerated windmill motion and the ability to throw to any base without turning from the batter.

Born Clementina Brida in Italy in 1881, the young Maud Nelson found a

The Cambridge Club of 1907 won the championship of Maryland and Delaware. Few players are wearing Cambridge uniforms. J.F. Baker appears to be wearing an Athletics uniform. 1. Bonthron, catcher; 2. Townsend, left field and captain; 3. Corneil, second base; 4. John Franklin Baker, third base; 5. Norman (Patsy) Baker, umpire; 6. Coolin, first base; 7. Wilson, pitcher; 8. Dawson, center field; 9. Cunningham, pitcher; 10. Bonthron, second base; 11. Bassett, catcher and manager; 12. Gallagher, shortstop; 13. H.C. Byrd, pitcher; 14. Norman Meekins, mascot (author's collection).

doorway to American culture through baseball. Maud began her career in the late 1890s as a teenage pitcher for the Boston Bloomer Girls. In 1903 she left women's baseball to play for the Cherokee Indian Baseball Club, where she met her future husband, John B. Olson, Jr., who managed the team. During those years she primarily pitched and played some third base. In 1911 she and Olson married and left the Cherokee for the Western Bloomer Girls, operating out of Chicago. By the age of 30, Nelson owned, managed, and was the pitching sensation for the Western Bloomer Girls, considered the most successful of the female clubs of the time. They were billed as clean, moral, and refined. After her husband died in 1917, Nelson continued to play, coach, own, and manage other women's teams. She died in 1944 in her home near Wrigley Field.[14]

While there is plenty of evidence to indicate the significant role women played in financing town teams on the Eastern Shore through auxiliaries, there is little to show of actual game participation on the Shore. No game accounts have been found, but this does not preclude activity. A local photograph of women in a team picture pose with baseball equipment includes three men in women's clothing. It was customary practice for women's teams of the early 1900s to use three male players, but all in this photo are in women's dress, not uniforms, suggesting a local team rather than a barnstormer. That they were members of a local team with competitors or were part of a fundraising event are two plausible explanations.

The most avid of Cambridge fans was Lee Fong. Fong was a first-generation immigrant who managed to wander his way from China to Cambridge. The two worlds could not have been more different, but Fong adjusted quickly to the culture through a shared love of all sports, particularly baseball. It was Fong who led the opening day parade through the streets of Cambridge in 1908: "To begin with there will be a grand parade through the town, led by our famous Citizens' Band, accompanied by Lee Fong, our star rooter, and followed by both teams, seated in large vehicles and attired in brand new uniforms; following the teams will be several carriages containing the president and other officers."[15]

It is easy to assign Fong the role of team mascot. Adopting a person for a mascot as a talisman for baseball teams had started in the 19th century. Considered to be the most coveted of good luck charms were boys, the developmentally or physically disabled, dwarfs, and African Americans, or some combination of these. Fong was no mascot, token, or talisman.

Fong emigrated from China to Ottawa in Canada in 1888. He worked his way down the East Coast with short stays in Boston, Hartford, Baltimore, and Washington before ending up in Cambridge in 1895. His brother owned a large restaurant in New York City. Fong opened up a laundry on his arrival in Cambridge and was immediately accepted into the community. He was an industrious worker and his money was always among the first to go into the coffers to secure a quality baseball team. It was his $5 that was put up for the Cambridge player to hit the first home run of the season. But Fong had many more interests than just baseball. His name also appears prominently in fund drives for the new hospital, food relief, World War I causes, and other community projects.

One reason that Fong assimilated so quickly may have been that he eschewed politics, even though he did like to see his friends win, regardless of party affiliation. But the primary reason for his acceptance in the community may have been his athletic nature and quick adaptation to American sports. In addition to playing baseball, he was considered a world-class bowler, traveling to tournaments in Baltimore and Philadelphia. Fong also bought horses and often placed challenges for match races and wagers in the local newspapers. During the bicycle craze of the 1890s he even took to competitive racing, and he rarely said no to a "friendly" game of pool.[16]

When Cambridge failed to put a strong team in the field after the expenses of the previous two championship seasons, Fong took matters into his own hands. He put together Fong's All-Stars and took on all comers, and they quickly emerged as the best of the teams competing in town. Fong would often foot the bill for Cambridge teams for the next few years. Business sponsorship was not entirely new. A couple of hardware stores in Salisbury had fielded teams as early as the 1870s, and Johnnie George had his squad in Sudlersville, but only George could afford the first-rate teams the town fans demanded. Fong's teams may not have equaled the success of the two state champions of '07 and '08, but it was quality ball as he helped carry Cambridge through a couple of lean years.

Many metropolitan newspapers provided some coverage of notable and regional games, but like their rural counterparts, they provided scant insight into black baseball and its impact in those communities. Even the *Baltimore Afro-American* was incomplete in its coverage of baseball in the early 1900s. The newspaper did have embedded correspondents for a time, reporting from many Eastern Shore communities that sometimes included baseball activities. Teams from across the state were encouraged to send in their baseball news. While these reports are sparse, they do provide a couple of line scores and box scores, the briefest of narratives, and a handful of names of the participants.

Racial violence, retaliation, and recurrent lynching, like in most other parts of the country, occurred on the Eastern Shore. In 1898 Garfield King was lynched by a mob in his Wicomico County jail cell, and similar incidents would continue over time. In spite of all of this, African Americans of the Eastern Shore tried to better their economic conditions, many starting businesses. In 1903 it was reported that Adeline Lewis had opened an excursion line up the Choptank River from Denton to Cambridge with an ice-cream parlor strategically located at the end of the line. The money generated from these nascent investments produced the funds needed to sponsor and present black baseball teams. As Eastern Shore towns courted the tourist dollar, it was realized that black money was just as green as anybody else's. Segregated steamboat excursions to the towns of Cambridge, Oxford, St. Michaels, Chestertown and Easton were regularly advertised in the *Afro-American* through the early 1900s. For years, at the encouragement of the railroad officials and steamboat lines, Cambridge advertised their town as a point of destination for excursions and vacations for African Americans in Baltimore. Those officials weren't always consistent in their encouragement. Most counties even held segregated county fairs with different dates, vendors, and events.[17]

Cambridge newspapers addressed black baseball at times, but usually only when some other reportable incident was related to the event. Such was the case in 1903 when a game with a black Baltimore team took a back seat to the scene of an irate mother that stormed the steamer before it departed, and dragged her daughter down the ramp, after she attempted to run off with one of the Baltimore players. When the same excursion packet returned a week later, the railroad officials, who previously promoted these excursions, refused permission for the steamer to dock. Another incident reports a Cambridge win, but the story was that someone from the hometown Easton team snuck off with all the gate receipts. Within a few years the citizens of Cambridge, despite continued promotional advertising, voiced their objections to what they called "negro excursions." One of the reasons Baltimore excursions brought these baseball teams to town was that the black Cambridge club was often considered one of the best teams in the state and the event was sure to fill the steamer and draw a crowd.[18]

But racially motivated violence continued. In 1906 law enforcement in Somerset County acted quickly to spirit away William Lee for safekeeping in a Baltimore jail after he was accused of assaulting two Crisfield women. After he fled across the Virginia border, he was eventually returned to Princess Anne, where an armed escort ensured his hanging was "humane." A year later an Officer Daugherty was brutally shot down in the streets of Crisfield by a man named Jack Reed. Daugherty had tried to arrest Reed, who went off and acquired a .44 caliber handgun and attacked the unsuspecting officer from behind. Minutes later Daugherty's wife and children turned the corner. A manhunt was immediately formed using gasoline launches in nearby marshes and creeks to track down the suspect. When found, Reed was dragged back to town, where he was beaten to death and strung up from a telegraph pole. The mob then turned on the black community of Crisfield in a rage as men were hauled from their houses, "mauled fiercely," and were told to leave town. In the spreading hysteria, the citizens of nearby Onancock, Virginia, ran all African Americans out of town. Not long after the Crisfield incident, the citizens of Princess Anne also expelled their entire black population from the community. Research done by the *Baltimore Sun* indicates that 44 African Americans were lynched in Maryland between 1854 and 1933. At least 10 were hanged on the Eastern Shore of Maryland. This does not count assorted abuses and atrocities that did not reach print.[19]

William Johnson lived in the middle of all of this in Snow Hill in Worcester County. He worked as a merchant seaman, and had seen enough in his travels to know that the violent racial environment on the Eastern Shore was not the norm everywhere. To protect his children and raise them in a safer and more productive environment, Johnson did as many others did, and followed the old Underground Railroad and moved his family to Wilmington, Delaware. Only about 125 miles north, Wilmington's less brutal segregation was deemed safer. William's son was Judy Johnson, who would go on to become one of the best players of the Negro Leagues and was selected for the National Baseball Hall of Fame in 1975. (See Appendix A for a biographical sketch of Johnson.)

In the face of these difficulties, black baseball persevered. Sol White pointed out that in 1907 there were nine professional teams within a hundred miles of Philadelphia. The optimistic White proclaimed, "From a scientific point it outclasses all other American games. It should be taken seriously by the colored player, as honest efforts with his great ability will open an avenue in the near future where he may work hand-in-hand with the opposite race in the greatest of all American games—baseball."[20]

One feature of this decade was the proliferation of high school teams. They had existed in Baltimore since at least the 1880s but there is no mention of their activity on the Eastern Shore until the turn of the century. Youth teams had started as the offshoots of the adult teams, and in fever seasons several age levels of youth teams had been active. Many adults did not see the arguing, fighting, language and violence of baseball as a good thing for young boys. At one time many thought of baseball as the pastime of the uneducated Irish and other assorted rogues and idlers. That was changing. Si Nichols' parents would soon find themselves in a minority.

Baseball had started on the Eastern Shore as a physical and social activity to give "social standing." Within 10 years, rule changes, aggressive tactics and attitudes had devolved baseball to "a game worse than folly." More rule changes, strategies and organization culminated with the modern pitching distance in 1893. By this time, lower income parents were not alone in perceiving baseball as a means to an end. Attendance in the major leagues doubled from 1900 to 1909. Minor leagues and independent baseball were also enjoying a boom. Much of that increased interest came from the middle class. Much of baseball information of the early years came from national publications like *The Sporting News, Sporting Life,* and the *Police Gazette,* hardly considered suitable for mainstream or upper middle-class reading at the time. Now, such staunch middle-class national periodicals such as *Collier's, Scribner's, Harper's,* and *Literary Digest* carried regular baseball stories and extolled the sport's virtues. This media was distributed into every middle-class community in the land. When C. Starr Matthews wrote his "Work and Win," on Buck Herzog in 1911, he stated that "Horatio Alger could not find a better hero." Baseball, properly supervised and coached, taught essential American values. First was the importance of individual effort. Perseverance, stamina, guile, and fair play were the other attributes a lad needed to succeed in the world. It also provided the basis for teaching the value of teamwork, emphasized communication, sacrifice, and assistance to obtain a common goal. All were found in a nine-inning game. Adleman surmised, "Modern athletics resulted from the social system's attempt to channel the play instinct into socially productive outlets." A potential Horatio Alger hero was any young man coming of age in a small town. Baseball was perceived to be the perfect format to teach a boy to be that hero.[21]

Once adults were alarmed with the childish enthusiasm for baseball, whether it came from youths or young adults. Many now saw it as an effective educational tool. This fit in neatly with the Progressive movement that was making inroads into American education. The philosophy of Progressive education had been initiated in the 19th century and included the importance of physical exercise. By the early 20th century it had become the foundation of American school systems. The philosophy stressed sound minds and sound bodies in forming productive young adults. Once local education boards accepted this mode of instruction, budgets were allocated for athletic facilities for students. Educators who implemented these methods found eager pupils flocking to the diamond. A new way was found to sponsor a baseball team.

One of the offshoots of this concept was the playground movement. Many of the children of the era did not, or could not, complete the full term of schooling. Many children on the Eastern Shore, like those in other rural areas, had to leave school early to help on the farm or work on the water or in the canneries to support their families. It was felt they, as well as adults, needed access to healthy exercise. The Playground Association was formed in 1906 with the journal *The Playground,* and other popular national periodicals noticed the movement, promoting and supporting the need for community playgrounds. The magazines showed an individual, or a town, how to set up facilities in a cost-effective manner, and how to adapt existing activities to the reality of space. This was an issue in urban areas. The flat wide-open spaces of the peninsula did not present such problems. Organizational methods for the efficient management of these facilities were offered as park and recreation boards became more prevalent.

In 1908 Chestertown native Dr. John L. Wethered returned for a visit from his Midwestern home. While visiting he suggested that his hometown was ready for a funded playground facility that could accommodate baseball, tennis, and football, to be available to all citizens.

The progressive ideology of athletics was also making headway into collegiate sport, defining a firm delineation between amateur and professional. It was claimed that Washington College's philosophy had always been "purity in athletics over victory," but that was merely lip service. Burris had ended his 10-year career playing for the college in 1902 but was still an influence on the team as a faculty member. In 1908 he left the school to pursue a medical degree, and turned over the reins of athletic director to M.L. Thompson, who implemented the transition to purely amateur status: "his object has been to raise the moral standard of college sport and to imbue students with the idea that a game fairly played and lost is preferred above a victory dishonestly won ... through his influence the ethics of athletic sports in Maryland will be raised."[22]

7

End of an Era

> The finance committee represented by the business men and ladies is collecting a reserve fund of several hundred dollars to guarantee the success of the team. The idea is to get as good a team as we can afford and to play as long as we can afford and no longer. It is intended to give the fans just what they are willing to pay for. It is believed that with so many good teams on the shore there never was a better time for Cambridge to have one.
> —"Cambridge Catches Baseball Fever,"
> *Cambridge Daily Banner*, July 19, 1921

A young boy on the Eastern Shore of Maryland in the early 1900s read about his favorite major league players. Stars like Napoleon Lajoie and Ty Cobb were the next Baltimore newspaper, Sporting News, or Literary Digest away. But these were distant heroes. A trip to Washington or Philadelphia to see a major league team was rare, and out of the reach of most Eastern Shore children. Yet they read of the exploits of major league players, going over every box score, and sometimes reading of their personal lives. They might covet a picture of them on a dog-eared tobacco card, but that was all on paper and in the imagination. To see a baseball game, and experience its sights, smells, and sounds, a man, woman, or child, went to see the local team. Whether it was the Driving Park in commercially booming Cambridge, or the Crumpton grounds surrounded by corn or wheat fields, or on diamonds at river's edge, these were the places where most people knew baseball. On these grounds rural baseball fans found their stars. From those grizzled old pros in their 40s to the latest teenaged phenom, a boy could find a local hero. Mere accessibility was not the only reason for looking for heroes so close to home. The media told them that was where to look. Small towns were where they said all the skillful players came from. Historian Richard Crepeau referred to it as the Agrarian Myth and Steven Riess addresses the concept in his works on baseball in the Progressive era.

At this point in time the country was a hundred years into the industrial revolution, but few Americans saw themselves as urban or cosmopolitan. Most of the country perceived themselves as rural, and they were. Baseball in its earliest unorganized forms had been a rural, bucolic pursuit. The New York game was thought to reflect the new urban and industrial persona of the nation, but by the early 1900s perceptions of baseball had been reshaped and it was now perceived

Postcard of the Berlin Ball Grounds in 1912. Penny postcards of town teams were popular. Outdoor action cards appear to be more common after 1900 (Nabb Research Center).

as a bastion of rural values. Ballplayers were supposed to be men close to the soil who were protectors of women and children and had a strong work ethic and Christian moral values.

People wanted to see their heroes in print, factual and fictional. The *Cambridge Daily Banner* ran a piece of serial fiction called "The Ferncliff Pitcher," a clear copy of the Alger formula. C. Starr Matthews certainly did his part with the 1911 article on Herzog on his farm, portraying a city boy gone country. In 1912 New York sportswriter Bozeman Bulger took the 10-hour trip from New York to Cambridge, where "those trains run by sight and stop whenever the engineer sees something of interest." When Bulger made it to his destination of the "little berg," "Home Run" Baker greeted him with "Somewhat to the bush, eh?" Baker was usually depicted as a man of the soil whose family could trace their three farms to before the Revolutionary War. An interview with Helen Berry portrays Baker as a youthful representation of the myth. Of Baker she said, "He came in (to school) late in the fall after the farm work was finished ... a rather clumsy country boy ... so dark he seemed almost sun-baked, with thick black lashes and dirty hands ... the typical Baker grin ... so good natured and sympathetic.... Frank was always the one to sharpen slate pencils, turn the jumping rope and climb the mulberry tree and throw down mulberries to the girls ... very quiet and easy going." Like all Eastern Shore boys he learned and loved to hunt and fish. Everybody knew the best time to talk to the quiet Baker was after a successful duck hunt. Posed with a string of waterfowl laid at his feet for photos, rural men like Baker were considered the backbone of American society and culture.[1]

Steven Riess' seminal work is probably the first set of data used to explore the agrarian perception of Progressive-era baseball in the early 1900s and indicates most baseball players came from urban areas. Yet the data may explain why many people on the Eastern Shore boasted of the quality of their baseball, and why so many believed in this agrarian self-perception. Using Dr. Riess' definition of a rural community as one with a population under 2,500, the data provided in his works indicate that over 41.6 percent of major league players of the era came from small towns like those that were the heart of the Eastern Shore of Maryland. If Riess' definition of communities considered rural is extended to those of 5,000, to include the larger towns of Salisbury and Cambridge, it would suggest that 49.9 percent of major league players came from towns like those on the Eastern Shore of Maryland. In a geographic area of 3,000 square miles, and an aggregate population of around 170,000–200,000 during the period, Maryland's Eastern Shore and its scattered commercial centers and villages hardly comprised an urban or urbane population with cosmopolitan mores. The Eastern Shore of Maryland certainly contributed to the proliferation of this myth.[2]

Many fans clung to this notion that their most wholesome baseball heroes came from rural areas. When "Home Run" Baker repeatedly told the press during his 1915 salary holdout that he was equally content working the family farms as he was playing baseball on local teams, everyone knew he meant it. When he sat out his second season five years later to take care of his children after their mother died of scarlet fever, Baker was admired for his actions as a man of principle and integrity, with the proper values and priorities. City players cultivated this cultural perception. Many, like Herzog, and those who decided to live on the Eastern Shore, actually accepted and embraced rural culture, then lived the reality of it. Others, including Babe Ruth, would pose on their "working farms" to cultivate this image. Whether it was real or romanticized, many contemporary observers and the media saw rural towns and country ball as the heart and soul of American society and its cultural values well through the 1920s.

Starting around 1910 baseball begins to shift somewhat in these rural towns. Lee Fong tried to uphold the quality of the game in Cambridge, but one year his All-Stars went rogue, and he had to print a retraction of sponsorship in the local newspaper. Most towns continued to field fast teams, only maybe not as fast as in the previous decade. There was a lot of activity, and there were big games and the usual defiant independence. Fewer in number were the veteran independent and organized baseball players who in the past had filtered in from the cities. They were finding other places to play.

In 1913 and '14 it was the Chinese Nationals of Hawaii that rolled down the peninsula. Chinese immigrants were a sizable portion of the population of the island territory, and the sponsors promoted the team as all Chinese. Research has shown that by the time of the Eastern Shore tours, the team was composed of players who were of Chinese, Japanese, Native Islanders, and of mixed blood. Several would later remain in the Philadelphia and Wilmington areas, where they played minor league, semipro, and college baseball. Though described as undersized by Anglo standards, the Nationals were a quality club that beat most of the town teams they faced. Like the Nebraskans and the Cherokee, the Chinese put a "fast" team on the field. Rest assured that the main attraction of most barnstorming teams was their ethnicity or gender. When the Chinese Nationals played in Dover, Delaware, in 1913, Fong was amongst those included in the motorcade of Cambridge baseball moguls, which was described as part pleasure and part scouting expedition. Other barnstorming teams now appeared on the Shore. Former major league players, with baseball as their only skill, formed touring teams. Pete Kilduff and Cub Stricker were well enough known from their major league days that their all-star aggregations drew well playing in small rural towns.[3]

The baseball information sent to the *Afro-American* by its rural correspondents offers a glimpse of what was happening. In 1910 a "colored" league was formed on the Eastern Shore as the Salisbury Business League. The same year, the independent Crisfield Corkers won 13 straight, and then sat idle because no one else would play them. Nehemiah Henry won a seat on the Cambridge Town Council, and 10,000 people were expected for a grand parade in Salisbury to mark the 45th anniversary of emancipation in Maryland. In Trappe it was "Uncle Nace Day," named for Union veteran and event organizer Nathaniel Hopkins. The *Afro-American* remained positive in this volatile environment, citing "silent forces ... at work for the general uplift of the Negro," perhaps alluding to the Progressive movement now in full swing.[4]

The Washington, D.C., and Chicago race riots of 1919 rocked those cities, and two years later there was the deadly Tulsa unrest where the entire black community was burned to the ground. On the Eastern Shore, many who had worked at skilled maritime professions had been gradually forced out. Some took to the bay and its tributaries as watermen and lived in a handful of segregated communities along the Shore. Most were relegated to manual labor or other unskilled positions on farms or in canneries and seafood packing houses.

But the national economy was good and a black middle class was emerging in urban areas despite the 1918–19 unrest. African American communities looked to leaders like Booker T. Washington, Marcus Garvey and W.E.B. Du Bois. The cultivation of arts and intellectual pursuits created the Harlem Renaissance. Star black pitcher Rube Foster decided it was a suitable time to form a professional Negro league to wrest their proceeds from the white booking agents who reaped most of the profit from their games.

After 16 years of being one of baseball's premier players and managers on the Eastern Shore, Burris hung up his spikes and glove. Burris had more than his own financial prospects on his plate. Baseball was never far from his mind. In 1911, Burris and other baseball citizens on the Shore circulated a letter in newspapers with a proposal. It was an effort to form a bona fide independent professional league with a schedule, roster rules, umpires, and administrative oversight. Cambridge was enthusiastic about the proposal, and a meeting was actually called at the Masonic temple for all baseball advocates. The meeting was well attended, and the idea warmly received. The *Cambridge Daily Banner* was correct in at least two of its observations. The league could provide good baseball without the deficits that usually outpaced gate receipts by thousands of dollars, and it could, through parity, prevent weaker teams from folding as they fell out of contention.

Where they were wrong was that fans were ready for any limitations on their baseball. No one else appeared to respond so there was no league. It took time for the seed to germinate. Everyone was fine with their independence.[5]

Hope for baseball on the Shore in 1915 started with S.E. Gordy of Salisbury. He announced that he was willing to undertake the expense of a first-rate team in what was not an entirely solo venture. A local movie theater held a "monster" benefit to help manager Green's new squad in June. Gordy's team was to be composed of locals with "a few outsiders" to be "selected with special care." The local players would be paid as well. Gordy pumped $4,000 into the grounds for a new fence and grandstands.

Salisbury started the season with wins over Baltimore teams, then hired pitcher Doc Twining from Philadelphia fresh off a victory over holdout "Home Run" Baker's team in the Delaware State League. Baker was defiantly playing under Connie Mack's nose for the independent Upland team in Chester, PA, during his salary holdout. Salisbury then dropped two extra-inning contests to Easton, the first before a crowd of 1,200 fans. It was obvious the local players would not be enough, so Salisbury again turned to Philadelphia for more talent, then hired a new manager. In addition to Salisbury, Cambridge, Easton, and St. Michaels emerged as the other top teams on the Shore, and a meeting was held in Easton on July 22 to organize those four squads into a league.

It was decided to begin play July 26 with three games played in each town every week. Officers were selected at the second meeting in Hurlock on the thirty-first. Dr. Al Burris was selected president of the league. An eight-week season was established, to be governed by the rules and regulations of the National

This 1912 postcard features the Crisfield Reds. Whether an assertion, or the result of a playoff or tournament, the Reds have the confidence to proclaim themselves "Champions of Eastern Shore Maryland" (Nabb Research Center).

League. It was further agreed no club would "interfere in any manner with any players of other teams … unless said players be released, sold or traded. Such tampering could result in fine or forfeit." Salisbury hoped for the services of "Home Run" Baker, while Cambridge thought he should rotate his services amongst all four teams, but Baker, Tom Kibler, Jack Enright, and Joe Knotts, all of whom had played for the Upland Club, were conceded to Easton.[6]

Twenty-nine years old and at the peak of his major league career, Baker was locked into a three-year contract with the Philadelphia Athletics while the upstart Federal League was throwing around big money. Unable to extract a raise from Connie Mack, and threatened with expulsion if he bolted to the Federal League, Baker chose to "retire" to his family farms and "hit a few around with the boys." Baker lived up to that promise. Small towns and villages up and down the peninsula held "Home Run" Baker Days. The deal was that Baker would play a few innings for his hosts, after which he was well fed and feted and presents were given. When Baker found the time from the Upland squad and his banquet tour, he joined the Easton Diamondbacks in the newly formed independent Peninsula League. He had a pretty full season of retirement.

Even with Baker, a major league star, playing in a third of the games in the 30-game schedule, and with key players from the excellent Upland club, Easton could muster but a third-place finish in the hotly contested season. St. Michaels would finish last but the scrappy squad from the watermen's town was competitive to the last day of the season. Cambridge was described as a "heavy hitting" club, and with the workhorse Mike Cantwell on the mound, managed a second-place finish. Salisbury jumped to an early lead in the standings behind the pitching tandem of Doc Twining and Lefty Clunn, and never relinquished it.

When the dust settled on the season, Salisbury claimed the championship with a 21–9 record. Finishing the schedule in St. Michaels, the team was met on its return home at the train station by a brass band, a program of honor, and supper at the Elks club. A baseball autographed by the team and tied with a ribbon of the team colors of black and gold was presented to Mr. Gordy for his liberal financial support. Mayor Bounds declared in his speech that members of the team would always be welcome in the town for winning the first championship of the first successful league on the Shore. The young ladies of the town presented the team with a 12-foot-long pennant reading "Peninsula League Champions 1915," and it was unfurled from the fourth floor of the B&L Building.

But the glory was not over for the peninsula champions. An exhibition was arranged in late September with Connie Mack's American League Philadelphia Athletics. The A's were not a good team, as Mack had dismantled his club in one of his periodic rebuilds. The heat was intense for late September, but it did not deter baseball fans from around the peninsula from pouring into Salisbury by train and auto. A crowd of over 2,500 began to gather at one o'clock for the 3:00 p.m. game, and there was a mighty push when the gates were finally thrown open.

The Athletics, with future Hall of Famer Nap Lajoie, were fresh off a 9–0 victory over the Wilmington All-Stars. Doc Twining took the mound, and with no additions to their roster, paced the Salisbury team to a 6–3 win over the American League team. The Philadelphia players were impressed with the quality of their opponents and the enthusiasm of the crowd. One was heard to remark as he walked off the field that they had not played in front of a crowd that size at Shibe Park all year.[7]

Discussions started early in the summer for a Peninsula League for 1916. Eight towns vied for spots in the circuit, four now being from Delaware. Four teams were chosen for the league, with Seaford and Milford in Delaware, and the two largest Maryland towns of Cambridge and Salisbury. Alex Johnson was named president and other officers were selected. The schedule expanded from 30 to 58 games. No team would carry more than 12 players and they would refrain from hiring players from other league teams. The officers had the complete authority of the league to change dates, rules, and review decisions made on the field of play. Umpires were empowered to banish players for misconduct, and to levy fines up to $10. The league was determined to enforce good conduct. Its umpires were Barnes, Glatts, Morgan and Bill McGowan. This was seen as a significant improvement as the usual umpires in 1915 had been reserve players from both teams. Although no rowdy events had been reported, the usual weakness of that system had to be evident.

Many familiar players returned for the new season. Baker was gone, however, Mack having traded him to the Yankees, where being in pinstripes meant more money. Twining was back for Salisbury and Cantwell for Cambridge to provide a strong pitching matchup when those teams met. A young kid landed on the new entry in Seaford, Delaware, where the 16-year-old future Philadelphia Athletic Eddie Rommel of Baltimore anchored the pitching staff. He was ably assisted in the field by future major league players Jimmie Dykes and Joe Boley.

At the request of the "country people" and factory workers, Salisbury decided to play some of its games on Saturdays to allow more fans a chance to see the team. The grounds kept the name Gordy Park, even though its namesake made it clear that he was not footing the entire bill this time around. One thousand dollars each was raised in fundraisers in Cambridge and Milford. Salisbury subscriptions were set at $50 for the estimated $3,000 a week needed to maintain the team in the field. Buck Herzog, now managing in Cincinnati, plucked the promising Twining directly from the Salisbury roster, but he was soon returned when Herzog was again traded back to the Giants.

If 58 games were not enough in a nine-week schedule, teams filled in many of the open dates. Berlin picked up independent journeyman pitcher Rube Vickers for a game with Salisbury, but he was soundly clouted. Then the high minor league Orioles came to Cambridge, only to watch three of their pitchers get pounded for 16 hits and eight runs, the home team taking an 8–2 win. Cambridge had now won 15 straight against league and outside opponents, but the people were showing "poor appreciation" for the team's accomplishments. Attendance was falling and the unlikely reason given was people were tired of seeing the team win. Opponents in the league had something to say about that. For a time, the race was close before Salisbury jumped in front with a six-game lead.

The four umpires hired had a tough time living up to the league's promise of good conduct. All four expected trouble from the turbulent nature of rural baseball, and got it. In one game between Cambridge and Seaford, Barnes got into a scrap in the first inning and his partner, Morgan, had to finish alone, both teams "kicking all the way." McGowan's integrity was questioned after one game. He lived in Milford, Delaware, and often rode the train with that league entry to the games. It was thought he was too friendly with that member of the circuit and should divide his time more evenly with the other teams. McGowan was originally from Wilmington and had gotten his start umpiring as a teenager by going to the baseball directors in small peninsula towns and offering his services as an independent professional umpire. This was his first league job. McGowan was selected for the National Baseball Hall of Fame in 1992.

The Peninsula League drew wide attention, and not for its umpires. Scouts from Detroit and St. Louis were spotted at early contests. Governor Harrington, a Cambridge native, brought an entourage by automobile to see his home team. The *Baltimore Sun* was taking a more active role in Maryland sports and expanded its coverage of the league. Sporting editors and reporters from Baltimore were frequently at games. So thorough was the *Sun* coverage that when the local *Cambridge Daily Banner* published a list of the league's leading hitters in August, it compiled the statistics exclusively from the box scores that appeared in the Baltimore paper, rather than from any official scorebooks.

Arrangements were being made for the league champion to play the winner of the Blue Ridge League of western Maryland despite rumors that the league might "blow" in a week. The players insisted they would continue if crowds were large enough. But after another week, 31 games into the schedule, the league did blow when Cambridge and Milford disbanded. Salisbury was on top of the standings with a 20–11 record at the first of September. Fifty-eight games may have been too many for these small towns to support.

The series against the Blue Ridge League champion would be played on the Eastern Shore with four games in Salisbury and one in Milford, Delaware. Chambersburg was the pennant winner in the Blue Ridge League and with them was Eastern Shore–born Hanson Horsey on the mound. Salisbury added an additional pitcher. As evidence of his reputation early in his career, Bill McGowan was brought back to work the series from the New York State League, where he had gone when the Peninsula League had abruptly folded. The series was anticlimactic. Chambersburg easily took the series with only Twining gaining a win for Salisbury.[8]

Newspapers began to fill with ominous war news from Europe, and it was inevitable that America would enter a conflict in which people were being slaughtered in unprecedented numbers. Attention and dollars were being diverted from baseball. In 1917 the greatest war effort since the Civil War and the subsequent popularization of baseball began. Young men of semipro and minor league age enlisted or were being drafted into service. By 1918 there were few minor leagues left, and many semipro and independent associations had suspended operations.

War hysteria gripped the region. Some thought a German submarine had made it across the Atlantic when a periscope was sighted in the Chesapeake Bay, but it turned out to be nothing more than an oyster stake in the bobbing seas. Most of the local baseball talent went with the National Guard, and teams were formed and games played amongst the different peninsula units as they took the place of many town teams. Admissions went to the war effort. The economy was also in transition. Light, durable manufacturing was moving in to supplement the seasonal canning and packing jobs. This increased emphasis on manufacturing forced people into extended rigid workweeks where labor responded to the pace of machines rather than the rhythms of nature or the idiosyncrasies of an employer who might love baseball. One advantage the baseball-loving cannery worker had was that there were so many canneries that he had no problem finding another job if he was fired for missing work to attend a game. But those with better-paying year-round manufacturing jobs did not have as many options.

It took a couple of years for most in the armed services to be mustered out and return home. Town teams become active again in 1919 and enthusiasm picked up from there. Early in the 1920 season it was observed,

> Base ball seems to be attracting greater attention this year than usual. Lovers of the sport have frequently remarked that interest in the game seems to run in wave like periods; for two or three years there will be manifested the deepest interest, then enthusiasm seems to lag for a time, then take on a new spurt and so on. This seems to be one of those "on" years; there are base ball teams in every sector; there are "Babe" Ruths and "Home Run" Bakers in every vacinity (sic), and while their reputations may never reach that of those celebrated above, they all have their supporters and boosters.[9]

The season had started with an understanding that town teams could be composed only of players from that town or immediate area. It was proposed that any violations would result in forfeit. There was no league or governing association for enforcement. Winning was all that mattered. From Chestertown in the north to Crisfield in the south, and all points in between, the smallest communities were supporting quality teams. Even towns and villages like Berlin, East New Market, Fishing Creek, Mardela, and White Haven were fielding strong clubs. Many independent players found their way back to Eastern Shore money. Easton was said to have two pitchers able to "serve up the beandips" to the many professional players they faced. Some were coming over on game contracts from the Blue Ridge League. Future major leaguer Jake Flowers finished his high school season in Cambridge, then played with the independent White Sox and then the Federalsburg and Cambridge town teams. He later played at Washington College for his mentor, Tom Kibler, who had taken over as coach.

Crowds grew through the early season in most towns. Cambridge complained they had some of the smallest crowds for one of the larger towns. Fans were encouraged to support the team with the thirty-five-cent admission rather than the usual subscription method. Despite good crowds on the Fourth of July, the team decided to allow all ladies free admission the rest of the season in the hopes that it would provide an added attraction for the male fans and assuage their sometimes insolent behavior. In the last 20 years Salisbury's population had surged 32 percent to more than 7,000 by 1920. Only Cambridge came close to that number. When Salisbury drew just 1,200 to a game with Cambridge, it only piqued the pride of their sensitive opponents.

The 1921 season started no differently than the two that had preceded it, yet the events of the summer led the Shore directly into the minor league era. Fiscal prudence induced many towns to organize with local talent. The usual happened when they succumbed to the lure of foreign men. Those who were willing to pay quickly bought up the better players from neighboring rivals to supplement their imported ones. What happened in Cambridge was typical. In the middle of July, concerned with the fact there were a dozen or so fast teams around them, the businessmen of that town held a series of meetings to form committees for the improvement of the local team. With the help of the ladies, several hundred dollars was raised to put the best team possible on the field, for as long as the money lasted. Considering the caliber of ball being played on the rest of the Shore, it was deemed imperative that Cambridge meet the standard.

Virtually every town on the peninsula had a baseball team, and again, many small communities fielded teams competitive with the larger towns. Easton and Cambridge were eager to form a league with the smaller communities of East New Market and Hurlock, but nothing came of it. Familiar players appeared on the rosters, with Philadelphia, Wilmington and Baltimore providing much of the talent, along with a few players from the Blue Ridge League who continued to cross the bay. The local players proved to be better than usual.

Herb Armstrong of Baltimore, and a colleague of Jack Dunn of the Orioles, managed the Snow Hill club. He noticed Princess Anne's young player-manager Dickie Porter. Dunn signed Porter before the season was over. Porter won two International League batting championships before the tightfisted Dunn sold his contract to the Cleveland Indians. Porter retired from the majors with a lifetime average over .300. In fact, by 1921 a wave of homegrown talent was working through the ranks of this dynamic baseball environment. In addition to Dickie Porter of Princess Anne, there was Vic Keen, who pitched for Snow Hill and had already had a tryout appearance in the major leagues, with Connie Mack in 1918, and would be a late-season callup with the Cubs before the '21 campaign was over. Jake Flowers of Cambridge would also make good. Frank Bennett of Mardela Springs, and Doc Wallace of Church Hill were other local players that came out of the Eastern Shore headed for the major leagues.

So intense were these summers of baseball that the novelty of the touring Bloomer Girls Baseball Club barely turned the heads of local enthusiasts. All towns were now preoccupied with the expense of their clubs. Salisbury needed $2,000 just to keep their team in the field until the end of July, and a meeting was held at the chamber of commerce for this purpose. Receipts from a recent gate were insufficient. Of the $313 grossed at a game in Dover, Delaware, $33 went to the war tax; $70 to the visitors, $1 to each of three police officers; $5.50 to the ticket seller and collector; $12 for six new balls; and $10 for advertising and circulars. This left but $176 for salaries. The guarantees of the last three road games had barely met payroll. Six hundred dollars was the estimated weekly expense for the team. Crisfield's payroll was said to be between $300 and $400 a week.[10]

Cost and competition took a toll that month of July. Some were surprised when manager Hanson Horsey disbanded the Centreville team, his players hitting the open market. Salisbury changed management when R. Felton Waller resigned after being called away on business. The dependable Dr. A.B. Burris was named to take his place. Before he left, Waller had to put money into the treasury for the new regime until they could generate their own funds. By the end of August another $600 had been spent on the grounds, and $160 on uniforms, but only $458 raised through subscriptions. Three players were released. Just when all the hubris and cash seemed about spent, the *Baltimore Sun* stepped in with an idea.[11]

Sun sporting editor C.E. Sparrow proposed a championship of Maryland. A meeting was called in Baltimore to discuss how to select a representative from the Eastern Shore from the seven teams left standing. Snow Hill was immediately eliminated because they used a contract jumper from organized baseball. They could not play against Frederick of the Blue Ridge League, since that league had been accepted into organized baseball. At the urging of the *Sun*, and time being crucial, and as much because of the financial pressure on the independent Eastern Shore towns to keep their teams on the field, the remaining top six teams were split into two three-team brackets for an elimination tournament. One team in each tier was to draw a bye, and the winner of the play-in game would embark on a two-out-of-three series with the team that had drawn the bye. St. Michaels and Salisbury of the northern tier refused to participate under the format. Burris pointed out that the single elimination round was not a practical measure of the best team, and whoever drew the bye would have unfair advantage. Cambridge took the northern tier by default. Burris' fears came true in the southern tier. Led by Dickie Porter, Princess Anne was considered the weakest team in the field. All their players were considered local, even if paid, five being native to Somerset County. They did not even have an enclosed field. Pocomoke City beat the favored Crisfield, and after taking Pocomoke City in the series, Princess Anne completed their upset with two wins over Cambridge, who had been idle for a week. All games were fully covered by the *Baltimore Sun*.

For the championship series arrangements had to be made for Princess Anne's games to be played in Salisbury, where there were grounds suitable to the standards of organized baseball, and whose size and location made the town accessible to more Eastern Shore fans. Each team could pick up an extra battery from their respective territories. Frederick was expected to use their intact roster, while Princess Anne picked up a pitcher. The series was to be played under the rules of organized baseball. The first two games were to be played in Frederick, the second two in Salisbury. The next two games were to be played at Oriole Park; the seventh game location decided by a coin toss. The administration of the series was by the Maryland Commission of C.E. Sparrow, J. Vincent Jamison, and L.D. Wallop of Princess Anne. They chose five umpires, two from the independent Shore and three from the Blue Ridge League. They were paid $15 a game and an additional $5 for the second game of the doubleheader in Baltimore.

The first game in Frederick drew 1,200 fans, 1,300 if passes and fence-hopping boys were considered. Receipts of $1,066.75 had to pass through the sticky fingers of the National Association of Professional Baseball Players, the Maryland Commission, and Uncle Sam before anything was to be reserved for the players. The "underhand," or submarine, delivery of Bill King had the Somerset County boys swinging for pitches at their necks. Local pitching standout Frank Hummer evened it in the second game for Princess Anne.

Travel was now by auto caravan. Cars had drastically improved in the last 20 years, and the road system with them. The old steamboats were being replaced with gasoline- and diesel-fueled ferries and boats with gasoline motors. Traveling by train now seemed confining compared to being on the open road by car to the bay, ferried across, and then more open road to Frederick. The freedom of dusty roads was favorable to smoky, crowded, lurching trains. It was an exciting trip for the teams, hangers-on, and the nabobs of the commission. On the way back from Frederick, they backtracked to Annapolis, by ferry to Claiborne, then by road to Salisbury. There, 2,308 Shoremen paid their way into the grounds, and with passes and fence sitters, the crowd exceeded 2,500, greater than Frederick's two-day attendance. The receipts of $1,833.50 and the rooting of the fans did little good in an 11–4 drubbing. The loss showed up in the second-day turnout of 1,409 as Princess Anne absorbed their third loss. When the series reached Oriole Park it was billed the biggest event of its kind ever in Maryland, as 3,671 fans turned out for the doubleheader conclusion. Frederick won the series in the first game, and the second was played as an exhibition for the fans. In all, the attendance for the series had been 9,567 with net receipts of $6,591.41. The Maryland Commission took 10 percent to pay the umpires, the rest divided amongst the participating teams from both territories. The two opponents took over $1,000 in profit from the series and the players were handsomely rewarded. Based on a 14-man roster the winners took $138.78 each and the losers $92.50.

The profits generated by this event, along with Frederick's announced net profit for the season of $4,000, caught the attention of Eastern Shore baseball magnates. Even they could get it through their heads that this might be a more economical path to town baseball. Discussions started immediately after the series.

Initially, the newly formed peninsula league was not specified to be a minor league. Individual meetings were held in different towns, including Easton, Princess Anne, Centreville, and Crisfield. Still reluctant to let go of their independence, some proposed following all the rules of minor league baseball without naming it that. They would follow the rules of organized baseball with restrictions on both managers and players. Management would be prevented from enticing players, and players prevented from seeking to change teams, under the threat of being barred from organized baseball. Salary caps and paid umpires were considered. A meeting was held in Salisbury for next year's team and the agenda included formulating a financial plan, upgrading the grounds, and deciding whether to go independent or organized. Editorials began to appear around the peninsula pointing out that salaries on the Shore had run between $600 and

$1,000 a month, while the Blue Ridge attracted better players with a salary cap up to $2,000 a month, and still, they managed to make money. In September J. Vincent Jamison was invited to various meetings on the Eastern Shore. Some were held at chambers of commerce or other civic organizations, or directly with town baseball directors. Jamison, who many considered the best president of the most stable Class D minor league, hit the road, and brought home the advantages of organized baseball and the Class D minor leagues.

By October, the consensus was with starting a minor league. A meeting was called in Salisbury as 200 representatives from 11 towns maneuvered for position in the proposed eight-team circuit. Relying on and encouraged by the organizational skills of Blue Ridge League president Jamison, and the promotion of *Baltimore Sun* sports editor C. Edward Sparrow, a board of directors was chosen from Crisfield, Berlin, Pocomoke City, Cambridge, Snow Hill, Laurel (DE), Princess Anne, and Salisbury. A player salary limit of $1,750 was imposed as well as a limit per team of no more than three players with experience at a higher classification. The purpose of Class D baseball was to find and develop new talent. Winning, at least in theory, became a lower priority. How to split receipts was decided, and a $875 forfeit fee established. Several towns had to raise additional funds to upgrade or build new parks in order to conform with the standards of organized baseball.[12]

There was one thing baseball fans of the Eastern Shore could not see. Population and prosperity had increased steadily after the Civil War, but by 1900 population had peaked, It leveled off at just under 200,000 and stayed there for 50 years. While commercial centers like Cambridge and Salisbury continued to grow, some Shore counties actually lost population. But by 1920 baseball was as much a part of the Eastern Shore summer as sweet tea, shade trees, watermelon, and crab feasts. The next growth spurt on the Eastern Shore wouldn't begin until the 1950s with the building of the Chesapeake Bay Bridge, which further expedited travel and commerce to the urban centers of the western shore.

Part II

The Baby Loop

8

No Town Too Small

> Game Near Killed by Independents
> The land of the potato, oyster, crab, and fish long has been a fertile field for rustic baseball ... the enthusiasm of its inhabitants knows no bounds.
> While the men talk franchises, player deals, and the coming series with the Blue Ridge champions and the little tots argue over the relative merits of the hit-and-run and the sacrifice, the women—passing entirely over the ever appealing subject of handsome and unhandsome players—discuss everything from the rulings of Commissioner Landis to Hewell's fielding and Fisher's batting.
> —"Organized Ball the Answer,"
> *Sporting News*, September 7, 1922

By the 1920s baseball was completely absorbed into American culture, particularly on Maryland's Eastern Shore. Fifty years of rule changes, equipment modifications and evolving strategies and tactics had established the modern game. Baseball, and the perception of it, had been shaped, molded, and defined to fit the spirit and myths of American culture. The region entered a period of commercial and cultural stasis piqued by developing technologies, an increasingly global world, and expanding material opportunities. Yet, it was all blunted by an ingrained and isolated ethos considered unique to the region and perplexing to the uninitiated. Baseball was now just as much a part of the daily rhythm of Eastern Shore life as going to church, threshing wheat, shooting ducks, or eating hard crabs. What remained to be seen was what hold the extending grasp of organized baseball would find in these small rural towns . While independence had always been the preferred method of operation, Jamison and Sparrow had pointed them in a new direction.

Local newspapers give a feel for what it was like to live on the Shore as technology barged into the reserved peninsula. The *Salisbury Times* ran a weekly feature of photographs, with an emphasis on persons of note, from movie stars to politicians to sports heroes, spurring on the cult of celebrity. Great attention was given to the latest flapper hairstyles and dresses for the more daring Eastern Shore women. It was noted that loops, chains, and bracelets, once the symbols of slavery, were now in vogue. Movies made it to the peninsula and were extremely popular. Budding movie stars Gary Cooper and Fay Wray made a film on location on Tilghman Island about a romance between a waterman and his girl. Movies were often used as fundraising events for baseball clubs. Business advertisements now included their three-digit telephone numbers, and the new radio station in Salisbury published its daily schedule for the "radio bugs" with their new crystal sets.

Canning factories and seafood packing houses were still a significant source of employment, with several in every county. The industry continued to improve its technology and processes leading into the 1920s. In the 19th century conversion was made from glass to tin cans for most products, and beginning in the 1870s continued improvements made to the pressure kettles modernized the industry. Between 1870 and 1960 the eight Maryland Eastern Shore counties counted nearly a thousand vegetable canneries in operation at one time or another.

It was said that the Ku Klux Klan numbered 9,000 members on the Eastern Shore of Maryland alone, and the organization had the political influence and support to sue the State of Maryland when they were denied use of the Baltimore Armory for a convention. The automobile, the very conveyance that made the Eastern Shore League possible, became the catalyst for a wave of crime. Road bandits held up businesses and individuals, as the auto afforded the culprits a quick getaway. The Volstead Act provided opportunity for those who had no qualms in breaking an unenforceable law by running alcohol. Mother ships would lay off the three-mile limit of the Delmarva coast as new high-performance gasoline motorboats ferried in copious quantities of illegal spirits to high-powered autos for distribution. Others made their own beverages in stills tucked back in the woodlands that comprised much of the peninsula. The Roaring Twenties roared just as loud on the Eastern Shore as it did anywhere else.

If population growth had leveled, a different kind of immigration took place. Many who increased their wealth during the 1920s sought property on Maryland's Eastern Shore. They came from Baltimore, Philadelphia, Wilmington, New York, and Europe. The Delmarva Eastern Shore Association took a page out of Halstean's old business book of the 1870s and printed a guide for residents of Washington, D.C., looking for a "White House," or summer home. They listed some of the finest estates on the Eastern Shore for $45,000 to $100,000. The guide promoted large private properties rich in fishing, hunting, historical features, golf, horse trails, and an array of outdoor sports, all just a short distance from the nation's capital. People came from all over the world and bought up old waterfront estates or sought vast tracts of property to build new. For some it was a grand weekend getaway, while others had bold if eccentric schemes. One family bought up much of Wye Island and converted their portion to a cattle ranch, worked by Colorado cowboys. The new money mingled with the old. The Eastern Shore was an odd contrast of the isolated yet linked.

One winter George Ponzi was arrested in Florida for fraud and the term "Ponzi scheme" was born. In Maryland, the building of a bridge across the Chesapeake Bay to connect the Eastern Shore of Maryland to the western side was proposed. The process would take 30 years to see fruition. Watermen complained of an "oyster crisis," and when the crab season opened in the spring, a Crab War broke out between the watermen of Tangier Island in Virginia, and those of Tylerton, Maryland, on Smith Island. They fought over the location of the state line and their crab lays. Boat crews carried tommy guns to protect their nautical turf, just like Capone's gangsters in Chicago. Little had changed on the bay since the Oyster Wars.

Floating theaters, popular before the turn of the century, were still a fashionable entertainment in the 1920s. These boats plied the Chesapeake, usually towed by power boats. With shallow drafts of as little as 14 inches, they did not require a dock and often worked the shorelines near towns. To announce their arrival they disbursed handbills on shore, and sent their brass band out on a towboat and into nearby coves so the music would carry over the water to people's homes. People knew what the music meant. Each of these boats had an ample stage for plays and vaudeville acts. One didn't have to go to the theater; the theater came to you. The Adams Floating Theater worked out of Trappe and featured Beulah Adams, "the Mary Pickford of the Chesapeake." Novelist Edna Ferber spent a week with the theater, taking notes for an idea for one of her novels. She changed the venue from the Choptank to the Mississippi and called it *Showboat*, later made into a Broadway play and movie musical.[1]

The Eastern Shore League of 1922 was the latest of the new Class D minor leagues that organized baseball was using to make inroads into the bastions of independent and outlaw baseball, and the Eastern Shore of Maryland and the Delmarva Peninsula were well known for just those things. Peninsula towns were smaller than those of most teams in comparable Class D leagues, hence the nicknames in the national papers such as the "Baby League," or the "Baby Loop." Still, they were considered an important baseball market despite their lack of numbers. But there was another reason for organized baseball to go into small towns other than the outlaws, and it may have been influenced by the Agrarian Myth. They feared they were losing rural youth to other modern distractions. Mike Sexton, president of the National Association of Professional Baseball Players, proposed a classification lower than D to aid small towns in developing the sport.[2]

The stated purpose of the D classifications was to develop young talent for the major leagues, but there were other reasons for organized baseball to encroach into these rural areas. Outlaw leagues and independent teams competed for the same talent, incited by small-town enthusiasm to pay more money. By 1920 most of the outlaw leagues had been corralled under the auspices of the National Association of Professional Baseball Players. In many areas, like the Eastern Shore, rowdyism, rioting, gambling, and corruption, often downplayed or ignored in the local newspapers, were unwanted and unpleasant facts. These conditions further sullied the game's reputation, and the public perception of baseball was already reeling from the Black Sox Scandal of 1919. For the small towns of the Eastern Shore, the motivation for the transition from independent to organized baseball, as seen in the Maryland series of 1921, was simply money. The new commissioner, Judge Landis, was attempting to clean up and control the game at every level. The gambling and corruption that plagued major league baseball continued at the grassroots level. To encompass ever smaller communities under the umbrella of organized baseball seemed a logical way to curtail these activities. The Class D minor leagues had been around long before Landis was brought in, and he was merely supporting the efforts of Mike Sexton and J.H. Farrell of the National Association of Professional Baseball Leagues to extend their reach.

When the National League existed as the only major league, any other association was designated as "minor." Then the American Association declared itself a major league in 1882, establishing some franchises in the same cities as the National League. With the National Agreement between these two entities, and the founding of the Northwestern League, the concept of minor leagues came into being. Many of these minor leagues accepted the National Agreement, while others did not, making them by definition, independent or "outlaw." From 1884 until the formation of the National Association of Professional Baseball Leagues in 1901, the situation was fluid. Joining the agreement did not mean a total commitment. During this time, a classification system was also devised, but it had nothing to do with the size of the city or the level of play. It was a system based on the degree of protection of team rosters, and a league could apply for several levels of protection from the major leagues. Some leagues were designated independent.

This all changed with the formation of the National Association of Professional Baseball Leagues, with Patrick Powers as president. Several minor league moguls had come together for the express purpose to provide solid opposition and provide protection from the major leagues, eliminate havens for contract jumpers, punish and suspend violators, provide a selection or draft system, institute salary limits, and protect reserve lists. Teams were now classified by level of play rather than level of protection sought. Organized baseball seemed more worried about the independents, rather than the other way around. The outlaw leagues were not bound by the salary limitations, reserve clauses or other contractual limitations of organized baseball, so they often ignored those agreements and bid higher for a major or minor league player's services. The threat from these outlaws was real for a time, if overstated.

In 1905 there were 35 minor leagues registered in the National Association, with 12 of them at the Class D level. Mike Sexton took over the Association in 1909 and the following year membership increased to 50 minor leagues, 29 of which were designated as Class D, and there were no designated independent leagues left in the association. By 1916 independent leagues were few, and usually relegated to the smaller towns, industrial leagues, or commercial sponsorship. The renegade player now faced a dwindling market for his services. The towns of the Eastern Shore that participated in Class D were about the smallest in the association. Although the *Sporting News* provided weekly coverage of the Eastern Shore League, it was never included as a circuit in the "Directory of Organized Baseball" listed in its pages every week.

Even with increasing participation rates in the National Association, teams and leagues frequently folded. At Class D this led to secret deals with both major and higher minor league clubs for financial and player support. Mike Sexton and new commissioner Landis were dead set against affiliation. Both felt that smaller cities and towns would not support absentee ownership and corporate control of their clubs. They thought that these clubs could only survive through local ownership and management. J.H. Farrell, the association's longtime secretary-treasurer, was another adamant "stand patter." The reality was that the very leagues that could infiltrate the havens of contract jumpers and free agents were rarely financially sound. By the time the Eastern Shore joined the fray in 1922, joint ownership and affiliation with minor league clubs by major league and other high minor league clubs was legal again. The National Agreement dropped the farming prohibitions that had been routinely ignored since 1903. These changes took little time to have an impact.[3]

Salisbury was now the largest of the towns on the peninsula. At 7,000 people, it was much larger than Easton, and now outstripped Cambridge, its two nearest commercial competitors. Salisbury served as the commercial and cultural center for the lower peninsula. They were inevitably the center of the league. The automobile revolutionized travel on the peninsula much the same as the steam network that had brought baseball to the region. Like steam transportation on the Shore in the 1860s, it quickly became more available and was reaching its culture-changing potential. Only now were vehicles becoming affordable through assembly line production, and the road system was in its early development. The fact that there was now a set schedule, and each team was required an enforceable forfeit fee for failure to appear, influenced who would be members of the league. The early Class D league was sometimes referred to as The Wheel, and Salisbury was its hub, as it had been with the local Eastern Shore League of the early 1900s.

Adopting guidelines from the National Association, the new Eastern Shore League forbade the use of blacklisted players and contract jumpers from organized baseball. The league also promised to abide by the rules of the National Association and the National Agreement. The advantages of the National Association's oversight were obvious, even as they proved difficult to live by.

> Previous to this season independent ball was the rage on the shore. Baseball of any kind is sure of the support on the Shore ... but lack of organization has provided a hinderance to the full development of the game. With scheduled games cancelled at the last minute, teams not showing up for games booked, no league umpire staff, players unsigned and able to go and do as they pleased and other things of a like nature, it was no wonder the game was not fully developed.
>
> Worst of all was the cost of independent ball. Where towns were bitter rivals each town could go forth and get the best players to be had and pay them accordingly when a "big" series was to be played. The player could demand almost anything and get it for their services and many were the clubs which came out on the wrong side of the ledger through paying high salaries.[4]

During the 1921 season an Eastern Shore team had picked up a pitcher for a best of series with Onancock, Virginia. He was paid the considerable sum of $300 to pitch two games for what amounted to no more than a county championship. The same pitcher could not find a roster spot in the new Class D Eastern Shore League when he offered his services at $50 a week for the season. Even with the stipulations imposed by organized baseball, the teams more closely resembled their independent past than a cooperative future.[5]

From the rabble of representatives that met in the fall of 1921 through the winter, six teams were chosen. In an attempt to curtail expenses, no team was admitted from north of the Choptank River. This relegated the league to the southern peninsula and effectively omitted the larger towns of Easton, Dover, Delaware, and other dens of baseball activity like Federalsburg, Centreville and Chestertown. An independent upper Shore Tri County League formed with Easton, Centreville, Chestertown, and Oxford. Such smaller and independent leagues would continue throughout the minor league era. Often they were semiprofessional and competed for fans with the Class D minor leagues. As for the Eastern Shore League, the towns of Salisbury, Pocomoke City, Crisfield, and Cambridge came from Maryland, with teams also in Laurel, Delaware, and Parksley, Virginia.[6]

As in the past, each town had a local independent board of directors and team officers. From these groups, or prominent men in their communities, league officers were selected. Walter Miller of Salisbury was chosen as the first league president. The various team directors then set out to choose their managers and sign many of the veterans who had played on the independent town teams in recent seasons. The 1922 version of the Class D Eastern Shore League seemed little different from that of the recent past to its directors and fans. Managers and directors signed most of their players from the same places as in the independent years. An early roster indicates that a few players were farmed out to local teams, but the list is heavy on players from the Baltimore and Philadelphia regions, with a few locals sprinkled in. Many favorite players returned from the previous independent seasons.

Early proponents of modern major league affiliation were just getting started, led by Branch Rickey and Sam Breadon of the St. Louis Cardinals. They were not alone. Most teams were making strides towards the new management model through the use of negotiated working agreements, but Farrell, Sexton, and

Gordy Field in Salisbury, Maryland, was named for an early member of the White Cloud. It served as the main baseball grounds there until War Memorial Park was built after World War II. The club had to purchase land behind the short right field in the 1920s in order to expand it to the 250-foot minimum required by organized baseball (courtesy Eastern Shore Baseball Hall of Fame).

Landis seemed to be working against it. Eastern Shore League directors in the league's first season were looking for managers with experience and personal connections in organized baseball. Salisbury's Izzy Hoffman was said to be a personal friend of Connie Mack and was sure to receive players and leads from that astute judge of talent. Cambridge went with Herb Armstrong of Baltimore. Armstrong was a longtime player who was familiar to Eastern Shore fans from his years playing and managing in the independents. He had played minor league ball, coached in college, and had close connections with Jack Dunn of the high minor league Baltimore Orioles. The small town of Parksley hired Baltimorean Poke Whalen, a veteran of organized baseball and the semipros of Baltimore. Laurel, Delaware, went with Sam Frock, well known on the peninsula from the triplet rivalry years between Easton, Cambridge, and Salisbury in the early 1900s.

After a period where independent professional town teams were simply referred to by the name of their town—e.g., the Eastons, or the Easton Club—teams returned to the familiar custom of using a nickname. Many of the financial backers in Salisbury came from old members of the White Cloud, their earliest town representative. Locally owned and operated, Salisbury's entry into organized baseball reverted to the White Cloud, or, more commonly, the Indians. Such designations clung well into the next decade when affiliation and working agreements became more prominent. The other teams took names indigenous to the region and the occupations of which people partook. There were the Crisfield Crabbers, Cambridge Canners, Laurel Blue Hens, the Pocomoke City Salamanders, and the Parksley Spuds.

Poke Whalen of the Spuds got the drop on the rest of the league. He began to sign players out of the Baltimore semipros in March and kept the team there to play exhibitions against the best teams he could find throughout the spring. This must have been an expensive proposition, since league play did not begin until June 12. The investment paid off as their competitors got a much later start on the season. Poke's Spuds jumped to an early league lead. At one time five of the six league members were playing under .500 ball. Newspapers pointed out that the league leader was a town with a population of somewhere between only 700 and 900 souls. As a regional representative for the Eastern Shore of Virginia in the league, the Spuds routinely drew as many as 1,500 fans to their games, sometimes more. *Baltimore Sun* headlines read "Diamond Fans Mildly Insane." To quote from the *Sporting News*,

"No one seems immune from the malady, peculiarly American, which has been known to seize whole communities and temporarily transform them into medleys of rabid ball bugs.

"Parksley is proud of her team, proud of her franchise and the league to which it belongs, and the success she has enjoyed on the field." By mid–August the team was 12 games ahead. The rest of the league had already reverted to their independent ways by "cramming" their rosters in an attempt to catch up. There were wholesale releases and fresh players signed. Many suspected both the salary cap and the class player rules were extensively violated, but there was no catching the Spuds in the pennant race.[7]

One way around the league rules was to enter into creative, illegal contracts. Laurel entered into such a deal with manager Sam Frock. Class D leagues often used player-managers and their salaries were considered part of the cap, but Frock angled for a profitable twist in his negotiations. In addition to his salary, Frock had sole control of signing players and managing the salary cap. He was allowed to keep any of the monthly salary cap of $1,750 not spent. In the first two months of the season Frock signed and released more than 50 players, most to cheap tryout contracts. With the constant rotation of bargain players he was able to realize a substantial bonus. It eventually became obvious to the Laurel directors that Frock was profiting at the expense of the team as the Blue Hens wallowed towards the bottom of the standings. He was fired in mid–August and Laurel withheld his last payment. Frock did not remain unemployed for long in a musical chairs of managers that saw four of the six skippers released. Frock was immediately hired by Pocomoke City.

Frock appealed his case to the National Association. He wanted the balance of his $1,500 in wages plus the money he had gleaned from the salary cap. It was determined that between June 16 and his dismissal on August 10 Frock had pocketed the shortfall of the cap. When other teams were trying to find legal or illegal ways to bypass the cap, the Blue Hens were consistently under it to Frock's benefit. There was also the matter of the $300 loan advanced to Frock at the beginning of the season, plus the additional "slush" fund he tried to raise amongst the enthusiastically gullible Laurel fans. Farrell ruled that Frock owed Laurel $1,200 to be paid by September 12 or he would be placed on the ineligible list.[8]

Rowdyism was another carryover from the independent era that was hard to shake. Opening day in June saw governors Ritchie of Maryland and Denny of Delaware in attendance. Former governors Harrington of Cambridge and Pennewell of Delaware also made appearances. But the league got off to a rocky start as there was a "cowardly attack" upon umpire Knowlton at Crisfield. A spectator alleged to have imbibed in too much "Volsteadism" spirits struck the umpire on the back of the head, resulting in the official's confinement in the Crisfield Hospital for several days. Doc Dolan didn't last a week as Cambridge interim manager before umpire Truitt banished him. President Miller gave "explicit instructions" that order was to be maintained at all games.[9]

Despite Miller's mandate, and a runaway pennant race, the "ball bugs" continued to root, encourage, and fight for their home teams. On July 26 umpire Elwood Dixon was "roughly treated" at Cambridge in a game against Pocomoke City. Dixon was jumped and rapped across the back of his head with a club as he was halfway in the dugout. He was said to be in "pretty bad shape" for several days. Several stories were now spinning out of Cambridge trying to shift the blame, but the fact remained that Dixon was "trampled upon and hit." Miller sent him home to Baltimore to recover. Even with hospitalized and convalescing umpires, some saw an improvement in the league. One newspaper stated that the umpiring was better than during the independent years and rowdyism among spectators and players had decreased, all the while blowing their own horn in the formation and success of the league. The Spuds took the league championship, with Parksley perhaps the smallest town to ever win a pennant in organized baseball. They capped the season with what was now dubbed the Five State Series.[10]

The continued effort to establish a series between the two Class D minor leagues based in Maryland was primarily through the continued efforts of Vincent Jamison and C. Edward Sparrow. It was now referred to as the Five State Series because the Eastern Shore and Blue Ridge Leagues represented towns from Virginia, Delaware, Maryland, Pennsylvania, and West Virginia. The series began in 1916 with the Blue Ridge and Peninsula Leagues and disappeared during the war years, then returned as the championship of Maryland in 1921 when Jamison and Sparrow presented that much ballyhooed event that led the Eastern Shore into the minor leagues. Now, the 1922 version not only had the backing of Jamison, Sparrow, and the *Baltimore Sun*, but organized baseball as well.

Mike Sexton, president of the National Association, saw that this fit perfectly into his plans. Sexton was promoting what he called the "Little World Series" between neighboring leagues throughout the country. Since this event was already organized and running, Sexton merely had to sanction it. Similar events were being planned between the Texas and Southern Leagues, South Atlantic and Virginia Leagues, and the Western Association and the Southwestern League. Sexton decided to appear at as many of these series as he could. Also jumping onto the promotional bandwagon for these postseason contests was American League president Ban Johnson. Johnson promised a pennant for the series winner. It was 15 feet long and five and a half feet at the base and read, "1922 Five State Champion Blue Ridge Eastern Shore." The donation included an intent to attend, and was backed by a letter of support from association secretary J.H. Farrell. The

The Spuds—from a town of "600–700 souls"—won the Class D Eastern Shore League's first pennant in the 1920s. They took three pennants and one second place in the league's six full seasons (courtesy Eastern Shore Baseball Hall of Fame/Donnie Davidson Collection).

series proved profitable for the participants, and fit Sexton's promotion of Little World Series.

Parksley hosted the first two games of the 1922 series, with a third to be played at Gordy Park in Salisbury. From there the series returned to the western side of the bay with two games at Blue Ridge champion Martinsburg (WV), one at Hagerstown, and the last at Oriole Park if needed. The first game in Parksley saw the Spuds lose before 1,445 fans. Second-day attendance was 778. The third game brought in 2,229 to see the ceremonial raising of the Eastern Shore League pennant by Samuel E. Gordy at Gordy Park in Salisbury. Over a dozen had "motored" all the way from Martinsburg. The crowd ran several feet deep along the ropes set up inside the field. Several hundred more people were lined around the outside fence. The Eastern Shore games drew 4,452 people with receipts of $5,108.25.

Not deterred by three losses, 25 Parksley fans planned the trek to Martinsburg, first by boat to Salisbury, where they boarded a bus covered with banners and placards. Sixty miles later they caught the ferry across the Chesapeake from Claiborne to Pier L on Pratt Street in Baltimore. Then it was by train to Martinsburg, where the series ended in a sweep by the Blue Ridge representative. If local and national magnates loved the publicity generated, the players loved the money. They took a 60/40 split based on 70 percent of the total revenues after the war tax. The clubs split 25 percent and the leagues 5 percent. The total take was $6,440.50, over a thousand dollars more than the '21 series. Martinsburg's winner's split was $176.92, and Parksley's share $117.92. This was a significant payday. This time the two umpires split a winner's and loser's share. Each league netted $144.91. Each club received $688.33. Even with a four-game sweep, the series had been a financial success.[11]

All agreed that the league had been a great accomplishment, and an improvement over baseball in the past:

> That the almost limitless extravagance of independent ball was killing the game in a territory where the national pastime is as much of a necessity as water, all agree. They point to the fact that the larger and wealthier towns were not able to go out and, by the expenditure of fabulous sums of money, actually buy baseball supremacy. Of course, Cambridge, Salisbury, and Crisfield had an equal show with the smaller towns for the pennant, but not one whit more.[12]

Somewhere along the line Sam Frock appealed the National Association ruling and his case was one of many to cross Judge Landis' desk that offseason. Frock had started his career with the semipros of Baltimore and the town teams of the Eastern Shore of Maryland as a pitcher and outfielder. After his stint in the major leagues, Frock's career then took a turn in another direction. Frock had profited from spendthrift independent clubs in his early years, so he turned his career and efforts there, often acting as a recruiter for independent teams. That led the *Sporting News* to refer to him as a "former notorious enticer of players from Organized Ball to outlaw clubs." This was the kind of man Landis was gunning for, and he had the full support of Mike Sexton and J.H. Farrell.

Frock admitted that he received $558.65 from June 9 to August 10 from the player salary pool. With a 14-man roster he had gone through 51 players in a little over eight weeks. Thirty of those had been tryout contracts receiving minimal compensation. Landis' response helped extend his power into the lowest rung of the minor leagues. Landis ruled against the Laurel contract in that it violated Article II, Section 1 of the major-minor league rules that no club shall make a contract different from the "uniform" player's contract, and "not only is it obviously an improper basis for the manager's compensation, but it puts a premium on the wrecking of the team." Frock lost his money, and Laurel was not punished for offering the illegal contract in the first place. Hospitalized umpires, roster cramming, and the Frock case caught Landis' attention, and may have even raised one of his furry eyebrows.[13]

Landis then announced his intention to visit the Eastern Shore League in 1923. It would all be portrayed as a social call by the new commissioner. In reality, Landis wanted to get a closer look to make sure the "baby member of John Farrell's family" was living up to its responsibility to develop new players. Reports of roster cramming, illegal contracts, drinking, gambling and violence may have also attracted his attention.[14]

9

The Eyes of Landis

Most towns made money in the 1922 season and the league was considered a success. This local heady outlook was echoed in the prestigious *Sporting News* with headlines like "Organized Ball the Answer" and "Eastern Shore's Story Shows Benefits of Organized Ball." M.B. Thawley of Crisfield was elected league president for the new season, and the circuit expanded to eight teams. Joining the league were the Dover Dobbins and the Milford Sandsnipers, both in central Delaware. The distance between these two northerly towns and the southernmost member in Parksley, Virginia, was well over a hundred miles. The tight little wheel was broken already.[1]

The new season started well enough with significant attendance, but early on a protest was filed against the Sandsnipers for the blatant use of six class players. For pitchers there was a limit on appearances and innings at a higher level. For position players it was the number of games. The league decided that Milford had to forfeit the games in question. Rather than accept the punishment, the Milford directors abandoned the season and arrogantly forfeited the franchise back to the league. Many in that town thought it just as well since they were of the opinion that independent ball was better quality than this Class D version. There were rumors that there was sufficient backing in Easton to assume the spot, but the league assumed control of the franchise as a road team. They became known as, and were now precariously listed in league standings as the Free Lancers.

At the same time the Pocomoke City Salamanders were having trouble making payroll due to poor attendance and insufficient backing. None of this could have come at a worse time. Commissioner Judge Landis had previously announced he would visit the Eastern Shore League, and the dates and arrangements had been made. Landis Day would soon be upon them, and they did not want to present the grand "Czar" of baseball with two failed franchises. Both teams were still listed in the standings on July 19 when he found his way to the peninsula.

Landis had been in Washington and met *Baltimore Sun* sports editor C. Edward Sparrow and Blue Ridge League president Vincent Jamison en route to Salisbury. They crossed the bay on a banker's luxurious yacht and landed at the ferry dock at Claiborne, Maryland. They were met by the first ever Maryland state trooper, who escorted the entourage on his motorcycle. Included in the motorcade was the *Evening Sun*'s brass band of boys and a flock of Baltimore street urchin newsboys. After covering the first 15 miles from Claiborne, Landis decided he needed some more cigars so the speeding caravan came to a halt in Easton. Landis was recognized, a crowd gathered, they pressed towards him, and a speech was given. With tobacco in hand, the trip to Salisbury was completed.

The *Baltimore Sun* account on July 20 explained, "The Eastern Shore League is a small pink pearl in the great American baseball necklace, and Judge Landis is the custodian of that necklace and now and then he has to count those pearls. That is the brief story why he is here." The boys' band hopped out in khaki and red uniforms with hats and pompons, looking like the "Duchy of Luxembourg," and began to play as a parade proceeded through Salisbury. Fourteen thousand people lined the curbs of the town of 7,500 to gawk and cheer the man who promised to clean up baseball. Main Street was decorated with flags and the town shut down two hours before the 3:30 game. "The bankers took a last look at the day's business. Lawyers locked their office doors, the barbers opened the cut-outs of their razors, the businessmen threw odds and ends together and shut their desk, and the sudden deaths of eighteen office boys' grandmother were reported."

After lunch at the home of league vice president Walter Miller, the commissioner proceeded to Gordy Park, named after old White Cloud catcher S.C. Gordy. Landis met with three of the five surviving members of the founding team, L.W. Gunby, S.S. Smith, and H.S. Todd. Absent was the old curveballing Judge Stanley Toadvine, whom Landis would meet later at the banquet, and his catcher Gideon Jordon. Landis was amazed that so many from the team were still alive more than 50 years later, and even more surprised they all still lived in the same town. They had backed Salisbury's independent professionals in the 1890s, and again in the early 1900s, and over a half century after first taking the field and starting baseball in Salisbury, all were still ardent rooters and among the financial backers of the league entry.

Landis walked around the perimeter of Gordy Park, waving to the more than 4,000 fans crammed in and around the facility. A third of them were thought to be women, most of whom were directed to the covered grandstand. This caused one wag to observe that the women had misread Landis Day for Ladies Day. Then Landis, in support of the Laurel Club, and defiant of outlaw miscreant Sam Frock, donned a Laurel Blue Hen cap to throw out the first pitch. The Cambridge Canners proceeded to best Laurel 10–5 in the game.

It was then to a local church where 300 sat down to an Eastern Shore dinner of Maryland fried chicken and seafood of all kinds and styles. After the repast, the doors of the church were thrown open to the throng outside. When on the Eastern Shore, where Landis saw a crowd, he made a speech. Fresh on his mind were hospitalized umpires, crammed rosters, illegal players, and Sam Frock's antics in 1922. He was also aware of the Milford story and had to know that the vagabond Free Lancers would not survive his departure, and the Pocomoke Salamanders weren't doing much better. As he spoke, he complimented the people of the Shore for their efforts in the Great War, and the league officials for an outstanding job. He thanked everyone for their wonderful hospitality, and promised, or threatened, to return in the near future.[2]

Commissioner Landis shakes hands with Cambridge manager Herb Armstrong on his 1923 visit to Gordy Park in Salisbury. Landis seemed to thoroughly enjoy his visits to the Eastern Shore, even if they were more than social calls (author's collection).

Dover (DE), Cambridge (MD), and Laurel (DE) proved the strongest teams in the circuit. The Dobbins were led by the bat of second baseman and catcher Frank King. King's real name was Cochrane. Mickey Cochrane was playing for Dover under an assumed name to protect his amateur status. The Free Lancers did not last long after the judge's departure. Pocomoke City hung on in a catch-22 scenario. They were forced to sell their better players to meet expenses. Putting cheaper players on the field resulted in an inferior product which only exasperated their inadequate attendance. It was not until August 21, less than two weeks before the end of the season, that Pocomoke finally called it quits, and it was only through a reorganization where the players took over operations that Crisfield avoided the same fate. It looked like the little pink pearls had lost some of their luster. But the finish to the season was an exciting three-team race with the Dover Dobbins taking the pennant and securing entry into the profitable Five State Series. The *Sporting News* reported that the Eastern Shore League would "Limp Along to Wire."[3]

The Five State Series for 1923 attracted even more attention than it did the year before. American League president Ban Johnson threw his full support behind the "little world series" concept of Mike Sexton and even made suggestions to the bi-league committee. In addition to Johnson's valued pennant was now the *Baltimore Sun* silver ball and the Ned Hanlon Trophy for the winner. Games were scheduled in Martinsburg (WV), Hagerstown (MD), Dover (DE), and

Salisbury (MD). Dover made it clear that the quality of play in the league had improved. Frank King, alias Mickey Cochrane, led his team in hitting en route to Johnson's pennant. In a game at Dover, Cochrane grabbed umpire Sipple by the arm after a called third strike. Several teammates rushed the plate before the umpire regained control by tossing Cochrane and fining the others. Cochrane was suspended one game for the series and fined $25. Whether in reference to this game or another, Cochrane would later tell of an incident with an umpire. He had been ejected and the umpire held up his open hand to indicate a $5 fine. The problem was the umpire had only three fingers. Looking at the two stubs, Cochrane countered, "Okay, okay. I'll settle for $3.50." Dover won the series in six games, and the financial success was posted.

The league may have limped to its finish, but it ended the season on the highest of notes.

The Five State Series drew 9,115 fans in the six games with net receipts after the war tax of $9,300.50. The player pool netted the 14 winning Dobbins $128.77, and the 13 losing Martinsburg Red Sox $92.75. The two umpires made $112.50. Attendance in Martinsburg for two games was 2,076 with total receipts of $2,307.00. Dover's two games drew 2,807 with net receipts of $3,259.25. Salisbury drew 2,320 for its game for $3,259.25, and Hagerstown attracted 1,912 for $2,165.75. The Eastern Shore League had beaten the Blue Ridge at the turnstiles, at the bank, and on the field.[4]

With Sparrow's silver ball already in Dover's hand, "Foxy Ned" Hanlon made the trip to Dover to present his trophy. More than 70 political and baseball dignitaries were on hand for the ceremonies. Hanlon made his speech and gave his trophy. It was described as solid silver with bats for handles. One side was inscribed with "The Ned Hanlon Cup," and the opposite inscribed with the name of the year's winner. As a permanent trophy it could not remain with one club or organization but had to pass from year to year to the winner. The *Baltimore Sun* was entrusted with its keeping.[5]

While many old-timers still longed for the independent days, most were fully satisfied with organized ball and financially supported the teams in their towns. Dover, Salisbury, Cambridge, and Laurel, with a population of around 3,000 each, were certain for the '24 season.

Landis Comes Again

The Salisbury Indians returned to the league in 1924 along with the Cambridge Canners, Parksley Spuds, and the Dover Dobbins. The Crisfield Crabbers were considered a new franchise after their previous financial problems. Lawyer Harry Rew was elected to his second term as president of the league, and rowdyism and vulgarity would not be tolerated. But the real excitement was the admission of the Easton Farmers. The Rev. Thomas Donaldson, a former semipro player from Baltimore and pastor at the Episcopal Christ Church in Easton, was instrumental in founding the franchise. "Home Run" Baker was brought in to manage.

The local slugger seemed an ideal choice. One of the best players of the day, the world series hero was signed as a player-manager. That in itself made him a box office draw. He had played for the Philadelphia Athletics and the New York Yankees, and with baseball's newest sensation, Babe Ruth. Sensing his own value to the league, Baker proposed a salary of $1,000 a month, a percentage of the gate and a share of all players sold, none of which was likely to meet anyone's approval. Baker settled for less.

A call went out for volunteers to get the field in shape for the inaugural season. People responded in typical Eastern Shore fashion when it came to baseball. A throng of doctors, lawyers, merchants, farmers, and laborers answered the call and rolled up their sleeves. Some brought shovels and spades for the tons of dirt to make up the new infield. Others brought hammers and saws for the posts and lumber for the new fence. Much of the work was done in a day. The Farmers were asked by the league to transmit game results over the Easton broadcast station 3UI three times a week. This was an amateur venture of Raintree Andrews, who had built the station with $400 of his own money. Andrews had received several responses from "radio bugs" throughout the county, and as far away as Salisbury, to messages he had sent out. Dover, Cambridge and Salisbury were "anxious" for these baseball reports. Although cautious of federal restrictions, he hoped to take his equipment to Federal Park once the games became exciting, to "broadcast every play that is made." Salisbury and Cambridge were also considering radio broadcasting of some type. Andrews was encouraged by the responses he had received from his broadcasting of music played on his Victrola. The station was located in Taylor's garage on West Street, up the street from Federal Park.[6]

Easton offered stock at $25 a share and needed to sell 200 to get in the league. By the middle of March Easton had $5,000 in the bank from stock sales and other fundraising activities. Salisbury needed another $4,000, so the Lions club and their 30 members subscribed for $600. The soda concession was awarded to the appropriately named Whistling Bottling Co., since so many were hurled through the air at ball games. Cushions and programs went to Hearstler and Holden for $100, and Oscar Catlin got the bus contract at 21 cents a mile. All of these were typical annual business transactions for the locally operated clubs. It was estimated the population of the six towns in the league totaled 23,000, with Parksley having the smallest.[7]

Opening day 1924 was Decoration Day, and the total attendance cited for the three games was from 8,000 to 9,000. The league provided the fans with talented players. Veteran Poke Whalen returned to Parksley as manager, where he joined ex-major league player Ralph Mattis. Mattis would lead the loop in hitting. Charles "Red" Ruffing, a Red Sox signee, was farmed out to Dover in July. Some have described Ruffing's debut as lackluster, but the national press saw him as a "sensation." His pitching record was but 4–7 and included a six-game losing streak, but Ruffing also spent time in the outfield and won several games with the long ball, garnering the attention of the *Sporting News*.[8]

The other can't-miss prospect out of the Eastern Shore League that year literally came off a farm. The 16-year-old Jimmie Foxx was signed to the Easton

Farmers as a local prospect out of Sudlersville, Maryland. Foxx had been playing for the small semipro town teams in Sudlersville and Goldsboro by the age of 14, where he was already attracting notice. His father was his biggest supporter. How Foxx was discovered fostered several colorful stories. Yankee pitcher Lefty Gomez would later quip of the muscular slugger, "Jimmie Foxx wasn't scouted—he was trapped."

Jimmie's father had played independent professional ball for Johnny George's Sudlersville Nine and was contemporary to Baker's early independent career on the Shore. They were friends, and Dell Foxx made a trip to Baker's home in Trappe and asked his old adversary to give his son a tryout. Baker and Easton did not regret it. The 16-year-old Foxx played 76 games, mostly at catcher, and hit .296 with 10 home runs and 77 RBIs. It was thought he would go to the Yankees.

Yankee ownership thought Baker could still play when he retired to his family and farms. They still had him reserved when he sought the Easton job and his release had to be negotiated. There may have been some lingering bitterness between the two. Now Baker attended a game between his two old employers, the Yankees and the Athletics, to make his pitch about Foxx before the game. Baker went to Yankees manager Miller Huggins and Babe Ruth first. They laughed at Baker's estimation of the prospect's ability. He then walked across the diamond to Connie Mack. "Bake, if he's as good as you say he is, I'll take him. I don't even

The Sudlersville team, early 1920s. Jimmie Foxx (front row, right) played for semipro town teams while still in high school. Here he is closer in age to the batboy than to his adult teammates (courtesy Federalsburg Historical Society).

have to see him" was Mack's response. Baker then counseled Foxx that he would get a shot at the major leagues sooner with the Athletics, so his contract was sold to Mack for $2,000.⁹

Some local fans cried that he had been sold too cheap, and that Baker focused too much on player development at the cost of winning. As an example, one player walked 56 miles on his journey from Baltimore to Easton and took a ferry across the Chesapeake Bay, just to play for his childhood hero. On learning Baker lived in Trappe, not Easton, the young lad continued the extra eight miles on foot, and unannounced, knocked on the manager's door. Baker, impressed with his enthusiasm and initiative, signed and kept him on the roster.

Rew had his chances to address the rowdyism prevalent in minor league baseball, and he had a challenging time keeping players out of jail, sometimes by the busload. Before two weeks could pass in the season two Salisbury players were arrested for drunkenness. Al Burris suspended outfielder Christian Fitzberger and catcher Lee a week for breaking training. Fitzberger was in his third year with the league and had been hard to handle in previous seasons with the Spuds and the Blue Hens. He had promised to do better when he signed with Salisbury. He didn't. Fitzberger and Lee got mixed up in a drunken "affair" in the "colored" section of town near the railroad tracks. With charges pending, both caught the next

The Easton Farmers of the 1924 Eastern Shore League. This was a popular postcard. Foxx is in the top row, third from left behind the seated Baker (courtesy Talbot Historical Society).

train out of town with no intention of returning. Police were holding charges over Fitzberger if he did come back.[10]

Doc Burris was hard-pressed to keep up with his baseball duties as Salisbury manager. His dual medical practices and businesses were flourishing and running the team was taking its toll on him. He relinquished on-field duties, naming Dick Early as field captain to manage those responsibilities soon after the season started so that he could focus on the administrative end of the franchise.

It was shaping up into an exciting four-way race between Cambridge, Parksley, Crisfield, and Salisbury. A big game came up in Dover between the Dobbins and the Salisbury Indians. Hanson Horsey was a local hero of the independents and semipros of the northern Shore and the Tri-State League. He had gotten his cup of coffee with Cincinnati and returned to the peninsula to umpire. In the seventh inning Horsey called veteran catcher and Dover Dobbins manager Jiggs Donahue out on strikes. It appears that Donahue was headed back to the bench before his temper got the best him, as he suddenly turned, rushed Horsey, and struck him several blows to the body. Nobody could get the raging backstop off the field. Horsey calmly, in the expression of the day, "pulled his watch on him." Then a 275-pound Delaware state policeman appeared by his side and escorted Jiggs to the bench. Box scores and game accounts do not indicate that Donahue was ejected.

Five days later Rew was interviewed regarding the league. He noted that there had been little to do, with rowdyism being on the wane from last year. He had fined Donahue $50 and meted out a three-day suspension. He praised his umpires Derby, Horsey, Cloak and Verecker. As the four-team pennant race was generating great excitement amongst the local fans, he pointed out that umpires were only human. He asked fans and management to give them the respect they deserved and the protection they needed. Then he pointed out that a second Landis visit would be soon.[11]

Cambridge and Salisbury had been rivals since baseball began on the Eastern Shore, and the pennant race stoked the old fire. The Indians had come back to take a game from Cambridge with no reported incidents. The team had stopped for supper before boarding the bus for home. As they drove through town a player called out "Yea, Hawkshaw," the nickname of a friend he saw working as a lineman on the street. Officer Hurley, a "guardian of the peace" in Cambridge, thought it was directed at him and it must have had "deep significance," as he took it as an insult. Hurley commandeered a fast Ford and chased the bus down. Once stopped, Hurley boarded the vehicle and demanded, "Which one of you ____ called me Hawkshaw?" Freddie Fitzberger, who had gained confidence after securing a starting role in Salisbury's outfield, replied, "There are no ____ on this bus." The Salisbury players began to "razz the cop." Hurley decided to arrest everybody.

In the contentious time at the station, the verbal exchange between the officer and the Indians continued, with captain Dick Early being charged and put in a cell. After teammates sent back cigarettes and chewing tobacco, expecting an extended stay, they then passed the hat to raise the $100 bail. They had just spent their meal stipend, and Freddie Fitzberger knew they could pass six hats and not produce $100 on their salaries, so he dashed out of the building. He soon returned with Robert Matthews of Cambridge, who was treasurer of the league. It was Matthews who bailed out Early. The detained Indians were jubilant upon their release. Many buses of the 1920s had a bell in addition to the horn. The bus pulled away from the jail and they began their departure out of town—slowly. One player laid on the horn, while another rang the bell incessantly. The rest of the players hooped and hollered in their slow, deliberate, revengeful procession out of town. The Salisbury account stated that the only thing the Indians were guilty of was "snatching victory from the hands of the Cambridge Canners and robbing the fans of an upward march for the pennant." Matthews managed to have the charges dropped. Landis was but a week away.[12]

The "Supreme Dictator Landis" said all the right things prior to his second coming: "I have always taken a great deal of interest in your small and efficient leagues, and Frank Baker should give much color and punch to the one on the Eastern Shore. He should be just the man to help make baseball even more popular." And then later, "Tell them I am coming to the Eastern Shore again this summer to meet all my friends in the Eastern Shore League."[13]

The Landis visit was set for August 15 at Easton, and he had a busy itinerary. He left Baltimore at 8:00 a.m. and stopped over in Annapolis for what must have been a whirlwind inspection of the Naval Academy and St. John's College. From there he caught the 11:15 ferry to Claiborne, and then traveled by motorcade to Easton. The county seat of Talbot County had already been abuzz for hours. The *Baltimore Sun* bold print declared, "Easton in Holiday Dress." They described the small town as it readied itself for the event. "Shortly after daybreak the residents of Easton were up and stirring.... Everything was ideal for the occasion, the sun rising in a cloudless sky, with just enough breeze to make things comfortable."[14]

Across Washington Street hung a large banner: "Welcome Judge Landis." And just in case the judge was not looking up, the message had been painted on the street. Flags and bunting covered the streets and businesses. Proprietors had opened early to accommodate the arriving crowd, and the clerks anticipated closing early for the game. When the motorcade reached Easton it proceeded to the New Theater ballroom, where lunch and program were presented by the Rotary club. Landis played to his audience. He praised the league for its sportsmanship in the midst of a hotly contested pennant race. Then he declared that the two things he looked forward to the most in his job were the World Series and his annual trip to the Delmarva Peninsula. He was sorry it had taken him 53 years to discover it, and he hoped he could return for the next 50 years. Then it was on to Federal Park.

Official attendance was announced at 2,645. Others estimated the bustling mass at 3,700 "crammed in to every nook and cranny." A big cheer went up when Landis shook hands with Baker, but when it came to the ceremonial first pitch the curmudgeon "fooled Frank Baker with a high spitter." The 16-year-old Foxx, now property of the Athletics, treated the commissioner to a three-run home run, as Baltimore native George Klemmick pitched a four-hitter in the Farmers' 4–1 win over the Crisfield Crabbers. League statistics printed that day in the *Salisbury*

Times showed the young Foxx hitting .301, pitcher-outfielder Red Ruffing hitting .298 in limited action, and Freddie Fitzberger—hero of the Salisbury bus—at a solid .311.[15]

The presence of baseball moguls on the Eastern Shore was not a rare occurrence. Landis never did return despite his promise to visit for the next 50 years, but the league would continue to draw his attention in the future. Ban Johnson was also drawn to the peninsula. Johnson had been the dominating presence on the triumvirate commission that had overseen organized baseball prior to the hiring of Landis. When the Judge was brought in, Johnson had lost much of his power but was still president of the American League. Whether out of competition with Landis, or genuine interest, Johnson made his appearances, involving the Five State Series. A week after Landis appeared in Easton, Johnson showed up to personally unfurl the Five State Series pennant won by Dover the previous year. Of course, he was feted, and speeches given.[16]

John Heydler was president of the National League and a longtime Maryland resident. While his visits to the Shore were never known to be in an official capacity, he had friends who resided in Cambridge and was often seen there. Neither president Mike Sexton nor secretary-treasurer John Farrell of the National Association were strangers to Delmarva.

Well into late August four teams had records over .500 with a realistic shot at the pennant. With the season scheduled to end on Labor Day, the August 30 standings show Salisbury in front with a 44–33 record. Parksley was a game behind, with Cambridge another game behind that. Crisfield was grasping to hold on.

As the final days approached, nerves were on edge and tempers flared. Tommy Vereker had formerly been a pitcher for Parksley, but signed on to umpire in the league. Salisbury was playing Parksley at Gordy Park in Salisbury with a one-game lead in the waning days of the season. Vereker called a Salisbury player out on a force at second which ended the game 3–2 for his former team. No sooner had Vereker made the call than the fans swarmed the field trying to get at him, but the police had been at their ready and surrounded the young arbiter and escorted him from the park. The mob that followed shouted threats as the police buffeted Vereker from any violence, all the way to the Salisbury jail, where he was locked up for the night as the only safe place in town. Parksley was now tied for the league lead.[17]

Easton, wallowing in last place, was distracted during the final days of the season. Baker's sister-in-law had been assaulted by a farmhand. When it was reported, Sheriff William Hopkins immediately formed a posse of more than a hundred armed men, including members of the National Guard, Frank Baker, and his Easton Farmers baseball team. The heavily armed band followed a bicycle trail through the mud to what was termed a "negro festival" north of Trappe. When Baker laid his hands on the suspect, a cry went up to hang him on the spot, but he stopped it, telling the posse to let the law take its course. By midnight, the accused was locked up.

Following a signed confession, a crowd began to gather, and two unidentified men took clubs to the jailhouse door and broke it down. Sheriff Hopkins ran them off, and then bravely dispersed a crowd of more than 50 men who were milling about the lamplit street. It was realized that the prisoner was not safe there. While the local Ku Klux Klan met across the street to plan their next step, the prisoner was boldly secreted from under their noses and sent to the Baltimore City Jail to await trial.[18]

Three teams were still in the hunt when the season ended with doubleheaders on Labor Day. Salisbury dropped both to the lowly Dover Dobbins, the second contest a 2–1 loss that was described as "11 bitterly contested innings." Parksley came off with two "lucky" wins over the competitive Crisfield Crabbers to secure the championship. Poke Whalen had returned to Parksley after a year with the Laurel Blue Hens to add the "punch" to take Parksley to its second pennant in three years. It was on to the Five State Series.[19]

The *Baltimore Sun* enumerated the number of Baltimoreans in the 1924 Five State Series, but it was two Eastern Shoremen that took the first day. Frank Hummer of Trappe blanked Martinsburg while battery mate Jimmie Foxx, picked up for the series, clouted two home runs and added a sacrifice fly to pace the 17–0 route at Parksley. Martinsburg of the Blue Ridge League then turned the tables with an 8–0 rain-shortened romp. The size of Parksley got smaller with each telling as attendance at "a town of 600–700" was 2,328 for the first game and 947 for the second. Total receipts were $2,647.50 before the series moved to Easton. The third game in Easton drew 1,848 with receipts of $2,037.50 as the fans watched the new phenom, Foxx, blast one over the center-field fence in the first inning to take the lead. It was said to be the farthest hit in Federal Park. Tom Glass of Cambridge pitched and was denied a shutout by a misplayed fly ball. The series then went to Martinsburg as the Blue Sox evened the series, but not before the sixteen-year-old Foxx had blasted another home run. The Spuds then took the series lead 3–2. The attendance was the smallest since the series had started in 1921, with only 519 in the stands. The final crowd in Chambersburg, Pennsylvania, was even smaller with Hummer earning the victory. Hummer was the proclaimed star of the series, but it was Foxx's performance that stood out. The entire series had drawn 6,401 fans, but only one game on the western shore had exceeded a thousand. The winning share for the Spuds was $141.63 for 14 players. The Blue Sox took home $94.42 on the same split. The umpires took $118.02 each. The two teams received $1,174.52 each and the leagues received $391.15. The Five State Series was now a proven moneymaker for both leagues and the players.[20]

To end the season the Salisbury Indians could not arrange an exhibition series with Hagerstown so they scheduled a doubleheader with the Baltimore Black Sox at Maryland Park in Baltimore and 10,000 fans were expected. A year later the Eastern Colored League was in competition with Foster's Midwest-based league. The two best teams in the ECL were scheduled to play on the Eastern Shore. It was Jud Wilson and the Black Sox against the Harrisburg Senators and Oscar Charleston. Charleston was often compared to Ty Cobb and considered the best black outfielder in the game, and he alone was considered worth the price of admission. Games were scheduled for Salisbury (MD), Easton (MD), and Dover (DE). Large crowds of both races were expected. City newspapers in Wilmington, Harrisburg, and Baltimore covered four of Harrisburg's wins in Dover and Easton. Wilbert Pritchett of Ridgely, who would play eight years for Negro League teams, won one of those games pitching for the Senators. These Negro League teams that came over were billed as the "class of professional colored baseball."[21]

The *Afro-American* continued to print a box encouraging baseball teams across Maryland to send in their activities. Many Eastern Shore teams responded with meager details. In 1920 at a doubleheader in Easton, Cambridge brought along their favorite musicians, the Merry Band, to play at the dance afterwards. Then the Cambridge team felt strong enough to take on the highly regarded Hilldale Athletic Club, and again, the Merry Band went with them to assure some entertainment. More black leagues were beginning to form. Both the Negro National League and the Eastern Colored League were active in the 1920s as major leagues. The Southern League also came into existence. The Boston League featured five white and five black teams. The Texas Colored League formed, and in Baltimore there were independent black semipro teams and the Baltimore Universal League.

A handful of the Eastern Shore games mentioned in the *Afro-American* do offer a hint as to some of the participants. The Cambridge Orioles, the Crisfield Giants, the Denton Tigers, and the Carmichael Speed Boys appear to have been the better of the teams reporting in the 1920s. Some accounts included the name, usually the manager, with contact information for arranging future games. M. Wicks ran the Crisfield Giants, and it was James Frazier for the Chestertown Gray Sox, who played some of their games at Worrell Field. For the Denton Tigers the contact was N. Wayman and for the Bellevue All Stars it was Russell Bailey. Daniel Hutchison managed the Carmichael Speed Boys, and they were led by the hitting of John R. Winston

BLACK SOX AND GIANTS TO PLAY TWO GAMES HERE

Two Best Aggregations In Colored League Play Tuesday And Wednesday

OSCAR CHARLESTON TO BE IN GIANTS LINEUP

Large Crowd Expected To See Final Game Of The 1925 Season

The Baltimore Black Sox and Harrisburg Giants faced each other in a series of games on the peninsula in 1925. The Black Sox featured Jud Wilson, and the Giants, Oscar Charleston. Both are in the National Baseball Hall of Fame. Wilbert Pritchett of Ridgely pitched for the Giants and appeared in the series (*Salisbury Times*, September 21, 1925).

with his 15 home runs. Centreville was paced by Albert Bowsen with a 6–1 pitching record and managed by Edward Trusty.[22]

Along with occasional exhibitions on the peninsula by the Eastern Colored League in the 1920s, Baltimore semipro teams came over frequently. The Bellevue All Stars beat the Oval Blues and the Crisfield Giants took care of the Maryland Eagles in 1925. Bellevue and Crisfield were cited in the *Afro-American* as members of an Eastern Shore League that year. Whether this was a formal or informal circuit is uncertain. No standings or box scores have been found to date. The Crisfield Giants did play one game against the white Crisfield High School, and they were negotiating to play the Crisfield Crabbers of the Class D Eastern Shore League. In an undated oral recollection, a white team from Chester, PA, came down to play the Centreville Black Sox. Not knowing the way, the players stopped to ask the county sheriff for directions to the Black Sox headquarters. The incredulous sheriff explained that the Sox were a black team, but the Chester players already knew that. After their loss, the visiting players stuck around for the postgame hospitality.[23]

There were far too many teams active for all of black baseball to be in one league. Teams came from every little community on the Shore, including Crisfield, Fruitland, St. Michaels, Ridgely, Hebron, and Pondtown, with its Wasp-jackets. There were also teams from Still Pond, Pocomoke City, Federalsburg, Barclay, and Chestertown (the Gray Sox). When the obscure districts of Broad Neck and Wye

The Bellevue All-Stars, c. 1930. Bellevue was a tight, segregated, hardworking watermen's community on the Tred Avon River. Manager Russell Bailey and the All-Stars were a fixture on the black baseball circuit. They were particularly active in the Tri-State and Bi-State leagues of the 1930s (courtesy Talbot Historical Society).

Neck played, it was at a carnival picnic in Queen Anne's County at Rolph's Wharf. Another game in little Greensboro drew 350 spectators.[24]

The Baltimore Black Sox played in a city with the fourth largest black population on the east coast. They billed themselves "Champions of the South," and like other Negro League and independent teams, toured their immediate region playing exhibitions to raise additional funds. It is estimated that while white major leaguers made a minimum of around $2,000 a year, the best Negro League players topped out at about $500, so any additional money from these games was highly sought after.[25]

10

Umpire Uprising

The report to Salisbury stockholders after the 1924 season declared a surplus of $3,273. That included their purchase of the Laurel Blue Hens and the sale of the players, the net profit of which was $3,100. Easton reported a surplus of $4,000 despite a woeful last place finish. As in Salisbury, whose profits were from player sales, Easton's gains were boosted by the money received for Foxx. A dividend to the stockholders was proposed. There was talk of renovations to the park on Federal Street. It was proposed to extend the grandstands and bleachers, add two club rooms with showers and baths. It was said all of the members of the Eastern Shore League made money on the year.[1]

All of the existing franchises returned for the 1925 season. Most players continued to come from the same sources as they had for the last 40 years. Others came from eastern colleges. It was decided to keep the class limit at three, the schedule was set at 90 games, and the salary cap was raised to $2,200, with a promise to try the two-umpire system. The first hint of trouble came when, for unspecified reasons, all Salisbury players returned their contracts unsigned in February, and new manager Homer Smoot offered to walk out with them. They were, in turn, threatened with being blacklisted by organized baseball.[2]

Baseball was getting outside competition from many new sources and the sometimes loosely conceived high school teams of the era were becoming more formalized. Instruction was given so that "youth won't take to the putter and the mashie, or autos or movies" now vying for their attention. While many minor leagues suffered in attendance, the two Maryland leagues gained renown for their prosperity and propensity for developing talent:

> Through many hard, lean years of uncertainty two baseball leagues fought for their very existence in Maryland. Today they stand prominent among the Class D organizations of the United States. Everywhere their names are heard when the national pastime is discussed, because they have sent to the majors some of the brightest stars of the sport. Everywhere they are known as firmly established circuits where the town folk support their teams and have in them civic pride which made baseball the greatest of American games.[3]

Flush with profit and popularity, others saw that last-place Easton upgraded their facilities, announcing the addition of a new "colored section," and the rest of the league followed suit with improvements. Gordy Park's grandstands were increased by 500 to a total of 2,000 with 500 bleacher seats, all at the cost of

$1,700. Cambridge businessmen were matching funds for their improvements as Dover, Crisfield, and Parksley all announced increased seating. Soon all would be adding clubhouses and showers to meet the standards recommended by organized baseball.

An early headline declared that all Eastern Shore highways led to ballparks, but opening day 1925 revealed another portent of trouble for the league as attendance failed to meet expectations. The first home game of the season usually drew capacity crowds, but Salisbury drew only 1,298, and Cambridge about the same. Neither Parksley nor Crisfield did well, and only Easton drew 3,000. Getting fans to come to the ballpark would be a problem all season.[4]

Before the middle of June, the man who had single-handedly won the 1911 World Series, who had poems written about the clouts that earned him his sobriquet, the man who was idolized and respected from Elkton, Maryland, to Cape Charles, Virginia, was unceremoniously pushed out as manager of Easton. The Farmers had started well out of the gate, but attendance had dropped from 2,000 to a mere 300 a game. In the face of growing criticism of his relaxed management style, it was announced that Baker had submitted his resignation. The players threatened to revolt and not play, placing the future of the franchise in jeopardy, but for the second time in a matter of months, player threats were countered with the prospect of blacklisting. The team and the league continued on. Baker explained his resignation, stating he had never had full control of the team as promised. The board of directors and the fans were disgruntled with the results on the field.[5]

Baker was replaced by an old friend and teammate residing in the area. Buck Herzog had come to the Eastern Shore from Baltimore 20 years earlier to captain the Ridgely town team, met and married a local girl, and now lived on his Caroline County farm. The *Sporting News* once referred to him as the "cantaloupe king" of Ridgely. Herzog's management style was in contrast to Baker's. He was considered a college type with a "rah-rah" style of team building. He also had connections with Jack Dunn of the high minor league Baltimore Orioles, and it was hoped they could get a couple of players farmed out from them. Another reason for his hiring was that the Easton Club drew many fans from Caroline County, where Herzog lived. Despite his Baltimore upbringing, Herzog was honored as a "native son" at Caroline County Day in late August. But the problems of Easton paled in comparison to what else was going on in the league.[6]

Dover complained early that Cambridge was using four class players but nothing came of the protest. New president Harry Rew had pleaded for "honesty" to be observed by all teams in such matters. Herzog complained that many local scorers were urged to pad the books to raise the batting averages of their players to boost their sale value. Manager Ted Smith in Cambridge was said to be a John McGraw–type manager and then he resigned without comment in August. The rumor was that the club had fined him the hefty sum of $150 for misusing a pitcher in a game. It was said that one of the reasons the Blue Ridge and Eastern Shore Leagues had become one of Ban Johnson's "pet circuits" was that gambling persisted in organized baseball, and the interference of gamblers was still happening, particularly at the lower levels, where communities and leagues lacked the resources to police these activities. Johnson thought his influence might help.

It appeared that Rew had done a good job of curtailing rowdyism and umpire baiting the previous season. Reports had been few and little comment made as punishment was meted out quickly. Now it seemed that as the attendance dropped the players, management, and the dwindling fans left in the seats vented their frustrations primarily at the men in blue. Two weeks into the season, the scrappy Jiggs Donohue protested a game he lost, complaining the umpire did not have "just cause" to call a game for darkness and rain. Umpire Mitchell ruled a forfeit to Dover of a July 9 game at Parksley. Mitchell had ejected catcher Joe Tagg and then manager Poke Whalen. Harassment continued from the bench, so Mitchell ordered it cleared. When the players did not move he took the "shortest route" and declared a forfeit. On the heels of the Mitchell forfeit, umpire-in-chief Murphy had his run-in. Crisfield manager Herb Armstrong was ordered back to the coaches' box by Murphy during an argument, but he defied the umpire. He was then ordered to the bench but refused again. Murphy quickly forfeited the game to Salisbury and had to be escorted from the field. After the umpire had left, Armstrong talked Homer Smoot and Salisbury back off the bus to finish the game as an exhibition for the fans. And there, the matter seemed to rest.[7]

By the middle of July a special meeting was held to discuss the deteriorating state of umpire protection. The situation was believed so bad that it affected attendance. This time, it was not the fans at issue.

> Constant disputes and wrangling of the players and managers with the umpires has brought disapproval of the fans throughout the league, it is sad. Disputes between managers and umpires last week caused the forfeiture of two games. Players who have disputed decisions of the umpires in situations appearing similar in every respect have drawn heavier penalties then others. Acquisition of umpires, whose work please the majority of the clubs have been an enigma for some time.

In the same edition of the *Salisbury Daily Times*, yet another incident was reported.

> The tragedy tale is not complete. In the sixth the cash customers rose as one to hoot umpire Haines for a decision made while Fitzberger was at bat. The little trouble seemed to pass but at the end of the session the player made his way to the plate and again protested the third strike decision. A few words, inaudible to press box or grand stand, and the two were exchanging blows. Fitzberger was replaced in center."[8]

Another meeting was held and it was decided to go to the double umpire system that the league had promised prior to the season but failed to implement. After a raucous beginning to the meeting, Rew took and held the floor the full hour and a half that it took to review the incidents and instruct the umpires, "while he stated he did not approve a player attacking an umpire, but where such incidents did occur severe penalties should be imposed." Someone, again, pointed out all punishment should be equal, Salisbury just had two players fined $25 and $50 each in separate incidents for attacking umpires which included five-day suspensions. In a similar incident another player was fined only $15 for knocking over an umpire, but several Crisfield fans attested that he had knocked the umpire over in pursuit of the ball and later apologized.[9]

Apparently the umpires were not satisfied with Rew's meeting and decided to meet on neutral ground in Laurel, Delaware, in what was described as the first "uprising of umpires versus Organized Baseball." They threatened to quit if not given an increase in pay and more on-site protection. They released a public statement: "We are tired of having pop bottles and other missiles thrown at us and hear club officials applaud the miscreants, some officials joining in the yell, 'Kill the umpire!'" An agreement was reached a day before the scheduled strike. Treasurer Robert Matthews' excuse was he had inadvertently forgotten to include their traveling expenses in the umpires' paychecks. This was to be reinstated and reimbursements made. Two umpires were let go, while the respected arbiters of McFarlane, William Rusk, and Hans Horsey were brought in. Mitchell reported ill.[10]

Easton had its ugly incident in late July. "Near riot was precipitated in the seventh inning when Skelton took exception to the remarks of Woods on the Dover bench and advanced towards him. Both Easton and Dover players mixed in a free for all fight that ended only when the sheriff and a city policeman with drawn clubs separated the athletes and rushed the crowd back in the stands."[11]

While things settled down for the last month of the season, one incident spilled over afterwards. The game that had been forfeited to Salisbury and finished as an exhibition was awarded to the Crabbers by Rew based on new evidence. The game had been attended by now vice president Thawley. According to his testimony, and that of others, umpire in chief Murphy was drunk. He had walked up the third base line during the dispute with the Crisfield manager, uttered something inaudible, and was then escorted, or helped, back to his hotel. Now Rew reversed the decision. Salisbury tried to reverse the reversal with an appeal to the "Supreme Arbiter" Landis. If he were not going to come see his friends in the Eastern Shore League anymore, they would find another way to catch his attention.[12]

Cambridge, Parksley, Dover, and Salisbury emerged as the contenders for the season. The Cambridge Canners took an early lead and held on to it. At first it was Dover at their heels before the Spuds made their move. In the middle of the pennant race, Ban Johnson appeared in Parksley to present his cherished Five State pennant from the year before. He visited Cambridge first, where he was feted by a hundred of the town's best citizens before a game against Parksley, last year's league winners. Johnson stayed the night in Salisbury before proceeding to the game in Parksley, where he was entertained by the Pennsylvania Railroad Brass Band. During the second inning the game was stopped as Johnson personally hoisted the prized banner before the cheering crowd. The Canners took a doubleheader on the last day of the 1925 season from the lowly Easton Farmers to take the pennant and a shot at the Five State Series, now sometimes referred to as Johnson's Pennant.[13]

Rather than jump around to various towns in the leagues, the first three games were to be played in Hagerstown and the second three in Cambridge. The seventh, if needed, would be played in Baltimore. After veteran Nig Clark turned down a position on the team, the Canners loaded up on pitching. They were little help in the slugfest series. The Hagerstown Hubs took two of three at home before the series moved to Cambridge, where the Canners evened the series. The final game took place at Oriole Park, where the Hubs prevailed and the Hanlon Trophy was awarded on the spot.[14]

Nobody came out and said that teams lost money, but the signs were there. Before the season even ended Easton announced a fundraising six-card boxing program to be held at Federal Park on a hot, humid August night, and their fire department promoted a street dance to benefit the baseball club. Salisbury put on a Seven Day Exposition that included vaudeville acts, an auto giveaway, a better baby show, an indoor circus, and yodelers. All of these were the fundraising methods used in the independent era. The league treasurer reported the circuit had a balance of a little over $2,000, but a convoluted report from Salisbury gave the overall tone that attendance had fallen. Herzog promised Easton fans a better team. He proposed to collectively house the players during training so they could listen to the radio or records, read, and play games and mesh as a team.[15]

C. Edward Sparrow proposed to lobby the government to remove the amusement tax left over from the war that cut into the teams' profits. He thought all clubs in the league had lost $1,000 to $1,500 due solely to the tax. Circuits like the Eastern Shore League did not operate for profit but for "civic pride." Money could not be made year to year, the best one could hope for was to break even. The first joint administrative meeting between the Blue Ridge and Eastern Shore Leagues was called. At the national meeting of the National Association, Mike Sexton and John Farrell were to propose that the government remove the amusement tax so the smaller minor league markets would have a chance to make money.

The ladies of Salisbury put on a card party with prizes at the armory to raise money, and Wicomico High School sponsored a pin drive for the Salisbury Indians. In Cambridge money was raised for the Canners with a three-day fashion show at their armory. The merchants set up booths and activities included an indoor carnival. On Thursday there were vaudeville acts and dancing; on Friday it was a Charleston contest; and Saturday it was old-fashioned square dancing. All of this was to benefit the baseball team.[16]

The league returned all of its officers for the '26 season. The league agreed to keep the class player limit at three and the 90-game schedule, but raised the salary cap to $2,400 a month, including the manager. Resin bags were banned, and in an effort to curtail creative contracts, the time-honored tradition of awarding players presents and "property" by team management would no longer be permitted. Fans, however, considered their private presents and rewards to players a given right and a separate matter, and would never relinquish that right. It was also agreed that clubs would try to honor the organized baseball recommendation of a 250-foot minimum on outfield fences. The Gordy Park board negotiated with their neighbor Messick Ice Co. for an extra 50 feet in order to comply. The board required $1,300 for the second consecutive year of renovations, to include dressing rooms. In prior years, the players had to go to the local YMCA to shower. A "Kiddie Stand" was added with the hope that local fraternal organizations would help build it, and then pay the youngsters' way. As an example of what clubs were charging, Salisbury offered season tickets at $50 a year for reserved box, $15 for front seats, and $10 for rear seats. A season pass in the grandstands went for $7.50. Crisfield was said to have run up a deficit of $3,500 over its four-year existence, considered "remarkable" compared to others.[17]

11

Chaos

The 1926 season was described by one scribe as "epochal." Buck Herzog was named vice president of the Easton Farmers. Jack Dunn and the Baltimore Orioles sent him five "farm hands" to anchor the team. Some of John McGraw's rough style must have rubbed off on Buck Herzog while he was with the Giants, as his aggressive and brash style inspired letters to the editor at the *Baltimore Sun*. One side referred to him as a "rough neck," while others considered him an asset to the game. The ever-vocal Herzog berated everyone in earshot while encouraging his players. He still found time from his managerial and administrative duties to write a regular feature on the national baseball scene for the *Baltimore Sun*. Herzog's style must have worked as the Farmers found their way to the top of the league by early August.

There appeared to be fewer incidents of rowdyism and umpire baiting, but three new umpires had to be brought in at the end of July. Such occurrences were overshadowed by the last few weeks of the season, which were described, in an understatement, as "chaos." After wallowing in the lower rungs of the league for two years, the Easton Farmers had finally clawed their way to first-place respectability. Yet their fans had little opportunity to enjoy their lofty position as the league kicked the legs out from under them. Salisbury claimed Easton used five class players, while Dover protested Parksley also had five. Easton and Parksley were in first and second place, respectively, Salisbury and Dover third and fourth. At a hearing on August 13 the Farmers were penalized with 34 forfeits and Parksley was later assessed 20. Winn Clark of the Crisfield Crabbers and Buck Herzog correctly pointed out that the league bylaws defining a class player were contradictory and more rigid than those used by the National Association and most other leagues.

Easton had letters from the other league or team officials attesting to the validity of their players. They appealed to the league's mediation board and were denied. They then appealed to their old friend, Judge Landis, but nothing came of it. Despite a telegram in hand from National Association secretary J.H. Farrell saying that at least Parksley's best player was not a "class man," Miller upheld the ruling that he was. Miller and the board stuck to the decision of using the local bylaws to define a class player, and Rew confirmed it. All of this catapulted Dover and Cambridge into first and second place. Easton threatened to quit after their appeal before the mediation board was denied, but they stood to lose a $1,000 bond and the franchise in doing so. Easton complained attendance had fallen so badly because of the penalty that only 500 turned out for Governor Ritchie Day.

Somewhere along the line, Crisfield had to forfeit one game, paltry compared to what happened next. An outfielder who played for both Dover and Cambridge during the year was now accused of being a class player. Rew imposed penalties of 23 forfeits to Dover and 22 for Cambridge. They appealed. With a telegram in hand from the president of the Eastern (Canada) League that the player had only pitched two games and played in two others, Miller and the board reversed the earlier decision in Rew's absence. Rew came back and directed that the original decision of the board was binding. Dover was knocked out of first place by the ruling just as Easton had been. Accusations and protests flew around the boardroom for two league meetings, including one charge that Crisfield was using 10 ineligible players. There was more than one ineligible player to pick from on most teams. At the third and final meeting when the league ended on Labor Day, the Crisfield Crabbers emerged from the closed boardroom as the declared league champions.[1]

The Five State Series came off as usual in 1926 with it opening on the Eastern Shore with two games in Crisfield and one in Easton. From there, three games were scheduled for Hagerstown, and the last in Baltimore, if needed. Ban Johnson did not attend the contests between his two pet leagues due to a bad foot. Crisfield left for Hagerstown with a 2–1 lead in the series. It was reported after the Easton game that total attendance on the peninsula was 3,556 with total receipts of $4,020. Hagerstown swept the three games at home to clinch the series. The *Sporting News* reported good crowds and the players made a tidy sum for their efforts. The series drew 5,227 fans and receipts of $5,968.25.[2]

The Eastern Shore League was not done in capturing the attention of the baseball world just yet. Alexander Jackson, president of the Salisbury Indians, was suspended by the National Association for one year for illegal "side dealings" with his players. The league had started the season emphasizing that extra payments and properties given to players by the club were not permitted. Jackson had signed the manager without consulting his board of directors and he never reported details of player sales in 1925. In July, the team finances were taken over by a committee and all transactions were to pass through them. The side dealings were Jackson's way around the committee. An appeal was made, and by the time the National Association met, Sexton and Farrell lifted Jackson's suspension and he was reinstated.[3]

Jesse Linthicum of the *Baltimore Sun* summed up the season, "Sensations and upsets have not been confined to the majors. The Eastern Shore League race was spoiled by wholesale forfeits ... because of the use of ineligible players."[4]

Rew was again elected president of the league for 1927, with all of the officers returning. The league finally agreed to use the National Association definition of a class player. All class player protests had to be filed within 15 days of the contract being registered with the league, and the penalty would be the loss of the player rather than the ugly wholesale forfeits that had nearly ruined the league. Six umpires had cost the league $6,500, so to save money the number was pared to four with an umpire-in-chief working selected games. Cambridge went on with its now annual fundraising fashion show at the armory. In Salisbury $1,428 was raised and more than 40 businesses and individuals were listed, but the sum only represented one-half of the team's operating budget. A benefit motion picture was shown at Salisbury's Arcade Theater featuring, appropriately, "Casey at the Bat," and the business and individual sponsors were listed. The concessions were put up for public auction on the steps of the courthouse. A prosperous season was seen for the league.[5]

Two hurdles had to be surmounted to start the '27 season, one of which threatened the existence of the league. Five teams had been slapped with forfeits, four of them with 20 or more. Of all the teams affected, only one, the Dover Dobbins, would not go quietly into the good night. They had hired player Jiggs Donahue as business manager and the league ruled that no team business manager could also don a uniform and take the field as the Dobbins proposed. After this, and the bitter taste of forfeits still in their mouths, Dover threatened to withdraw from the league, and then did. Their letter to Secretary McAllister stated, "We cannot get the pennant even when we win it." The league refused to back down on either account and considered Dover no longer a member of the league. A group of Dover fans attacked Rew and the league in the local newspaper in an attempt to discredit him. They did not seem to remember that the team was not the first to lose its hold on first place because of wholesale forfeits and was among the first to turn in an opponent. All of this prompted the observation, "The Dover Club officials remind one of the boy who knows he has committed an offense but resents the spanking before the public eye." Adding Cape Charles on the southernmost Virginia peninsula to replace Dover was already in the works. With a distance well over a hundred miles from the most northern league representative in Easton, the railroad officials stepped forward. They would add a Pullman car to the southbound train, and the northern teams could motor to Salisbury, catch the train, and then lay over there on their return. The league discussed Cape Charles paying a stipend to the two most northern teams for travel in order to enter the league.[6]

The second hurdle involved the league's old friend Judge Landis. He was not coming all the way to the Shore this time, but the commissioner summoned the Eastern Shore League moguls to Baltimore. It seems that one of Jackson's side dealings in Salisbury had been to sign a player who was subsequently sold to St. Louis for $2,500. Turns out the player was playing under an assumed name and had signed under an alias as a minor to protect his amateur status. The Yankees claimed to have already signed him, but they failed to report that illegal contract to John Farrell and the National Association because of his age. It was baseball business as usual. The Yankees were willing to pay $2,500 outright for the contract. Landis ruled the player a free agent and allowed him to negotiate with the Yankees on his own.[7]

By this time, the league was about ready to get started on the 1927 season. Cape Charles was admitted as Northampton, the county in which the team played. Patton Field was quickly erected with all the amenities the other towns had recently adopted in their upgrades. An overflow crowd of 2,500 turned out for the Memorial Day weekend opener to see Virginia governor Byrd throw out the first ball. Big crowds were reported for the other openers. Dan Pasquella was back for a second stint as manager in Crisfield with a promise from a big-league manager to send him a second baseman and two hard-hitting outfielders. Paul Richards was moved from third base to shortstop. Independence Day also brought decent crowds with 1,900 in Salisbury for the morning game, and 1,500 turned out in Easton as an influx of fresh players were brought into the league. Other towns on the Shore still had their baseball. Among those independent operations the Delmarva Baseball League was entering its fourth year of play with teams in Snow Hill, Pocomoke City, Chincoteague, Virginia, and Newark.[8]

The pennant race also proved a good one. Parksley was the best, but Crisfield and Salisbury provided stiff competition throughout the season. Yet in spite of standout individual performances, a good pennant race, and encouraging holiday crowds, much of the season played out in front of mostly empty seats. By the middle of August Cambridge was already talking of folding for the next season for lack of local support. They said the fans were "tired of baseball." Only 288 turned out to one contest. "No one expects baseball to be profitable," they declared. The talk was that they should sell the grounds, take their losses, and surrender their franchise to the National Association. They were only averaging 300 a game. At 50 cents a ticket they needed $450 a week to meet the $2,400 monthly salaries plus transportation for 14 or 15 men. They needed $8–9 for balls and security at the gate, and groundskeepers cost another $100. The total cost was $3,500 a month and they were only generating receipts of $1,800 to $2,000 a month. That was not counting money going to the league, commissioners, and umpires. A minimum of 600 people a game was needed. People had simply run out of enthusiasm and money.[9]

To further dampen the mood of the season, the league's first president, and now first vice president, Walter Miller, was hospitalized when his car was struck by a train. In a few days he succumbed to brain injuries. In the face of these somber portents, Salisbury filed a class player protest reported on August 29, but the meeting was postponed and no further action taken. Parksley took their third Eastern Shore League pennant in six years.

Parksley picked up Dan Pasquella and Paul Richards from the Crisfield Crabbers for the Five State Series in 1927. The "borrowed" Richards, chosen for his "big noise" bat, blasted the Spuds to a 6–4 win with a pair of two-run homers before 1,266 fans in Chambersburg. The Maroons evened the series before a diminished fan base of 773. Hagerstown hosted the third game before 1,250 and saw the Spuds take the series lead. Chambersburg evened the series in front of 1,437 Parksley fans before Richards again took charge in the second game in Virginia. Richards hit two more home runs for a total of five for the series before a crowd of 824. Still, *Baltimore Sun* sports editor C. Edward Sparrow pointed out that the series was outdrawing that of the previous year when 5,554 people had shown up to shell out $6,310.50. Parksley took the series in six games in a rain-shortened contest in Salisbury. The Spuds were presented with a silver ball by the Sunpapers.[10]

Much of the offseason hot stove news of the Eastern Shore League was overshadowed by prominent sportsman Tony Luciana and the Crisfield Crabbers.

Luciana had persuaded the Pasquella brothers, Dan and Tony, to take their team on a tour of Puerto Rico and South America. Tony Rensa, Paul Richards (now the property of the St. Louis Americans), and a team made up "almost entirely" of Eastern Shore League players would make the trip.[11]

The tour was introduced in the *Sporting News* with a roving report that player Dolph Luque had bitten the ear of an umpire in a game in Havana, that 25,000 had seen a game in Japan, that baseball was growing in popularity in Australia, and that in Puerto Rico it was a "national institution." The Class D team players fared well on the island, playing games in Ponce and San Juan. Twice they had to face the pitching of San, star hurler for the Cuban Stars of the Eastern Colored League. The Crabbers failed to get a man on base against Ponce until they plated two runs in the eighth for the win. On Thanksgiving Day, San returned the favor with a run-scoring double in the ninth to break up a Crisfield no-hitter.[12]

In the offseason finances dominated league talk. Salisbury was negotiating the sale of three players to Beaumont, Texas, for $4,000, while Easton declared they would be back in '28 despite falling receipts. Their directors were "deep in their own pockets" and unsuccessful in raising adequate funds in the community. Easton suspended four players and two more jumped. The new year would bring more of the same.[13]

Confidence was not at a premium to start the 1928 season for the league officers, the town directors, and the fans. Rew was elected to his fifth term as president of the league, and proposals were made to allow only one class player per team and set the salary cap at $2,400 a month. Cambridge made the valid point that the class player rules and salary limits were irrelevant, since no one adhered to them anyway. The league could only survive if the cap were enforced, since it would "minimize likelihood of several unpleasant episodes which have taken place in the past." Having no class players on the roster would make more room for young players. A deadline of April 19 was set for the $500 entry deposit and Crisfield did not have it.[14]

Even at the earliest stages, Salisbury was not a sure entry into the league and a meeting was held at the Chamber of Commerce. The league came out in opposition of the new draft instituted by organized baseball. The teams that did manage to break even only did so through the signing and sale of their own players as Salisbury had done with the sale of five players at the end of the previous season. The draft would eliminate this potentially lucrative source of income. It would result in mostly farmed players which local management could not sell. Easton needed $4,000 to wipe out existing debt and pay for spring training. They could save $1,000 if they eliminated travel and rooming expenses. Things were so financially "shaky" that a four-team circuit was proposed with an 80-game schedule. Home teams would keep all receipts while visitor's shares and rain guarantees were eliminated. Pocomoke City, Snow Hill, and Dover were said to be ready if Crisfield folded. Then, to add to the uncertainty, three Salisbury officials resigned citing lack of financial support from the community. The team did not have the $3,000 needed to start the season. This "attitude" concerned the rest of the faltering league.[15]

There was more talk of the league's demise during the hot stove season than at any other time in its existence. One reporter noted in reference to the lucrative Five State Series, "The Shore League holds a rather unique place in baseball in this part of the country and followers of the national game in Maryland would hate to see the organization forced to curtail its membership or go out of existence. A similar regret would arise if anything should bring about the abandonment of the interleague series." When Crisfield expressed doubt about survival, its management acted, and a meeting was held at the Elks club, where former major league player and Eastern Shore League umpire, manager, and college administrator Billie Lush of Baltimore was called in. He would act as a "committee of one" to assess Crisfield and its ability to continue. A Baltimore sportsman was rumored to be ready to put a franchise in Laurel, Delaware, or Pocomoke City if Crisfield failed to enter the league. In a moment of foresight and optimism, it was reported, "The officials were of the opinion that radio broadcasting station WSMD, which is to open here (Salisbury) later in the month, would prove a stimulus for baseball."[16]

As the spring progressed it appeared that the six teams would include Northampton and Parksley from Virginia, and Salisbury, Crisfield, Easton, and Cambridge from Maryland. Poke Whalen was hired to manage in Salisbury, while its board raised $1,100. It was still $3,000 short. Billie Lush managed to raise the funds to keep Crisfield in the league.[17]

The league got started with little fanfare. Catcher Joe Tagg was with Salisbury, the only player to participate in all six years of the league. Paul Richards came back for his third season. Salisbury and WSMD were determined in their radio experiment. WSMD was scheduled to broadcast the July 3 contest between Northampton and Salisbury. The announcer's voice would be transmitted from Gordy Park by amplifier to WSMD in the Wicomico Hotel. From there, "out into the ether waves" to all of the radio bugs in the region. The following day it was announced that the station had inexplicably gone off the air before game time and was working to restore service. On July 10, a second attempted broadcast was scheduled for the 3:30 game that day, but the league put an end to the innovation when it abruptly shut down operations less than six weeks into the season.[18]

The National Association was notified that day of the decision, and poor attendance was cited as the reason. Even local newspapers had showed less attention and enthusiasm in their coverage. Leading teams in Salisbury, Northampton, and Crisfield hoped to keep the league alive by adding a fourth team, but it was too late. The league had already officially, and prematurely, surrendered all the franchises and privileges of the towns back to the association, and most of the players had already departed the scene as they scrambled to find new jobs. Seventy-eight players of the Eastern Shore League were declared free agents, and the excess of players on the market was compounded by the folding of the Class D Florida State League. In an article heavy with medical metaphor the author spoke of the "demise due to malnutrition and faulty assimilation." Within days the *Baltimore Sun* announced the Five State Series would continue with the Mid–Atlantic

League, an arrangement the former circuit had lobbied for since rumors first circulated about the demise of the Eastern Shore League in the spring.[19]

Some have surmised that the Great Depression hit the Eastern Shore a year and a half early and brought on the end of the league. Newspapers do not indicate any downturn in regional economics. Jobs seemed plentiful, the canneries, packing houses and farms relying on local and migrant labor were going strong. There is no evidence that some parts of the country hit the depression sooner than others. Financing and attendance declines were less likely the result of the national or regional economy than other local influences.

Affiliation was just developing and had not reached its recognizable model. Local franchises continued to be owned and operated the same way in these small towns as independent teams had been for over half a century. They were made up of directors of local athletic associations, and management and fundraising efforts were community enterprises. As previously noted, profligate independent teams lasted three to five years before enthusiasm and financial backing waned. There would be a break of a couple of years before enthusiasm for baseball would return, along with the willingness to spend whatever money was needed. The passing of the first incarnation of Class D baseball on the Eastern Shore of Maryland appeared no different than the cycles generated by the nature of independent baseball in the past. The fact that the league lasted over six years was remarkable in itself, and a credit to the league leadership. Yet it was the historical inability to abide by roster and salary restrictions, and the ensuing forfeits, that created an environment of animosity, frustration, and disgust that discouraged any continued enthusiasm from the townspeople. A telling statement was written 20 years later when baseball had returned to the Eastern Shore after World War II: "An overstep in payment for a player's services could result in the death of a league, which happened in 1927." When organized baseball returned to the Eastern Shore a decade later, things would be different.[20]

12

Promise Kept

The new concept arising from the Eastern Shore League was the promise to develop talent over winning. While many of the early teams looked no different from those of the independent years, and in spite of roster cramming and a high turnover of players, the league lived up to that promise. It was pointed out that the league sent 17 players on to higher classifications after the 1923 season, but not all went smoothly. In other significant player movements that season, Laurel released manager Poke Whalen and then sold its reserved players to the Salisbury White Cloud to pay off debts, so there was little hope it would return to the league. The National Board of Arbitration then ruled all of the Crisfield players as free agents as they had not received their full salaries after the struggling franchise was taken over. The best that could be hoped for in that 1924 season was a six-team circuit.[1]

In late September 1924 it was reported 10 players from the Eastern Shore League had advanced to higher levels of competition, including locals Frank Hummer to Norfolk and Jimmie Foxx to the Athletics. By November, the *Sporting News* was singing the league's praises, "Little Shore Loop Real Incubator." Over two dozen players received major and minor promotions from six small towns. Thirty-three had already been promoted from the previous two seasons. Sixty players had moved up in three years. If the quantity was there, the quality was to be determined. The Hall of Fame did not exist yet, but four from the "Little Shore Loop" who played the first three years would make it there: Mickey Cochrane, Red Ruffing, and Jimmie Foxx, along with player-manager "Home Run" Baker.

It was with the 1925 season that *Salisbury Times* sports editor C. Truitt was asked in a letter signed "Baseball Hounds" to select an all-star team and a most valuable player. Later it was announced that Nig Clarke, who had started his professional catching career in 1900 and caught an Addie Joss no-hitter in 1908, was awarded a trophy as the most valuable payer of the league.[2]

The entire league was well stocked with talent, resulting with Parksley in first place at one point during the 1926 season with only an 18–15 record. George Selkirk, the man who replaced Babe Ruth for the Yankees, was starting his career with Cambridge as a catcher, and Tony Rensa was in his second year with the Crabbers. Even with Rensa, Crisfield was looking to shore up its infield and picked up a skinny kid from Waxahachie, Texas. named Paul Richards to help out.

Paul Richards would go on to a solid big-league career before taking turns as coach, manager, and general manager. With the Baltimore Orioles he teamed up with the innovative Jim McLaughlin in a productive, if fractious, relationship. The one thing they could agree on was that it all started with pitching. Richards was known for his "bonus baby" signings and brought many young pitching talents to the major leagues. He also implemented an approach to the game in his book *Modern Baseball Strategy* in 1955, which was taught at every level of the Baltimore minor leagues. With significant contributions from the many that he worked with, and from those who followed him, this style of fundamentals, coaching, and play was the beginning of what became known as the Oriole Way. It served as a model for other major league clubs, and kept the Baltimore franchise in consistent contention for 30 years.[3]

Tony Rensa led the Crabbers and the league batting at a .388 clip. He was ably assisted by their new second baseman, Paul Richards, who finished with a .301 average. Even though they ended up in fourth after forfeits over class players, Parksley, once again, appeared the strongest club in the baby loop. Accused of being a class player, McDougall anchored the Spud lineup with a .342 average and 19 home runs.

Parksley also fielded the best pitcher in the league. Johnnie Firth of Messick, Virginia, pitched shutouts in both ends of a doubleheader. He dominated the league with most wins with a 21–8 record, had the most strikeouts with 143, and logged a league-leading 246 innings while appearing in 37 games in a 90-game schedule. At the urging of C. Edward Sparrow, the league had formed a committee to choose the best player each season. The twenty-six-year-old Firth was named MVP of the league for 1926 and was presented with the Sun Medal from the Baltimore newspaper. Freddie Fitzberger, formerly with Salisbury, won the Blue Ridge League version.[4]

Eastern Shore fans also had much to cheer for in the major leagues in the 1926 postseason. Local products from the late independent days, Jake Flowers and Vic Keen, former competitors on the Shore, had made good and were playing together with the St. Louis Cardinals. Branch Rickey's Birds were going against the Yankees in the World Series. Many were surprised with the Cardinals' ascension. It was reported that the 31 players used on their roster had only cost the team $39,000. Some estimated that Comiskey in Chicago, and Mack in Philadelphia had spent a half a million apiece to put together a winner. Rickey said he built the club with his "farms," and strong scouting. Rumors began to circulate that Easton was now willing to give full control of the club to an American League team. The Farmers would be just as their name implied and function as a "farming place," receiving all their players via that route. This was in contrast to the preferences of Sexton, Farrell, and Landis, but Rickey's model of affiliation had produced quick results. It was later rumored that the Yankees were consorting with the Farmers. Once staunchly independent, the Eastern Shore League was flirting with the advantages of affiliation.[5]

Individual exploits were many in 1927. Paul Richards played short, did a little pitching, and led the league in home runs with 24. George Selkirk qualified for third in the league for hitting with a .349 average. The Canners' veteran starter,

Trippe, tossed a no-hitter. Rose of Crisfield won both ends of a doubleheader against the Canners, and little more than a week later Slim Perry of Easton duplicated the feat against the Northampton Red Sox. In spite of all its troubles, the league did live up to its promise to develop players for the major leagues. It would do the same in later editions of the league.[6]

13

Transition

If the Depression did not cause the collapse of the Eastern Shore League in 1928, it certainly hindered its later reforming. And the Depression was different in this rural region than urban areas that were plagued with rampant unemployment, homelessness, and starvation. Most manufacturing on the Shore revolved around the seasonal canning of oysters, crabmeat, tomatoes, peas, and corn. But things were changing in the marketplace. In 1920 there were 249 canneries in operation on the Eastern Shore of Maryland. By 1931 there were 178. Advertisements for chain grocery stores began to appear in local newspapers, eventually beating out the small independent grocers. Chains placed larger orders which required larger factories. With a stagnant population growth, and a limited number of available migrant workers, Eastern Shore canneries found it difficult to find the labor needed to expand their operations.

Year-round manufacturing was making strides with a hosiery factory in Seaford, Delaware, and the Coca-Cola bottling franchises in the larger towns of the Shore. No community on the peninsula could yet refer to itself as urban. The Eastern Shore and the Chesapeake Bay continued in its breadbasket role. Cash crops like soybeans, wheat, and field corn were becoming more prominent. It was during this time that a handful of farmers, notably Arthur Perdue, were pioneering the concept of large-scale chicken farming which became so vital to the region's economy. While most natives still flipped an axe or twisted a neck for a chicken dinner, these entrepreneurs raised them by the thousands, established processing plants and then shipped the product to chain grocery stores in metropolitan markets. The industry was supposedly spawned by a mistaken shipment of 500 chickens that was kept and raised. In 1923 a thousand broiler chickens were raised on the peninsula, and in a scant seven years the number grew to six million. By the onset of World War II 77,000,000 broilers were raised, and by its end, 110,000,000. Then the industry took off.[1]

Most people of the Eastern Shore participated in the food industry, whether directly or indirectly. A sizable portion of the population were farmers or watermen. Many were both. The economy revolved around them. Every farm had its household garden that might include some combination of tomatoes, squash, zucchini, potatoes, peas, bush and pole beans, and other foods raised for home use. Cash crops of wheat, peaches, tomatoes, soybeans and corn kept the farm going. Potatoes were a more recent addition to the cash crops that proved successful in some areas, if not lucrative. By 1937 the FBI was conducting a probe of a racket to control the potato crop. It was feared organized crime, having lost the bootlegging business, was trying to "muscle in on potatoes."

Cattle were kept on farms for dairy products and meat, swine for slaughter, chickens for eggs and meat. Those farming on or near the water supplemented their diets with a variety of readily available seafood. Rockfish, hardhead, flounder, trout, and perch were preferred fish, but other species supplemented diets as well. They also scooped up piles of oysters and indigenous soft-shell clams. Terrapins were harvested from the bay. Muskrats, rabbits and racoons were trapped to sell the pelts for fur coats, and the meat went in the pot. Tamed ducks, geese, and guineas roamed the barnyard as wild waterfowl like Canada geese and several species of wild duck and swans covered the skies, fields, and rivers, and were hunted personally and commercially.

By this time the once respected waterfowl marketers, who had provided for the posh tables of East Coast restaurants, became outlaws. The Migratory Bird Act of 1918 eliminated many of the hunting tactics used as overhunting had depleted the skies, field, and rivers of the waterfowl population. Traps were banned, as were the big guns, and battery-rigged skiffs. But market shooting had gone on for generations; many individuals had been at it for more than 30 years. There was still a market, and many ignored the laws that forced them into more menial occupations than that of the fiercely independent gunner. The outlaw gunner usually went to church, coached sports, and contributed to his community in countless ways, but he lived in remote areas and was loath to give up his Eastern Shore ways. During the depression outlaw gunning provided both food and cash for its participants. Paying fines and doing time were the cost of doing business. Many who lived through the depression on the Eastern Shore claimed they never had two nickels to rub together, but they always had plenty of good things to eat. Neighbors took care of neighbors. What little money circulated went for essentials, and it was money that was needed for baseball. It took time for money to come back into circulation. Many couldn't wait.

Town teams continued their independence following the abandonment of the Class D minor league. Each community had their team and field. They played who they wanted when they wanted. Most appear to have been amateur, or nominally semipro. Smaller towns followed the previous business model of a core of well-heeled sponsors with the community at large adding their contributions. Many were content with intercounty rivalries and occasional forays into neighboring counties or farther. Most were truly local teams with players from close to home. Historical societies have collections of pictures from these small-town teams and glimpses of the fields they played on. Yet there were significant differences between the independent teams before and after the Eastern Shore League of the 1920s.

Independent town baseball had been a drain on organized baseball for years. Organized baseball in the form of Mike Sexton, John Farrell, and later, Kennesaw Landis, had effectively curtailed that independent environment. The number of Class D minor leagues peaked at 30 in 1911, and the number of independent leagues dropped from four to zero. World War I caused a significant drop in the number of minor leagues beginning in 1915. Down to barely a dozen leagues by the 1920s, the minors were just rebounding when the Great Depression came. When the minor leagues ventured into the "Baby League" on the Eastern Shore in 1922, they had shown a willingness to go into the strongholds of independent baseball, regardless of size, and take over. At the same time, they were luring outlaw strongholds into their fold. There were fewer places for the independent entrepreneur/baseball player to ply his trade. Prior to 1910 outlaws and independents were healthy and noticeable. By 1930 they were usually havens for those of marginal talent, or those suspended or blacklisted from organized baseball.

Another goal, at least for Landis, was the gambling. He came into power on the promise to clean up baseball after the Black Sox scandal of 1919, and he knew that if he was to be successful, he had to go beyond the major leagues and clean up gambling down to its grass roots. If he had no power outside of organized baseball, organized baseball would simply expand into the vacuum. The Eastern Shore League fit the bill and had served that purpose. His two trips to the peninsula were evidence of his concern. The league was rife with violations of class players, illegal contracts, beaten umpires, and betting was still a prominent part of the typical game. There was also the important expectation that this league would fulfill its promise to groom young players for promotion.

When the Eastern Shore League folded in 1928, independent professional players were being absorbed into organized baseball, and gambling appeared to be on the wane. There did not seem to be as much loose talent for the Eastern Shore towns to spend their money on as in the past. If the town teams were not as good as they once were, they retained their importance in the community. Every town had one, and everybody went out to watch them; it just did not cost as much money.

One difference now, as opposed to the earlier independent years, was an increase in corporate sponsorship. Where the towns seemed to shy away from expenses, these new moguls were willing to pay for equipment, management, infrastructure, and what few quality players that might be available. The best example of that was what happened in Cambridge. The two prominent sponsors in that town were the local Coca-Cola franchise, one of the many companies undergoing national expansion, and the Phillips Packing Company, a local seafood packing and canning factory. They were the best teams in Cambridge, some thought the best on the Eastern Shore of Maryland, being among the few that could afford imported players. It seems these two teams met in a best of seven series at the end each season to determine the city championship. The championship escalated in 1936, resembling the old days of independent town ball.

The series was stretched out, playing mostly on Sundays, providing plenty of rest between games. Having fallen behind, Joe Fowler of Coca-Cola brought in a few International League players who were quickly recognized. Col. Albanus Phillips of the packing company promptly called on his good friend Jacob Rupert of the Yankees for some help. Phillips brought in Max Bishop of the A's and ex-major leaguer and Eastern Shore native Dickie Porter, along with some other minor league players. Fowler also continued his addition of players. With the series tied at two games apiece, Phillips put in a call to Jimmie Foxx, who was getting together a postseason barnstorming team. Foxx was only too happy to play in front of his fellow Shoremen and, unannounced, brought a few of his barnstormers with him.

The series started with a crowd of a thousand that grew to 2,000 when the professionals started showing up. Three thousand showed up, not even knowing Foxx and his friends were there, and they were treated to a home run from the local hero. Word spread and 4,000 Eastern Shore fans showed up for the next game. Phillips and Foxx took the series 4–2. The picture of the winning Phillips Packing championship team featured none of the players that had played for him all year. Six of the nine players that posed wore major league uniforms, and one of the two minor league players was Dickie Porter, who had just finished a six-year major league career. Foxx wore his barnstorming uniform. It has been said that other professionals had played incognito. The major league players known to have played in the series included Foxx, Porter, Bishop, Frankie Hayes, Jimmie Deshong, Billy Werber, and Roger Cramer.[2]

While some have proposed that this series led directly to the formation of the second Class D Eastern Shore League, a look at the Federalsburg semipro team of those years provides a broader perspective of baseball activities in most towns on the peninsula. Team ledgers from 1935 and 1936 are the source. The books for 1935 show that the Federalsburg team, playing for a town of 1,300 people, participated in a season that lasted from early May through October 10. During that stretch they played 93 games, sometimes six or seven days in a row with doubleheaders. They compiled a record of 63–25–5 in a schedule exceeding the length of the previous minor league. The ledger shows that expenses for paid players ranged from $9 to $34 per game. In all, the player expense for the year was $827, with total expenses of $1,048.25. Their total receipts were $907.18. The team broke even in providing the town and community plenty of quality baseball entertainment.

The 1936 ledgers, though probably not as complete, may be even more revealing. Recording games from June 30 through October 25, Federalsburg played in 89 games with a record of 55–32–2. Four of those games came against Phillips Packing of which Federalsburg won all four recorded contests. When they went up against Coca-Cola of Cambridge during the season, Federalsburg posted a 7–3–1 record. Phillips and Coca-Cola may have received all the attention for their "war on the shore" at the end of the '36 season, but they were by no means the dominant teams on the peninsula prior to the ballyhooed series. Little towns up and down the Shore like Federalsburg were fielding teams as good or better, well before those two magnates got carried away in their postseason series. The peninsula was ready for another try at minor league baseball.[3]

As in white communities, most black teams preferred the independent model. In the words of local participant Leon Taylor, there was a "baseball team in every hamlet…. That was all you had to do." They were usually relegated to "playing on back lots, scrub fields, any clean place you can play baseball." Yet Taylor recalled that in 1932, in the middle of the Depression, J.O. Chapman was instrumental in

From 1929 to 1936 towns reverted to their independent ways after the minor league folded. Perhaps not as talented as before, town teams still might play 80 to 120 games a season for their fans. This ledger page reflects the daily finances of a town team, including player expenses (courtesy Federalsburg Historical Society).

forming the black Eastern Shore League. If it seemed an odd time to attempt the expenses associated with the administration of a peninsula wide-league, one participant observed. "We were already poor so the depression didn't bother us." The eight teams that composed the league came from the mid- and upper Shore towns of Centreville, Vienna, Easton, St. Michaels, Denton, Batt's Neck, Cambridge, and

Bellevue. The season opened on Easter Monday, an important holiday in the African American community.[4]

Games were usually played on holidays and Sundays once church let out. While white communities were subject to Sunday blue laws, it appears the laws were not always enforced in black communities. There was some commercial sponsorship and the degree of professionalism was restricted by availability of resources, "There were a lot of black businesses in town.... They would give you $2 if you got to first or second base, and if you won the game they would give you a party." Despite Taylor's observation of the depression having no impact, many black individuals and families did move to the nearby cities of Baltimore and Philadelphia to find work, but the bonds of home and family brought many neo-urbanites home on weekends. On Sunday it was church, baseball, and the party for the big send-off for another week of work, until next Sunday's game.[5]

During the 1930s the direction of the *Afro-American* newspaper changed, and less news was solicited from the rural hinterlands with an increased focus on urban and national news. But Eastern Shore correspondents sent enough reports to indicate consistent, widespread baseball activity throughout the Shore. To the south were the Oaksville Eagles, Crisfield Tigers, the Maryland Flying Clouds and the Princess Anne Black Hawks. On the mid- and upper Shore were the Federalsburg Bearcats, Preston Tigers, and the St. Michaels Red Sox. The talented Black Hawks and "Wild" Bill Bailey were slated to play the Philadelphia Red Sox and the Johnson's All Stars of Atlantic City. In 1934 the Bi State Loop standings began appearing in the *Afro-American*. With two teams from Delaware, the six Maryland teams were Denton, St. Michaels, Cambridge, Vienna, Federalsburg and Bellevue. This resembles the Eastern Shore League founded by Chapman and recalled by Taylor. They played one game a week in a split-season format. Batteries and line scores were often provided to the *Afro-American*. By 1936 this circuit had become the Tri County League with all the teams coming from the mid-Shore region of Maryland. While most of the *Afro-American* coverage focused on league play, the Salisbury All Stars were beaten by the white independent Salisbury Indians, and played some of their games at nearby Harmon's Beach.[6]

By the 1930s the combined efforts of Landis in the major leagues and those of Sexton and Farrell in the minors had an impact on baseball in small towns. They imposed rules, standards, and expectations. During Sexton's and Farrell's tenures, the minor leagues were promoted and expanded. But now Sexton and Farrell were gone, Landis was ensconced in his role as aging commissioner, and minor league matters seemed removed from his purview. The money backing minor league teams was less local now.

While these three executives had touted independently owned, operated, and supported minor leagues, the current was flowing in the opposite direction. The 1921 National Agreement allowed for multiple ownerships of major league and minor league clubs, and reinstated the practice of farming players under contract. This was something always done on the sly, but it became open again. Many players of the Eastern Shore League of the 1920s were such players. While farmed players cost teams no money, neither did they profit from them, since they did not own the players' contract. The fact was that the minor leagues were well along in giving definition of affiliation or working agreements.

Branch Rickey, running the cash-strapped St. Louis Cardinals, along with team president Sam Breadon, saw the advantages to minor league ownership and affiliation. They were not alone in their observations and efforts, but they may have been the most determined in following affiliation to its logical conclusion. While Landis saw this emerging system as a form of slavery, and often referred to it as a "chain gang," depriving players of their rights, others saw it purely in the light of competition. In 1926 Rickey was frustrated in a bidding war for a minor league player. Breadon declared, "If we can't buy the contracts of the players, we'll have to start raising our own." The Cardinals president soon realized that they already had. Rickey had built a network where players could be signed, and then designated to teams to be groomed for the major leagues, keeping them out of the bidding wars. The year Breadon announced they would have to raise their own players, the Cardinals made it to the World Series against Ruth, Gehrig, and the Yankees. The Cardinals lineup included future Hall of Fame players Jim Bottomley and Chick Hafey, and also included Eastern Shore products Jake Flowers and Vic Keen. In five years Rickey's "chain gang" produced a World Series champion.[7]

Again, it is Federalsburg that provides some insight into this new type of affiliation and its variations. The town had an agreement with Connie Mack for most of the years that the Federalsburg team was in the Eastern Shore League in its final versions from 1937 to 1941, and again, from 1946 to 1949. Writing after the league folded in 1949, an unknown author (probably Dr. W.K. Knotts) recorded the three means by which Federalsburg financed its minor league team.

The first option was affiliation. This format was noted to have been used in 1939 and 1947, if not other years as well. In this scenario Connie Mack, or his son Earl, would own the franchise outright and were responsible for all expenses, business operations and decisions and usually leased the field from the local athletic authority.

The second option was known as a working agreement. These arrangements varied and were usually the result of demands of the major league club, or negotiations between the parties. It was under these arrangements that the Philadelphia Athletics and Federalsburg mostly did business. In their particular arrangement Mack owned the franchise, furnished the players, and held all rights to them. Philadelphia signed the players to contracts and had the authority to promote, trade or release them. Mack further agreed to help renovate the ballpark or otherwise help out financially if needed. In return the town of Federalsburg had to produce a set fee as a guarantee to Mack. To do this an athletic association was formed to put up the main portion of the money. It also raised funds through advance ticket sales and box seats, and sold stock at $10 a share. This was a business arrangement only. The association did not own or control the players but might be responsible for paying their salaries, providing lodging, and covering all other operations. It raised additional money through the regular methods of promotions, concessions, scorecards, and advertisements painted on outfield fences.

13. Transition

The author of the one-page document noted that in both of the first two options the Philadelphia Athletics and the Macks were the bosses. They made the decisions "most of the time."

The third option, an exception by the late 1930s, was to go independent. This usually happened when no working agreement could be found but a community

> Operation of Class D Baseball Team — 3 Systems —
>
> *1 - Affiliation with a Major League Baseball Club (Phila. Athletics)
>   - a - A's owner, Connie Mack (son, Earl) would own minor league team outright
>   - Fed. tried this system - years? - 39 or 47' (don't know) (used this!)
>
> *2 — Working agreement with Major League Club — (majority of time)
>   ① Connie Mack of the A's owned the Franchise, would furnish the players with all rights to them —
>   Signed to contracts, authority to promote, trade, release them.
>   - would help renovate old ball parks,
>   - Helped financially if needed.
>   ② Fed had to come up with a set fee (example 1,000⁰⁰) as a guarantee
>   ③ In order to do this, they had advanced ticket sales, and box seats. They also sold stock to citizens (fans) 10⁰⁰ a share
>   - That's when a group of businessmen formed an association — they put up the main portion of the money —
>   It was a business arrangement only - They did not own the players!
>   ③ The Assoc. was responsible for paying the players salaries, finding housing for them, + all other operations -
>   - they raised money by, promotions, concessions, sold some cards, tickets, etc, business ads painted on fences!
>
>   *In both of these systems, the Phila. Athletics (Connie Mack) was the boss. They made all of the decisions most of the time -
>
> *3. Independent —
>   1 - Put up own money for the guarantee fee to the league - plus - furnishing the players (had to do own recruiting)
>   + all expenses of the operation - Fan support along with the backing of an association
>   - a - 1949, Fed operated under this system, + made a profit according to records (Dr. Knotts, Bus. Mgr.)

These are probably the handwritten notes of Dr. W.K. Knotts. They outline options for financing a minor league team. Knotts was the steward of the Federalsburg purse strings. He was acknowledged for having an almost enigmatic knack for keeping a small town's baseball ledger in the black (courtesy Federalsburg Historical Society).

had the funding through an athletic association or a private franchise holder. In this model someone put up the guarantee to the league. The franchise holder was responsible for the scouting and recruiting of players, and had to meet all business expenses. The club was entirely reliant on fan support and a strong athletic association. It might pick up a couple of farmed players from other organizations, but could only make money selling players when it owned their rights. Often it had to raise additional funds during the season. Independents usually struggled in this era without the financial support of a major or minor league team. Federalsburg operated as independent in 1949 when the Athletics backed out and, according to the books of business manager Dr. Knotts, showed a rare independent profit.[8]

Part III

Heyday

14

Another League

> The Sho' Loop was killed off once before when clubs began using more class men in the lineups than rules allowed, and nothing was done about it. First one started and then another followed until it got just a plain scramble for victories regardless. They couldn't stand the financial strain of the necessary increase in payroll and—blooie!
> —Jesse Linthicum, *Baltimore Sun,* June 18, 1937

Linthicum stated the real reason for the demise of the previous Eastern Shore League. Wholesale forfeits had not curbed the use of illegal players and the illegal contracts that threw the league into a maelstrom of financial deficits and frustration with no way out but to fold. Attempts to reform the Eastern Shore League during the Depression were described as halfhearted, but in 1937 that would change. Most of the old league directors and independent franchise holders from the 1920s were gone or uninterested. Much of the incentive in starting a new Class D league seemed to come from people in organized baseball and a handful of past participants. Joe F. Carr of the National Association lobbied hard for affiliated teams on the Eastern Shore. He was joined by John Ogden of the high minor league Baltimore Orioles, Patsy O'Rourke of the Philadelphia Phillies, Win Clark of the Bi State League, Carlton Molesworth of Pittsburgh, and Joe Cambria, owner of the Trenton minor league team and associated with Clark Griffith and the Washington Senators. Local representatives of Crisfield, Centreville, and Easton attended early meetings. Eastern Shore notables Poke Whalen and Dickie Porter tagged along as employees of Cambria. Early meetings to form the league had a decidedly nonlocal power base.[1]

It was touted that financial investment of major and minor league clubs in the franchises would cut costs. Enthusiasm swelled as at least a dozen towns were interested in a league planned for eight teams. The circuit was proposed to the towns in this way: "These owners in some instances would provide all the players and pay all expenses incidental to operations of the farm club, including players payroll. In other towns entering the circuit, a club owner would make a substantial contribution to the operation expense in return for the exclusive player purchase agreement." There were conflicting reports as to who was affiliated or had agreements with whom, but all was settled by opening day.[2]

Some could not help but compare it with the old league. Local pundits now crowed that the Eastern Shore League of the 1920s had produced 22 major league players, including Mickey Cochrane, Red Ruffing, and Jimmie Foxx. Could this new system do the same? Outside interests did not seem to be soliciting local backing or support. It was hoped that the lack of any of the old sponsors and directors did not indicate indifference. Ogden was thought to be the real power behind the scenes when his suggestion that Tom Kibler of Chestertown be brought on as president of the new league was accepted. Many thought the new president would have more power and authority in this position than even Landis in his. Where former presidents had provided their services for free, the new system allowed Kibler a salary of $1,000, or $1,200 if there were eight teams, with office expenses of $300. Once, baseball was a local entertainment with residents volunteering their efforts for the community. Now it seemed more like the imported entertainments of vaudeville, minstrel shows, or the movies.[3]

The league decided on a salary cap of $1,000 a month, managers and playing managers excluded. Players with experience at a higher level were limited to two per team, and a total of four were allowed to have two years' experience. Ten players had to meet the definition of a rookie. All the old ballparks were locally owned and leased to the new franchise holders. All were being rebuilt, repaired, upgraded, and expanded. Gordy Park in Salisbury would hold three thousand, 3,500 by season's end. Dover, Salisbury, Cambridge, and Pocomoke City announced they would play night games to make it easier for working fans to attend scheduled weekday contests. Other towns would follow. Maryland still had blue laws on the books that prevented Sunday baseball, but most towns were willing to ignore them for the convenience of the fans. Police were on hand every Sunday in most towns, not to shut down the game, but to keep the unruly players and fans in check. Robert M. Clark threatened to pull his Crisfield franchise and move it if he did not receive assurances from the town that he would be permitted to play on Sunday. Crisfield stayed. Kibler noted that "things are ready to roll." If some thought Kibler was Ogden's man, he was anything but.[4]

John Thomas Kibler was born in Chestertown, Maryland. Instead of attending local Washington College, he went off to Temple University in Philadelphia in 1904, where he excelled in football, basketball, baseball, and gymnastics. After graduation in 1908 he coached football at Lehigh University for a year before going on to Ohio State as freshman football coach and as a basketball and baseball tutor. He would stay at Ohio State until 1912. While there he was scouted by Branch Rickey and signed to play baseball for Chillicothe of the Ohio State League in 1910. He was but two weeks on the roster and he was made the team manager. He continued in his positions at Ohio State while playing baseball in the summer, until his contract was sold to the White Sox organization in 1912. Two weeks later, he broke his leg sliding into second base, and was later sent to the San Francisco team in the Pacific Coast League.

Kibler then went to San Antonio in 1913, where he played professional baseball in the summer while taking on the position of athletic director and coach at his hometown Washington College the rest of the year. Kibler managed in San Antonio in 1914 and returned as a player the following year. It was in 1915 that he was sold to Newark. During his spare time he also played for the semipro Upland Club of Chester, Pennsylvania. It was with this club that he met the Athletics holdout Frank Baker, following him to Easton to play for the Easton Diamondbacks in the independent Eastern Shore League.

Kibler took leave from his duties at Washington College and baseball, joining the army in 1915 in anticipation of the coming war. He reached the rank of lieutenant during the conflict and was gassed and wounded before returning to the college in 1919. At that time Jake Flowers was making a name for himself in Cambridge. Kibler, like Burris before him, took advantage of local talent and recruited Flowers to Washington College. Flowers considered his coach a mentor, and it may have been Coach Kibler and his connections with Rickey who steered Flowers to the Cardinals farm system.

By 1937 Kibler was well respected for the quality of the basketball and baseball programs at Washington College, which had produced National League future home run champion and all-star Bill "Swish" Nicholson of Chestertown. Kibler was widely acknowledged for his administrative abilities. He had excellent baseball credentials, having played and managed in the minor leagues for Branch Rickey. He was friends with Frank Baker, which gave him connections to Connie Mack as well, and he was well connected to Jack Ogden of the formidable minor league Baltimore Orioles. Kibler was the iconic taciturn Eastern Shoreman with a reputation for integrity, and a remaining vestige of the Agrarian Myth. Whereas his predecessor Harry Rew was a respected lawyer with little knowledge of baseball, but a reputation of being a man of good judgment, Kibler possessed the same reputation of judgment, only with the baseball background and contacts to go with it. There seemed to be no man better suited for the job.[5]

15

Wonder Club

> Nobody ever figured out how a chicken feels in the chopping block, but the chicken's experience must be something akin to the reactions of an Eastern Shore League team playing Salisbury. A few squawks and it's all over.
> —William Needham, Associated Press, *Salisbury Daily Times*, August 19, 1937

Throughout the spring the league had taken some shape. The Salisbury Indians had a strong organization, associated with the Senators, and they had the recently retired local baseball hero Jake Flowers at the helm. Then there was old Eastern Shore League stalwart Poke Whalen as general manager. Easton aligned with the St. Louis Browns, with Doc Jacobs and Ernest "Duke" Landgraf as franchise holders. Cambridge drew the Cardinals with Joe Fowler owning the franchise, and former major league player and Rickey protégé Fred Lucas as manager. The Baltimore Orioles were firmly in control of Dover and Gerald Nugent of the Phillies was enthusiastically expanding his farm system with the Centreville Colts. Joe O'Rourke, son of Phillie executive, scout, and Centreville franchise holder Patsy O'Rourke, was named manager. Federalsburg went with the Athletics as the four Philadelphia and St. Louis major league teams accounted for half of the eight franchises. Arthur Ehlers, a wounded World War I veteran, held the Pocomoke City Red Sox franchise, with local pitching hero Vic Keen as manager. Former major league umpire and Baltimore sportsman Robert M. Clark held the Crisfield Crabbers. The nature of their working agreements were still taking shape.

As opening day approached Cambridge was "just plain ball crazy." Salisbury lined up their 53-piece town band to lead the opening day parade, and L.W. Gunby, the aged founding member of the original White Cloud, umpired the first pitch. Ten thousand were expected at the four league openers. Great crowds were expected for the opening day parades. It was announced 2,000 paid for opening day in Salisbury. Franchise owner Joe Cambria was excited, and announced that he planned to expand Gordy Park to 4,500, even 5,000, seats. For the first 10 days of the schedule the crowds ranged from 1,400 for a game in Federalsburg to 3,000 for a night game in Dover. Night games were especially popular.[1]

Joe Cambria had more than his association with Clark Griffith and the Senators to work with. He had what was referred to as the "Cuban connection." He

15. Wonder Club 149

Federal Park in Easton, night game in progress, c. 1938. Night baseball was highly popular on the Eastern Shore when it appeared in 1937. It seems minor league attendance increased nationally with its inception. It took the major leagues a little longer to catch on (courtesy Talbot Historical Society/H. Robins Holiday).

signed pitcher Jorge Comellas, and catcher Fermin Guerra, and would later add Juan Montero and Joe Salazar from his Trenton squad. With a loaded roster and Fowler's astute baseball mind at the reins, Salisbury jumped to a quick and commanding lead. By the middle of June the Indians were already running away with the race with their 21–5 record behind the pitching of Comellas and Joe Kohlman.

At this time Cambria announced that Salisbury would not be playing Sunday ball, since it violated local blue laws and there was strong community sentiment against it. All the smaller towns saw Sunday and night games as the only way to survive financially. Since the gate was not shared with visiting teams, there was no harm done to the other clubs by switching those games to another day. Indian business manager M.E. Murphy even offered visiting teams a piece of the gate for that inconvenience, but the Salisbury situation rankled the league and team directors over the loss of solidarity. Although Cambria had no control over the town enforcement of the Sunday ban, his colleagues thought he should defy the ordinance. Newspapers implied that this minor disagreement about Sunday ball created the ill will that led to what happened next.[2]

Thirty days into the season all clubs were required to pare their squads to the maximum of 14 players. Without any accusations being made, Kibler was asked to review Salisbury's final roster. What he found was that in addition to the four declared veteran players of Kohlman, Comellas, Lynn, and Guerra, player Bob Bradley had signed a contract with Harrisburg in 1934. Salisbury explained that Bradley had been illegally signed as a minor, had never played a game, had been verbally released and sent home; the contract had never been registered with

National Association because the Boston Braves were hiding their illegal conduct; and Kibler had already approved Bradley when rosters were submitted for opening day. The class rule was now interpreted that anybody under contract for more than 30 days was considered to have logged a year's service at that level. Some recommended a fine and suspensions, since Bradley had never played in '34, but Kibler adhered to the letter of the law; ruled him a veteran player; and forfeited all 21 of the Indians' wins, assigning them a record of 0–26. It looked like 1926 all over again.

Flowers tried to reason with his old coach and friend, with no success. Cambria "burned up" the telephone and telegraph to Judge William G. Bramham (now head of the minor leagues), and Commissioner Landis, and anybody else he thought would listen. Clark Griffith was livid, telling Kibler, "You're doing nothing more than ruining the league." Kibler's response was true to his nature: "Mr. Griffith, if we can't play baseball according to the rules of the National Association, let's break up the league." Bramham deferred it to Kibler as a league matter, thereby upholding the forfeits. Cambria was confident in his appeal to Landis, since the commissioner's history had been to declare such illegal contracts invalid. Landis' affinity for the Eastern Shore was but a memory. His convenient response weeks later was that he did not have the authority over a minor league matter. Long before that Cambria had expressed both his frustration and determination: "Tom Kibler has always impressed me as being level-headed, but in this case he seems to have forgotten the words 'common sense' are in the English language…. The decision to throw out twenty-one games has floored the Indians, but they'll never quit. I've instructed the manager and the team to carry on the fight on and off the field."[3]

Carry on the fight is exactly what they did. The first game the Indians played after the forfeitures was at Gordy Park. Flowers was tossed in the sixth inning following a running harassment of plate umpire Jim O'Connor. In the eighth, Cambridge base runner Jimmie Ettenger attempted to score and Salisbury catcher Thomas put him out with a "hard tag." A bench jockey, utility man named Gaugain, began to ride Thomas, who then turned and strode towards the opponent's dugout. He didn't make it. Gaugain ran out and landed a right hook to the catcher's eye, and "Bedlam broke loose, players, umpires, and fans mixing in a free-for-all. When order was restored, Thomas, Gaugain and Danny Murtaugh, the Cardinal second sacker, were given the gate." Jim Boyer, a Templeville native in his first year of professional umpiring, was working the bases. He later remembered after the game that O'Connor had to beat off a gang of ruffians with his mask as he made his way to the car. The police were not to be seen. When Boyer was later pressed on how much tougher it was to umpire in the American League than the minor leagues, the veteran of the 1944 World Series and All-Star Game responded that "the big leagues are a Sunday School compared to that '37 Shore season," and "the major league wolves don't howl in the same ferocious manner as the Salisbury fans during the '37 season."[4]

Later, Flowers explained in an interview his managerial strategy at that point:

I called a club house meeting, and here's what I told those boys: "Don't let this get you down. Even if we can't win the pennant now, don't let this affect your own personal chances. You're all young and want to advance. The only way to get attention is to go out there on the field and do your best in every minute of every game. Make yourselves look good. If you do, you are bound to win promotion. And if you do win the pennant, they'll all be talking about you."

It was the emphasis on the personal interest of the player that did the job. I had a young, fast team, and it ran the other clubs off their feet. These boys were all striving to climb the ladder individually.[5]

Easton was catapulted into first place after the forfeits and grasped it firmly. Owned and managed by Doc Jacobs and with the talented Mickey Vernon in the field, they won 12 out of 14 in the heart of the season. With Fred Lucas at the helm, the Cambridge Cardinals put a solid squad on the field, led by second baseman Danny Murtaugh and the pitching of Ken Raffensberger. Umpires continued to be harassed throughout the league. Umpire Toach was charged by fans after Pocomoke City lost one in the ninth inning at home. He left the field under police protection. Then the newspapers focused on the two "countdowns."[6]

While the Indians were punished with their forfeits, all individual performances still counted for season statistics. Joe Kohlman lost his first pitching decision, then found his stride. Comellas started his winning streak right out of the gate. It was reported that one had won six in a row, and the other seven. Then it was 13 and 12 in a row, with no sign of ending. Flowers had more than two pitchers. Revolinsky's numbers were not as gaudy, merely excellent. Cambria called on Juan Monteras from Trenton to bolster his staff, while the lefty Brassler seemed to pitch into what little bad luck they had. The Indians had more than pitching. Jerry Lynn and Frank Treschock paced the league in hitting through the season, and Luzansky wasn't far behind. The second countdown was Salisbury's rise back up the standings, which coincided with the winning streaks of Comellas and Kohlman.

With Easton in the middle of its hottest run of the year, the Indians climbed out of the cellar after a night game in Federalsburg in late July. A young Easton boy remembered those heady days. With 14-man rosters, Doc Jacobs was always looking for help shagging flies in batting practice, and young Bill Perry was one of those kids always spending time at the ballpark. Mickey Vernon would give him rides to Federal Park in Easton on his bicycle, where Perry wore out his Chuck Klein model glove shagging flies in batting practice. He and his friends formed a knothole gang behind the right field fence but constable Stewart would not let them hang around there long. Instead, they retrieved balls hit over the fence, where a mad scramble of children ensued. The first to the ball had the choice of 10 cents or admission to the game. Money was not the object.[7]

Kohlman then won his 16th, and Comellas his 17th. This propelled Salisbury into sixth place ahead of Dover and Pocomoke. By August 16, the Indians leapt into third place with seven home games scheduled at Gordy Park in the coming week. By the 18th of August, Salisbury was one game off Easton's now shaky grip on first place. After six shutouts in a week, including a no-hitter by Revolinsky,

The Wonder Team Salisbury Indians of 1937. Their parent team was the Washington Senators, and their remarkable comeback inspired the frugal Clark Griffith into generosity. He bought seventeen bejeweled watches for the players. From row, from left: Batboy Morris (Maurice) Fields, William Luzansky, Joe Salazar, Fermine (Mike) Guerra, Charles (Q)uimby, Jerome Lynn, Edgar Leip; middle row, from left: Club secretary John Milton, Fred Thomas, Manager D'Arcy (Jake) Flowers, John Bassler, Leon Revolinsky, Joseph Garlan, Joseph Kohlman, and Business Manager M.E. Murphy. Back row, from left: Georg Comellas, Juan Montero, Frank Treschock, Frank Deutsch (courtesy Eastern Shore Baseball Hall of Fame/Donnie Davidson Collection).

Salisbury still trailed the Easton Brownies. On August 20 Salisbury had won 12 in a row. Comellas was 20–0, Kohlman 19–1, Montero 6–1, Revolinsky 9–2, with lefty Brassler absorbing most of the losses at 7–10.[8]

ERA was not an official stat for the Eastern Shore League but Jake Flowers was keeping track of his Indians. Kohlman posted 1.31, while Comellas worked to 1.38. Montero worked to a 2.44 and Brassler 2.85. Flowers seemed to apologize for Leon Revolinsky's astronomical 3.08 by pointing out he was 1.98 over his last 50 innings. One night heavy rains pelted Gordy Park, but the Indians were back in the pennant race and the game must go on. The park was drained, the water pumped out, and the infield set afire with gasoline to dry the basepaths in order to get in an 8–1 win.[9]

On September 1, Salisbury held a Booster Night at Gordy Park with Clark Griffith as guest of honor. More than 3,000 appreciative fans showed up to celebrate what had become known as the "Wonder Team" or the "Wonder Club." Not particularly known for his largesse, Griffith handed out 17 jeweled wristwatches to all the players, business manager M.E. Murphy, Secretary John Milton, and GM Poke Whelan. Other gifts went to pitcher Joe Salazar, scorekeeper Elijah Disharoon, batboy Maurice Fields, and bus driver Ernest Tosker. Jake Flowers was presented with a car. Griffith told the fans, "I do not remember, in my 50 years of baseball a team with the pluck, grit, and determination these boys had... (it is) your inspiration that made these boys come from behind." The next day they took first place when Kohlman, in keeping with the storybook season, pitched a no-hitter over the tenacious Easton Brownies. The Indians' climb to the top was called "probably the most epochal comeback in baseball history." After being "hurled" from first place on June 19 it took 58 games to complete the climb back to the top. Forty-eight of those games were victories.[10]

Salisbury took the league pennant over Easton. Before the playoffs, the Indians whipped Cambria's high minor league Trenton in an exhibition and Kohlman was named MVP of the league. Kohlman threw a second no-hitter over Centreville in the last game of the postseason playoffs. Five no-hitters were posted in the league on the season. The Centreville Colts surprised the Indians when the little town of 1,292 drew 2,735 to an upset win, but Salisbury prevailed in the series.[11]

More than 20 years earlier Connie Mack had brought his A's down to the peninsula only to be beaten by the independent Salisbury club. Now Mack brought five of his mainstays for an exhibition, but Flowers and his charges beat the Athletics 3–2 at Gordy Park for Mack's second loss on the Shore. The Indians capped their storied season with a win over the House of David. The players on the "Wonder Club" dominated the league as much as the team had. Joe Kohlman led the league in pitching at 25–1 with 227 innings pitched. Comellas was second at 22–1 with 206 innings, and Revolinsky placed fourth in the league at 13–2 behind ex-major leaguer, Pocomoke City manager, and Eastern Shore resident Vic Keen. Juan Monteros was ranked sixth at 7–3. Brassler evened his mark to 10–10. Second baseman Lynn led the league with a .342 average, and teammate Treschock was second with .338. Ruzansky placed fifth at .331. Kohlman, Comellas, Lynn, Treschock, and catcher Fermin Guerra received a September call-up by Griffith to the Senators. Seldom has a team dominated its league the way the Salisbury Indians did in 1937. The official minor league website ranks that edition of the Salisbury Indians as the eighth best minor league team of all time.[12]

Much happened during the offseason. Bill Terry and the Giants bought the Crisfield franchise and moved it to Milford, Delaware, with league approval. An earlier attempt to grab up the Easton franchise had met "vigorous" opposition. Doc Jacobs would retain the Easton club. Kibler then suffered a heart attack and he named Harry Russell to take over. In December it was announced that Salisbury, Cambridge, Federalsburg, and Dover had all shown a profit, and even struggling Pocomoke City broke even. Every park now had lighting for night games, and Salisbury's attendance of 88,000 set a Class D record. Then, at the end of the month, the *Sporting News* announced in a front-page headline story that Jake Flowers was named Minor League Manager of the Year for leading the Wonder Team to the Eastern Shore League pennant in spite of the 21 forfeits under their belt.[13]

The Eastern Shore League had stumbled into chaos and controversy in 1937 only to come out on the other end as the most recognized league in organized baseball with the Wonder Club and the Minor League Manager of the Year. Everybody in the league seemed proud, happy for the success, but they begrudged how Cambria got there. They did not consider his "Cuban connection" a level playing field. Most of these players were not previously known to organized baseball, and could have easily played at a higher classification. "Papa Joe" Cambria, as he was now affectionately known after winning a pennant, wisely moved his players around from his different minor league teams to create winners and boost the box office.

Salisbury continued to receive pressure from the Salisbury Ministerial Society over Sunday baseball throughout the winter, extending the aggravation of being the only town in the league to enforce its blue laws. To add to this constant irritation the league passed the "alien rule" as a bylaw. This action was aimed directly at Cambria. All aliens were now barred from the rosters and one had to be an American citizen to play in the Eastern Shore League. In addition, all Cuban players, regardless of previous experience, were declared class men. It was recognized that any protest to the enforcement of this by law was subject to being overturned by Bramham and the National Association rules. The alien rule was not included in the *Constitution and By Laws: Eastern Shore League of Professional Base Ball Clubs*, revised April 1, 1938. The rule may have come out in a later edition, or simply been an unspoken agreement.

The good news was that all eight grounds would be ready for night play. Mickey Vernon's contract was sent outright to Cambria and Trenton, making him a Senator. Eastern Shore native Art Ehlers bought and held the independent franchise in Pocomoke City. The league restated the alien rule before the season began, and when the weekly ladies' nights sponsored by the league were eliminated, the beleaguered Cambria vowed, "I'll fight for ladies prices all I can." Baseball comedian Nick Altrock was booked for Salisbury's opening day, which included the championship pennant raising. Cambridge planned to broadcast their season opener over the radio.[14]

Salisbury boosters met with business manager Murphy and Cambria, who promised their constituents another pennant. It looked like they might meet that promise when the Indians reeled off nine straight, but then they went into a tailspin. By the middle of June, Dover was the only team over .500 at 23–8. It was announced that the league had placed mor than 30 players in higher classifications from last year. Under severe "fan pressure" Arthur Ehlers had to fire veteran Joe Boley as manager. It seems the easygoing skipper did not partake of the Eastern Shore pastime of baiting, abusing, and assaulting the umpires to the degree the Pocomoke City fans expected. Ehlers took over on the bench. Val Picinich, an eighteen-year major league catcher, was managing in Milford. He brought with him the experience of catching three no-hitters, for Joe Bush and Walter Johnson in Washington and Howard Ehmke with the Red Sox. Doc Jacobs returned from his successful year coaching Villanova University to take over the helm in Easton. Jacobs was of the fiery sort. After a loss in Pocomoke City the team was singing on the ride home to pass the time. Jacobs, nerves obviously frayed, suddenly leapt up and shouted that they didn't have anything to sing about. He then told the driver to pull over to the side of the road, where he jumped out and fumed and swore for a while, then he hopped back on the bus and ordered it to be driven into the Pocomoke River. The driver ignored him. When Jacobs finally cooled off, they resumed a quiet journey home.[15]

Early in the year Cambria had tried to bring back pitcher Joe Salazar. Russell at first waived the alien rule, only to later reverse himself and allow Cambria a week to make a roster move. The ruling was the last straw for his catcher, Guerra, who declared before he departed, "No good for them, (other Cubans) no good for me too." Guerra was considered major league materiel and risked blacklisting from organized baseball with his decision. The team was in second place and Cambria was hampered in his efforts to improve his roster due to a rule designed specifically to thwart him. Having promised the boosters a pennant, and with the ministers of Salisbury preventing Sunday profits, a cartoon appeared of Cambria in Indian headdress with the caption "Startum Big War." There were rumors of impending class player forfeits in Dover, and the matter had been referred to Bramham, who had ruled it a violation. But Russell had softened league policy. Dover was allowed time to correct their roster before any penalty was assessed. By this time both Guerra and Monteros were reported to be back in Cuba.[16]

Fighting at ball games continued to be a problem for league president Harry Russell. In a Cambridge and Easton contest it was curtly reported, "At the close of the game, fans surrounded the car of the two umpires, and attempted to drag Clark out. Police intervened and escorted them out of town." The national press provided a little more detail,

> Police rescued umpire A. Clark from a group of irate Easton fans, who were trying to pull him from an auto after the Cambridge Cardinals handed the Browns an 8–3 setback the night of July 15. The trouble had its inception in the sixth inning when the pitcher of the Redbirds bunted down the first base line and the Easton hurler, fielded the ball and tried to tag the runner, whom Clarke ruled safe. A similar incident involving the same players occurred in the seventh stanza and again the arbiter ruled the runner safe, after which the pitchers sailed into each other with their fists. The pair were separated and both remained in the game.[17]

Barely a week later, there was another incident when the Cardinals faced the Centreville Colts. "Neither Joe O'Rourke, Centreville pilot or Joe Davis Cambridge manager suffered much damage when they tangled last night, but Francis O'Rourke, Joe's brother and secretary of Centreville Club, was knocked out by someone in the crowd." The manager's fight started at the same time that Cambridge fans went at umpires Arthur Gilbert and Hanson Horsey after they had called the game in the eighth inning for rain. The brawl had diverted the fans away from their usual pursuit of the umpires. Davis and O'Rourke were fined and suspended three days. A Cambridge pitcher was also fined and the club was assessed an undisclosed fine for failing to provide adequate police protection to the umpires.[18]

Russell wrote a letter to Easton on July 20, stating that they were the worst in

Federal Park in Easton, ca. 1938. Eastern Shore baseball was known for its "confabs" and "rhubarbs." This looks like a confab that might turn into a rhubarb (courtesy Talbot Historical Society).

the league when it came to umpire baiting. After an incident in Cambridge, Russell wrote another letter directed to Mayor Wrightson and Daniel Henry of the Easton Athletic Association. "I understand that at Cambridge last night there was a general disorder in the extreme, resulting in a free-for-all mix up in having to send several players to the hospital, one of the Centreville players, so the story goes, being in the hospital at the present time.... It is hoped that we have seen the end of such things." This prompted Wrightson and Henry to call on their chief of police for better protection. Henry expressed his frustration in a letter to Russell after another incident in Easton which the umpires did not bother to report to the league office. To Henry's thinking, what crossed Russell's desk and what did not seemed subjective.[19]

A week later a Dover Oriole hit a ball, ruled foul, which would have scored a run. A teammate took exception to the call and slugged umpire Frank Wisner in the eye. A complete investigation was ordered. By the end of August, six of the eight teams were playing over .500 ball, with seventh place Centreville at .455. The independent Pocomoke City team was mired in the cellar at 37–64. Sid Gordon took over with a league-leading .336 average and second-year man Danny Murtaugh was not far behind.[20]

Doc Jacobs was back in charge of the Easton Brownies September 1 after several weeks confined to bed. In a standard practice of the day, Jacobs and a crew member had poured gasoline on the infield and set it aflame to burn off the excess water and dry the diamond to avoid a rain out. Unfortunately, Jacobs caught fire in the process.[21]

Salisbury now stood alone in first place with Cambridge, Milford, and Dover in a virtual tie for a close second. Even Easton was only three games back with a mathematical chance. In the end, Salisbury won their second pennant and faced off against the trailers in the playoffs. Cambria managed to get Comellas back on the Indians roster for the stretch run, then beat Milford in the first round and went on to take both the pennant and the championship. The last game was before a capacity crowd of 4,000 in Cambridge. Manager Joe Davis and his wife were presented with wristwatches by the Cambridge fans. Jake Flowers was given a gold watch by league president Harry Russell, while the Indian fans collected $200 which was disbursed among the 17 players who had appeared for Salisbury. When the all-star team was posted, Murtaugh was at short and Jake Flowers was manager, but league-leading hitter Sid Gordon was inexplicably left off the team. When the official statistics were finally posted, Milford Giant Sid Gordon hit .352, with Cambridge infielder Danny Murtaugh fourth at .312. It was anticipated that 24 players out of the league would be promoted.[22]

16

Secret Deal

Salisbury had forfeited all those wins the year before, and now, there was the "Secret Deal," or the "Hidden Sale," that once again had the Eastern Shore League in national sports headlines. The antics of the local moguls always seemed to be on the desk of Judge Landis as he had to sort through yet another mess.

Doc Jacobs and Ernest C. Landgraf were the original Easton franchise holders of the Browns but the league had inexplicably failed to issue a formal franchise document of ownership. In June of 1937, shortly after the start of the season, Jacobs had reported Landgraf was no longer president of the club, and he had divested of his share. Attendance had been bad in '37 so Jacobs convinced the Easton Association to raise the $11,400 to rebuild Federal Park. Part of the deal was that Jacobs commit to a four-year lease with the requirement that he report any intent to transfer the club and give the association first option to buy the franchise. Jacobs represented himself on the lease as sole owner.

In February of 1938 league president Harry Russell wrote a letter to Daniel Henry, president of the Talbot Athletic Association, which stated, "I believe you have a fine man in the person of George Jacobs." By all appearances, he was, serving as coach in football, basketball, and baseball at Villanova University. Easton had a working agreement with the St. Louis Browns, and the team wore uniforms bearing the name. There were rumors of a sale, but no sale had been reported or filed. The rumors persisted through the 1938 league playoffs. Henry wrote a letter to the *Sporting News* on September 6. "I am anxious to obtain some information as to the records in organized baseball of George W. Jacobs and Lincoln Lenzi.... I would prefer to have my inquiry considered a private one."[1]

When Henry received the response, he notified the league. A letter from Russell revealed a league president reluctant to take any action. Easton learned enough from their inquiry that they wanted Jacobs out, and Henry wanted to raise the rent to do it. Russell did not want to "air" league business with a confrontation or open investigation that might make headlines. He preferred to work something out. Russell urged that the matter remain confidential. Henry was not satisfied. In November, Daniel Henry and Mayor Wrightson of Easton arranged to meet Commissioner Landis in Philadelphia.

Ongoing correspondence by letter, telegraph, and telephone began between Henry and Commissioner Landis. During the exchange Henry politely asked the commissioner for an autographed photograph to put on his desk with those

Aerial view of a game in progress at Federal Park in Easton, Maryland, in the late 1930s (courtesy Talbot Historical Society/H. Robins Hollyday).

The Easton Browns, 1937, before the "secret deal." Back row, far left, is the maligned Duke Landgraf. Beside him is Doc Jacobs. Back row, second from right, is future American League batting champion Mickey Vernon (courtesy Talbot County Historical Society).

of other famous personages he had met. Landis gladly complied, honored to be included in prominent pictorial company. The investigation lasted through November. The correspondence ended abruptly with a telegram dated November 30 telling Henry it was imperative he attend the National Association meeting in New Orleans when the decision would be announced. Then the story broke, and to Harry Russell's chagrin, the league's business made national headlines again.[2]

The investigation established that Jacobs had sold Brooklyn "all rights and title" to the franchise and contracts while holding an option to buy back the franchise, but not the players. None of this was reported to Henry and the Easton Athletic Association, Russell and the Eastern Shore League, or Bramham and the National Association, all in violation of the rules. The deal further stipulated any money received from player transactions would go straight to Jacobs, without reporting through proper channels. General manager Larry McPhail of the Dodgers characterized the arrangement in different terms. First of all, he claimed to be unaware of an option on the lease with the Easton Athletic Association. Then he explained that the deal was one of "straight employment," and that he had promised Jacobs all profits to be his salary. It was employment, not a purchase, he insisted, although he did not explain how the Brooklyn general manager became Jacob's boss without first purchasing the franchise. The St. Louis Browns, which were supposed to have a working agreement with Jacobs, seemed to have little to say as to what transpired.

Landis handed out his punishment. Larry McPhail of the Brooklyn Dodgers was fined $500 and Easton owner George Jacobs was suspended from organized baseball for three years. All players transferred in the transactions were declared outright free agents. In a letter Landis said he thought that Easton had been cheated. He had referred the matter of the franchise to the league directors, who allowed the Easton Athletic Association to buy the franchise for a nominal fee of $100. To Landis all of this seemed similar to a scheme McPhail had tried earlier of "leasing" into farm teams, which the commissioner had also thwarted. McPhail declared he did not need the money and that "the Easton arrangement proved unsatisfactory, anyway," so he appealed the ruling.[3]

Duke Landgraf had been implicated in the story even though he had been gone for over a year and was working for Kingsport, Tennessee, in the Appalachian League. He wrote to Henry that in the

> *Sporting News* official base ball newspaper quite some space was devoted to the mess created by Doc Jacobs. What riled me was that my name was so prominently mentioned. You know I had nothing to do with the 1938 club.... No man with any self respect could stay with that fellow. He double crossed me several times in the '37 season. He agreed to pay me for my half interest but never did so. We had assets at the end of the season.... The good people of Easton are lucky to get rid of that fellow and keep him out.... Mr. Henry I am going to ask you to please write to my associates at Kingsport Tenn. And tell them I was not connected with Easton in '38 and that I left Easton clean at the end of '37.[4]

The offseason was a busy one for the league. Organized baseball took a look at Rickey's "extensive farm," forcing him to reduce his operations from 33 to 25 teams for the 1939 season, while the Yankees were doing well with what was referred to as their "silent farm." Cambridge was one of the 25 teams that the Cardinals retained. The Philadelphia Phillies dumped the Centreville Colts, and the franchise was transferred to the Queen Anne's Sports Authority. What was referred to as a cushion fund of $2,500 was raised by local fans, refundable if the club made a profit from affiliation or attendance. Centreville worked out a deal with the Red Sox. Part of the paring of Rickey's system was that a hundred Cardinals players had been granted free agency. The Cambridge manager, twenty-four-year-old Joe Davis, was one of them, but he signed again with Rickey and was promoted to Portsmouth, Ohio. Fred Lucas was brought back to manage Cambridge, and Rabbit Powell was brought in to get Easton out of its "rut." Vincent Christy was still on the suspended list in March for punching Wisener in the eye the previous year.[5]

It took a special ruling from Judge Bramham that allowed Vic Keen as a player-manager on Salisbury without taking a roster spot. The aging pitcher declared, "I have a good game in me every 6 or 7 days." He had gone 9–2 for Pocomoke City in 1937. The Yankees wasted no time filling the void left by McPhail and Jacobs in Easton. New York vice president George Weiss came to town for the formal transfer of the franchise. They brought in H.M. Reilly as business manager. Groundskeeper Merkel of the Newark Bears came down to put in a new grass infield in the refurbished Federal Park, with new drainage and grading. In Federalsburg improvements included lockers and showers, umpire's quarters, an electric scoreboard, and a ladies' room.[6]

The Salisbury Ministerial Association had not gone away over the winter and kept Salisbury's feet to the fire. Legislation abolishing Maryland blue laws was waiting to be signed, but stalled on the reluctant governor's desk. The issue was scheduled to a vote by referendum on June 6. All other jurisdictions in the league agreed not to enforce the ordinances for the sake of their baseball. The league even passed a bylaw that failure to play a Sunday game would result in a $100 fine. Salisbury tried. The typical court fine levied on Salisbury for players and employees when they played on Sunday was around $90. But there did not seem to be "malicious intent" on the part of the Indians, so the fines were often reduced, and in at least one instance, when the judge was a former team scorekeeper, reduced to court costs. This, however, did not alleviate the inconvenience of time and money lost. Salisbury business manager M.L. Murphy went out on a limb and vouched for the conduct of the notoriously fractious hometown fans. Sunday sports were then voted down in the June referendum in a stunning upset at the polls. It was announced the next day that Salisbury would shift all Sunday games back to weekdays. As for the rest of the clubs, they would continue with their Sabbath ball, in spite of the referendum's results.[7]

For the third year, World War I veteran Arthur Ehlers, now living back in Baltimore, had held the Pocomoke City franchise. As an independent, it had struggled to provide quality baseball for the town. Now the Pocomoke team wasn't drawing 500 fans to the biggest home games. Ehlers was exploring other career options in scouting and administration for other organizations. Crisfield offered $1,500 for the ailing franchise, but Ehlers was looking for more. The league called a meeting to address the problem. Rather than take over the problem franchise, it decided to let Ehlers retain it, but all games would be played on the road. The team then became known as the Pocomoke City Orphans. Other clubs were reported "deep in the red." Some thought the league in danger of collapsing. When Ehlers was promised by fans that they would support the team better, he moved the club back to the fairgrounds for home games. Jake Flowers, who had failed to find a manager's job at a higher classification after two straight Class D pennants, was hired to take over in Pocomoke City and straighten out the club.[8]

Fighting and umpiring seemed to be of less concern for the season, but they were never far from a fan's mind. One columnist observed, "We realize this is a Class D league ... isn't there some way we can get better than Class Z umpiring?" Later he would offer, "Fans gripe about ball players: the ball players gripe about the umpires. Writers gripe about all of them." Continuing on the theme the journalist reported a Cambridge fan jumped up and yelled, "We wuz robbed!" on a close play at first base. League president Harry Russell was at the game and sitting nearby. The man turned to Russell. "That's the kind of umpiring we have in this league." Russell responded with an effective "That will cost you five bucks."[9]

Cambria didn't like the second division start his team stumbled to at the start of the '39 season, so he made a visit in June to evaluate his squad. Cambria complained of lack of public support and that the demanding fans expected .650 ball all the time. He brought in new players, and Salisbury climbed to within a sniff of first place before the formidable Federalsburg Athletics ran ahead of the rest of the league. Then the Eastern Shore League heard the roar of Landis once

Out at the plate in a cloud of dust. Centreville vs. Cambridge, 1941 (Donnie Davidson Collection, Dan Tabler photo).

again. He cracked down on Cambria, ordering him to return four players to the Senators for manipulating player contracts. Griffith was described as his "indirect boss," but the Senators' owner, speaking of Landis, made it clear that he was not involved. "He hasn't anything on me, and he won't have. I don't do things that way." On review, Landis agreed. Once the players were reassigned to his satisfaction, the matter was dropped.[10]

One of the lighter features of the season was the appearance of "Half Pint" Billy Hutt. A man of short physical stature, Hutt would participate in pregame warm-ups with a comedy routine. In one he was described as taking 80 steps to reach the base 90 feet away. A week later he was still warming up with the team and by July had his own downsized, left-handed catching glove and equipment. In August Laura D. Jefferson of the *Federalsburg Times* resigned her post as official baseball correspondent of the Eastern Shore League for the Associated Press and the Sunpapers, leaving the newspaper business entirely. Ralph Johnson replaced her.[11]

Easton had an ardent supporter in Nick Koste. He had been on the bus as a fan when Jacobs had ordered that it be driven into the river. He knew the players made little money and tried to help them out when he could. Future major league outfielder Bud Souchock recalled of Koste and the people of Easton, "The ball players would have starved if it hadn't been for Nick slipping us milk shakes and banana splits at the drug store.... I know that the way the fans treated us, invited us out was fantastic."[12]

In an effort to get his team out of the second division, Cambria brought Comellas back, his left hand recovered from a "nervous" injury of the previous year. While most of the league jockeyed for a playoff spot, Federalsburg ran away with first-place honors at 83–38. Six of their starters would make the major leagues: Ducky Detweiler, Gene Hermanski, Ron Northey, Joe Rullo, Elmer Valo, and Jack Wallaesa. Pitcher Les Hinkle dominated and set league marks when he pitched to a record of 27–6 in 282 innings with 309 strikeouts, completing 29 games with a 2.49 ERA. In the middle of the league pennant drive Connie Mack brought his Athletics "back to the bushes" for the third time to play an exhibition with his Class D farm league. It was agreed that Federalsburg could pick up a handful of league all-stars for the event. Mack's A's seemed to have little luck on the peninsula as the little A's took the big A's 6–2. Billy Hutt was brought in special from Salisbury to entertain the crowd.[13]

The teams jammed up for a Shaughnessy playoff spot were the Dover Orioles, Centreville Red Sox, Salisbury Indians, and the Cambridge Cardinals. The Shaughnessy was a new format out of the International League that did away with multiple elimination playoff rounds. The system seeded the first four teams with first playing fourth and second playing third in a single-game elimination round followed by a championship series.

As usual, not all teams played all the scheduled games in their season due to rainouts not made up. Salisbury, mere percentage points behind, appealed to the league to make up a game on a late off day. It was said a win would put the team in fourth place and the playoffs by a winning percentage of 0.000137. Russell ruled

Many major league players came to hunt, or just visit with their friends from the Eastern Shore, during the offseason. From left, Jimmie Foxx, Eddie Collins, and "Home Run" Baker pose in downtown Easton, c. 1939 (courtesy Talbot County Historical Society).

against it. Salisbury had ample time to make up the game previously, so the final standings were approved by the league. Salisbury congratulated manager Spud Narchard for bringing the team within "eight thousandths of a point" of the playoffs. Dover surprised Federalsburg in the first round and Cambridge beat Centreville. Cambridge won the final series. A total of 344 players circulated through the league during the season. Cambria and the Indians went through 50, and the Pocomoke Orphans and the Federalsburg A's 47 each. Easton went through 46, Milford 41, Dover 39, Cambridge 35, and Centreville only 33.[14]

The offseason was busy. The Dover Orioles shook up their front office, naming Ms. Jack Dunn president and eliminating the general manager's position. Longtime Oriole Tommy Thomas was named to manage. At least two offers were reported for the team, one from Cal Griffith on behalf of the Senators. The Yankees were disappointed with Easton. The town had no intention of taking over any further monetary responsibility. New York had been responsible for everything but the ballpark, but they had brought in their people to make the park "one of the finest ball orchards." Arthur Ehlers turned down an offer for his franchise in Pocomoke City as being short of his asking price. Ehlers then sold it to J.R. Eddington, described as a Federalsburg native and chicken magnate, and now owner of Reading of the Interstate League. He intended to use Pocomoke City as a farm team for Reading. He and Ehlers would run the team jointly.[15]

16. Secret Deal

Landis did not find anything on Cambria during the season, but he did afterwards. It was reported that 11 Indians were declared free agents for mishandled contracts, throwing a "monkey wrench" into the '40 season's plans. Then it was reported that Cambria was to lose the services of eight players, two from Salisbury, none of whom could sign again with Cambria for three years. Bramham announced a crackdown on these "fake contracts." The league was further stunned when Landis and company assessed Salisbury with a fine of $1,000 for using a blank contract, and an additional $500 for postdating another. Seven more players were declared free agents.[16]

It was now announced in the press that the 41 minor leagues had set yet a new attendance record of 18.5 million. That was three million more than the previous year. The Depression was ending. Seventh-place Easton led the league when it sent 32,000 fans through the turnstiles. Salisbury drew 23,000, and Federalsburg attracted 27,000 in winning the pennant by 14 games. Dover drew 23,500, Centreville 21,000, Milford 19,000, and the Pocomoke City Orphans 12,000. In the Eastern Shore League even the top drawer averaged less than 600 a game. The lowly Orphans barely averaged 200 a home game.[17]

17

Fog, Tomatoes, and Rabbits

Landis remained on his war horse to start the new year, riding rampant through the minor league systems along with Bramham. Rickey was ordered to withdraw from his present working agreement with Cambridge. Left with only five players, owner and former Coca-Cola sponsor Joseph Fowler put his franchise up for sale. Landis then went after the Detroit Tigers, awarding 93 players free agency for "fake agreements" and "cover up" deals. He warned that he had other clubs in his sights. It was in the dead of winter that Landis issued his letter that some referred to as the "7 point manifesto" on the minor leagues. Larry McPhail's response, showing he was still smarting from getting caught in the Secret Deal, was to call Landis a "bush leaguer." McPhail was armed with a letter from 15 minor league presidents declaring something had to be done to stop the commissioner. The Landis manifesto was said to threaten to wipe out nine farm systems and 100 working agreements in what was becoming known as the "Detroit decision." To the old school, unaffiliated-prone Landis, something did have to be done. In 1933 there had been 13 minor leagues and 3,501 player contracts. Through the combination of an improving economy and affiliation run rampant, in seven short years there were now 41 minor leagues and 13,154 player contracts. Landis always seemed to try and prevent the indefinite "careers of bondage" of minor league players. In the spirit of working out a solution, Landis conceded two of his seven points. In a heated February meeting it was revealed that the minor leagues classes B, C and D had outdrawn the major leagues, and their continued health was vital to organized baseball. Landis conceded two more points of his manifesto to get an agreement. The main sticking point was how long a major league team could hold the option on a player.[1]

For 1940 the Eastern Shore League set a 126-game schedule. Twenty-man rosters were allowed for the first 20 days, when they had to be pared to 15.

Many players were being signed from the semipro teams of the smaller Eastern Shore towns and leagues. At times there were as many as five thriving semipro and amateur leagues on the peninsula in addition to the minor league. The team from Ocean City won all 23 of its games that year, but most teams played far more. These little communities often drew crowds greater than the larger towns in the league attracted. Every little community had its own gala opening day parade.

Pocomoke City, no longer Orphans, were now the Chicks, named for the mass chicken farming taking hold on the peninsula, and where franchise co-owner Eddington had made his money. Eddington sent the Chicks pitcher/outfielder Carl Furillo on assignment from Reading. Jorge Comellas, one of the heroes of the Wonder Club, was back with Salisbury, still nursing his "nervous" injury. The previous year the curveballer had to rub his arm down with liniment and a wire brush, but he felt he had another 20-win season in it. Prospect Gene Hermanski was back and six of the eight league managers were catchers.

Many fans now complained of games taking 2¼ to 2½ hours. Often the second game of a twi-night doubleheader could not be completed before curfew. Someone complained that one inning took 20 minutes followed by one that took 18. Something had to be done. Players were slow getting on and off the field between innings and the umpires needed to speed things up. The main reason for the slowdown was that there were too many "confabs" and "rhubarbs." One visiting metropolitan sports scribe referred to the Eastern Shore League as "camp meeting baseball," and as usual, the men in blue took the blame for it.[2]

Hanson Horsey and George Ekaitis were two returning umpires, but familiarity bred contempt. A game in Salisbury was played in a "dismal fog" where many fly balls were lost until they hit the ground. A Milford player held up the proceedings with a 10-minute argument and would not leave until the umpire called in the police. Russell suspended the player for five days. Umpire Bock thought the manager should be fined $25 as well for "pushing and shoving" him all over the field. Whether it was the fog or a blind eye, officials at Gordy Park denied the shoving incident as described, and press box observers did not see why the player had been ejected from the game in the first place.[3]

It was not always the umpires in the middle of an incident. In Salisbury a fan at an extra-inning game offered $5 to the player with the winning hit. When it happened, the fan ran for the clubhouse and handed the "kid" $2.50. Whether just excited or inebriated, the fan realized he had the wrong clubhouse and the wrong man. The Centreville player, backed by his teammates, had no intention of returning the money and told the man to get out. Salisbury business manager M.L. Murphy and manager Brittain had no luck trying to get the money back either. Murphy then called in the police to settle the matter.[4]

Sometimes it wasn't even people that caused the problem. Hans Horsey stopped a game in Milford when rabbits took over the outfield. An "ambitious farmer" yelled out from his seat, "Wait five minutes till I go home and get my twelve gauge and I'll shoot 'em for you." Some spectators, less patient, or more animal friendly, jumped from the stands and chased them back under the fence. That must have relieved Horsey, since usually when fans jumped from their seats they were chasing him.[5]

Not every umpire had rabbits for cover. Salisbury had a "family night" against the Dover Orioles where children under 16 could get in free with an adult. In the ninth inning the crowd had enough of umpire Bushman's balls and strikes and stormed the field in what was described as a "miniature riot." Bushman had to be escorted off the grounds by police. It was not reported how many in the riot were accompanied by an adult. Sometimes the fans just knew they were going to get angry before they got there and came prepared. One night Easton fans brought baskets of tomatoes to a doubleheader during which they hurled their red projectiles at the umpires with every adverse decision throughout the first game. Nobody thought to confiscate them. When it came time for the second game, umpire LeCompte saw the baskets weren't empty yet, and he had been pelted enough, so he "refused to brave another shower" in the nightcap. He left his partner to face the onslaught alone in the second contest.[6]

In a game between the Salisbury Indians and the Cambridge Cardinals, there is a rare report of players standing up for the umpires:

> Besides the ball game several members of the Tribe and the Cards went to the rescue of umpires Hanson Horsey and William Connelly when Cambridge fans, angered by a decision on the bases earlier in the game, and bearing a grudge, swarmed onto the field at the end of the contest, The arbiters, surrounded by a ring of Cambridge players, made their way to the exits and finally escaped without serious injury. It was reported by observers that Connelly was kicked about the leg in the melee.[7]

This is not to imply that such treatment of umpires was unique to the Eastern Shore. Harry "Steamboat" Johnson was a 55-year-old veteran arbiter with 38 years of experience, with one of those in the National League. Johnson estimated he had been hit by 25 bottles in his career. One, when he was working in the Western Association, required 17 stitches over his right eye, "I know how pop bottles sound whistling through the air," he explained, "and I know how they sound crashing near you. I know how they look coming straight at you and I know how they feel when they land on your head." Johnson had called over 5,000 games in his career and got a certificate every year validating his eyesight.[8]

The Dover Orioles took first place in a well-contested race over the Centreville Red Sox, Milford Giants, and Salisbury. Of the 12 leading pitchers in the 126-game schedule, six logged more than 200 innings, and three others had more than 190. Carl Furillo and Hermanski showed well offensively with the last place Pocomoke City Chicks, but Furillo was sent to the Cambridge Cardinals towards the end of the season, where they tried his strong arm from the pitching mound. Neither Furillo nor Hermanski could crack the season-ending all-star team. Furillo and the departed Mickey Vernon would win the batting titles of their respective major leagues in 1953.

Salisbury won their third pennant in four years. Before they even got there, Cambria was talking vaguely of a "big surprise." He wanted to see more fans in the seats. "I won't take a worse beating than I've gotten now." Cambria did not reveal his scheme but promised "faster ball." It was rumored he had his eye on moving Salisbury into the Class B Interstate League because attendance had dropped to the level of "sandlots." Cambria continued to talk in riddles, speaking of a "mutual cooperation proposition" and "You help me out this time, and I'll help you next." Then the Salisbury players went out on strike during the playoffs. The issue was salaries, and Murphy made it clear that league rules did not permit players being paid for the postseason. With Poke Whalen no longer at his side, Cambria was considered the Senators' one-man scouting staff. This would bring a new set of headaches to the Salisbury fans.[9]

Cambria's mysterious statements may reflect that he knew he could not be a major league scout and a minor league owner at the same time. It was soon announced that he had sold the club to Reuben Levin of Bennington, Vermont, and opted to be a scout. Levin was an attorney who had graduated from Cornell and Maine. He was 44 years old and a father of seven. Levin had owned the Bennington team in the independent Northern League, where he had shipped players to Cambria for years. His timing might have been better. The Eastern Shore League seemed to be in flux. League attendance was down by 40 percent.[10]

No franchise seemed safe. The Yankees were rumored to be parting ways with Easton. Former Coca-Cola sponsor Joe Fowler was actively trying to sell his Cambridge franchise, and Federalsburg chicken magnate J.R. Eddington was already trying to divest himself of the Chicks, while his partner, Arthur Ehlers, was angling for a position with the Interstate League. Herb Pennock said he had no agreement with Centreville yet, but they would be back if the league survived. To make matters worse, Landis declared Hermanski a free agent, so Eddington was trying to get his money back from Federalsburg, from whom he had purchased the contract.[11]

Many fingers were pointed at Russell for the league's financial condition. Certain disgruntled owners offered Dr. W.K. Knotts of Federalsburg as an alternative. A league meeting ended in a deadlock, leaving Russell in charge.[12]

The major Negro Leagues were in their prime in the mid- and late 1930s with regional franchises in Baltimore, Washington, and Philadelphia. As was the custom, the Negro Leaguers played exhibitions in their regions for extra money. Their proximity to the peninsula and the perception of the area as a hotbed for baseball drew these teams to the Shore. In 1939 the *Salisbury Times* printed an announcement that the colored baseball stars were to play in Salisbury:

> Supremacy in the negro baseball world will be sought in two games on the shore when the Philadelphia Giants of the Negro American League will cross bats with the Baltimore Black Sox of the Negro National League, tonight and tomorrow night.
> The first game will be held at Gordy Park at 8:15 o'clock and tomorrow night in Federalsburg. Championship will be determined by these games.

In a year when there was no official world series between the two Negro major leagues, these games were presented to the local fans as the Negro Leagues championship with the title being determined in the game in Federalsburg. The problem was that the Baltimore entry in the Negro Leagues was now the Elite Giants and there was no Philadelphia Giants in the league. How much of this report was in error, and how much was hype is yet to be found.[13]

From 1939 through 1941 several of the best Negro Leagues teams played on the Shore. They included the New York Eagles and the New York Black Yankees, the Newark Eagles, Baltimore Elite Giants and the Philadelphia Stars. Those rosters included future National Baseball Hall of Fame inductees Jud Wilson, Oscar Charleston, Leon Day, Biz Mackey, Mule Suttles, Monte Irvin and Satchel Paige. A game between the Newark Eagles and the Elite Giants in Salisbury in 1939 included the raising of the Elite Giant 1938 championship pennant. This series of games may have been arranged through Joe Cambria and his former connections as a Negro Leagues owner.

Cambria was born in Italy, and like Fong and Maud Nelson before him, fell in love with baseball and found it the quickest way to assimilate into American culture. He made good with the Baltimore Bugle Coat, Tie and Apron Company, and owned Bugle Field, which was one of the better playing facilities available to black teams in the city. For a time he owned the Baltimore Black Sox and sponsored exhibitions at Bugle Field. It was through his connections with the Negro Leagues that Cambria learned of the talent pipeline with Cuba, but Joe was looking for Hispanic players with enough Iberian blood to fill the white rosters of his minor league teams, including the Salisbury Indians in 1937. Those connections may have led to some of the best Negro Leagues baseball in the country to be played on the Eastern Shore. It was known that the star players on these teams would attract not only black fans, but white fans too given the opportunity to see the star players. That these events were popular is suggested by an advertisement for admission at 40 cents and box seats for 65 when the New York Eagles squared off against the Black Yankees. The prices were only slightly less than those for Shore minor league games.[14]

Through the 1930s many black Americans were still struggling financially. Many followed the old Underground Railroad to jobs and schools in the Philadelphia area and other points north. They often mailed money home to their families. This migration may have resulted in a drain of the player pool as the Bi State/Tri County League standings disappeared from the pages of the *Afro-American*. When the Baltimore Elite Giants thrashed the Newark Eagles in Salisbury, it drew 500 fans.

Most local black teams cobbled together resources where they could. The Church Hill Red Sox adopted that name when a disbanded team from the Class D minor leagues donated their old uniforms. When those threads were worn bare, Church Hill reverted to the name of the Hawks. Ralph Deaton was a player on these teams and his father helped sponsor the club. He owned the Country Boys Inn and supplied most of the team's equipment. The inn had an outdoor beer garden, and every game day the benches from the garden were loaded on the back of a truck and carted to the game for the spectators. When Linwood Baines began playing for the St. Michaels Red Sox in 1957 he noted, "We were still a black league; it was still segregated." And in a familiar refrain he said, "We played on Sundays and holidays. It always drew a big crowd because there was nothing else to do so everybody flocked to the baseball game after church." St. Michaels had two white players and according to Baines, "We didn't bar anybody from the league. If the white players wanted to play, we let them. We just wanted to play baseball." The black Eastern Shore League lasted through segregation of the 1960s and did not fold until 1979.[15]

18

Be Careful What You Wish For

Things started to settle for the league during the winter. Russell narrowly won his fourth term as league president at a January meeting. Federalsburg found a working agreement with the Wilmington Blue Rocks of the Athletics farm system. Joe Fowler brought in Rickey disciple and former Eastern Shore League veteran Fred Lucas as a franchise partner in Cambridge. Eddington found a buyer for his Reading team, and eventually, Pocomoke City. The Yankees threatened to part ways with Easton, so the stockholders brought in Frank Baker as president for credibility and to sell $3,000 of stock at $10 a share to convince the Yankees to stay. Ehlers, who had run Pocomoke City for Eddington, was selected vice president and treasurer of the Interstate League. The Centreville Red Sox reached an agreement with Greensboro of North Carolina in the Piedmont League. Reuben Levin, operating as an independent owner, was excited about purchasing the Salisbury franchise for $2,000 with a $1,800 per annum five-year lease on Gordy Park:

> In 1937 I picked up a sports newspaper and read about the Salisbury wonder team of minor league baseball. I read how the Salisbury Indians, after being pushed down in last place midway the season arose again to take the championship. Baseball fans in Salisbury were daffy; everybody was a fan and attendance records for Class D cities were set. I said to myself then, "What a baseball town, Boy! How I'd like to own a team in a town like that." And now I do own it, it's just one of those things we dream of but seldom realize.

Levin discovered that Salisbury might not be the baseball town it once was. The Ministerial Association in Salisbury continued its relentless attack of Sunday baseball in the dead of winter. Under the headline "Pastors Fight Sunday Baseball, Opposed in Sermons Here," Pastor Fox expounded that baseball patrons were the "enemies of a vital force in our nation," and they were behind an "attempt to break the historic American Christian Sunday."[1]

Levin, more of a fan than an owner, wanted the fans to run the team. He had done that in Manchester, Vermont, and was once fined by his own fans. He now arranged meetings with Salisbury boosters to that effect. Levin then called a second meeting of 75 to 100 boosters and it was agreed the fans would have a say in running the team. Independent baseball remained active throughout the peninsula. The MarDel League on the northern peninsula was composed of three Maryland and three Delaware semipro teams and was just one of the many leagues and independent teams looking to compete with Levin in the Class D league. In any town on any given day one could find a quality, well-attended baseball game.[2]

Easton wooed the Yankees back with the best attendance in the league despite second-division finishes. Dover and Pocomoke City were out, with 10 of the Chicks players declared free agents. Six umpires were named, with Hans Horsey and George Ekaitis the familiar faces. It was now a six-team league playing 110 games. Rickey was being touted as the "daddy" of the "farm chain." It was noted that the best way to the big leagues was the Cardinals system, where 60 current major leaguers had begun their careers. This was more than any other system. Rickey, seemingly under constant scrutiny from Landis, was proud of his accomplishments and explained his strategy: "The chain saved the minors and thereby saved baseball. We carried them through the depression. And when we go into a league we don't look for the best team, but the best strategic one—the one that 'carries' the league. We help the players give the fans better baseball and help the minor leagues, and people point the finger of scorn at us." Of Levin it was observed, "At the moment he's having his big long-dreamed-of fling in baseball and seems to be getting a whole lot of fun out of it." With the return of Bill Hutt as clown prince of the league, things seemed to be shaping up for a fun, exciting season. Levin contracted with WBOC radio to broadcast home games.[3]

The former business manager at Pocomoke City, Fred Herring, took a job with London, Ontario, of the Pony League. He was 30 years old and a native of Washington, D.C., and bemoaned the lack of an organized team in Pocomoke City: "This is a good baseball town. And if you put a good team down here, the fans would support it. The big trouble has been Pocomoke in three years finished last three times. The fans get sick of that stuff year after year." With the league streamlined to six teams, most agreed the season would be pivotal to the league's survival. Russell remained optimistic. "As far as the league itself is concerned, we are in excellent shape and ready for the best season since the league was organized in 1937. But the action of the farms will make or break the year." Russell did admit that this was the last year if the league was not supported by the fans. The big advantage during the 1930s had been the introduction of night baseball. But the league also had to stop the constant arguing between umpires and players. "The fans don't like that stuff"—then he qualified the statement—"unless some fists are thrown in for good measure. And that is dangerous." Pastor Fox felt he had good reason for his crusade.[4]

Less than a month into the 1941 schedule Milford was 23–4 with the two closest competitors at 13–13. Salisbury's manager was conscripted into the armed services during the season as the general draft had been implemented the year before in anticipation of war. Fortunately for the league, the draft age at the time was older than that of the many teenaged players. As much as Levin promised to let the fans run the club, he seemed to have a difficult time letting them do that. It reached the point where Levin had to be phoned in Vermont to okay calling a rainout in Salisbury. On another occasion Levin pulled into Gordy Park on a rainy night after his 600-mile drive and insisted the game be played for the 25 fans who had braved the elements. It cost him $200 to play the game. He promised to move his family to Salisbury, but continued to commute between the two states, tracking his teams in Vermont and Maryland. So much for the fans running the team. Salisbury was the first to be hit by lagging attendance. By the end of June Levin had already lost $5,000 and slashed his prices in an effort to sell 25,000 tickets. He was selling strips of 10 for $2.50.[5]

The country was six months from Pearl Harbor, but it was more than the draft that had people on a war footing. There was already a silk shortage for the making of parachutes for use overseas. A gasoline "curfew" was already in effect. Observation towers would be erected on the Maryland and Delaware beaches, and the shorelines patrolled for the landing of spies. The war felt pretty close to home.

The peninsula sportswriters selected an all-star team, managed by Tom Kibler, which played at midseason against league-leading Milford before 2,000 fans at Cambridge. Ed Nichols of the *Salisbury Daily Times* alluded to some justification of players' and fans' opinions of umpires. He noted that league umpire Jambeau never looked at the plate when calling balls and strikes. "You see it, but you don't see it," Jambeau explained. Diminutive lefty Tommy Boland paced the streaking Milford Giants with 18 straight wins to start the season before returning to reality. Cambridge was the only other team out of the six to be playing .500 ball.[6]

Not making that all-star team was Centreville Red Sox pitcher and future Boston starter Mel Parnell. It appeared that the young lefty was singing his way to the big leagues. His catcher Stu Hoskins would croon love songs behind the plate during the game, entertaining or annoying the umpire, opposing players, and nearby fans. When a batter went for a bad pitch, Parnell would chime in his own refrain from the mound, "I love you truly."[7]

At the end of July, Indians fans showed up at Gordy Park only to find it padlocked. They acted immediately to "Rescue Indians from Sheriff." Levin owed $230 and all equipment had been hauled to the courthouse. Two fans came forward to vouch for the bill and allow the night's game to be played. A suit had been filed in circuit court asking $500 in damages. The club secretary then sued for back pay, and Ms. Charlotte Cambria sought $600 for park rental. Creditors went as far as to go after Levin's car, but it was registered in his wife's name. Then they went after a bat, three balls and the uniforms, but the players refused to give them up. A Salisbury judge placed the franchise in receivership and appointed two local attorneys to the job.[8]

It was "finish-out-the-season-or-bust" at this point for Salisbury. The team was flat broke and free admission was announced for the coming game. Businesses pitched in $140 to keep things going. The money went for balls, the light bill, gas for the bus, and food for the players. "We're going to try and get along on what we have," one receiver said. "We'll give the players as much as we can so they can get something to eat. But it's going to be a tight squeeze.... If it rains tonight," he moaned, "we don't know how we'll get through." The hungry players were not praying for rain. More than a thousand "full throated" fans turned out to support their Indians. Levin was in Vermont for the funeral of his mother. One court-appointed representative was as much the Indians fan as he was the court-appointed receiver. He made two phone calls to Centreville for updates on the game, and his long-distance "rooting" cost him $1.05.[9]

Milford stumbled down the stretch, but their lead was too big to catch. Cambridge, Centreville, and Easton made it over .500 and to the playoffs. Milford and Easton made it to the championship series, and the seven-game series drew 14,000 fans as Easton took the playoff honors. Each Milford player, mascot Snowball Hill, and the groundskeeper received envelopes of cash, and manager Gruber got a wristwatch. Easton fans released several hundred dollars to the players, and traveling bags for the manager and Ms. Warren, a much valued gift for a Class D league manager. Easton booster James N. Bennet treated the team to a beefsteak dinner.[10]

It had taken the seven-game championship series between Milford and Easton for those teams to realize a profit, the only two in the league to do so. Still, Russell announced that the league was in good shape. Salisbury was a different story. Bills of $2,500 to $3,000 needed to be settled before Salisbury could be readmitted; $1,800 of that was in player salaries. They needed major league backing. The Salisbury team went barnstorming to try and raise some money.[11]

Salisbury became the "Phantom Franchise." The league discharged the receivers after the league voted to vacate the franchise. The receivers and local boosters called it "unfair." Joe Cambria was back and claimed rights to the franchise, since Levin had defaulted. Cambria's potential return did not sit well with the board. Russell explained, "The league directors have been dissatisfied with the way the Salisbury Club has been operated the last two years. We took up the franchise in order to put it in other hands." It was rumored Branch Rickey, now working for Brooklyn, might move into Salisbury.[12]

Even after Pearl Harbor there was some talk of continuing the league, but the full scope of the war effort had not sunk in yet, and the draft did not help the future of the league. In time it was realized it was best to put the league on hold.

In 1938, 30 players were promoted out of the league and another 44 in 1941. It was noted that since 1937 the Eastern Shore League had sent 150 players to a higher class. Art Gunning caught for the Milford team for three years, married a local girl and stayed put. He thought the league was equal to a modern AAA team. Elmer Valo hit .374 for Federalsburg in 1939, and was speaking as a 10-year veteran in the middle of a twenty-year major league career when he said of the second incarnation of the Eastern Shore League, "I never found such spirit during my 10 years of baseball as I did during my one year of play in the Shore league. Sure, you read where there is 30,000 fans in the stands, but the game is soon forgotten when the last man is out. These Eastern Shore towns play each game over and over the next day. These people take defeat as a bitter dose." Even umpires, as harassed, beleaguered, and pummeled as they were, attested to the quality of the league.[13]

With short rosters, league leaders put up big numbers. Leading pitchers often won 20 games and pitched more than 200 innings. Hitters also posted good numbers, relative to the length of the schedules. There were no future Hall of Fame selections on these rosters but plenty of solid major league players. (See Appendix B.)

Part IV

G.I. Jitters

19

Will Greenville Yield?

> There was a time when the village boasted three baseball teams—the big nine, the second club, and the little fellows hardly out of their pinafores.
> At every cross-road and in the cow pastures one could see ball games being played, marked by bitter rivalry between the contestants. Now, in most instances, baseball is as dead as a herring in the corner grocery.
>
> —Ed Nichols, "Shore Sports,"
> *Salisbury Daily Times*, January 28, 1946

Gas rationing during the war put a serious dent into baseball activities. Trips to towns up and down the peninsula were restricted to necessity by the scarcity of fuel. Such ventures for entertainment were out of the question. There was a booming black market in every community for commodities like chickens, eggs, meats, flour, sugar, silk, and gasoline. Like many another time and place, there were Eastern Shoremen who profited from the war while others died or came home physically or mentally scarred. More than 4,000 Marylanders died while in service during the war, 400 from the Eastern Shore. The war affected the lives of everyone, whether in the armed services or not. People were anxious to get back to normalcy. The shipyards of Baltimore had drawn workers for war production. Natives and nonnatives flocked to the port, and then many came to the Eastern Shore after the conflict, anticipating opportunity once the Chesapeake Bay Bridge was built. Houses sprung up in the adjacent farms and fields around these small towns and villages. In these postwar melting pots, able seamen did business on an equal footing with ex-colonels and privates with commodores. The common denominator was all had lived through the depression, and most served in the armed forces or in war-related industries. So determined was everybody to put those years behind them and get on with their lives that a nurse who cared for more than 10,000 casualties in a 200-bed field hospital in Europe attended the same church every Sunday as an ex-navy fighter pilot. It wasn't until more than 70 years later that each learned what the other did during war.

The Central Shore League based on the lower peninsula kept baseball alive during the war using the old concept of Salisbury as the hub of the wheel. This had proven a dependable model on several occasions. Several communities were close enough to scoot a few miles down the road for baseball. The players were either too young, too old, or too something to be in the armed services. When the war did end and the boys started coming home, and rationing gradually lifted, everybody was more than ready for baseball.

Among the many were Dr. W.K. Knotts of Federalsburg, John Perry of Centreville, Dr. Walter Grier of Milford, and Tom Kibler of Chestertown. All had been active leaders in past leagues. Added to this mix was Fred Lucas of Cambridge. Baseball had brought Lucas to the Shore as a player, manager and owner in previous incarnations of the league. He married and settled in Cambridge to raise a family. Rickey was the acknowledged expert of the modern farm system, and Lucas surmised that if he could get his old boss Rickey to commit to coming to the Shore, others would follow to help get the Eastern Shore League back on its feet. If Rickey built it, they would come.

It helped that Rickey bought a farm near Chestertown in 1944 for his "peace of mind," and where he kept up his friendship with Kibler from their earlier years in the Midwest. Rickey took to the Eastern Shore life, and loved the many outdoor activities indigenous to it. Fred Lucas used this to his advantage, inviting Mr. and Ms. Rickey on a fishing trip. Fortunately, Ms. Rickey caught the first of 96 hardheads, a favorite eating fish of many local anglers. Every one of the fish was packed on ice and put on the refrigerator car for shipping to their main house in Brooklyn. But Rickey did not commit and Lucas still had work to do. When winter rolled around, he arranged a duck-hunting trip on Hoopers Island. Rickey bagged the only bird, but the idle time provided Lucas the chance for some duck-blind chatter. It took 96 fish, one duck, and a little bull to convince Rickey to build a new ballpark in Cambridge. Even if they did not form a league it could at least be used as a training and tryout facility. With Rickey on the line as live bait, the rest of the major leagues were sure to school up and follow. Kibler being an old friend and Chestertown neighbor did not hurt the cause either. Kibler returned as president of the league.[1]

In February 1946 parks were already being built or remodeled, and negotiations started for affiliation with major league teams. At the league meeting in Milford, Delaware, Connie Mack was named president of Federalsburg, with sons Roy and Earle filling the other offices. By April it was said major league clubs had pumped $120,000 into local ballparks. Improvements included new lighting systems with aluminum reflectors, "deluxe" ladies' rooms, better press boxes, umpire rooms, and covered seats and backrests. Centreville corralled the minor league Orioles as their parent club. The Yankees returned to Easton as did the Cardinals to Salisbury and the A's to Federalsburg, Red Sox to Milford, and the Phillies to Dover. It was just like old times. Only Seaford went independent with Baltimore native Walter Youse at the helm. The St. Louis Cardinals were even willing to pay off the five-year-old lien of $988.15 left over from the '41 season to clear the Salisbury franchise for the coming 126-game schedule.[2]

There were now 51 minor leagues throughout the country and 20 of them were Class D. The thirty-three-year-old Chuck Wamsley, a native New Englander with previous experience with the Cardinals at Class B, Allentown, Pennsylvania, and AA, Columbus, Georgia, took the job of business manager in Salisbury

Tom Kibler (left) and Fred Lucas talking baseball, c. 1938. Both were Branch Rickey protégés, Kibler starting in the 1910s and Lucas in the 1920s. Both maintained lifelong friendships with Rickey, and both served as president of the Eastern Shore League (author's collection).

and made it clear, "No, this assignment is not a demotion, I requested it. I wanted to have my wife and family with me this year and was advised this location was one of the most progressive communities in organized baseball." Sportswriter Ed Nichols expressed the tenor of the coming season, "The typical Class D rookie is usually a rip-muscled kid, busting with ambition—a Yankee-Doodle-Dandy, who figures he can out-play, out-holler, out-fight, anybody, anyplace, anytime." Everybody was ready when spring came.[3]

The Central Shore League beat the resurrected Eastern Shore League to opening night with more than 6,000 fans attending their slate of games. Even many of the amateurs and semipro leagues featured lit fields now, but because of the war the country was plagued by a coal shortage. Four of the Eastern Shore League towns imposed brownouts, which meant no night baseball in those places. There were opening day parades and large crowds that continued through the '46 season. Crowds well above a thousand were common, and 2,000 not unusual. The amateurs and semipro leagues consisted of more than 30 teams peninsula-wide and all these small towns were drawing significant crowds. This did not count community teams playing independent of any league or association. The coal shortage was short-lived and everyone was soon back to night ball.

The small town of Centreville became the story of the season as little Parksley had been 20 years earlier. With a meager population of 1,114, its team drew as well as most teams in the league and by July was playing over .700 ball. It wasn't long before Centreville fans were calling themselves "Baseball Town U.S.A." Jack Dunn III was from the Baltimore family that owned the Orioles franchise. He attended Princeton and was a pilot during the war. He made the team in an unusual dual role of utility player and club president. Before the season was over he had filled in as starting catcher when that player was suspended, managed for two weeks when the skipper went in the hospital, and was the groundskeeper when that employee was out for an extended illness. And he washed the uniforms. Dunn then added security to his resume when, after being ejected from a game as a player, he, as team president, had to ignominiously help escort the responsible umpire off the grounds in order to protect him from the angry crowd he had just incited. In his early twenties, Dunn learned about every aspect of the baseball business in one season.

Centreville, if smaller than other towns in the league, was typical in its relationship to its team. Mrs. C.P. Ivins housed several of the young players. After the war, meat was scarcer than coal, but when she went shopping for the boys, the butcher always supplied only the best cuts of meat. Financial incentives to the players were common, and merchants routinely offered prizes of $5 or $10 for home runs or other game-winning feats. In big games the fans often spontaneously raised a kitty. Many of the Centreville fans were farmers with dairy cows. A game with the Milford Red Sox was tied 1–1 and going to extra innings. The exuberant home-fan farmers challenged each other around the intimate-sized stands, and as the kitty grew, the players could hear it. When Bunky Langgood finally knocked an inside-the-park solo home run in the bottom of the 11th inning to win the game, he collected his prize of $100 in cash and 64 quarts of milk. He effectively doubled his monthly salary with one swing of the bat.[4]

Hans Horsey was back as chief of umpires, and when the Baltimore Orioles cut outfielder Jim Honochick, he was hired to the staff, most of whom were now graduates of the Bill McGowan School of Umpires, where Horsey worked in the offseason. Loved in local baseball circles, Horsey was a "nice guy as far as umpires go" and was known as the Squire of Millington. But the squire could be gruff with players and fans alike. One night during the '46 season, Dick Waldt was pitching

The Centreville Orioles, 1946. While Jack Dunn III scrambled to keep things going, the Orioles kept winning, drawing 52,000. Local reporter Dan Tabler promoted the team, the town, and its fever season, and the national press soon saw little Centreville as Baseball Town U.S.A. Top row, from left: Don Smith, Mike Gast, Stan Coulling, George "Red" Cave, Alvin Heuser, Dick Waldt; middle row, from left: Don Marino, Nick Malfara, Dru Schupp, Jim McLeod (manager), Jack Dunn III, Fred Pacitto, Bunky Langgood; bottom row, from left: Lou Isert, James Stevens, Frank Thalheimer, Bill Dornbusch, Chuck Price, Ray Hilton. Bat boy unidentified (courtesy Eastern Shore Hall of Fame).

for Centreville and yelled to Horsey, "You're having a pretty good night, Hans. You missed only two on the last hitter." Horsey glared back. "Miss that junk you throw?" He bellowed, "Anytime I can't count the stitches on your fastball I'll give up. Why, when you pitch I shut one eye just to rest it and work the other one." An older story was when he turned to the scorekeeper in the grandstand for a lineup change and a heckling fan asked who was umpiring the game. The squire's retort, "You are, but I'm getting paid for it."[5]

The Eastern Shore League was considered a tough place to work, but a good place to learn for umpires. Nichols cited an unnamed umpire who knew "if you are lucky enough to endure two years in that league, you will be fully equipped to call 'em anywhere in the country." He then attempted to explain the irrational Eastern Shore fan,

> They are kindly, fatherly men who make good husbands and enjoy a laugh as much as the other fellow.

Some arbiters have asked "why do the people take the game so serious, it is a matter of life and death to some." Many large city newspapers have asked the same question, and have devoted numerous articles to the Peninsula fans' habitual heckling of the boys with the windpad and mask. They have been accused of drastic measures, ranging all the way from slashing tires of the umpire's cars to actual physical violence. Speaking as an Eastern Shoreman, the writer is not proud of these unsportsmanlike acts. However, on the other hand, we regret our metropolitan brothers do not understand the heart beat of the average Peninsula ball fanatic.

Well, the Delmarva Sector has been considered by many as the country's "hot-bed" of the National Pastime, and today is no different.... It is their blood, their favorite life line to recreation.... Eastern Shore addicts appear to derive more kick out of the game than do our big city friends. Summing it up, we are more rabid rooters.

There are approximately 70,000 people in the area covered by the eight-wheel circuit, all the teams averaging 700–1,000 nightly. That means everyone in the league-affiliated towns must attend a game once or twice a week. How can you match more loyalty in organized baseball?

Cambridge, current occupant of the cellar position, is near the top in league attendance at 40,000 with the season half over. The Rochester Red Wings, last year's tenants of the International League basement, only drew 77,000 patrons with a seventy-seven home game schedule. This in a population of 350,000 competing against a small Class D town of 10,000. Where else can you find such community spirit?

Centreville, considered the smallest town in organized baseball, has a population of 1,100 but has outdrawn that figure five times this season. Again, we point to the contrast of Peninsula baseball to that of large cities.

Although some of the umpires may disagree, the average Eastern Shore baseball fan is easily riled, but soon forgives. He is on the whole a gentle, patient, cheerful individual.[6]

A week later Nichols ate some crow when he had to report, "Disorder that reigned throughout the Eastern Shore League last night when three umpires needed police protection from several hundred angry rooters, can be traced to the office of the league president, the respective managers, and the fans themselves." He thought Kibler too patient, and that players, managers, and even front offices blamed every loss and adverse decision on the umpires, and purposely whipped fans into a frenzy. In the same issue, it was reported that Centreville outfielder Nick Malfara was subjected to a "glass bombardment." When manager Jimmy McLeod pointed the culprit out to the police, hoping to see the man escorted out before play resumed, he was told, "Go on and play ball, we'll handle the situation." Visiting players were not always safe either.[7]

Lt. Col. Kibler called an emergency meeting of the league and team executives where he chewed them out "with a salty G.I. tongue.... We're sitting on a keg of powder, and it can be blown skyward with another outburst." Kibler was worried about the Shore's reputation, and the outburst he feared came a week later when an "ardent rooter" was arrested at a Monday night game in Salisbury. He had been drunk and disorderly and several women had left the park and reported him. When Officer Sidney Fields went to arrest him, the intoxicated Paul Tankersley threatened the officer's life. When released on Tuesday, the defendant went straight to Gunby's Hardware, where he found Fields. Fields testified, "He threatened to kill me several times and said, 'the only reason I don't blow your brains out right here is because I don't want to splatter blood around the store.'"

Tankersley's explanation in court was "I just said that for something to say. I had no intention of doing it." Judge Henry Hudson fined Tankersley $100 for assault, $25 for being drunk with 30 days in jail. The $25 fine and 30 days were suspended on payment of the $100 for assault.[8]

Kibler took to the pen with an angry letter sent throughout the league complaining that only Dover provided adequate police protection at games. An indignant Salisbury fired back that five officers were on duty every night. Jim Honochick was a longtime major league umpire who started in the Eastern Shore League. Long before making beer commercials in the 1970s, he had a strange take on the situation, noting that "umpiring in night games is more concentrated, what do I mean by that? Well, put 2,000 fans in the stands on a bright Sunday afternoon. There is a lot going on in the stands, the crowd milling about, an occasional argument. The picture in the stands is interesting. Put the same amount of people in the same park during a night game and the distraction leaves. The umpire finds there is more concentration on the ball, on the infield, on the players." It must have been pretty dark in those stands. Blame it on the lights.[9]

It was a conflicted fan base. At once rowdy, threatening, and violent to the men in blue and opposing players and fans, then generous, caring, at times fraternal, always maternal to the local team players. Little Centreville was enjoying the positive side of that duality. Playing consistent .700 ball helped bring in crowds from throughout the region. The Orioles did not dominate among individual league leaders but were considered a veteran team. Actually all the teams were older than before. In the past the typical Class D player was just out of high school or had played a couple of years of college. Now, many of the players were picking up where they had left off before joining the armed services three and four years ago. Those who would have come up during the war years had tried to stay sharp on regimental teams if they were fortunate enough not to be on the front lines. Those just coming of typical Class D age may not have had the chance to play high school or college baseball because many athletic activities had been curtailed during the conflict. Many in baseball realized it would take a few years for the situation to straighten itself out.

At the end of August, Pittsburgh scout Poke Whelan, who had been shaking the bushes of the Eastern Shore for baseball talent for nearly 25 years, signed local semipro pitcher Joe Muir to a contract. The "bulky" Steve Bilko, not considered much of a prospect by most, was proving his detractors wrong with his season in Salisbury. He had previously earned a different kind of reputation tearing up many of the locker rooms he came across. The Cardinals had secured the final playoff position despite a record under .500. Salisbury had already drawn over 70,000 fans, and many thought the local semipros and amateurs could draw as well if more of their fields had lights.

The Eastern Shore League and all the amateur and semipros started their playoffs at the same time. Salisbury drew the largest Eastern Shore League crowd of 2,843 in a game with Milford, while the leagues of the smaller towns drew as many as 1,300 to 1,400 during an unusually chilly September. The Salisbury Cardinals then set the new league record again with 2,940 when they were knocked

The Federalsburg Athletics, 1946. When the Class D Eastern Shore League resumed after World War II, Connie Mack and his sons were no strangers to Federalsburg (courtesy Federalsburg Historical Society).

out of the playoffs by Milford. As Centreville and Milford played a final series for the championship, the Salisbury Cardinals took on the Central Shore League all-stars at Wicomico War Memorial Park before 1,346. But the local leagues were still at it. The northern peninsula MarDel League agreed to play the Central Shore League in what was called the Shore World Series.[10]

The Eastern Shore League series between Centreville and Milford was not without a disturbance. Centreville players Irving Shipp and Bunky Langgood were fined $15 each, Kibler pointing out, "The conduct of the Centreville team during this particular evening was detrimental to the game of baseball." But the Eastern Shore was not alone in this regard. Bottles were thrown at a game in Orlando, Florida, and the location of a playoff game in East Texas had to be moved after the threat of a riot and the flashing of a knife. Centreville went on to take the championship, and Jack Dunn III recalled that the team had little to show for it. The team received $500 from the league, to be split 20 ways. With no other acknowledgment coming, young Dunn III went out and had rings made for all the players, paid for out of his own pocket. The smallest town in organized baseball had won the pennant and the championship, and its claim as Baseball Town U.S.A. grew louder. Dunn would later go to work in the front office of the Baltimore Orioles when they came back into the American League. He recalled of his season in Centreville, "I've had a lot of thrills. The first major league game in Baltimore in 1954 and sweeping the Dodgers in the 1966 World Series stand out in my mind. But winning the Eastern Shore League pennant in 1946 with the Centreville Orioles ranks among my top memories."[11]

19. Will Greenville Yield?

In the first season after the war, the *Sporting News* reported that the minor leagues eclipsed all attendance records, drawing 30,078,400, shattering the 1939 mark of 18,500,000—and that with 36 of 314 clubs not yet reporting. During the off-season 10 small communities on the Virginia portion of the peninsula raised the funds for a park and lights if an opening became available in the minor league. Enthusiasm continued to run high. Parksley, Pocomoke City, and Crisfield were also clamoring for franchises in the league. Salisbury led the circuit in attendance with 92,152 with receipts of $50,655.25, and Cambridge had drawn 62,468 with receipts of $36,188. The total eight-team league attendance was 428,962. Centreville sportswriter Dan Tabler challenged Greenville, Texas, to the title of "biggest little town" in organized ball. He pointed out that the Greenville Majors were in the Class C East Texas League and its population of 14,000 had drawn 160,195 in nearly 70 home games. The Centreville Orioles had drawn their 52,000 in 62 home games and six playoff contests with their meager town population of 1,100. Tabler figured that was 46 times the population of the town: "Will Greenville yield?"[12]

Dunn, the Ivy Leaguer, fighter pilot, team president, and utility fielder, in 1946. Other duties included catcher, manager, groundskeeper, laundryman, and security guard. He bought surplus military rings for his players and had them inscribed for the champions when the league failed to provide a token of their accomplishments (courtesy Eastern Shore Hall of Fame).

Frank Baker, always a respected voice, weighed in on the season that had been especially rough on umpires in what were described as "riotous attacks." He repeated what others had offered before. Better exits, separate umpire dressing rooms, and properly uniformed police protection were needed. Much of the rowdy fan behavior was seen as a reaction to the release of wartime restrictions and discipline. In addition, Baker complained that players, managers, and executives urged fans to bait umpires in an effort to distract them from the teams' failings. He also pointed out that gambling was at the bottom of some cases. Many leaders of attacks had large wagers on the games, and "the fans have a nervous hangover condition from the war, everyone appears keyed up to a high pitch."

Many agreed that people seemed "keyed up" and that the postwar sports boom would continue. Baseball, harness racing, boxing, scholastic football, and basketball now frequently drew local crowds in the thousands in these small rural communities. The growing popularity of golf and tennis spurred the formation or expansion of country clubs, all driven by "lush, free spending GI days."[13]

Baseball continued as an important social and cultural focal point in African American rural communities. After World War II, over the course of 12 contests among local black teams at War Memorial Field in Salisbury, there were more than 6,000 paying customers. Oaksville was one of those isolated black enclaves located about five miles east of Princess Anne on the lower part of Maryland's Eastern Shore. It consisted of 30 to 40 families, most of whom worked as laborers on local farms. This tiny community fielded one team or more a season from at least 1910 to the 1980s. With the team still going strong in 1949, a handful of families pooled their resources to build Eagles Park. Tickets sold for a dollar to cover the cost of equipment and travel. Many former Eagles credited their success in life to their baseball experience in this small enclave, citing work ethic, the importance of community, and teamwork as valuable lessons learned on the playing field. Many future businessmen, administrators, teachers, and community leaders played for the Oaksville Eagles.[14]

Newspaper snippets, advertisements, and oral history offer, at best, adequate if tenuous evidence of the vibrant enthusiasm for baseball in rural black communities, and the difficulties faced in pursuing it. Separate and silenced as the black leagues were, baseball was as important in black homes as anywhere else. Those who remembered noted that the players were heroes in their communities, large or small. They played for now forgotten teams like the Chestertown Twins, Rock Hall Tigers, Millington Eagles, and the Batt's Neck Clowns. There were the Church Hill Hawks; Oaksville Eagles; and teams from obscure districts like Pondtown, Coleman Corner and Big Woods. And for 40 cents and a ride, one

A few of the Oaksville Eagles posing. Baseball was at the center of social life for the enclave of thirty to forty farm-laboring families. They put one or more teams in the field for more than seventy years beginning in 1910. They probably started earlier (courtesy Eastern Shore Hall of Fame).

had a chance to see some of the best Negro League players in the country take the field on the Eastern Shore when those circuits were in their prime.

There is some evidence that speaks to the quality of black baseball on the peninsula. Eight native Eastern Shore Marylanders played in the major Negro Leagues. Other Delmarva players from Delaware and Virginia would also see action in the Negro Leagues spanning 50 years. Long before Harold Baines was drafted out of the Little League and high school fields of St. Michaels, Robert Harvey of the same town preceded him. Harvey was a star athlete at Bowie State, and was discovered playing for one of the Phillips Packing teams in Cambridge. He played in the Negro League World Series in 1946, and All-Star Games in 1948 and 1950.

Howard "Toots" Farrell of Chestertown pitched in the Negro Leagues and was selected to the Delaware Sports and Delaware Afro-American Halls of Fame. The earliest of these players was Charles "Bugs" Hayman, born in 1885 in Salisbury. Hayman was in his third year pitching for the Philadelphia Giants when he was killed in an automobile accident en route to a game. In 1909 he pitched

The Nanticoke Tidewater Giants, one of countless forgotten teams that played on now forgotten grounds. Front row, from left: Pat Barclay, Grant Waters, Charles Perry, Wilson Jones, James Conaway, Dol Bradshaw, Wilmer Wright; middle row, from left: Freeman Nutter, Orville (Bully) Nutter, Sam Turner; back row, from left: John Pinder and Floyd Wright (courtesy Eastern Shore Hall of Fame).

a 12-inning no-hitter. Goldie Cephas of Preston also appeared in the Negro Leagues.

Knowlington "Buddy" Burbage of Salisbury had a career that spanned from 1929 to 1943 with some of the best teams in the Negro Leagues. Wilbert Pritchett of Ridgely pitched for the Harrisburg club in their Shore series with the Black Sox in 1925 while John "Neck" Stanley of Kent County, Maryland, had a pitching career that spanned 20 years in the Negro Leagues. Elmer Wicks of Crisfield also played for Harrisburg, 1922–24.[15]

20

Watermelon, Skunks, and More Tomatoes

The smallest town in organized baseball had won the league pennant and playoff championship. It had drawn over 52,000 fans, 46 times its population. The team had made its parent club a $2,000 profit, and newspapers across the country ran stories on Baseball Town U.S.A. The thanks the people of Centreville got from the Orioles was to be dumped. The Baltimore Orioles severed ties for "not sufficient materiel" before the new year even began. Centreville's only hope for affiliation was the St. Louis Browns, but before that organization would commit to a working agreement, Centreville had to produce 150 rooms to house participants for a proposed baseball camp; 150 haylofts they could do, but not extra rooms. Centreville would have to settle for an independent team in 1947.[1]

Kibler did not want to do a second year as president of the league. There had been some criticism from team executives. He turned down a three-year, $1,800 contract, but within a week, relented. "Baseball is more than a sport to me, it is a religion." Kibler said, "I didn't want to let the boys down and will agree to serve another year." Kibler clearly saw the problems he faced, and was determined to resolve them. The problems were gambling, rowdyism and drinking, and they were all usually linked. While these were the same problems that hampered the Eastern Shore leagues of the 1920s and 1930s, they were magnified by the many fans and players returning from the war. As a wounded veteran himself, Kibler had personal experience:

"There's too many servicemen returning home with a bitter attitude toward life.... Our returning GI's need help, and there's nothing better for them to expend their nervous energy than athletics." The challenge was keeping the enthusiasm from boiling over onto the playing field and in the stands. Kibler was agreeing with Shore native and ex–major leaguer Dickie Porter's observation that baseball had attracted "more fans this year than ever before" and the war left many with the "GI jitters, nervous and high strung."[2]

Kibler was genuinely concerned about gambling and bribery coming to Class D ball. There were recent reports of fixed sporting events in football, boxing, basketball, even Ping-Pong. There was an ongoing probe of the Class D Evangeline League by organized baseball, which implied there might be other gambling investigations initiated. Kibler announced, "We know who the gamblers are in most towns. The small one and two dollar bettors are harmless. The big spender is who we're looking for." Ed Nichols expanded on the president's statement: "Gambling on the Eastern Shore has never been too open, but the situation may have loosened up during the war when money was plentiful." Many throughout the industry seemed worried about gambling in baseball at this time. When St. Louis scout Pop Kelchner spoke at the Salisbury Kiwanis club, he expressed that he was worried about the rackets getting into sports for betting.[3]

Then Kibler addressed the drinking: "We're going to put the drunks out of the ball parks. We've got the dignity of the game to uphold.... I stopped taking my wife and daughter to ball games simply because there was usually some filthy mouthed drunk nearby, making life miserable for everyone. This condition existed in most every park. There were no exceptions." Teams were to make sure games were patrolled by uniformed and plainclothes officers. George Trautman, now president of the minor leagues, was going to be sending out inspectors throughout the country to make sure order was maintained in all the leagues. He seemed to think that the public was gradually drifting back to their prewar level of sanity and fiscal responsibility.[4]

Veteran umpire Leo Tournier wrote a letter to the *Sporting News* editor that proposed a common theme in much of minor league baseball, and echoed Baker. He suggested that there needed to be better uniformed police protection within fifty feet of the umpires at the end of the game, adequate separate dressing rooms, and more spacious exits so the umpires did not have to leave in the middle of a hostile crowd. But most rural ballparks were rudimentary, and often crammed into small lots. Kibler's solution was to ask the sportswriters in the league to help promote better sportsmanship. Drinking, profanity, and umpire baiting were "detrimental" and cheapened the towns and the major league organizations they represented. One of Kibler's first moves was to bar the sale of bottles so soft drinks were only dispensed in paper cups. Steamboat Johnson would have to learn the sound of a crumpled-up paper cup flying at his head if he worked in the Eastern Shore League.[5]

Rehoboth, Delaware, made the best pitch for Centreville's old franchise. It may not have had a park, but the population of 2,000 in the tiny beach resort swelled to 30,000 in the summer, far surpassing Salisbury in size during the baseball season. It promised 100,000 fans for a 5,000-seat park, and already had the backing of the Pittsburgh Pirates. The other clubs had their working agreements by now as well. Most stayed put with the Dodgers in Cambridge and Cardinals in Salisbury; there also were the Dover Phillies, Easton Yankees, Milford Red Sox, and the Seaford Giants. Pocomoke City native Art Ehlers, now head of the Athletics farm system, struck a working agreement with Federalsburg.[6]

Like Kibler, Ehlers was a wounded World War I veteran. Jack Dunn of the Baltimore Orioles had signed the left-handed hurler, gave him a tryout, and thought he would make the big leagues. But instead, Ehlers joined the army prior to World War I. He served with the 25th Infantry in a machine gun battalion and was thrown on the front for eight days in the Battle of the Meuse-Argonne. It was while operating his "chopper" that a bursting shell nearly took off a leg and two machine gun slugs ripped into his pitching arm. Ehlers spent a year in hospitals, used crutches for two years after his discharge, and used a cane for two more years. He eventually became involved with the Pocomoke City club. Then there was the stint with the Interstate League, and then the National Association. His wife and son now lived with him in Baltimore. Of his wounds and new job as farm director for Connie Mack, Ehlers told the *Sporting News*, "There's no crying over spilt milk.... I think I've got the best job in baseball."[7]

Ehlers would later become general manager of the Phillies with Jimmie Dykes as manager. The two then went to Baltimore in 1954 in the same roles. Ehlers was replaced the next year by former Crisfield player Paul Richards. Ehlers remained as his assistant.

Business in the minor leagues was booming. Many of the teams made money and were using it to modernize their parks. Salisbury improvements included a roof for the stand to block the sun during those new Sunday doubleheaders. After so many years winning so many battles, Pastor Fox and his allies had finally lost their blue law war to the euphoria of a world war won. Salisbury added concrete walks and ramps, new box seats and plumbing. In Easton tons of dirt were brought in to shift the drainage towards the fences. Seaford added bleachers. The CPA halted construction on the Rehoboth diamond after previous approval, withholding $25,000. The project was held up for three weeks before the money was finally released, with the season just two weeks away.[8]

When 5,000 turned out for the six Central Shore League openers in the middle of April 1947, the season looked promising. Return to pre–World War II thrift was not happening just yet. The Central Shore League was drawing from the high hundreds to more than a thousand for games, and the Eastern Shore League trended a little higher. The new War Memorial Park in Salisbury hosted amateur boxing matches on some nights that baseball was not played there. Typically, crowds ran from 1,300 to over 2,200. Harness racing in small towns was also drawing crowds, sometimes in the thousands, and now power boat racing, popular since the 1910s, became more prevalent.

Players continued to be treated as royalty by their fans. Kibler did not like the idea of fans raising money for player incentives, but it continued just the same. The BB Diner in Easton offered a steak dinner to players for a home run, and passing the hat in the stands was still commonplace. But not everyone was as accommodating to their baseball team. The complaint in Salisbury was that many restaurants raised their prices for the baseball season. Some charged as high as $2.25 for a steak, $1.25 for a platter, 65 cents for breakfast, and 10 cents for coffee; ice cream went for 25 cents. Some player salaries topped out at $150 a month, but most made far less. Typical meal money ran from $1.25 to $1.50 a day. The situation prompted Salisbury to raise its meal stipend to $2.25, the highest in the league. The other teams had to improvise.[9]

Bill Torrey and Carroll Beringer were two players who recalled pulling the bus over and stealing watermelons out of the fields on road trips so they had enough to eat. And there were always folks like Kate Taylor, who put up players at the Maryland Inn in Easton. The players called her Mom, and she was not going to let her boys go hungry. Catcher Tim Thompson almost quit baseball during the '47 season with Cambridge. He was making $110 a month, and he and his wife rented an apartment. His furniture had been repossessed, as he could not make the payments, and he faced eviction. Now the grocery bill was overdue. He went to Fred Lucas to tell him he was going to quit baseball and get a real job. Lucas picked up the phone, called the landlady and told her to send the bill directly to the Brooklyn Dodgers. He then called the grocery store and told it to send the bill to the Cambridge ball club. Thompson stuck with the game and saw action in four major league seasons, and was still supervisor of scouting for the St. Louis Cardinals in the early 1990s. He had the fondest memories of the Eastern Shore: "Cambridge was one of the nicest towns I ever played in. The people were really nice. I enjoyed that year as much as any I've had in baseball. I have a lot of friends in Cambridge today."[10]

Fred Lucas was a part of the Rickey feeder system. Brooklyn, now under Rickey's tutelage, was responsible for 700 of the 1,000 players on 25 minor league teams. They had 18 full-time scouts, 60 "bird dogs," along with tryout camps and schools. The efforts of the "father of the farm system" paid off in Cambridge.[11]

Nebraskan pitcher Carroll Beringer had signed a $90 contract with the Dodgers for the '46 season and would have never come so far to Cambridge if not promised train fare home. It had been a dismal year for the players with a seventh-place finish, but the fans had backed them all the way. Beringer returned for 1947 and the club added a fellow Midwesterner in Chris Van Cuyk from Wisconsin, who started the season with 12 consecutive wins. Together they would post 25 and 22 wins, respectively, while teammate Mike Quill accounted for another 18. Their offense was led by catcher Tim Thompson, and a 150-pound "string bean" outfielder from Aberdeen, Maryland, named Bill Ripken. They posted a winning percentage of .728. The Federalsburg A's made the playoffs with a losing record of 62–63. Four of the top 10 hitters were either exmajor leaguers or older player managers, and included Bobby Westfall in Seaford, Harry Contini in Salisbury, along with Ducky Detweiler and Pop Lambert in Federalsburg. In May the Salisbury Cardinals pulled off what was called a "grand slam strikeout." With the bases loaded, the runner broke for the plate, and the pitch was called a third strike, but the runner's slide knocked the ball from the catcher. Contini got his players to circle all the bases after the Pirates ran into the dugout, under the impression that the inning over. The botched play at the plate was ruled a dropped third strike. There were no reports of a confab or rhubarb.[12]

Detweiler was back playing for Federalsburg, where he had started his career in the late 1930s. Coming back from the war, Ducky had played a year with the Boston Braves, but did not feel he had gotten a fair shot. A good family and a good home were more of a priority for Detweiler than traveling across the country as an unappreciated utility player.

Beringer noted that the Cambridge team posted an amazing 57–6 home record, averaging more than a thousand spectators. He explained, "It was always important to win at home because the rivalries were fierce. On the road, crowds were usually hostile." After 70 years, nothing had changed when it came to peninsula baseball. One such incident came in June when Seaford played in Cambridge. Eastern Shore fans did not wait for the game to harass visiting players and fans. One particular fan was on Bobby Westfall during warm-ups, and his wife had already taken considerable abuse in the stands. An errant warm-up throw from Westfall zoomed toward the fans doing the heckling. He was accused of doing it purposely. Westfall responded, "I don't play that kind of baseball." But there was plenty of "chin music" during the game, and the crowd became threatening, until a thunderstorm rolled in and doused the situation. Somebody on Seaford left all the showers turned on before boarding the bus, creating a minor flood in the clubhouse before it was discovered. Some fans took a lighter approach. Kitty Knox of Easton told of the time the team went to a game in Cambridge and the lights went out. The next trip, the Easton contingent took flashlights with them to tease the hometown fans.[13]

Kibler's crackdown on drinking seemed to be effective. The visible presence of authority and the threat of immediate punishment may have deterred many. In the past Salisbury and Cambridge had been the biggest offenders, and only two had been arrested in Salisbury, while the lone person arrested in Cambridge was fined $25. Seaford and Dover reported no problems. The "little Yanks" in Easton were on an 11-game losing slide at the time, which prompted association president J. Howard Anthony to respond, "Goodness knows the performance of our club would drive a normal fan to drink, but the crowds have been mannerly. Anyway there's nothing much for us to get steamed about." The *Sporting News* added that the cooperation of local police had reduced drunkenness at league games "to a remarkable degree. Drunks are escorted out of the park and fined under the new policy." Umpire baiting was a different matter.[14]

President Trautman of the National Association declared that preventing fans from storming the field had become a priority. Kibler responded when the opportunity presented itself. He fined one player from Dover $15, and two more $5 for protesting a decision of the umpires down the pennant stretch. All three were on the disabled list and in civilian clothes when they incited a riot from the stands. Even Beringer pointed out that players and managers were still employing the old trick of luring over umpires to ask questions in order to get them closer to fans the team had already whipped into a frenzy. But Beringer was more worried about tomatoes. The tasty food had become a staple crop of the Shore and every county boasted several canneries. He does not mention Easton as the culprit but it could have been any town in the league. Perhaps tomato chucking had become a league tradition from the 1930s. The young pitcher did not seem offended by the projectiles, but pointed out how difficult it was to concentrate and learn new mechanics and techniques while always on the lookout for incoming objects.[15]

And then there was Seaford's skunk problem. In the fifth inning of a game between Cambridge and Seaford a skunk ambled out of the bushes and onto the diamond. All the players, including two base runners, made for the dugouts. Manager Pederson of Seaford demanded that umpire Bob Hanks act. Hanks was not so willing. "I've argued with a lot of things, but darned if I'm going to get spat on." Patience worked. The malodorous critter halted play for 10 minutes and all were relieved to see him wander off. Beringer also relates a story, perhaps the same incident, when he was knocked out of the game in Seaford and was sent to the showers. He heard a noise and turned expecting to a see a teammate, only to find himself in a stare down with a polecat.[16]

Closing the season, Dover catcher Jack Werner belted three grand slams in three days. He had five on the season. But it was Cambridge that walked away with the pennant. Fred Lucas was against raising the prices for the playoffs, sounding a now common complaint that for two adults, a child, a couple bottles of pop and a bag of popcorn, the family would be out $4. Lucas lost out. In the playoffs, "history and hysteria" were made. The series between Cambridge and the Dover Phillies was hotly contested. Just two weeks before four Dover players and the team were fined for not providing adequate police protection to the umpires. Now, early in the playoffs, Kibler fined Dover manager Dick Carter and infielder Bill Scull $15 each, and the team an additional $50 for "inciting a near riot." Scull had run to the stands, screaming at the fans, "Get those umpires!" It was reported that this time the fans "exhibited mild physical violence" with their bombardment of pillows, caps, and clothing, and then they doused the umpires with soda and water. Cambridge set a single-game season high attendance of 3,692 at the final game of the series. The overflow ringed the outfield and sidelines. Every hot dog and peanut was sold by the second inning. There "wasn't enough room to twist your neck to talk to your neighbor." The members of the crowd were so excited by Van Cuyk's performance that they raised $44 for their hero. In the middle of all this Kibler informed committee chairman Lucas he was resigning.[17]

The championship was between Seaford and Cambridge and continued to draw crowds in excess of 2,200 a game. The Dodgers' pitching juggernaut of Van Cuyk, Beringer and Quill faltered down the stretch, however, primarily because their catcher Tim Thompson was in a violent collision at the plate and missed most of the series due to separated ribs. Seaford reset the league game attendance high with 3,705 at the sixth game, and 3,009 Cambridge fans watched their team lose the seventh game and the playoffs. Seaford won $500 for the championship. Cambridge had won $700 for the pennant while the fans pitched in another $200. The final seven-game series drew 18,209, 1,800 more than the '46 series.[18]

The minor leagues set attendance records again by another eight million with 40,635,336 in 1947. The Eastern Shore League drew 334,671, with an additional 39,749 for the playoffs. This was a drop of about 75,000 from the '46 season, but still a significant number. Salisbury showed the sharpest drop of 32,000. Dover showed a slight increase while Cambridge and Federalsburg matched attendance figures for the previous year. Rehoboth delivered only 30,000 of the 100,000 promised. Rehoboth reported a $3,900 deficit, and the '48 season would be crucial as two or three clubs were reporting heavy financial losses. Only Seaford reported a profit, although Dr. Knotts in Federalsburg had a knack for keeping their books in the black. The Talbot County Athletic Association continued to hold the Easton franchise but turned over total control to the Yankees in a sweetheart deal. The New Yorkers would pay yearly for the park, supply all players and equipment, operate concessions, and pay all expenses for upkeep of Federal Street Park. J. Howard Anthony was told that he could throw away his aspirin.[19]

More than 300 attended Kibler's testimonial dinner for his thirty-five-year association with Washington College. Part-time Chestertown resident Branch Rickey was the surprise guest and speaker. He described his onetime protégé as a symbol of American boyhood. Dallas Culver, a player in the Eastern Shore League of the 1920s, was named the new president by Fred Lucas' search committee. His first challenge came from Arthur Ehlers, who planned to move the Athletics farm team to the larger western shore town of Annapolis, a move which Connie Mack had already approved. Ehlers thought the league needed to expand into larger towns to survive, but the league was not about to sanction the move. Annapolis was across the bay and there was no bridge yet. The costs of taking the ferry, meals and accommodations were met with opposition. There was also the fact that the Eastern Shore was immensely proud of their baseball heritage, and their decades-long reputation in the national pastime. They weren't going to allow interlopers from the western shore to horn in on their parade.[20]

21

And Take Your Batboy with You

George Trautman of the National Association was one of the many admirers of baseball on the Eastern Shore, despite its problems. Of the league and Tom Kibler, he said, "If all my leagues functioned like the Eastern Shore.... I wouldn't have too much to worry about." Umpire Roman Bentz was another. He was a professional football player in the fall with the New York Yankees and worked with Hans Horsey at Bill McGowan's Umpiring School in Florida in the winter. Bentz had stayed on with the circuit and turned down offers to work in higher leagues, stating, "I think the Eastern Shore League is the best operated minor league in the country for an umpire to get good training." Certainly, they faced every obstacle imaginable in these country parks. Chief umpire Horsey got things off to an antagonistic start for the '48 season, saying, "You can be sure the umpiring will be better than the playing." Then he added fuel to the fire after the season started, saying the pitching in the league was the worst he had ever seen.[1]

The league made some changes, raising the salary limit to $2,600 while staying with a 126-game schedule. The biggest change came in rosters. There had been concern about all the young prospects having to grind through the long schedule, and often play while injured. Each club was allowed a roster of 21 players the first and last 30 days of the season. For the middle of the season 17 was the maximum.[2]

Culver, the "fertilizer magnate from Delaware," promised to continue with Kibler's policy, and he was going to oversee matters with an "iron fist." While Kibler made inroads on drinking and gambling, umpire baiting was ever present. Culver stated his position: "The spectator has the privilege of voicing his opinion—that's baseball. Who are more rabid fans than the club officials themselves?" But he was concerned about repeated incidents where heckling comments from the front office personnel during games encouraged fans to "show mob violence." He planned to come down on any "business manager, office employee or official scorer who exhibits conduct detrimental to the game." Philadelphia Athletics scout Chief Bender spoke to 300 Kiwanis in Salisbury and reminded his audience, "These kids are barely making enough money to exist. Boos from the grandstand may ruin a youngster's career." Culver added that there were two types of rookies in the league, players and umpires, and asked fans to give both a break. Art Ehlers, just removed from threatening to dump the Federalsburg franchise for Annapolis, now promised the town the best of talent.[3]

21. And Take Your Batboy with You

The Central Shore League had its problem with umpires as well. All efforts to stop the arguing and fighting had failed, and now few wanted to work the league's games. Horsey conducted a clinic for them with 17 aspirants, but few signed on with the independent league. Even before the clinic, local leagues took the rare, if not unprecedented, step of hiring female umpires. Dot Williams and Minnie Windsor were local fans who knew they could do a better job than umpires they were seeing in the local leagues. They worked the Central Shore and the MarVa leagues regularly that year and were hired to call Salisbury Cardinals exhibitions as well. Another woman who caught notice was nineteen-year-old Becky Shockley. She preferred jeans and a baseball cap to dresses. Long before analytics Shockley kept statistical index cards on major league players, often writing to major and minor league clubs for information on the business end of running a team. She also wrote baseball columns for many of the small-town weekly papers. Two years later she was writing minor league clubs looking for a job. She landed one as club secretary with the Newport News Dodgers of the Class B Piedmont League.[4]

Ernie DeFazio of the Easton Yankees proved a one-man wrecking plan to Culver's cleanup efforts. Barely three weeks into the season he was one of five players fined by the league. DeFazio's infraction was "trading punches" with fellow player Tex Whitfield of Federalsburg. Two days later DeFazio was suspended and fined for heckling an umpire. Culver had handed out eight penalties in three days. Ernie had been ejected three times the year before and was on a pace to shatter that record. Culver planned to get tougher.[5]

Tom Kibler may have been justified in his concern about gambling in Eastern Shore baseball. Barney De Forge had briefly managed and pitched for the Cambridge Dodgers in 1946. After an investigation, Trautman banned De Forge from baseball for life for bribery, gambling, and game throwing in the Carolina League, and then turned the findings over to the police for prosecution.[6]

Gene Corbett was brought in as manager of the Salisbury Cardinals for 1948. Corbett was on the tail end of a nineteen-year career, mostly in the high minor and major leagues, and he brought his family with him. They came early, bought a house, and settled in and made friends. His wife had traveled over 10,000 miles with him since 1939 from St. Paul to Kansas City, to Sacramento, Newark, Baltimore, Decatur, and now Salisbury. The decision seemed as much Anne Corbett's as the skipper's. She was not going to have their four children be a stranger to their father half the year. "Life of a baseball manager's wife is never dull. It's definitely stimulating, a challenge," she explained. "There's no chance to get in a rut." The children were described as friendly, lively, and adaptable, and Gene took to the Eastern Shore and its culture, "He could stay up all night and crack hard crabs," Anne mused. The fans took to Corbett as he took to them. The Corbetts would make Salisbury their home. Gene got his Cardinals out of the gate at 15–3, helping establish his popularity. The Milford Red Sox, Easton Yankees, Seaford Giants, and the Federalsburg A's were all playing above .500. Early attendance seemed down, but this was blamed on the weather.[7]

Once again, Ed Nichols tried a little public relations for the umpires. The eight arbiters lived in a 12-room house in Denton, a logistically neutral location.

Federal Park in Federalsburg, 1948. Note the light pole in the middle of foul ground. Other photographs indicate most Eastern Shore ballparks had light poles inside their playing territories (courtesy Federalsburg Historical Society)

They rented from a widow, Mary Garton. "I love my boys," she enthused, and they all called her Mom. "Why they're just wonderful," she told everyone of the umpires. "First, they are clean of habits and speech ... the rooms they keep as neat as a pin. Those boys are not fussy.... I hear the boys in the morning tell about the gripes which some fellow gave them the night before.... Still, I have yet to hear one of 'em say anything about anyone." They kept five radios in the house. "We all sit and listen to the A's, Phillies, Yankees and Brooklyn games and root for our favorite teams." Ed Nichols chimed in, "Mom says the lonesome part of the day is about six o'clock in the evening when the boys grab their bird cages and inflated bibs and trudge off to the nightly grind." Then Mom finished the piece on a melancholy note.

"The house is just like an empty ball park then after the fans have left—all the cheering and chatter has gone."[8]

Salisbury continued to draw crowds of 1,000 to 2,000 to War Memorial Park for boxing matches. Other parks around the league also sponsored fights when their baseball teams were on the road. The village of Fruitland boasted a stable of 28 amateur fighters. Then one night Dover's Mickey Micelotta went 10 feet out of his way to take a Cardinals infielder out on a force at second and "bing, bing, bing," there was a round of fisticuffs and ejections. One did not have to go to a fight to see one. Just go to an Eastern Shore League game.[9]

Umpire supervisor Hans Horsey was not happy with all of Mom Garton's boys. He had a new umpire en route but did not say who he was replacing. Two umpires had taken part in several rhubarbs, and "talking back to the fans and jockeying the hitters with insulting remarks is nothing more than inviting trouble." An unnamed umpire was being investigated for yelling profanities at Rehoboth fans, and another challenged a fan to a fight after a game. There were going to be some new faces at Mom Garton's, and then Ernie DeFazio momentarily took some of the heat off as he was "pasted" with a hefty $25 fine for punching somebody.[10]

One night the volatile Marty Vogel was working the plate in Salisbury and it was a tight game. The Salisbury runner steamed around third and Vogel threw up his fist to signal the out in a close play at the plate. In the ensuing argument, manager Gene Corbett and his batboy, Paul Murrell, were tossed from the game. The 12-year-old troublemaker was interviewed for posterity afterwards. "I guess I'm sorry now," the boy started half-heartedly. "Should have known better. I was mad, that's all, and manager Corbett really blew his fuse. All I said to the ump was to get in the game, and keep his eyes open. The next thing I knew I heard the umpire tell Mister Gene to get off the field and take his bat boy with him." Ed Nichols described the boy being interviewed. "He took a tug at his baseball cap, hitched his trousers like a veteran pitcher on a 3–2 count." Not at all repentant, Murrell continued, "Any way, it won't happen again. Doggone it all, Ted Zaharczyk was still safe on that play. Everyone in the park knew it but the umpire.... What are they going to do with me, fine me, throw me off the squad, or what?" The manager did scold his charge. "Mr. Corbett told me he would do the beefing for the ball club and my job was only to take care of the bats and the water bucket." Then, to be sure, a backup batboy was added just in case Murrell ever blew another fuse. The incident led the *Sporting News* to observe that no one was safe from banishment in the Eastern Shore League.[11]

That may have been because Murrell was not the only batboy to feel the wrath of Horsey's umpires. Squirrel Dyott held the same position as Murrell for the Easton Yankees. They were playing in Cambridge and it appears Roman Bentz was working the game. In a scenario where it appears he may have been set up by his own manager, Dyott was instructed to take a towel and wipe off the plate for the umpire. Squirrel did just as he was told. "When I stood up here was this great big umpire, he played in the National Football League, and all he said was 'You're outta here.'" Squirrel spent the rest of the night in the grandstands.[12]

It was acknowledged that there was trouble with the umpires. A replacement was being openly sought for one, and another had quit, but was willing to work until a replacement was found. One replacement called Horsey explaining that someone had thrown a brick through the window of his car, taking seven white shirts, two uniforms, a radio, and a suitcase with all his clothing. Horsey, thinking it a story concocted to avoid working in a tough league, called the Philadelphia police to verify the report. There were managerial changes as well with veteran scout Socks Seabold taking over at Seaford, and Stew Hofferth taking the reins in Cambridge.[13]

By the end of July, attendance was down in most towns and it was rumored Rehoboth might fold. Cambridge reported a terrific skid, drawing 20,000 fewer than this time last year. Seaford dropped by 14,000, and Dover another 14,000 with a total draw of only 7,789. Rainy weather was blamed again. Jack Downing and WBOC radio were broadcasting all the Cardinals home games, but some thought it hurt attendance. The good news was Salisbury had a commanding lead with a record of 61–22 for .735 ball, but Milford and Easton were playing over .600 ball while the rest were stuck under .500. Horsey's assessment of the pitching proved true, or there were just some good hitters in the circuit.[14]

Frank Malzone was on his way to a very productive major league career with the Red Sox but found himself overshadowed by his teammates. From that Milford squad, Norm Zauchin led the league in home runs with 22 and Ray Jablonski had 17. Both Zauchin and Jablonski would be future major league players. If '47 had been the year of the grand slam, '48 was the no-hit season. On the same August night Eugene Kern of Cambridge and Ed Black of Salisbury pitched no-hitters in their respective games. Three nights later Ed Santulli of Rehoboth joined the group. Towards the end of the season, a typical Fan Appreciation Night was held in Salisbury where each player received a new wallet with $50. Corbett received an FM radio from the players and the batboys each received a pocketbook with $5.[15]

Nearing the end of the season Norm Zauchin had broken three of the new league's hitting records and was approaching two more. For 1948 Ray Jablonski set the pace in hits with 172 and Don Maxa in batting average at .382. Zauchin set the standard with 44 doubles, 33 home runs, 138 RBIs, and 323 total bases. The only pitching mark of note was Johnny Andre of Seaford with 29 complete games, and hits allowed at 272.[16]

Earlier in the year, Dr. W.K. Knotts of Federalsburg had sold the league and the National Association on a round-robin playoff. Salisbury had walked away with the pennant behind what little pitching the league had with the top three league leaders. Amongst them they won 53 games and logged 608 innings. But it was Milford's young bats that took the championship tournament. The parent clubs could not wait for the season to end to act. A couple did not.

At the beginning of the year three major league clubs owned franchises outright. They were the Dodgers in Cambridge, the Red Sox in Milford, and the Cardinals in Salisbury. The rest were held by local associations with working agreements. Even in Easton, where the Yankees were allowed full control, the franchise itself was locally held. Their business manager was a local attorney, Walter Claggett. In later years Claggett could not recall if he ever applied for the job or the Yankees just forgot to replace him when they took full control.

Now the Pirates bailed out on Rehoboth and the Phillies dumped Dover before the playoffs even finished, and a third club was rumored to be willing to pull up stakes. Attendance in the league had seen another significant drop of 100,000 from 334,671 to 233,963. Only Salisbury's pennant winners showed an increase. Dover drew but 9,967 in 63 games and lost more than $65,000 in operating expenses. There was an emergency league meeting that included Eugene Martin of the Yankees, Harold Roettger from Brooklyn, Tom Sheehan of the Cubs, and Art Ehlers of the A's. Ehlers pulled the plug on Federalsburg and lobbied to get Frederick of the western shore into the league. The Athletics had committed to a 10-year lease on their ballpark, and mentioned the possibility of some other western shore teams coming in, proposing some combination of the old Blue Ridge and Eastern Shore Leagues. Two other Blue Ridge towns were said to be interested. Only the largest towns of Salisbury, Cambridge and Easton had major league backing.[17]

George Trautman and Branch Rickey both called for a reduction in the number of farm teams. Four hundred thirty-eight minor league teams had operated in 1948. Rickey issued an eight-point letter which boiled down to saying the supply could not meet the demand of 58 minor leagues. The postwar "mushroom growth" could not continue. "The number of farms must be predicated on your need.... It must be regulated by the number of contracts you need to protect." Rickey was saying that creating a team before knowing where the players were coming from was putting the cart before the horse. This came from the man who two and a half years earlier had committed $60,000 to building a new park with no team or league to accommodate it, all based on 96 fish and a duck.[18]

Another factor was that the operating costs of the small-town teams were escalating. Most towns held the franchise, and working agreements left many expenses to the town. With only the three teams with committed affiliations, the others scrambled to raise the money in their communities to operate independently. Dan Pasquella represented Crisfield in gaining a franchise and it was said $30,000 was needed to start. Another problem was the bonus rule that had been initiated. Teams were now allowed to attract players with significant signing bonuses. Money that once might have gone to running small-town teams was now going straight into players' pockets. Dallas Culver resigned as president of the league but said he would serve another year if needed, but Fred Lucas became the new president. Dover and Milford dropped out and it ended up a six-team league.[19]

Fred Lucas, as the new president of the league, announced, "The league is going to operate this year a little differently than in the past. I'm looking to the press and radio to help me do the job. There's got to be a big public relations program." He was looking for a more organized distribution to the fans of what was going on in the league. While some still doubted the positive impact of radio, WBOC continued to broadcast games and provide commentary from the great sportswriters like Grantland Rice and Red Barber. The Phillies worked out a deal with Seaford when that town promised accommodations for 150 for a baseball camp. The town was four times the size of Centreville and better able to handle the demand. That left only two unaffiliated teams. Those towns that had the backing, as in Easton and Salisbury, continued improvements on their parks. Lucas wanted to curb players' talking to fans during games, not just because of the violence, but for gambling reasons. He thought players could be accused and convicted if seen talking to professional gamblers. Said Lucas, "The Eastern Shore League has always kept its skirt clean."[20]

In April Betty Carey of Pittsville got a tryout with the All-American Girls Professional Baseball League. She was described as 5'4" and 140 pounds. She could "gobble up grounders" better than the boys and catch. She swung a thirty-six-ounce Charlie Keller model bat. Although he could not let her play, the Pittsville High coach referred to her as "Tom Boy," or "Little Toughie." She held her own on boys' teams in the Pittsville playground league and four of her brothers played or umpired in the Central Shore League. Carey was a big Stan Musial fan.[21]

The Eastern Shore League was the last of the now 59 minor leagues to open their season in 1949. Easton's manager, Jack Farmer, bemoaned there "aren't enough good ball players available today." The response was to go older, particularly the independent teams. There was no mention of a class rule. Federalsburg had veterans Ducky Detweiler, Bob Westfall, Cal McQuillan, Johnny Caputo, and later added Buck Etchison. Rehoboth relied on the older durable arm of Johnny Andre for another season. Federalsburg complemented their veteran position players with the experienced pitching of Len Baker. Baker had broken both arms on two different occasions, the last at six years old playing cowboys and Indians with his brother. His glove hand did not heal and withered as he matured. At the end of August Baker had appeared in 39 games. He had completed all five starts and appeared in the rest in relief posting 11 saves. Still, there were a few talented kids coming to the league, including Stu Miller and Don Zimmer.[22]

The standings posted for June 7 show Rehoboth in first place at 13–10, Cambridge in last at 8–12, and everybody else squeezed in between. Rainy weather was again blamed for the slide in attendance 30 days into the season. Rehoboth showed an increase while Federalsburg and Seaford matched last year's pace. But two of the larger towns, Easton and Cambridge, showed significant declines, and Salisbury was already 8,000 behind the previous year. Not everything could be blamed on the rain. A horse racing meet drew 3,500 to Ocean Downs track and produced a $100,000 betting night. Boxing at the ballparks on sweltering summer nights continued to draw good crowds. The league could not have been more balanced, but it soon became apparent that the Easton Yankees and their young pitching prospect Wally Burnette were the team to beat.[23]

The rowdy and violent behavior, whether an Eastern Shore tradition, or the GI jitters, seemed to abate. Future major league player and manager Don Zimmer did have an incident in Cambridge one night. Zimmer was known for his glove but had been charged with six errors in one game, and his hitting was anemic. Zimmer sometimes drew the ire of even the most loyal hometown Cambridge fans. One night Zimmer was getting it good from his own crowd in Cambridge. "In the din and the smoke of the bleachers," a bellowing voice rose out of the darkness above the others. When Zimmer finally had enough, he turned to the screened backstop and challenged the hecklers. The booming voice went silent. Out of that darkness and smoke emerged a burly 6'4" Hooper's Island waterman to confront the then diminutive Dodger infielder. The quick-thinking Zimmer turned to his dugout and cupped his hands around his mouth and yelled to his manager so all could hear, "Hey Johnny, I got him down for you!"[24]

Easton manager Jack Farmer, the man who had sent Squirrel Dyott to his fate with Bentz, conceded that 20 percent of managing was "bench jockeying," and Fred Lucas did crack down. A doubleheader between Seaford and Cambridge prompted Lucas to levy $110 in fines to two managers and four players. And like any other year, fans showered their appreciation on players and managers. Jack Farmer Night in Easton netted the manager and his pregnant wife $400 and a baby carriage. A few hours later, word hit the streets of the small town that Mrs. Farmer had just delivered twins. Money for a second stroller was quickly raised.

On Gene Corbett Night in Salisbury, the players and groundskeeper received $25 each and four other men who had played received $10. The players gave their manager the unusual gift of a typewriter, and presented corsages to Gene Corbett and his wife. Business manager Nick Greer received a bathinette for his troubles. Then the fans rolled out Corbett's real gift, a Chevrolet replete with seat covers for their popular manager who had led them to a third-place finish.[25]

Capt. Jim Walls had been a loyal rooter of Salisbury since the 1920s. He considered Corbett in the same class as Jake Flowers when it came to managing. It appears that Walls was not one of those field-storming rowdies as he repeated the refrain of Culver and Bender the year before, "A few encouraging remarks from the stands can go a long ways in helping these kids. Let's not give up on the kids, and remember they are kids." Fact was, because there were only two independent teams, and a shortage of players, the league was a little older than usual.[26]

Many of the league leaders were veterans. Johnny Andre in Rehoboth was the only pitcher to top 200 innings to go with his league-leading 17 wins. Second in wins was Federalsburg veteran Len Baker with 14. The hitting side was dominated by experienced player-managers and veteran players. Among the leading hitters were Bobby Westfall, Ducky Detweiler, Buck Etchison, all of Federalsburg, and Gene Corbett of Salisbury. The twenty-seven-year-old Bobby Westfall led the league in seven categories. Only Bragg in Easton topped his batting average. Home runs were down, but so were innings pitched and wins for pitchers, as it appeared that management was no longer expecting 200-plus innings from their young prospects.

After years of play in the Class D minor leagues, mostly in the second division, Easton took the pennant. The Yankees finally provided the young players that manager Farmer needed. The playoffs were in the round-robin format again, and fourth-place Rehoboth with a record of 56–63 prevailed in the series, taking the last game at Federalsburg before 2,318 fans.[27]

Preliminary figures from four of the six teams showed slight increases in attendance, as Cambridge was about even with their '48 figures. But Salisbury, the league's largest town, hub of the wheel, again took the sharpest decline of 20,000. From 92,000 in 1946 it had experienced a steady and significant decline to 40,000 in '49. Before the bats and balls could be put up, the Cardinals were talking about pulling out.[28]

Fred Lucas was sure the league was in better shape than last year, and Art Ehlers was still angling to open the league up to some old Blue Ridge League towns. Branch Rickey and George Weiss, competitors at every level of professional baseball, including the Eastern Shore League, feuded over who had the better farm system. Weiss asked, "Where would Brooklyn be if it had not raided the Negro leagues for Jackie Robinson, Roy Campanella and Don Newcombe?" Rickey took offense to the use of the word "raided." Rickey pointed out that Dodger teams had finished in the first division in nine of the 13 leagues they played in while the Yankees had only four rank that high. What Weiss did not point out was his Easton Yankees had won the pennant of the Eastern Shore League while the

Cambridge Dodgers finished last. What neither mentioned was they were both looking to downsize their minor league operations. There was already talk around the peninsula that the Eastern Shore League might have to go to rookie, local, or back to independent baseball.[29]

Salisbury continued to court the Cardinals, but hedged that bet by soliciting Cleveland for an agreement. Rehoboth tried to sell itself as a training camp with 4,500-seat modern park and, with a bit of exaggeration, boasted a beautiful spring climate tempered by southeast trade wins. Rickey stuck to his guns with Lucas and backed Cambridge outright. Seaford got a working agreement with the Phillies, and Ehlers was still trying to get Frederick in the league, as Chambersburg, Pennsylvania, made appeals. Then 200 Easton fans pledged the funds to operate the club as an independent. Ehlers then declared he would not enter Frederick in the league if Salisbury dropped out. Lucas was optimistic, but Harry Oliphant of Salisbury had only three weeks to raise $20,000. By the first of the year Cleveland pulled out of talks with Salisbury, and the Dodgers and Yankees, recently feuding, ganged up on the unattached Rehoboth club, and gave it only two weeks to get affiliated or get out of the league.[30]

Dr. Knotts, who had kept little Federalsburg operating with his meticulous budgeting, advised Salisbury to go independent. Knotts' club had expenses of over $40,000 the last year and he had $5,000 in cash on hand. He accomplished this with only 29,000 regular season admissions and another 8,000 for the playoffs. The working agreements being offered did not amount to much. Some major league teams were only looking to provide five or six players and a manager. Both Salisbury and Rehoboth were trying to get limited agreements with Ehlers and the A's, but the Athletics executive stuck to his Frederick policy, and Rehoboth could not meet the Yankees/Dodgers demands for affiliation. The Cardinals and Yankees then pulled out of their own agreements citing league instability. When the Yankees dropped Easton and seven other teams from their system, Walter Claggett considered the move a "body blow" to the league. Salisbury sportswriter Ed Nichols wrote the epitaph, "Resting here is the Eastern Shore League, 3rd. A faithful friend. Born November 1945, Easton, MD, died January 31, 1950." National papers were a little less dramatic: "Sho' Loop Tosses in Towel: Operating Costs Too High." They went on to cite the optimistic Lucas' plan, to hold all franchises for the future, rather than turn them back in to the National Association as was done in the 1920s. He explained, "The league feels it cannot continue to operate with the present cost of operations and the competitive field in obtaining rookie players. The financial aspect plus the player difficulties are too great to overcome for the independent clubs." Bud McCarter, writing to the *Sporting News*, gave this laconic history of the Eastern Shore League: "The league resumed operations after the war (1946), but during the past two seasons attendance declines resulted in several major league backers pulling out."[31]

Afterword

Baseball didn't just disappear after the 1949 season. Salisbury tried to carry on in the Class B Inter-State League in the early 1950s. At one time affiliated with the Athletics, the team then latched on to the Cardinals. It found its niche in the lower end of the standings. Money and attendance were the usual obstacles. Salisbury fans didn't seem to get as excited watching the out-of-state York White Roses, Harrisburg Senators, or Allentown Cardinals. They longed for the old rivalries with Cambridge and Easton. Baseball just wasn't the same without those passionate local Shore rivalries that had grown in these communities over the last 80 years. Organized baseball lacked a degree of intimacy that did not work in these smaller towns. There may have been an element of truth in the thinking of Landis, Sexton, and Farrell. Local fans did not seem ready for a regional representative against unfamiliar and distant opponents.

A bona fide attempt to revive the league came in 1954, but did not generate enough support. New diversions continued their assault on the Eastern Shoreman's activities. After 30 years of talk the Bay Bridge was finally completed, connecting the Eastern and western shores and making the metropolitan centers of Washington, D.C., and Baltimore that much more accessible and affordable. Some diehard Eastern Shoremen thought the bridge should be blown up. As much as it was the bridge, it was television that had a most immediate and profound impact on Eastern Shore culture. In addition to the novelties of visual live drama, variety and game shows, and news, there was baseball. One could sit in the comfort of one's own home and pick up broadcasts of major league games. Regional coverage from Washington, D.C., Baltimore, or Philadelphia could be received on most of the peninsula, and there was a national game of the week. Add the luxury of more affordable air-conditioning, and there seemed little sense to sit out on a muggy night, swatting mosquitos, dodging errant tomatoes and bottles, and listening to profane and belligerent drunks.

Not everybody was lured to the cities, or owned a television, much less an air conditioner. Many still sought those heated summer rivalries, as town baseball tried to adapt to its changing environment. The Central Shore League in the south, the MarDel League in the north, and the Negro League were among those that carried on. Most players were local, and often compensated to some degree. The hold of baseball on the smaller communities remained firm for a time, with a twist. Ironically, Sunday was now the big day for baseball.

A Rock Hall player from the 1950s tried to describe those typical, yet significant Sunday events with a bit of hyperbole. A doubleheader would start soon after all the churches let out. Some didn't bother to change out of their Sunday best only to chafe through their hot summer entertainment. Others were a little more heathen in their dress. Church and baseball on Sundays became a small-town staple. The man tried to describe the intensity, fervor, and distraction of this weekly ritual. He proposed that a gang of thugs from Philadelphia could descend upon the town while the games were in progress, blow the safe to the bank, pilfer the church's collection baskets, rob every business and house, and be back in the city and having dinner before anyone knew what happened.

By the 1960s the newest generation seemed to diverge from the 100-year tradition of small-town baseball and gravitate toward the broader cultural influences reaching the Shore through technology. The remaining leagues and independent teams eventually folded for lack of support. Modified softball rose to take baseball's place. Leagues and teams proliferated on Maryland's Eastern Shore. One county might have three leagues and as many as 30 teams. As it had in the past with baseball, the region quickly obtained a reputation as a hotbed for this particular version of the game, and the quality of the teams sent to national tournaments.

Baseball tradition has survived with the Eastern Shore Baseball League that currently functions on the lower Shore as an amateur circuit, and the Class A Delmarva Shorebirds, which represent the region in the South Atlantic League. The Eastern Shore of Maryland and the peninsula continue to produce players for the major leagues.

Appendix A
Selected Biographical Sketches

The following three biographical sketches are included in an effort to illustrate the times, places and people of the narrative, and help put events on the Eastern Shore in historical context. These individuals are of different backgrounds with different personalities and had different experiences in baseball. The pieces on Al Burris and Bob Unglaub originally appeared on the SABR Bio Project site. The one on Judy Johnson was recently written and influenced by the previous efforts of John Holway and Thomas Kerns on the SABR Bio Project site.

William "Judy" Johnson

William "Judy" Johnson was born October 26, 1899, in the isolated Worcester County seat of Snow Hill, Maryland. Judy fondly remembered some of those early childhood mornings on the Eastern Shore. He and his sister shared a sleeping area in the loft of their home that was accessed by a ladder, where on some frosty mornings, they would awake to the smell of a country breakfast cooking. His father, also named William, was a merchant seaman whose travels gave him a broader perspective of the world than many other African Americans confined to the Shore at that time. He was also a licensed boxing trainer, and the sport was rising in popularity in the region in the early 1900s. Along the way, the elder Johnson befriended Jack Johnson, the flamboyant heavyweight champion of the world.[1]

Around 1907, on the heels of recent lynchings, assaults, and wholesale racial expulsions, the elder Johnson made the same decision many other black families on the Eastern Shore faced at that time. He followed the migration north to the less violent segregation practiced in the Philadelphia/Wilmington area. In Wilmington Judy's father took on the role of athletic director of the Negro Settlement Home in the family's neighborhood. Sports were a very important part of the Johnson household, and the main emphasis was on boxing. Mr. Johnson saw his son following in the footsteps of the first black boxing champion, Joe Gans of Baltimore, or his friend Jack Johnson, into prizefighting. Judy's sparring partner was his sister, who was three years older than him. It soon became apparent that

Judy's future did not include pugilism. Quiet and shy, but consumed with determination, the younger Johnson preferred baseball, and played on youth teams that faced both black and white opponents. Often he would go to the home of his team captain to discuss baseball, but he may have been more interested in his teammate's sister, Anita Irons. Judy always tried to wrap up his baseball discussions with a visit with Anita on the porch, until her father would chase him away. Anita would then walk him down to the corner, where he would steal a kiss from her in the budding relationship.[2]

Johnson dropped out of high school to take a job on the docks of Deep Water Point, New Jersey. This did not deter him from his love of baseball. He took to the local semipro circuit at $5 a game, eventually going full-time with the Hilldale Club playing in Darby, Pennsylvania, in 1921. Hilldale was one of the best black teams of the era. Along the way Judy picked up his nickname for his resemblance to a first baseman, Judy Gans. With Hilldale the Negro League great John Henry "Pop" Lloyd took the young Johnson under his wing. Of this mentorship Judy later said, "John Henry Lloyd is the man I gave credit to for polishing my skill. He taught me how to play third base and how to protect myself. John taught me more about baseball than anyone else."[3]

Johnson was small in stature, rarely playing at more than 150 pounds. He was described as a tough out, doing anything to get on base, often leaning into pitches to accomplish that goal. He was a contact hitter and a man to be counted on to drive in the clutch run or make the clutch play in the field. Johnson was known to be a student of the game, quiet, confident, and a steady influence on the team. Johnson's abilities as a teacher and a leader were recognized early as he served on many of his teams as mentor, captain, coach or manager.

Early on his road to accomplishments and accolades, Johnson had continued his courtship of Anita Irons. While Judy had been learning his baseball trade, Anita had attended normal school to become a teacher. Now Judy was making a decent monthly salary that was augmented by the countless exhibitions played during the regular season. Negro League teams might play as many as 200 games a year. Judy added to these earnings with barnstorming teams in Florida and Cuba in the winter. In 1923, Judy and Anita eloped to his childhood home of Snow Hill to be married.[4]

Judy helped lead the Hilldale Club to three consecutive pennants from 1923 to 1925, and the first two Negro League World Series in 1924 and 1925. Both the *Chicago Defender* and the *Pittsburgh Courier* named Johnson the Negro Leagues' most valuable player for 1929. Johnson's nine-year tenure with Hilldale was most unusual in the unstable environment of the Negro Leagues of the 1920s.[5]

The Negro Leagues succumbed to the Depression, but monied teams continued as independents. Johnson signed with Cum Posey and the Homestead Grays. His coaching ability and steady influence were recognized, and if not in name, he acted as field manager. It was during his time with the Grays that Johnson, in a game with the Kansas City Monarchs, found himself in mid-game with an injured catcher. Josh Gibson, who played on a local team, was in the stands. Gibson's talent was well known, so Judy invited him from the stands to complete the game. Like Pop Lloyd had done for Johnson, so Johnson did for Gibson. Their relationship was close enough that Gibson had his own nickname for Johnson and called him "Jing." The two spent many hours talking baseball, and setting up infield plays to take advantage of Gibson's rifle arm. Johnson is also given credit for working with Gibson on the intricacies of catching, including his early weakness on pop flies.[6]

Johnson went back to independent Hilldale as player-manager, but eventually returned to play with Cum Posey with the Pittsburgh Crawfords of the newly formed Negro National League. From 1933 to 1936 he was again an integral piece of the best team in the Negro Leagues that boasted four consecutive first-place finishes. The lineup also included, among others, Josh Gibson, Oscar Charleston, Cool Papa Bell, Jud Wilson, and Satchel Paige. After the 1936 season Johnson was dealt back to the Homestead Grays. The move was a salary dump, but Johnson was a bit rankled that he was no more than a throw-in on the deal, so he retired. Pioneer Negro League historian John Holway pointed out that most considered Johnson the best third baseman to play in the Negro Leagues, over such standouts as Jud Wilson, Oliver "Ghost" Marcelle, and Ray Dandridge. Cool Papa Bell later summarized Johnson's career, "Johnson was the best hitter among the four top third basemen in the Negro Leagues, but no one could drive in as many clutch runs as he would. He was dependable, quiet, not flashy at all, but could handle anything that came up. No matter how much the pressure, no matter how important the play or hit, Judy could do it when it counted."[7]

Johnson tried a number of jobs and business opportunities after retirement, settling on none, usually coaching sandlot teams until Jackie Robinson was accepted into major league baseball. Of this event Johnson said, "I never dreamt it would happen. I was thrilled I lived to see the day." Now, many major league organizations sought out scouts to track down this new source of talent. Johnson's personality and ability to spot and teach young players was well known in white baseball circles, and Connie Mack's was one of those. Of Johnson, Mack had once proclaimed during his playing years, "If only Judy were white, he could name his own price." Mack hired Judy as a scout in 1951. In 1954 he was sent to Florida as a spring training coach for the newly signed black players, but Johnson would teach anyone who would listen. When the Athletics moved to Kansas City in 1954, he continued to scout over the years for the Braves, Brewers, Phillies, and Dodgers. While the Mack Athletics failed to heed his advice on Hank Aaron and Minnie Minoso, he is credited with finding Richie Allen and Bill Bruton. Bruton would become his son-in-law.[8]

When Braves general manager John Quinn took the same position with the Philadelphia Phillies, he sought out Johnson and hired him as scout and spring training instructor until 1974. Throughout his years in baseball, Johnson always saw himself as a teacher first. "I tell the kids baseball is like school and you get promoted if you learn." He would later go on to explain, "I love to teach baseball and would rather do it than anything. It's like putting seed in the ground, you like to watch it develop. As long as they're ballplayers, they're my kids. I love 'em all."[9]

In 1971 Commissioner Bowie Kuhn named Johnson to the newly formed

Negro Leagues Committee for selection to the National Baseball Hall of Fame of deserving players from that era. For one of those early meetings, Johnson asked his neighbor to drive him to Cooperstown. James Knott knew the quiet and unassuming Johnson had been a ballplayer "back in the day," but knew little else. When they pulled up to the Hall, "They were hollering at him, and I thought 'Who is this man?' That's when I realized this man was a great baseball player. The magnitude of his abilities, I had no idea. He was a legend." In 1975 Johnson was required to step down from the committee in order to accept his own nomination into the National Baseball Hall of Fame. While giving his acceptance speech, the normally steady Johnson's emotions got the best of him and he broke down. Son-in-law Bill Bruton took the stage to console him.

Johnson's personality was reflected in his favorite saying, "The sun is shining and there's a ball game going on." James Knott and his wife remained friends with Anita and Judy, eventually helping them out in their later years. "He had an impact on my life," Knott would say, "and he was an amazing guy." Anita passed away in 1985. "She was the most important thing in my life," said Judy of the girl he first kissed on a street corner in Wilmington.[10]

Al Burris

Alva Burton Burris was born on January 28, 1874, in the small village of Warwick in Cecil County, Maryland. Census records available only list the family for 1910 in Kent County, Delaware, showing Burris had two brothers (Frank and Eli) and three sisters (Amanda; Linda; and Elizabeth, a schoolteacher). The census lists his mother, also named Elizabeth, with an occupation listed as "own income."

Burris' contributions to his community and local baseball are forgotten. Variously, and respectfully referred to as "Pop," "Doc," or "Prof," Burris was the most prominent player, manager, and organizer in baseball on the Eastern Shore of Maryland through the first incarnation of the Class D minor leagues in the 1920s.

The right-handed throwing and hitting Burris was signed to pitch for the Washington College team in 1892. The formation of the Maryland Inter-Collegiate Athletic Association in 1888 had created an ardent competition for the collegiate championship of Maryland. Young Dick Hawke had already pitched for the college. When Burris reported to the school that had a student body of only 70 young men, he found the 25-year-old Dave Zearfoss as his catcher. Serving four years as his battery mate, Zearfoss would later play in the major leagues. Burris' leadership abilities were recognized early when the college named him coach of the baseball team and athletic director as he entered his junior year.

It was an eventful time for the young scholastic standout. He got a one-game shot at the major leagues that year when he pitched for the Philadelphia Nationals against the world champion Baltimore Orioles, soon after the college season ended on June 22, 1894. Of the game, the wire services reported, "For several innings professional ball was played, but after that it was a regular lot game."

Burris came on in relief of Kid Carsey in the fifth inning of an 18–14 slugfest loss to Baltimore. He managed to shut down the feared Orioles lineup in three of his five innings, but surrendered six runs in the sixth inning and four more in the eighth. Giving up 10 runs on 14 hits and two walks (the box score counted one), Burris was not credited with the loss. He did show well at the plate, however, going two for four. One of the opposing Orioles pitchers that day was Stub Brown. Ten years later they were playing with and against each other on Eastern Shore town teams.[11]

Upon his graduation, Burris would continue to serve the college for 10 more years as a professor, athletic director, and baseball coach. Although he did not always manage on the field, Burris was at the reins of the team from 1894 through 1906, which arguably included the best teams in the college's history. He was responsible for recruiting "imported" players to bolster the roster, and his teams held their own against larger schools such as Maryland, Syracuse, Villanova, and Pennsylvania over the years. In an era of less stringent college rules, Burris would often take the field for his team as pitcher, catcher, or third baseman. Burris went to great lengths to field a competitive team. In addition to Zearfoss, several future major league players came under his tutelage.

Once the college season ended, Burris' talents as player and coach were in high demand on the professional small-town teams of the area. With his rosters of future, former, and even current major league players, they excelled at this prominent level of semipro competition. Having developed an effective curveball, he was known as a "master of the pitching art" and "the wizard, the puzzler." Box scores show that on local town teams he caught; played short, third, and center field; was occasionally a starting pitcher; and excelled in relief. His reputation as a leader attracted the best talent coming to the region to the teams he played and managed.[12]

Burris played for Cambridge in 1896 and 1897. While continuing in his duties at the college, he spent some summers playing in the Silver Lake Assembly in New York. He then played for Salisbury in 1902 before returning to Cambridge in 1904 to play in the Eastern Shore League, the first peninsula-wide league that featured teams in Cambridge, Salisbury, and Easton. Among the future major league players on that team were Pete Loos, Chappy Charles, Buck Herzog, and Stub Brown. Somehow, during that busy season, Burris found time to manage and play for the team from the resort town of Betterton, Maryland. Their schedule against some of the best semipro teams in the Baltimore and Philadelphia regions was widely circulated and the team drew large crowds. Their star pitcher was future one-game major league left-hander Hanson Horsey.

A picture of the Pocomoke City team of 1905 shows the short, stocky Burris with a solid team composed of several of his old cohorts: Si Nichols and Chappy Charles, and newcomer Frank "Home Run" Baker. In 1907 Burris helped Cambridge claim the informal Maryland state championship under the management of former Pocomoke teammate Leonard Bassett and featuring Frank Baker. The town was determined to put an equally good team on the field the following season. When Burris was named manager of Cambridge prior to the 1908 season, it was announced that he had "never managed a losing team." Cambridge claimed the Maryland-Delaware championship that year, after a hotly contested series against Seaford, Delaware, which brought back Buck Herzog from the Giants to manage and play shortstop.[13]

The 1908 season would be Burris' last as player and field manager. In 1906 he had begun work on his studies at the College of Physicians and Surgeons in Baltimore, and he completed his degree in homeopathic medicine at Hahnemann College in Philadelphia in 1908. After two brief internships, he set up practices in Salisbury and Ocean City, opened a drugstore located on Main Street in Salisbury, and served as superintendent of the Pine Bluff Sanatorium.[14]

Although no longer on the field, he remained an influential factor in regional baseball. In 1911 Burris, along with Ray Truitt and R.V. Rich of Salisbury, proposed an independent league with strict rules limiting player transactions. Most towns were not ready for such restrictions on their independence, but the effort eventually succeeded with the formation of the independent Peninsula League in 1915 with entries from the towns of Salisbury, Cambridge, Easton, and St. Michaels. Burris was chosen president. Under his leadership, the Peninsula League was the first independent league on the Shore to abide by a set of bylaws and successfully complete a season.

Burris did not take part in the return of the Peninsula League in 1916. His medical practice and community service were now taking up most of his time as he advertised his thriving drugstore for sale. But Burris made his influence felt once again on the baseball scene in 1921. He was tapped to manage the independent Salisbury team when its manager was called away on business. The Class D Blue Ridge League of western Maryland offered to play the best independent team on the Eastern Shore for the championship of Maryland with the *Baltimore Sun* promoting the series. The Sunpapers sports editor C.E. Sparrow insisted that the Shore decide its representative through a single-elimination tournament. Burris protested that such a format was not a fair way to pick the best team to represent the region. As a result of his influence, two teams boycotted the playoff tournament.[15]

The extent of Burris' involvement in the formation of the Class D Eastern Shore League in 1922 was as general and business manager of the Salisbury Indians. A lifelong bachelor, in the absence of an immediate family, he settled into a quiet life and devoted his energies to his community. He split his medical practice between Salisbury and Ocean City, Maryland, which was 30 miles away and isolated from most medical care. In the winter it was a sparsely populated strand of sand while in the summer it teemed with thousands of tourists. He refused his services to no one, and paid little heed to their ability to pay.

It was during this time that Burris shifted his athletic focus from professional adults to the youth of the community. Before the era of organized youth leagues, he used his passion and knowledge for sports to influence children of all ages and all genders. It was said of Burris during these years,

"Always a sports enthusiast, he taught scores of youngsters the rudiments of baseball, football, and tennis. However, his interest was not only in the physical development of young people, but he sought to inculcate in their minds the principles of good sportsmanship in competitive sports and clean, wholesome living."[16]

Burris suffered a paralyzing stroke in November of 1937, and the citizens of Salisbury rallied to his support and voted him the prestigious Salisbury Award. This was the equivalent of a Man of the Year award in the local community, and the winner was usually not announced until the night of the banquet. Because of his condition, and his need to use a wheelchair, he was informed prior to the event. Dr. H.C. Byrd, Burris' former teammate on the championship Cambridge clubs of 1907–08, and then president of the University of Maryland, presented the certificate, which read,

> In recognition of his contributions to the youth of the community, and for his own exemplary life which has been an inspiration to old and young alike. As a physician he offered his services and skill unsparingly without thought of compensation or discrimination. Yet his public service did not end there. In his active years he contributed his time and talent to teaching youth the rudiments of athletics and, more important, proper physical development, and sportsmanship and clean, wholesome living.

Byrd added his own praise for his lifelong friend: "The spiritual contributions an individual makes toward the betterment and progress of humanity is everlasting; it endures long after his material contributions have been forgotten."[17]

Many thought the esteemed doctor was on the road to recovery when Burris suffered a second massive stroke three weeks later and died on the morning of March 24, 1938, at Peninsula General Hospital in Salisbury. He was buried at the Hollywood Cemetery in Harrington, Delaware.

Alva Burris was a college baseball star, major league player, a college coach and athletic director by the age of 20. He was a college professor, baseball manager and an influence on many young men aspiring to the major leagues at the lowest professional level. Burris was a dedicated and unselfish doctor, a businessman, administrator, and league organizer. But what he was remembered for most at the time of his death was as a mentor and inspiration to the youth of his community.

Sources

Family composition came from a combination of the HeritageQuest census data for Kent County, Delaware, for 1910; the census for Salisbury, Maryland, in 1920 and 1930; and Burris' obituary, which appeared in the *Salisbury Daily Times*, March 24, 1938.

Bob Unglaub

Robert Alexander "Bob" Unglaub was, at best, an average major league ballplayer, yet he was representative of the many city players coming to the Eastern Shore to play baseball seeking the economic environment in which it operated. One newspaper referred to Unglaub's career as a "meteoric rise," but in reality it was anything but. In fact, little in his professional or personal life was out of the ordinary, and his career was typical of the players of the dead ball era, with one exception: Unglaub was continuously at odds with organized baseball over his salary.

Unglaub was born July 31, 1881, to John M. and Minnie H. Unglaub and grew up three blocks from Union Park on 25th Street in Baltimore, where Ned Hanlon was building an Orioles juggernaut that would soon dominate the National League. The young "park rat" hung around the grounds, a self-professed member of the "knothole gang," peeping through the boards to watch the games. He soon talked the groundskeeper into letting him do chores and run errands in exchange for admission to the games. Unglaub later recollected that before long "I had butted my way into being bat boy and mascot." All his spare time from school was spent at the park shagging balls at batting practice for the likes of Joe Kelley, John McGraw, Hughie Jennings, Steve Brodie, and Wilbert Robinson. He learned his baseball from one of the best teams in the history of the game.

When Unglaub graduated from high school in 1897, he was approached about attending college. Unglaub answered that he would rather play ball. The man went on to explain that he could do both. He was offered $75 a month for four months of the year to play baseball for the University of Maryland, and was allowed to attend classes if he chose to do so. Unglaub played catcher for the university under his middle name of Alexander and took up engineering, professing to have completed his degree in three years.[18]

During the summer months Unglaub accepted the job he was most qualified to perform—he crossed the Chesapeake Bay to play for the semipro teams that were emerging in the rural towns of the Delmarva Peninsula. Here the Baltimore native used his own name.

In 1897 he appeared for the crack club of little Federalsburg, Maryland, where he took the field with two others destined for the major leagues. Three teenagers with diverse backgrounds came to this small town in pursuit of their dreams. Unglaub was the city boy already with a glimpse of what the big leagues were like. Also with the Federalsburg Club was the young, scrappy Raymond "Chappy" Charles, who had changed his name from Charles Auchenbach when he came down from New Jersey. Charles would eventually spend three seasons in the majors as a utility player. The pitcher was the carefree Jack "Happy" Townsend. Also known as the "Whirlwind," he was blessed with a blazing fastball and little command of it. He had grown up on his father's farm in nearby Delaware.

Unglaub followed Townsend as his battery mate to the Millington Club of Maryland that same year. When Unglaub finally made a name for himself in the major leagues, newspapers of the area noted that he had also played on the peninsula for Crisfield, the Cambridge Club, and Washington College during this time.

The skills Unglaub picked up through constant playing served him well. Upon graduation from college he signed with Meriden, Connecticut, for 1900, where he batted .321 while playing catcher and first base in the Connecticut State League. Towards the end of the season he was moved to Worcester of the Eastern League, where he played third base the following year. There was some "trouble with the salary question" so he "jumped" to Sacramento of the outlaw California State League in 1902, where he played first base and shortstop. In 1903 he returned to organized baseball, moving up to Milwaukee of the American Association, where he batted .304 after being shifted from first to third base.

A story is told of Unglaub during his stay in Milwaukee. His manager, Joe Cantillon, and several players were walking the streets of Indianapolis to kill time during a road trip. They stopped on a corner to take in the spectacle of a Salvation Army gathering, complete with brass band. Much to their amazement, out of the crowd stepped Bob Unglaub, who did not see them. He repented his evil ways, "I am sorry to admit it," he said, "but I am a baseball player. I don't know how I ever got into such a degrading, sinful business. It is an awful game and the men who play it are sinners, not fit for God-fearing people to associate with."

Cantillon had to restrain his teammates from going after Unglaub as he finished his testimony, and they then went their separate ways. When telling this story a few years later, Cantillon was asked if Unglaub had quit baseball after his epiphany. "Hell no," snapped the manager. "He was the first man in line at the pay window on the first and fifteenth of every month."[19]

At the end of the season his contract was sold to the Boston Americans, in exchange for George Stone and Jack O'Brien, but before the 1904 schedule opened, manager Jimmy Collins told him to report to New York. Unglaub sat on the bench there as a utility player until August when he was transferred back to Boston to complete the deal for Patsy Dougherty. He played in only 15 games for both clubs.

Unglaub finally got a chance to play more frequently for Boston in 1905. He appeared in 43 games that year, including a 15-inning pitching duel between Cy Young of Philadelphia and Rube Waddell in which he accepted 32 chances at first base without an error. But Unglaub now encountered a situation faced by many other major league players of modest stature: he was now making less money than he had in the minor leagues. The National Agreement between organized baseball clubs provided that a player would make more money at each step up in class. Unglaub did not feel this had been the case when he signed his contract with the Boston Americans. He had already jumped organized baseball over a salary dispute, and he was willing to do it again, even if he was now in the major leagues.

Unglaub's salary with Milwaukee had been for $2,000 and through his travels with Boston and New York it had remained the same, even though he claimed to have been verbally promised $2,400. In a letter to August "Garry" Herrmann, president of the National Commission, dated March 15, 1906, from his winter residence in Crisfield, Maryland, where he had met his wife, Unglaub explained he felt "compelled" to accept the pay since the only alternative was to sit out another season as a contract jumper. Unglaub then went public with a letter published in the *Sporting Life* on April 7, 1906, where he spelled out the terms of his contract for the 1905 season.

He was to be paid a $2,000 base salary with another $500 if he "made good" at first base, or $250 if he appeared in a third of the games as a utility player. Unglaub's letter did not explain how he had made good, whether as a first baseman or as a utility player, only that according to previous communications with Herrmann, he was entitled to a "substantial increase." Unglaub had written 12 letters to John Taylor, owner of the Boston Red Sox, between November 14, 1905, and February 14, 1906, asking for his pay—none of which received a reply. The lack of response had prompted the plea to Herrmann. By the time the piece appeared in the *Sporting Life*, Herrmann had responded to Unglaub's letter, stating he had been entitled to a raise all along.

Henry Pulliam, fellow member of the commission, wrote to Herrmann with the opinion that this was not the case of a new player coming into the league, implying that Unglaub had defaulted on his raise by accepting his pay as a utility player the previous year. Pulliam stated in the letter, dated March 21, 1906, "I fail to see where we have any warrant for interfering in the matter." American League president Ban Johnson, who was the real power behind the commission, also sided with Taylor, saying in his correspondence on March 26, 1906, "In my judgment he was handsomely compensated."[20]

The *Sporting Life* would later allege that Taylor might have instructed manager Collins to keep Unglaub out of games at the end of the season to prevent him from making good at first base. It also hinted that the Boston club might have doctored official records to squelch the utility bonus.[21]

In 1906 the Tri-State League gave Unglaub the leverage he did not have the previous two seasons. The league had dropped out of organized baseball and gone outlaw and was attracting quality players. Unglaub was angry enough that the prospect of rejecting organized baseball a second time did not seem to bother him. He signed with Williamsport, Pennsylvania, for the 1906 season. The offer from the outlaw league member for 1907 was for $4,500 a year for as long as he wanted to play there. This was more than double his previous American League salary. Garry Herrmann was not only president of the commission but also owner of the Cincinnati Reds. During the holdout he tried to lure the renegade player from Williamsport. With an offer of $5,000 a year to play for his National League club. Unglaub was determined to stand by his Tri-State contract. Unfortunately for Unglaub, the commission was in the process of reinstating the upstart outlaw league. Before the 1907 season began, the Tri-State League was readmitted into organized baseball and Unglaub's contract reverted back to the Boston Americans.

To rub salt into the wound of the malcontent, Unglaub was informed on March 13, 1907, that he would be fined $200 for not reporting to Boston. Boston had already generously paid the fine and it was now to be deducted from his pay. This prompted an indignant letter from Unglaub to Herrmann, written from the Hotel Marion in Little Rock, Arkansas, on the following day, indicating that Unglaub may have actually inked an offer from the Cincinnati club. In the letter the disgusted Unglaub restates his case to the commission and goes on to complain, "Again, you as Chairman & President of the Cincinnati Club sign me to a Cincinnati contract where I am the rightful property of the Boston Club and there after tampering with another club's player the National Commission has the audacity to fine a man $200 for asserting his rights as a man. So far as I can see it is a case of pure blackmail to extort money from a man to let him make a living for himself & family and so far as I am concerned there will be no fine paid."[22]

It is little wonder that many players opted for independent baseball as on the Eastern Shore. Unglaub went on to threaten to publish "every bit of evidence" so that the truth would be known before he was found guilty by the National Commission. This evidence may have been the allegations against Taylor and Collins that later appeared in the *Sporting Life*.

Unglaub's "meteoric rise" came about when he returned to Boston in 1907. He became the starting first baseman, appearing in 139 games and batting .254 for the season. He would set career highs with 13 triples, 62 runs and 49 RBIs. But Taylor's team was in disarray. Chick Stahl, manager of the team in 1906, had committed suicide in the offseason. Cy Young had started out as manager but stepped down six games into the campaign to be replaced by George Huff. When Huff abruptly resigned eight games later, Taylor turned to his former rebel utility man to take the helm. Unglaub would later muse over his stint as manager,

> After I was appointed the team went mad, raving mad, for some reason, winning four out of the first five games. The winning was done entirely by bunting. We didn't swing at the ball once an inning. We bunted to get on and bunted the happy ones all the way home. It was a great system all right. And the newspapers spent columns talking about our tapping. I was naturally puffed up like a toy balloon and dreamed of teasing our way to a pennant. Then, just to show what fans are made of when they get thinking too much, I began to get letters asking me why, if I had taught the team to bunt, I could not teach the men to drive the ball smartly on a straight line, over the heads of the infielders, when said infielders were playing in! What do you think of that! They were handing me a roast because I did not make the players turn off straight singles in these days when .300 hitters are so scarce you can count them on one hand! I have some of those letters yet.[23]

The fans may have been justified in handing him the roast. The bunting tactics failed to work for long, and with the team posting a 9–20 record, Unglaub was replaced by Deacon McGuire. Only the Senators would post a worse record in the American League in 1907. Despite his problems with management, Unglaub had been appointed captain of the team during this time. Then the fickle Boston fans, and in particular the press, began to roundly blame his shoddy fielding and weak hitting for the team's poor showing. One correspondent wrote in an article, "Wanted—A good first baseman, who can handle fast balls, occasionally stop bounders, who won't confuse base ball with bowling, and who won't draw back when at bat."[24]

McGuire insisted Unglaub would remain as long as he hit, but it was a known fact that the maligned captain now wanted out of Boston. In midseason his wishes were met when he was dealt to the Washington Nationals, where he was to rejoin Joe Cantillon, his former minor league manager. But days after the announced trade, Unglaub was still in Boston where he cried a familiar refrain, "The outlaws for me."

> I have heard nothing from the Washington Club about my transfer to that city. I do not intend to go there unless I am to be paid the same money that I was to get from Boston, and when Cantillon was here he told me he would not give me as much as I was getting, so there can be no misunderstanding to the matter. I would be foolish to make a change without surely doing as well financially as I have been doing, and you may be sure I will not give myself the worst of it. I have been approached by the Stockton, Cal, club and have been offered a very good thing, and if the matter is not fixed up otherwise, I shall leave next Saturday night for California.[25]

In the same report, Cantillon stated that the ever salary-conscious player was to receive the same money as in Boston, but all attempts to reach him had failed. He soon reported to Washington, with the change of scenery reviving the maligned Unglaub. He finished the second half of the season hitting .308. In his two and a half seasons as a regular with the Senators, Unglaub was a valuable commodity to the club. He reported for 1909 with a new attitude. "It's whatever Joe says," he remarked. "If the team needs me anywhere at all, it is satisfactory to me, for I shall try and deliver the goods. I would, of course, prefer the infield, but if there is not room there, it is all the same to me."[26]

During his tenure in Washington, Unglaub was alternately praised and criticized for both his hitting and his fielding. His managers, Cantillon and Jimmy McAleer, thought enough of his offensive abilities to often bat him third or cleanup, as he was considered a clutch hitter. A local reporter said of him, "There is not a man on the local team more dangerous to the opposing pitchers when there are men on the bases than Bob Unglaub. When it comes to wielding the ash he fits in mighty nicely with the local aggregation. Unglaub is a batter whom any pitcher must fear, for when he hits the ball it usually goes on a long journey."[27]

Despite some defensive shortcomings, Unglaub was considered valuable in the field for his versatility, experience, and leadership. He played third and first when Bill Shipke and Jerry Freeman struggled, and plugged the gaps at second and outfield when Jim Delahanty and Clyde Milan went down with extended injuries. He also saw significant playing time in right field. It was in the infield that Unglaub made the biggest difference: "The fact that Unglaub is a valuable man to coach the infield as well as the pitcher gives him the preference."[28]

Unglaub's influence on the team may not have always been positive. In May of 1909 it was reported that the cause of an injury that kept Unglaub out of the lineup came when teammate Bob Ganley broke Unglaub's ribs when he struck him with a bat in an altercation. This incident was denied, with Unglaub saying the sore ribs were an old injury, but Ganley, who happened to be captain of the team, was conspicuously released around this time.

After two and a half seasons with Washington, Unglaub was sold to Lincoln, Nebraska, of the minor leagues. He was a player-manager for Lincoln in 1911 and his contract was sold to Baltimore of the Eastern League prior to the 1912 season. He finished that year in Minneapolis. In 1913 he went to the Northern League as manager, and he usually finished the seasons playing a handful of games for Minneapolis of the American Association. It was a routine he followed through the 1916 season.

During the offseasons Unglaub utilized his engineering degree by hiring on with the Pennsylvania Railroad shops at Camden Yards in his hometown of Baltimore. On November 29, 1916, "while superintending repair work on a locomotive an accident occurred which crushed and mangled him so that all efforts to save his life failed."

One obituary characterized him as "a strong hitter and a brainy player and combined with these qualities a masterful knowledge of the game that made him an ideal team manager. Personally, he was always popular with players and fans alike. Bob Unglaub is a man who will be missed from the game that was better by his connection with it."²⁹

Unglaub was laid to rest in Loudon Park Cemetery in Baltimore. His wife, Minnie F. Unglaub, a Shore native, and her children left this final tribute to Unglaub the husband and father in his obituary in the *Baltimore Sun*, December 1, 1916:

> Oh how hard we tried to save him
> Prayers and tears were all in vain:
> Happy angels came and took him
> From this world of toil and pain.
>
> His heart was true, his life was young
> Yet not our will but God's be done.
>
> My husband gone, our father gone
> Gone to his last long sleep.
> His place and chair are vacant now
> And we are left to weep.

Appendix B

Players and Umpires

This appendix includes lists of major league players who were from the Eastern Shore of Maryland or were known to have participated on their independent and minor league teams, 1867 to 1950. They are categorized as local players, non-native players during the independent years to 1921, and the three Eastern Shore leagues by decade. Known major league umpires are included. Many of these players got their proverbial cup of coffee in the big leagues; others had more significant careers. It would appear the Eastern Shore lived up to its reputation as a hotbed for baseball and its promise to develop players for the major leagues. Nearly 200 major league players appeared for Eastern Shore towns. An asterisk indicates selection to the National Baseball Hall of Fame.

Eastern Shore natives who played in the major leagues.

Frank "Home Run" Baker*	Vick Keen
Frank Bennett	Joe Muir
Knowlington "Buddy" Burbage	Bill "Swish" Nicholson
Al "Pop" Burris	Dickie "Twitchy" Porter
Goldie Cephus	Wilbert Pritchett
Louis "Buttercup" Dickerson	Homer Smoot
Howard "Toots" Ferrell	John "Neck" Stanley
Jake Flowers	Jim Stevens
Jimmie Foxx*	Jack "Brewery" Taylor
Robert Harvey	Doc Wallace
Charles "Bugs" Hayman	Elmer Wicks
Hanson Horsey	Vic Willis*
Judy Johnson*	

Major league players who saw major league action for Eastern Shore town teams, 1867–1921.

Joe Boley	Jimmy Dykes
Steve Brodie	Jack Enright
Richard "Stub" Brown	Harry Fanwell
Mike Cantwell	Frank Foreman
Raymond "Chappy" Charles	Johnnie "Brownie" Foreman
Jack "Handyman" Dunn	Sam Frock

Charlie Gettig	Jimmie Mathison
Bernie Graham	Dan "Cap" McGann
Dick Hawke	Sadie McMahon
Buck Herzog	Harry Morelock
Ed "Lefty" High	Simon Nichols
Elmer "Herkey Jerkey" Horton	Eddie Rommell
Ken "Broadway" Jones	Otis Stocksdale
Bill Kellogg	Cub Stricker
Pete Kilduff	Jack "Happy" Townsend
Matt Kilroy	Earl "Doc" Twining
Mike Kilroy	Rube Vickers
Joe Knotts	Tom "Dutch" Walker
Flip Lafferty	John "Lefty" Wilson
Pete Loos	Dave Zearfoss
Nick Maddox	

Major league players in Eastern Shore baseball, 1922–1928.

Eddie Bacon	Jim Mahady
Clint Brown	Cy Malis
Ed Carroll	Ralph Mattis
Tim Cather	Joe Much
Oscar Charleston*	Roy Parmelee
Joe Cicero	Lerton Pinto
Jay Clarke	Pete Rambo
Mickey Cochrane*	Tony Rensa
George Durning	Paul Richards
Most Eggert	Red Ruffing*
Ferd Eunick	George Selkirk
Carl Fischer	Chick Tolson
Charles Fitzberger	Phil Voyles
Tom Glass	Mike Wilson
Bunny Hearn	Ron Woods
Bill Hohman	Ron Woods
Jimmie Johnson	Rusty Yarnell
Bill Knowlton	Carroll Yerkes
Jim Levey	

Major league players from the Eastern Shore League, 1937–1941.

Mel Bosser	Jorge Comellas
Ollie Boyko	Walter Cress
Gus Brittain	Ducky Detweiler
Allie Clark	Danny Doyle
Cap Clark	Eddie Feinberg
Joe Collins	Carl Furillo

Jim Glad
Sid Gordon
Mike Guerra
Irv Hall
George Hennessey
Gene Hermanski
Sammy Holbrook
Joe Holden
Dixie Howell
Tommy Hughes
Wes Kingdon
Joe Kohlman
Roy Lee
Fred Lucas
Jerry Lynn
Bob Maier
Hal Marnie
Chip Marshall
Ralph McCabe
Wallie Millies
Alex Monchak
Charlie Moss
Dick Mulligan
Joe Murray
Ray Murray

Danny Murtaugh
Ron Northey
Walter Ockey
Joe Ostrowski
Mel Parnell
Alex Pitko
Hugh Poland
Mel Queen
Ken Raffensberger
Bill Ramsey
Ed Roetz
Joe Rullo
Ed Sauer
Don Savage
Harry Sherman
Bud Souchak
Ray Stoviak
Max Surkout
Jocko Thompson
Frank Trechock
Elmer Valo
Mickey Vernon
Dick West
Johnnie Wittig
Yam Yaryan

Major league players from the Eastern Shore League, 1946–1949.

Johnny Andre
Joe Antolick
Joe Becker
Hal Bevan
Steve Bilko
Wally Burnette
Gene Corbett
Ducky Detweiler
Buck Etchison
Sam File
Chris Haughey
Bill Higdon
Stew Hofferth
Ray Jablonski
Lew Krausse
Frank Malzone
Duke Markell

Jim McLeod
Mickey Micoletta
Stu Miller
Herb Moford
Roy Nichols
Joe Pignatano
Tom Poholsky
Pep Rambert
Jack Sanford
Hank Schmulback
Nick Testa
Don Thompson
Tim Thompson
Spider Wilhelm
Grady Wilson
Norm Zauchin
Don Zimmer

Major league umpires who worked on the Eastern Shore. All but McGowan and Napp worked in the Eastern Shore League. Larry Napp played in the league before pursuing an umpiring career. McGowan worked the Eastern Shore prior to the minor league era. McGowan's school for umpires provided many of the arbiters, and at least three Eastern Shore League umpires taught there.

Jim Boyer
Frank Dascoli
Jim Honochick
Bill McGowan*

Larry Napp
Chris Pelekoudas
Ed Sudol

Appendix C

Eastern Shore League Standings,
1922–1949

1922	W	L	Pct.	1923	W	L	Pct.
Parksley Spuds	42	25	.627	Dover Dobbins	51	24	.680
Cambridge Canners	37	32	.536	Cambridge Canners	47	26	.644
Crisfield Crabbers	36	32	.529	Laurel Blue Hens	42	30	.583
Laurel Blue Hens	34	34	.500	Salisbury Indians	34	39	.446
Pocomoke Salamanders	29	41	.414	Parksley Spuds	31	45	.408
Salisbury Indians	27	41	.397	Crisfield Crabbers	26	47	.356

Note: Milford Sandpipers (Freelancers) DNF the '23 season.
Pocomoke City Salamanders DNF the '23 season.

1924	W	L	Pct	1925	W	L	Pct.
Parksley Spuds	46	34	.575	Cambridge Canners	51	38	.750
Cambridge Canners	45	35	.563	Parksley Spuds	48	42	.533
Salisbury Indians	44	36	.550	Salisbury Indians	46	44	.511
Crisfield Crabbers	41	39	.515	Dover Dobbins	46	44	.511
Dover Dobbins	41	39	.515	Crisfield Crabbers	42	48	.467
Easton Farmers	23	57	.281	Easton Farmers	36	53	.404

1926	W	L	Pct.	1927	W	L	Pct.
Crisfield Crabbers	63	21	.750	Parksley Spuds	60	28	.681
Salisbury Indians	59	29	.670	Salisbury Indians	48	38	.552
Dover Dobbins	40	46	.465	Crisfield Crabbers	44	43	.506
Parksley Spuds	40	46	.465	Cambridge Canners	41	47	.466
Cambridge Canners	32	54	.372	Easton Farmers	36	48	.462
Easton Farmers	24	60	.286	Northampton Red Sox	30	55	.353

Final standings, Eastern Shore League, 1937–1941.

1937	W	L	Pct.	1938	W	L	Pct.
Salisbury Indians	59	37	.615	Salisbury Indians	65	47	.580
Easton Browns	56	41	.577	Cambridge Cardinals	61	51	.545
Cambridge Cardinals	53	43	.552	Milford Giants	60	52	.536

Eastern Shore League Standings, 1922–1949

1937	W	L	Pct.	1938	W	L	Pct.
Centreville Colts	52	43	.547	Dover Orioles	58	54	.518
Federalsburg Athletics	52	45	.536	Federalsburg Athletics	56	56	.500
Pocomoke City Red Sox	42	55	.433	Easton Browns	55	56	.495
Crisfield Crabbers	40	57	.412	Centreville Colts	51	60	.459
Dover Orioles	32	65	.330	Pocomoke City Red Sox	41	71	.366

1939	W	L	Pct.	1940	W	L	Pct.
Federalsburg Athletics	83	38	.686	Dover Orioles	72	48	.600
Cambridge Cardinals	68	51	.571	Centreville Red Sox	68	48	.586
Dover Orioles	62	57	.521	Milford Giants	72	52	.581
Centreville Colts	62	60	.508	Salisbury Indians	65	58	.528
Salisbury Indians	59	59	.500	Federalsburg Athletics	57	67	.460
Easton Yankees	51	68	.429	Cambridge Cardinals	52	67	.437
Milford Giants	49	69	.416	Easton Yankees	48	69	.410
Pocomoke City Red Sox	43	75	.364	Pocomoke City Chicks	50	75	.400

1941	W	L	Pct.
Milford Giants	66	41	.653
Cambridge Cardinals	61	45	.575
Easton Yankees	57	53	.518
Centreville Red Sox	54	52	.509
Salisbury Indians	51	59	.472
Federalsburg Athletics	35	73	.324

Final standings, Eastern Shore League, 1946–1949.

1946	W	L	Pct	1947	W	L	Pct.
Centreville Orioles	88	37	.704	Cambridge Dodgers	91	34	.728
Milford Red Sox	77	49	.611	Seaford Eagles	74	49	.602
Dover Phillies	68	57	.544	Dover Phillies	68	57	.544
Salisbury Cardinals	61	64	.488	Federalsburg Athletics	62	63	.496
Easton Yankees	59	66	.472	Milford Red Sox	62	64	.492
Seaford Eagles	58	68	.460	Rehoboth Beach Pirates	50	75	.400
Cambridge Dodgers	53	73	.421	Easton Yankees	48	78	.381
Federalsburg Athletics	37	87	.298	Salisbury Cardinals	45	90	.360

1948	W	L	Pct	1949	W	L	Pct.
Salisbury Cardinals	89	32	.736	Easton Yankees	68	52	.567
Milford Red Sox	81	43	.653	Federalsburg Athletics	63	56	.529
Easton Yankees	71	50	.587	Salisbury Cardinals	60	59	.504
Cambridge Dodgers	65	61	.516	Rehoboth Beach Pirates	56	63	.471
Rehoboth Beach Pirates	60	65	.480	Seaford Eagles	56	64	.467
Seaford Eagles	56	70	.444	Cambridge Dodgers	55	64	.462
Federalsburg Athletics	45	76	.392				
Dover Phillies	26	100	.206				

Chapter Notes

Chapter 1

1. More than one nineteenth-century scribe was certain of an 1845 begin date for baseball. A similar reference comes from "Base Ball," *Chestertown Transcript*, October 13, 1866.

2. The Jamestown Poles is from David Block, "Polish Workers Play Ball at Jamestown, Virginia: An Early Hint of Continental Europe's Influence on Baseball," *Base Ball: A Journal of the Early Game*, Spring 2011, p. 5. Taken from David Block, *Baseball Before We Knew It: A Search for the Roots of the Game* (Lincoln: University of Nebraska Press, 2005), p. 101. Translated and excerpted in A. Waldo, *The True Heroes of Jamestown* (Miami: American Institute of Polish Culture, 1977), p. 128. The original volume: Z. Stefanski, *Memorialium Commercatoris* (Amsterdam; Adreas Bickera, 1625). Bradford's frustration is in William Bradford, *Of Plymouth Plantation* (Mineola, NY: Dover, 2006), p. 62. On Fayetteville, North Carolina, see Harold Seymour and Dorothy Seymour Mills, *Baseball: The People's Game* (New York: Oxford University Press, 1990), p. 541.

3. For a thorough understanding of the origins of baseball and the diffusion of the New York Game, the following are recommended: William Goldstein, *Playing for Keeps: The History of Early Baseball* (Ithaca: Cornell University Press, 2014); John Thorn, *Baseball in the Garden of Eden: The Secret History of the Early Game* (New York: Simon & Schuster, 2011); Peter Morris, *But Didn't We Have Fun? An Informal History of Baseball's Pioneer Era, 1843–1870* (Chicago: Ivan R. Dee, 2008); William Ryczek, *Baseball's First Inning: A History of the National Pastime Through the Civil War* (Jefferson, NC: McFarland, 2009); David Block, *Baseball Before We Knew It: A Search for the Roots of the Game* (Lincoln: University of Nebraska Press, 2005); Tom Gilbert, *How Baseball Happened* (Boston: David R. Godine, 2020).

4. An analysis that the 1850s was the beginning of the global age is in Ben Wilson, *Heyday: The 1850s and the Dawn of the Global Age* (New York: Basic Books, 2016).

5. Baltimore's early years of baseball are recorded in William Ridgely Griffith, *Amateur Baseball in Maryland, 1858–1871* (Baltimore: John Cox's Sons, 1897) and summarized in James Bready, *Baseball in Baltimore: The First 100 Years* (Baltimore: Johns Hopkins University Press, 1998); *The Home Team: A Full Century of Baseball in Baltimore, 1858–1959* (Baltimore: James Bready, 1992); and "Play Ball! The Legacy of Nineteenth Century Baltimore Baseball," *Maryland Historical Magazine,* Summer 1992, pp. 127–144. See also G. Tuohey, *The Story of Baseball: Scrap Book Vol. 1,* 1906, p. 442. Tuohey pushes back the year of baseball starting in Baltimore to 1857. Tuohey was an amateur player from New York c. 1879. Griffith was an actual participant in Baltimore events and a president of the Pastime club and the Baltimore Base Ball Convention. The author has deemed Griffith the more dependable of the two sources.

6. Newspaper accounts of the game include "Local Matters: A Gala Day Among Base-Ball Men: Arrival of Excelsior Club of Brooklyn; Match Game and Dinner at Guy's," *Baltimore Sun*, September 24, 1860, p. 1, col. 6; "Grand Base Ball Match at Baltimore: Excelsior of Brooklyn vs. Excelsior of Baltimore," *New York Clipper*, September 1860; and C. Waff, The Games Tabulation, origins website of the Society for American Baseball Research.

7. Quote is from W. Patten and J. McSpadden, eds., *The Book of Baseball, 1911: Our National Pastime from Its Earliest Days* (Mineola, NY: Dover, 2010), p. 17; Patricia Millen, *From Pastime to Passion: Baseball and the Civil War* (Berwyn Heights, MD: Heritage Books, 2009), p. 19.

Chapter 2

1. For population and general commercial conditions of the slave economy on the Eastern Shore, see Stephen T. Whitman, *Challenging Slavery in the Chesapeake: Black and White Resistance to Human Bondage, 1775–1865* (Baltimore: Maryland Historical Society, 2007).

2. On Fayetteville, North Carolina, cited from Harold Seymour and Dorothy Seymour Mills, *Baseball: The People's Game* (New York: Oxford University Press, 1990), p. 541.

3. The railroad schedule from Easton comes from the Edward Vernon, ed., *Travelers' Official Railway Guide to the United States and Canada* (Philadelphia: American Railroad Manual Co., 1870), p.157. In addition to the local papers on Eastern Shore railroads, see John C. Hayman, *Rails Along the Chesapeake: 1827–1978* (Salisbury, MD: Marvadel Publishers, 1979). Particularly useful for railroads on the Eastern Shore are Edward Vernon, ed., *American Railroad Manual, 1873* (Philadelphia: American Railroad Manual Co., 1873) and *American Railroad Manual, 1874* (Philadelphia: American Railroad Manual Co., 1874). See also Edward H. Hall, *Appletons' Hand-Book of American Travel, the Southern Tour* (New York: D. Appleton & Co., 1866) and *Appletons' Hand-Book of American Travel, the Southern Tour* (New York: D. Appleton & Co., 1867); Edward Vernon, ed., *Travelers' Official Railway Guide of the United States and Canada, 1868* (New York: J.W. Pratt, 1868), *Travelers Official Railway Guide to the United States and Canada, 1869* (New York: J.W. Pratt, 1869) and *Travelers Official Railway Guide of the United States and Canada, 1868* (New York: J.W. Pratt, 1868). Railroad guides were popular for regular commercial and casual travelers and promoted the idea of vacationing. They provided backgrounds of the many splinter lines and schedules along with descriptions of larger destinations and their points of interest.

4. For first quote see Hubert Footner, *Rivers of the Eastern Shore* (Centreville, MD: Tidewater Publishing, 1944); and "ground never trodden" is from Bayard Taylor, "Down the Eastern Shore," *Harper's New Monthly Magazine*, October 1871, pp. 702–708.

5. Gratton's role comes from William Ridgely Griffith, *Amateur Base Ball in Maryland, 1858–1871* (Baltimore: John Cox's Sons, 1897). Also see James Bready, *Baseball in Baltimore: The First 100 Years* (Baltimore: Johns Hopkins University Press, 1998), p. 9. Chestertown's response is from the *Kent News*, September 15, 1866.

6. Description of the New York Game comes from "Base Ball," *Chestertown Transcript*, October 13, 1866. The first game in Elkton is from the *Cecil Whig*, July 21, 1866. Taken from an essay on the beginnings of baseball in Cecil County by Chuck Desocio, "Cecil County Plays Ball," *Bulletin of the Historical Society of Cecil County*, Spring 1995, pp. 1, 4.

7. The 1865 begin date comes from one of the editions of Fred Usilton, *The History of Kent County*. In this edition Usilton has included a chapter, "Kent: A Breeding Ground for Sports Stars," that does not appear in other editions. Since Usilton was writing years later and based on memory or second-hand accounts, the year is questionable. Even the names are different. The activities in Chestertown and Kent County and Head of the Sassafras come from *Kent News*, September 15, 1866; the first box score is found in "Base Ball," *Chestertown Transcript*, September 22, 1866.

8. The anonymous old timer recollects the early years of the Salisbury White Cloud in "Gossip on the Diamond: Base Ball Players of Salisbury Past and Present," *Wicomoco News*, August 6, 1903; the Chestertown reunion is in the "Base-Ball Diamond," *Chestertown Transcript*, June 22, 1893. There is a temptation to ascribe proto baseball games to geographic regions. These two towns are in a confined geographic area 85 miles apart. Chestertown is northernmost, a college town and near the Philadelphia/Wilmington metropolitan area. It would make sense they would play a traditional and sophisticated ball and stick game like cricket. Salisbury is much further south and isolated from most urban influences. It is an easy assumption that they would be playing the more rural version of o'cat games. But the Salisbury founding pitcher threw a curve he had learned playing cricket. Looking back 35 and 25 years, respectively, does not preclude more than one form of ball games being played in each town. The declaration that 1867 was a great year was from William Ridgely Griffith, *Amateur Base Ball in Maryland, 1858–1871*, p. 49.

9. "Base Ball on the Brain," *Easton Gazette*, September 28, 1867.

10. "Base Ball," *Easton Journal*, September 12, 1867; "Base Ball," *Easton Journal*, September 26, 1867; "Base Ball," *Easton Journal*, October 3, 1867; and the match game and admissions is from "Match Game of Base Ball," *Easton Journal*, October 10, 1867.

11. "Communicated," *Chestertown Transcript*, June 1, 1867.

12. "Mr. Editor," *Easton Star*, August 7, 1869.

13. "Messrs. Editors," *Kent News*, April 15, 1871.

14. For the first recorded youth teams see "Base Ball," *American Union*, June 20, 1867; quote is from "Base Ball in the Streets," *Chestertown Transcript*, April 29, 1871.

15. "Base Ball," *Easton Star*, April 29, 1884. On East New Market see the *Dorchester Democrat-News*, August 4, 1888.

16. Gratton's brief story is pieced together from Peter Morris, et al., eds., *Base Ball Pioneers, 1850–1870* (Jefferson, NC: McFarland, 2012); Dwight Hall, *Memorial History of Syracuse* (Syracuse: H.P. Smith Co., 1892); *Nebraska State Journal*, February 25, 1873; *Nebraska Herald*, March 7, 1872; *Omaha Evening Bee*, August 6, 1874; *Grand Island Times*, August 20, 1873, December 1, 1881; *Syracuse Daily Courier and Union*, May 28 and September 28, 1859; and various issues of the *Baltimore Sun*, 1863–1870.

Chapter 3

1. "Base Ball," *Dorchester Democrat-News*, May 25, 1872, for the initial quote; the Cambridge

response is found in "Base Ball," *Cambridge Era,* August 24, 1878.

2. "Base Ball and Balloon Ascension," *Cambridge Chronicle,* September 20, 1871, and the *Easton Journal,* September 28, 1871.

3. *Easton Journal,* August 20, 1874.

4. "Grounds Rented and Well Shaded," *Salisbury Advertiser,* May 3, 1873; *Salisbury Advertiser,* June 28, 1873, has more on the grounds.

5. Quote is from "Base Ball-Two Exciting Games," *Dorchester Democrat-News,* July 27, 1872. See also "Base Ball Match," *Easton Star,* July 23, 1872.

6. "Base Ball," *Cambridge Chronicle,* August 28, 1872.

7. "Base Ball—Accident," *Dorchester Herald and News,* August 31, 1872.

8. "Base Ball, Cambridge vs. Seaford—A Warm Reception and Hearty Welcome," *Dorchester Herald News,* July 26, 1873.

9. "Gossip on the Diamond," *Wicomico News,* August 13, 1903.

10. *Cambridge Chronicle,* July 31, 1878.

11. "Base Ball and Murder," *Salisbury Advertiser,* June 6, 1874.

12. John H. Lancaster, "Baltimore, a Pioneer in Organized Baseball," *Maryland Historical Magazine,* March 1940, pp. 33–34.

13. "Not So Base," *Salisbury Advertiser,* April 3, 1875.

14. "Base Ball at Centreville," *Easton Star Democrat,* July 2, 1878.

15. The Mutual and Unique are from Todd Peterson, "May the Best Man Win: The Black Ball Championships, 1866–1923," *Baseball Research Journal,* Spring 2013. League and Newington Park is from Harold Seymour and Dorothy Seymour Mills, *Baseball: The People's Game* (New York: Oxford University, 1990), p. 539.

16. Leading quote is in Japheth Knopp, "Negro League Baseball: Black Community and Socio Economic Impact of Integration: Kansas City, Missouri as a Case Study," *Baseball Research Journal,* Spring 2016. Game citation from the *Cambridge Chronicle,* August 18, 1875.

17. "Base Ball at Greensborough—Easton Club Victors," *Easton Star Democrat,* June 18, 1878; for Easton vs. Centreville, see *Easton Star Democrat,* July 2, 1878; the challenge for the silver ball is in "Base Ball Challenge," *Cambridge Era,* July 6, 1878.

18. "Gossip on the Diamond," *Wicomico News,* August 13, 1903.

19. Wilmington's version is in the *Wilmington Morning Herald,* October 5, 19, and 28, 1878.

20. What happened to the ballists is in "Base Ball," *Chestertown Transcript,* July 17, 1879; Robeson is found in the *Easton Star Democrat,* September 9, 1879; Denton's dearth of players is from the *Denton Journal,* August 22, 1880.

21. From Harold Jopp, et al., eds., *Rediscovery of the Eastern Shore: Delmarva Travelogues of the 1870s* (Wye Mills, MD: Chesapeake College Press, 1984), p. 9; as cited from Robert Wilson, "On the Eastern Shore," *Lippincott Magazine,* August and September 1876.

22. Again cited from Jopp, et al., eds., *Rediscovery of the Eastern Shore: Delmarva Travelogues of the 1870s* (Wye Mills, MD: Chesapeake College Press, 1984), p. 71 as cited from Robert Wilson, "On the Eastern Shore," *Lippincott's Magazine,* July 1876; for other descriptions see Bayard Taylor, "Down the Eastern Shore," *Harper's New Monthly Magazine,* October 1871; Howard Pyle, *Harper's Monthly Magazine,* May 1875; and Alfred Townsend, "The Chesapeake Peninsula," *Scribner's Monthly,* March 1875.

Chapter 4

1. "Gossip of the Diamond, Salisbury Players Past and Present," *Wicomico News,* August 6, 1903; "Gossip of the Diamond, Base Ball Players of Salisbury Past and Present," *Wicomico News,* August 13, 1903; "Base Ball Notes," *Cambridge Chronicle,* June 16, 1884.

2. "Chestertown, Sudlersville, and Betterton," *Kent News,* August 9, 1884. The quote is from the *Kent News,* July 26, 1884.

3. See "The People of the Oyster War, Part 2," *Attractions, Easton Star Democrat,* August 2021, originally printed in the *New York Sun,* December 9, 1888. On the peach farm see Harold Jopp, et al., eds., *Rediscovering the Eastern Shore: Travelogues of the 1870s* (Wye Mills, MD: Chesapeake College Press, 1984), p. 110, as cited from Robert Wilson, "On the Eastern Shore," *Lippincott's Magazine,* July 1876. On market hunting see Harry Walsh, Sr., *Outlaw Gunners* (Cambridge, MD: Tidewater Press, 1971).

4. *Cambridge Chronicle,* June 9, 1887.

5. *Baltimore American,* June 15, 1887.

6. For quotes in order of use see *Salisbury Advertiser,* April 21, 1883; *Chestertown Transcript,* April 9, 1883; *Dorchester Democrat-News,* May 12, 1883.

7. "Base Ball Battle," *Dorchester Democrat-News,* June 16, 1883; "Taylor's Island Base Ball Skirmish," *Dorchester Democrat-News,* June 23, 1883; "A Truce," *Dorchester Democrat-News,* September 8, 1883.

8. *Dorchester Democrat-News,* July 7, 1883.

9. "A Base Ball Association," *Dorchester Democrat-News,* May 17, 1884.

10. *Easton Star,* July 22 and 29, 1884.

11. "Base Ball Notes," *Cambridge Chronicle,* July 16, 1884; see also "The Caroline Umpire," *Cambridge Chronicle,* July 23, 1884.

12. "Bad Row at Oriole Park—A Close Decision Raises an Ugly Spirit in the Crowd—A Run for Brennan—A Blow in the Jaw—An Exciting Game," *Baltimore News American,* June 13, 1884.

13. *Dorchester Democrat-News,* June 13, 1885.

14. "Muffers Reply to the Eclipse," *Dorchester Democrat-News,* August 22, 1885.

15. For Idlewild vs. Muffers, "Base Ball," *Easton Star*, August 30, 1887; "Base Ball," *Dorchester Democrat-News*, August 27, 1887; *Dorchester Democrat-News*, August 27, 1887.

16. See Todd Peterson, "May the Best Man Win: The Black Ball Championship, 1886–1923," *Baseball Research Journal*, Spring 2013. Quote is from *Dorchester Democrat-News*, May 7, 1887.

17. "Baseball and Other Topics," *Cambridge Chronicle*, May 16, 1889.

18. *Cambridge Chronicle*, July 25, 1889.

Chapter 5

1. Marty Payne, "Country Ball: Big Teams in Small Towns," *National Pastime*, 2009, p. 16. Marty Payne, "Bob Unglaub," *SABR Biography Project*, 2003. On Townsend see *Wilmington Morning News*, December 23, 1963. General history in this chapter comes from the *Chestertown Transcript, Dorchester Democrat-News, Cambridge Chronicle, Salisbury Advertiser, Easton Star,* and *Easton Gazette*. See notes for other sources and specific citations.

2. *Chestertown Transcript*, April 26, 1894.

3. Quote is from the *Salisbury Advertiser*, June 17, 1893.

4. "The Field of Sport," *Chestertown Transcript*, June 20, 1895.

5. For Hanover vs. Western Maryland Railroad see "Diamond Sketches," *Chestertown Transcript*, July 25, 1895; crowds in excess of five thousand at Tolchester from *Chestertown Transcript*, June 23, 1900.

6. Unless otherwise noted population figures used in this book are from Richard Forstall, *Population of States and Counties: 1790–1990* (Washington, D.C.: United States Bureau of Census, 1996), and the *12th Census of the United States Census Bulletin #28: Maryland* (Washington, D.C.: United States Bureau of Census, January 3, 1901).

7. For Adelman quote see Melvin Adelman, "Academicians and Athletics: Historians' Views of American Sports," *Maryland Historian,* Fall 1973, p. 129; Washington College subscriptions are in "The Base-Ball Season," *Chestertown Transcript*, April 21, 1897; on Easton see *Easton Star*, July 7, 1885.

8. For the women's New York team see "New York vs. Cambridge," *Dorchester Democrat-News*, May 20, 1893, and the *Cambridge Chronicle*, June 1, 1893.

9. Cited from the *Cambridge Chronicle*, May 17, 1894.

10. "Easton Boys Get Licked," *Easton Gazette*, July 20, 1895.

11. Quote and game account are from "Salisbury Still Playing," *Salisbury Advertiser*, August 17, 1895.

12. The Percy incident is found in the *Cambridge Chronicle*, July 11, 1895.

13. Excerpted from "Salisbury Wins," *Cambridge Chronicle*, August 15, 1895.

14. The Hope Lodge excursion is from the *Cambridge Chronicle*, May 29, 1890. The quote is from William Clarence Matthews to the *Boston Traveler*, August 9, 1905, cited from Karl Lindholm, "College Boys and Boozers: Vermont's Northern League and William Clarence Matthews," *Base Ball: A Journal of the Early Game*, Fall 2008, p. 83.

15. "It Was a Great Game," *Easton Gazette*, July 17, 1897.

16. Haddaway quote is from "Base Ball Notes," *Easton Gazette*, August 8, 1896.

17. *Cambridge Chronicle*, July 2, 1896.

18. Washington College game is from the *Cambridge Chronicle,* June 25, 1896; the Annapolis game is in the *Dorchester Democrat-News*, August 15, 1896.

19. Quote from *Dorchester Democrat-News*, July 25, 1896; the Starlight and the Salisbury invitation to the Orioles is found in the *Salisbury Advertiser*, July 25, 1896.

20. "The Wind Up with Cambridge," *Salisbury Advertiser*, August 29, 1896, has an account where Cambridge tried to sign Joe Corbett and Dad Clarkson from the Baltimore Orioles. For the contentious season see the *Cambridge Chronicle*, July 2, 1896; see also the *Salisbury Advertiser*, July 7, 18, and 25, 1896, and August 1, 15, and 29, 1896.

21. *Dorchester County Democrat-News*, August 22 and 29, 1896.

22. "A Great Game," *Chestertown Transcript*, July 22, 1897.

23. "Our Champions," *Chestertown Transcript*, July 29, 1897, and "Cambridge vs. Chestertown," *Cambridge Chronicle*, July 29, 1897.

24. "Notes of the Diamond," *Chestertown Transcript*, August 21, 1897.

Chapter 6

1. For the perception of social mobility in baseball see Jerrold I. Casway, *The Culture and Ethnicity of Nineteenth Century Baseball* (Jefferson, NC: McFarland, 2017) and Steven A. Riess, "Race and Ethnicity in Rural Baseball: 1900–1919," *Journal of Ethnic Studies*, Fall 1977, pp. 95–108.

2. Applications are in "Meeting of Cambridge Base Ball Association," *Cambridge Daily Banner*, May 22, 1908.

3. Art Rooney is from Harold Seymour and Dorothy Mills, *The People's Game* (New York: Oxford University Press, 1990), pp. 266–270.

4. "Baseball This Week," *Salisbury Advertiser*, September 10, 1904; "Baseball This Week, *Dorchester Democrat-News*, August 30, 1907, and "Cambridge Team Winning Streak," *Dorchester Democrat-News*, August 10, 1907.

5. For more on Nichols see Campbell Gibson,

"Simon Nicholls: Gentleman, Farmer, Ballplayer," *Baseball Research Journal*, 1989.

6. The 1900 season was pieced together from a combination of Salisbury, Cambridge, and Easton newspapers. See notes for other sources and specific citations. The Crumpton description is found in "With the Ballists," *Chestertown Transcript*, May 24, 1902.

7. For the Chicago Stars see *Dorchester Democrat-News*, May 31, 1902; report on the King Bees is from the *Dorchester Democrat-News*, July 19, 1902.

8. Eastern Shore assessment is from "Sporting Notes," *Chestertown Transcript*, May 24, 1903.

9. The league's season is primarily from the *Salisbury Advertiser* and the *Dorchester Democrat-News*, 1904. Assessment of the league is found in "Baseball Season Closed," *Cambridge Daily Banner*, September 8, 1904.

10. On Herzog see C. Starr Matthews, "Work and Win," *Baltimore Sun*, March 12, 1911. For more on Baker see Barry Sparks, *Frank "Home Run" Baker: Hall of Famer and World Series Hero* (Jefferson, NC: McFarland, 2006).

11. Guy W. Green, *Fun and Frolic with an Indian Ball Team* (Lincoln: Woodruff-Collins, 1907; reprint, Mattituck, NY: Amereon House, 1992) provides a lighthearted, contemporary view of a barnstorming team written by its manager.

12. *Ibid.*, p. 40.

13. The boat brigade is from "Base Ball Game Yesterday," *Cambridge Daily Banner*, June 28, 1907. The quote on the importance of baseball to small towns is in "Base Ball News," *Dorchester Democrat-News*, June 13, 1908.

14. On Maud Nelson and the Cherokee Indian Baseball Club see the *Dorchester Democrat-News*, September 12, 1908. For more on Maud and women's baseball, see Jean Hastings Ardell, *Breaking into Baseball: Women and the National Pastime* (Carbondale: Southern Illinois University Press, 2005) and Debra A. Shattuck, *Bloomer Girls: Women Baseball Pioneers* (Urbana: University of Illinois Press, 2017).

15. "Base Ball News," *Dorchester Democrat-News*, June 13, 1908.

16. This summary of Fong is from "Lee Fong Returns Home to China," *Cambridge Banner*, October 10, 1916, and numerous miscellaneous excerpts from the *Cambridge Banner*.

17. On King see the *Salisbury Advertiser*, May 28, 1898; for Lewis, *Afro-American*, August 15, 1903; on fairs, *Afro-American*, September 11, 1909.

18. Mother and her daughter are from the *Dorchester Democrat-News*, August 15, 1903; for railroad officials objections, see *Salisbury Advertiser*, August 24, 1903.

19. On William Lee, *Salisbury Advertiser*, June 30, 1906; Crisfield is in the *Salisbury Advertiser*, August 3, 1907, and "Lynching in Somerset," *Dorchester Democrat-News*, August 3, 1907; on Onancock, see *Salisbury Advertiser*, August 17, 1907.

20. Sol White, *History of Colored Base Ball: With Other Documents of the Early Black Game, 1886–1936*, 1907, introd. Jerry Malloy (Lincoln: University of Nebraska Press, 1995), p. 67.

21. Quote is from Melvin L. Adelman, "Academicians and Athletics: Historians' Views of American Sports," *Maryland Historian*, Fall 1973, p. 126.

22. The reference to Thompson is from "St. Johns vs. Washington," *Chestertown Transcript*, May 30, 1908.

Chapter 7

1. An example of a trip to Baker's is in Bozeman Bulger, "Home Run Baker's Rise," *Literary Digest*, April 16, 1912, pp. 718–21. The quote of Helen Berry is from Dickson Preston, *Trappe: The Story of an Old Fashioned Town* (Easton, MD: Economy Printing, 1976), p. 100.

2. For further discussion see Steven Riess, *Touching Base: Professional Baseball and American Culture in the Progressive Era* (Urbana: University of Illinois Press, 1999); see also Richard Crepeau, "Urban and Rural Images in Baseball," *Journal of Popular Culture*, Fall 1975. For a contemporary perspective see "Country Boys in the Big Leagues," *Literary Digest*, April 18, 1925, p. 602.

3. On the Chinese Nationals, see Joel Franks, "From Honolulu to Brooklyn: The Journeys of the Hawaiian Travelers," *Base Ball: A Journal of the Early Game*, Spring 2008, p. 5.

4. Salisbury league is in the *Afro-American*, July 23, 1910; for Henry see *Afro-American*, June 18, 1910; the Corkers are in *Afro-American*, September 3 and 17, 1910; silent forces in *Afro-American*, June 17, 1911.

5. "An Enthusiastic Meeting at Masonic Hall Last Night," *Cambridge Daily Banner*, June 10, 1911.

6. *Wicomoco News*, August 5, 1915.

7. Best coverage of the 1915 season comes from the *Wicomoco News* and the *Baltimore Sun*, 1915; the game against the Athletics is from "2,500 Turn Out to See A's," *Wicomoco News*, September 25, 1915.

8. Season events pieced together from assorted newspaper accounts including the *Wicomoco News*, *Chestertown Transcript*, *Baltimore Sun*, and *Cambridge Daily Banner*. See notes for other sources and specific citations. The playoff series is from the *Baltimore Sun*, September 14–29, 1916, found at the Enoch Pratt Library microfilm copy. The Pratt has a later edition than the digital source on newspapers.com, which does not have the detailed coverage nor the photographs found in the Pratt edition.

9. Quoted from "Fast Base Ball Game

Tomorrow Afternoon," *Cambridge Daily Banner*, July 12, 1920.

10. "Need $2,000 for Team," *Wicomico News*, July 28, 1921; "Crisfield Defeats Cambridge," *Cambridge Daily Banner*, July 14, 1921.

11. *Wicomico News*, August 25, 1921.

12. Much of the Eastern Shore season was well covered in the *Baltimore Sun*. See also the *Wicomico News*, August 25 and September 1, 1921, and the *Cambridge Daily Banner*. Much of the detail of the playoffs and subsequent series is included in a series of articles in the *Baltimore Sun* appearing August 28 through September 11, 1921.

Chapter 8

1. The real estate information is from the White House initiative of the Delmarva Eastern Shore Association, *Summer White House* (Salisbury: Executive Office of Salisbury, MD, 1929); the watermen's war is from *Salisbury Times*, February 19, 1926; the bay bridge and Ponzi are in the *Salisbury Daily Times*, January 23, 1926. For a brief glimpse of Edna Ferber and the showboats of the Eastern Shore see Dickson Preston, *Trappe: The Story of an Old Fashioned Town* (Easton, MD: Economy Printing, 1976), p. 87.

2. *Sporting News*, November 22, 1924. On Sexton's concern with youth see "To Rescue Baseball in Small Towns," *Literary Digest*, April 18, 1925, pp. 68–72.

3. This brief history of the minor leagues is from Lloyd Johnson and Miles Wolf, eds., *Encyclopedia of Minor League Baseball*, 3rd ed. (Durham: Baseball America, 2007).

4. Quote from *Sporting News*, September 14, 1922.

5. *Sporting News*, September 27, 1922.

6. Season accounts were pieced together from contemporary sources including the *Salisbury Daily Times, Cambridge Daily Banner, Easton Star Democrat, Baltimore Sun* and *Sporting News*, and secondary sources including Bill Mowbray, *Eastern Shore League* (Centreville, MD: Tidewater Publishers, 1989) and Jimmie Keenan, "Judge Landis Day in Salisbury, MD," SABR website. See notes for specific citations.

7. Quote and Parksley are found in the *Baltimore Sun*, August 25, 1922.

8. The Frock saga unfolds in *Baltimore Sun*, August 13 and 28, 1922; see also *Sporting News*, August 17 and November 29, 1922.

9. *Baltimore Sun*, June 18, 1922.

10. The Dixon account is in the *Baltimore Sun*, August 9, 1922.

11. For an excellent account of the Five State Series, see John P. Holl, "Baseball Braggin' Rights: The Five State Series, 1922–1927," *National Pastime*, 2009. For the 1922 series see *Sporting News*, September 14 and 21, 1922, and the *Baltimore Sun*, September 1, 3, 5, 7–11, 1922.

12. Quote from *Sporting News*, September 7, 1922.

13. Quote and ending of Frock story is from the *Sporting News*, November 9, 1922.

14. "Baby Member" is in *Sporting News*, January 23, 1922.

Chapter 9

1. General season events were taken as reported from the *Baltimore Sun, Salisbury Daily Times, Cambridge Daily Banner, Easton Star Democrat*, and *Sporting News*, and Bill Mowbray, *The Eastern Shore Baseball League* (Centreville, MD: Tidewater Publishers, 1989); headlines from the *Sporting News*, September 7 and 14, 1922; on the Eastern Shore League, see *Sporting News*, April 12, 1923. Specific citations are noted.

2. *Baltimore Sun*, July 19–21, 1923. See also Jimmie Keenan, "Judge Landis Day in Salisbury, MD," SABR website; William Mowbray, *The Eastern Shore Baseball League* (Centreville, MD: Tidewater Publishers, 1989); and *Fred Lucas Testimonial Program*, November 16, 1971.

3. "Eastern Shore Will Limp Along to Wire," *Sporting News*, August 30, 1923.

4. Cochrane's troubles are in the *Baltimore Sun*, September 12 and 13, 1923; other coverage of the series can be found in the *Baltimore Sun*, September 4, 8, 9, and 20, 1923. The hand story is from Ed Nichols, "Shore Sports," *Salisbury Daily Times*, April 19, 1947.

5. For Hanlon see the *Baltimore Sun*, September 26, 1923.

6. For Baker and the Easton Farmers see the *Baltimore Sun*, March 4 and 18, 1924; *Sporting News*, March 13, 1924; and an interview with Reverend Donaldson is in the *Star Democrat*, March 25, 1955. For the response of Easton volunteers see the *Easton Star Democrat*, May 3, 1924. For Raintree Adams see the *Easton Star Democrat*, June 7, 1924.

7. For Salisbury finances, *Salisbury Daily Times*, May 5 and 22, 1924; *Sporting News*, November 13, 1924.

8. *Sporting News*, May 29, 1924, offers total attendance of 9,000 while the *Salisbury Daily Times*, May 31, 1924, stated 8,000. On Ruffing's position play, see *Sporting News*, August 14, 1924.

9. Baker as told to Bill Perry, "Shore League Had Stars: 'Home Run,' 'Whirlaway,' and Ducky. A League of Our Own," part 2, *Easton Star Democrat*, August 31, 1992.

10. *Salisbury Daily Times*, June 11 and 16, 1924. There were three Fitzbergers playing in the league during these years. Charlie was a pitcher/position player with Laurel. Freddie was catcher and outfielder for Salisbury. This appears to be Christian Fitzberger of Baltimore listed on an early season roster.

11. *Salisbury Daily Times*, July 21 and 26, 1924.

12. *Salisbury Daily Times*, August 6, 1924.
13. First quote *Salisbury Daily Times*, May 9, 1924; the second is from *Salisbury Daily Times*, May 26, 1924.
14. Quote is from the *Baltimore Sun*, August 16, 1924.
15. Landis throwing a high spitter and the higher crowd number is from *Salisbury Daily Times*, August 16, 1924. Another account is from the *Baltimore Sun*, August 16, 1924.
16. For Johnson, see the *Salisbury Daily Times*, August 19, 1924, and the *Sporting News*, August 24, 1924.
17. The Vereker incident is from the *Baltimore Sun*, August 31, 1924.
18. Gibson was later hanged for the assault. For the posse and jailhouse attack see *Baltimore Sun*, August 28–30, 1924; *Sporting News*, September 17, 1924; *Salisbury Daily Times*, August 29, 1924.
19. *Baltimore Sun*, September 2, 1924; for quote, *Salisbury Daily Times*, September 2, 1924.
20. *Baltimore Sun*, September 5, 6, 7, 9, 10 and 14, 1924; *Baltimore Evening Sun*, September 11, 1924. See also *Salisbury Daily Times*, September 11, 1924; *Sporting News*, September 18, 1924.
21. The 1924 doubleheader is from the *Salisbury Daily Times*, September 5, 1924, and the 1925 series is found in the *Salisbury Evening Times*, September 21, 1925; other coverage for the six-game series appeared in the *Harrisburg Evening News*, September 23, 1925; *Baltimore Sun*, September 25, 1925; and the *Wilmington Morning News*, September 26, 1925.
22. *Afro-American*, May 30, 1925; on Centreville, see *Afro-American*, July 23, 1927.
23. See *Afro-American*, May 2 and 9, 1925. For the team from Chester, PA, Dana Carn, "Black Baseball Players Had a League of Their Own," *Easton Star Democrat*, February 21, 1993.
24. Picnic is from *Afro-American*, August 22, 1925; on Greensboro attendance, *Afro-American*, May 25, 1925.
25. On salaries, see Sol White, *History of Colored Base Ball* (Lincoln: University of Nebraska Press, 1995), p. 67; Also Steven Riess, *Touching Base: Professional Baseball and American Culture in the Progressive Era* (Urbana: University of Illinois Press, 1999), p. 199.

Chapter 10

1. On Salisbury, see the *Salisbury Times*, December 17, 1924; for Easton, *Sporting News*, November 20, 1924. On no teams losing money, see *Salisbury Daily Times*, April 15, 1925.
2. Salisbury contracts from *Sporting News*, February 19, 1925.
3. Quote from *Salisbury Daily Times*, April 15, 1925.
4. Ball park renovations are found in *Salisbury Daily Times*, April 4, 1925, and attendance is in the *Salisbury Daily Times*, May 29, 1925.
5. Baker's parting was reported as either a resignation or a firing. See *Sporting News*, June 18, 1925; *Salisbury Daily Times*, June 10, 1925.
6. *Salisbury Daily Times*, August 25, 1925, refers to Herzog as a native son; on the "cantaloupe king," see *Sporting News*, January 10, 1924; see also C. Starr Matthews, "Work and Win, Is Motto of Clever Charlie Herzog," *Baltimore Sun*, March 12, 1911.
7. Donahue is in *Sporting News*, June 18, 1925; Mitchell is from the *Sporting News*, July 16, 1925; Murphy is in *Salisbury Daily Times*, July 11, 1925.
8. Quote from *Salisbury Daily Times*, July 14, 1925.
9. Quoted from *Salisbury Daily Times*, July 15, 1925.
10. Umpire strike is from *Sporting News*, August 13, 1925; umpire reshuffle is from *Salisbury Daily Times*, August 3, 1925.
11. Cited from the *Salisbury Daily Times*, July 26, 1925.
12. The Mitchell appeal is found in the *Salisbury Daily Times*, September 3 and 4, 1925.
13. References to Johnson's Pennant are from the *Sporting News*, August 6 and 10, 1925; Johnson's concern for "pet circuit gamblers" is echoed in the *Sporting News*, August 13, 1925.
14. Five State Series of 1925 is found in the *Baltimore Sun*, September 11–13 and 15–18, 1925; *Salisbury Daily Times*, September 10 and 15–18, 1925.
15. For Easton finances, see *Salisbury Daily Times*, August 27, 1925; attendance, see *Salisbury Daily Times*, September 25, 1925; Salisbury exposition, *Salisbury Daily Times*, December 22, 1925; league reporting, *Salisbury Daily Times*, December 5, 1925; Herzog, *Sporting News*, December 24, 1925.
16. The Cambridge fundraiser is in the *Baltimore Sun*, March 22, 1926; pin drive is from the *Salisbury Daily Times*, April 10, 1926; card party is found in the *Salisbury Daily Times*, March 16, 1926.
17. For league rules and renovations, see *Salisbury Daily Times*, March 26, April 5 and 16, and May 23, 1926; for new rules and Crisfield, see *Baltimore Sun*, January 7, 1926.

Chapter 11

1. The forfeit story plays out in the *Salisbury Daily Times*, August 13, 16, 17, 19, 24, 31, 1926, and September 4 and 7, 1926; *Sporting News*, August 26 and September 9, 1926; *Baltimore Sun*, August 20, 24, 26, 1926, and September 4, 6, 7, 1926. See also the *Star Democrat*, August 1926.
2. The Five State Series of 1926 is from the *Sporting News*, September 23, 1926; *Salisbury Daily Times*, September 11, 14, and 16, 1926; *Baltimore Sun*, September 15, 16, and 18, 1926. See also Holl, "Baseball Braggin' Rights; The Five State Series, 1922–1927," *National Pastime*, 2009.

Totals are from the *Baltimore Sun*, September 19, 1926.

3. For more on Jackson, see *Sporting News*, December 23, 1926; *Salisbury Daily Times*, December 10, 1926, November 15, 1926, and July 19, 1926; *Baltimore Sun*, December 10, 1926.

4. Linthicum quote, *Baltimore Sun*, December 29, 1926.

5. On officers and class rule, see *Sporting News*, January 13, 1927; new class rule, *Salisbury Daily Times*, April 15, 1927; Cambridge threat, *Salisbury Daily Times*, February 18, 1927; fashion show, *Salisbury Daily Times*, March 23, 1927; Salisbury sponsors, *Salisbury Daily Times*, April 8, 1927; the Arcade theater, *Salisbury Daily Times*, April 28, 1927.

6. For the Dover reaction, see "Can't Win the Pennant," *Salisbury Daily Times*, March 10, 1927; the child comparison is cited from the *Salisbury Daily Times*, April 8, 1927; on the railroad and the Pullman car, *Salisbury Times*, March 11, 1927.

7. On contract and the Landis meeting, see *Sporting News*, April 28, 1927; *Baltimore Sun*, April 22 and 24, 1927.

8. Opening day and Delmarva League is from the *Salisbury Daily Times*, May 27, 1927; Independence Day, *Salisbury Daily Times*, July 5, 1927; Dan Pasquella, *Salisbury Daily Times*, March 22, 1927.

9. *Salisbury Daily Times*, August 10, 1927.

10. *Baltimore Sun*, September 13, 14, 15, 17, 19, and 20, 1927; *Salisbury Daily Times*, September 13, 14, 15, 17, and 20, 1927; *Sporting News*, September 22 and 29, 1927.

11. *Baltimore Sun*, November 8, 1927. There are 11 players listed, including two pitchers, two catchers, two shortstops, and only two outfielders. Due to fatigue, injury, and illness, players on short roster barnstorming teams were called on to play multiple positions, e.g., Richards could play third base, second base and shortstop and he could pitch. The team roster was listed as Tony Pasquella, Crisfield, manager and first base; Harry Tracey, Camden, N.J., outfield; Paul Richards, Crisfield and St. Louis, shortstop; G.H. Edmondson, pitcher; Ollie Jones, Kansas City, third base; Mike McAllister, Parksley, shortstop; Cecil "Slim" Rose, Crisfield, pitcher; George Eggert, Crisfield, infield; and Jimmy Lyons, Crisfield, outfield. Benny Artigiani of City College and Neil Rabe of Crisfield handled the catching.

12. *Baltimore Sun*, November 8, 1927; *Sporting News*, December 29, 1927.

13. *Salisbury Daily Times*, September 6 and 9, 1927.

14. Quote is from the *Baltimore Sun*, April 14, 1928; also *Baltimore Sun*, January 28, 1928; *Salisbury Daily Times*, January 13, 1928.

15. *Salisbury Daily Times*, January 13, 1928, March 24, 1928, and April 5, 1928; resignations are from *Salisbury Daily Times*, February 16, 1928.

16. First quote is from the *Baltimore Sun*, April 1, 1928; Lush and radio proposal is cited from the *Baltimore Sun*, April 7, 1928; the Baltimore Sportsman, *Baltimore Sun*, April 5, 1928.

17. On Lush see the *Sporting News*, May 3, 1928; on Whalen and funds, *Salisbury Daily Times*, April 11, 1928.

18. Plans for the radio broadcasts are in the *Salisbury Daily Times*, July 2, 3, and 10, 1928.

19. For the demise of the league see the *Baltimore Sun*, July 11, 1928; *Salisbury Daily Times*, July 11 and 12, 1928; also *Salisbury Daily Times*, July 13, 1928.

20. Quote is from Ed Nichols, "Shore Sports," *Salisbury Daily Times*, August 11, 1947.

Chapter 12

1. *Sporting News*, January 10, 1924.

2. *Salisbury Daily Times*, September 19, 1925, and *Sporting News*, November 5, 1925.

3. Warren Corbett, "Paul Richards," SABR Bio Project.

4. For league leaders and awards, see *Salisbury Daily Times*, September 16, 1926, and *Salisbury Daily Times*, December 4, 1926.

5. Rickey's roster is in the *Baltimore Sun*, September 18, 1926; Easton rumors are found in the *Sporting News*, November 21, 1926, and *Baltimore Sun*, November 21 and 26, 1926.

6. For Trippe see *Salisbury Daily Times*, June 21, 1927. For Rose and Perry, *Salisbury Daily Times*, July 2, 1927, and *Salisbury Daily Times*, July 12, 1927.

Chapter 13

1. For a general history of Eastern Shore canneries see R. Lee Burton, Jr., *Canneries of the Eastern Shore* (Centreville, MD: Tidewater Press, 1986). The growth of the chicken industry is found in Salisbury Chamber of Commerce, *Survey of Salisbury* (Salisbury, MD: Messick and Sons, 1951).

2. See William Mowbray, *The Eastern Shore Baseball League* (Centreville, MD: Tidewater Publishers, 1989), pp. 39–41; also "The Dorchester County Baseball War, Irving Lloyd as Told to Barry Sparks," *Baltimore Sun Magazine*, June 20, 1976.

3. Federalsburg records are found in ledgers from Federalsburg Historical Society.

4. Quotes of Leon Taylor are cited from Dana Carn, "Black Baseball Players Had a League of Their Own," *Easton Star Democrat*, February 21, 1993. Also used were notes from an undated presentation of Ralph Deaton at the Dorchester County Historical Society.

5. Quote is of Ralph Hollis from Dana Carn, "Black Baseball Players Had A League of Their Own," *Easton Star Democrat*, February 21, 1993.

6. For the Black Hawks see *Afro-American*, September 3, 1932; for Salisbury All Stars, *Afro-American*, July 27, 1935.

7. Landis's opinion and Breadon quote from Robert L. Finch, L.H. Addington, Ben M. Morgan, *Story of Minor League Baseball* (Columbus, OH: Stoneman Press, 1952), p. 77; for the reinstatement of joint ownership and the Cardinal '26 roster see Johnson and Wolf, eds., *The Encyclopedia of Minor League Baseball*, 3rd ed. (Durham: Baseball America, 2007), p. 304.

8. Anonymous and undated document from the Federalsburg Historical Society.

Chapter 14

1. *Salisbury Daily Times*, January 9 and 14, 1937.

2. Quote is from the *Salisbury Daily Times*, January 13, 1937.

3. *Salisbury Daily Times*, January 9 and February 17, 1937.

4. *Salisbury Daily Times*, January 30, February 17, and March 8, 1937.

5. For brief Kibler biography, see *Sporting News*, April 8, 1937; more also found in William Mowbray, *The Eastern Shore League* (Centreville, MD: Tidewater Publishers, 1989) and *Fred Lucas Testimonial Program*, November 1971.

Chapter 15

1. For preseason 1937 see *Salisbury Daily Times*, May 18, 19, 20, 22, 26, and 29, 1937.

2. *Salisbury Daily Times*, June 16, 1937.

3. The Griffith and Kibler exchange is quoted from William Mowbray, *The Eastern Shore Baseball League* (Centreville, MD: Tidewater Publishers, 1989), p. 43, original source unattributed. Cambria quote is from the *Sporting News*, July 1, 1937; for the forfeits, see *Salisbury Times*, June 18, 19, 21, 22, and 26, 1937; for Landis, *Sporting News*, August 3, 1937.

4. The fight and the quote are found in the *Sporting News*, July 1, 1937. See also Ed Nichols, *Eastern Shore League Record Book*, 1947, p. 59, and William Mowbray, *The Eastern Shore Baseball League*, pp. 47–48. The Boyer quote is from Ed Nichols, "Shore Sports," *Salisbury Daily Times*, January 3, 1948.

5. Flowers recollection of team speech from the *Sporting News*, May 15, 1941.

6. For Toach, see *Salisbury Daily Times*, July 16, 1937.

7. Bill Perry, "Youth Brigade Gained Early Baseball Fun, A League of Our Own," part 3, *Easton Star Democrat*, September 1, 1992.

8. The Wonder Club is from the *Salisbury Daily Times* and *Sporting News*, June through September 1937; climb out of last place, *Salisbury Daily Times*, July 29, 1937; climb to sixth place and Comellas' 17th win, *Salisbury Daily Times*, August 4, 1937; leap to third place, *Salisbury Daily Times*, August 16, 1937; pitcher records, *Salisbury Daily Times*, August 20, 1937; six shutouts in the *Salisbury Daily Times*, August 21, 1937.

9. *Salisbury Daily Times*, August 26, 1937.

10. Booster Night and Griffith quote, *Salisbury Daily Times*, September 2, 1937; taking lead from Easton, *Salisbury Daily Times*, September 3, 1937; quote and climb, *Sporting News*, September 2, 1937.

11. On MVP see the *Salisbury Daily Times*, September 5, 1937; on Trenton, *Salisbury Times*, September 8, 1937; attendance and Comellas, *Salisbury Daily Times*, September 12, 1937, and *Sporting News*, September 23, 1937; the Kohlman defeat is in the *Salisbury Daily Times*, September 15, 1937.

12. A's defeat is in the *Salisbury Daily Times*, September 21, 1937; for the league leaders, see *Salisbury Daily Times*, September 25, 1937, and *Sporting News*, October 7, 1937; call ups, *Sporting News*, September 9, 1937. For ranking see MiLB.com.

13. On Terry and the Giants, see *Salisbury Daily Times*, October 15, 1937; Kibler heart attack, *Salisbury Daily Times*, October 18, 1937; profits and attendance, *Salisbury Daily Times*, December 17, 1937; the Flowers award is found in the *Sporting News*, December 30, 1937.

14. The alien rule is from the *Salisbury Daily Times*, April 25, 1938; for the ladies, *Salisbury Daily Times*, April 26, 1938. For Salisbury ministers, see *Salisbury Daily Times*, February 5, 1938.

15. On 30 promotions, *Salisbury Daily Times*, May 19, 1938; Dover, Jacobs, and Ehler are in *Salisbury Daily Times*, June 16, 1938; the bus incident is found in Bill Perry, "Nick Koste Remembers All, A League of Our Own," part 15, *Easton Star Democrat*, September 3, 1992; for more on Picinich, see Bill Perry, "Baseball First Took Gunning to Milford, Now It's Home, A League of Our Own," part 20, *Easton Star Democrat*, September 27, 1992.

16. The second alien rule reference is found in the *Salisbury Daily Times*, June 14, 1938; Guerra and cartoon are in the *Salisbury Daily Times*, June 2, 1938; Montero and Guerra and Dover ruling are from *Salisbury Daily Times*, June 14, 1938.

17. First quote on the Clarke incident is in the *Salisbury Daily Times*, July 16, 1938; the national report is from the *Sporting News*, July 21, 1938.

18. Rhubarb quote is from the *Salisbury Daily Times*, July 26, 1938; fines and suspensions, *Salisbury Times*, July 27, 1938.

19. Russell letters and Henry response are found in the *Talbot County Historical Files*, FIC 2000.2256.

20. The Christy incident is in the *Salisbury Daily Times*, August 8, 1938; teams and Gordon, *Salisbury Daily Times*, August 27, 1938.

21. *Sporting News*, September 1, 1938.
22. Team standings are in the *Salisbury Daily Times*, September 2, 1938; capacity crowd, *Sporting News*, September 22, 1938; on gifts and promotions, *Sporting News*, September 22, 1938; All-Stars were reported in the *Sporting News*, September 15, 1938; official statistics, *Salisbury Daily Times*, November 8, 1938.

Chapter 16

1. Correspondence is from the *Talbot County Historical Society*, FIC 2000.2256.
2. *Ibid.*, telegrams and letters.
3. *Sporting News*, December 1 and 8, 1938; *Salisbury Daily Times,* December 7 and 8, 1938. Landis letter to Henry, Talbot County Historical Society, FIC 2000.2256.
4. Letter dated December 9, 1938, *Talbot County Historical Society*, FIC 2000.2256.
5. For the paring of the Cardinal system, *Salisbury Daily Times*, January 9, 1939; Centreville, *Salisbury Daily Times*, February 23, 1939; *Sporting News*, February 16, 1939; *Sporting News*, March 23, 1939; on free agents, see the *Sporting News*, March 2, 1939; Lucas is from the *Salisbury Daily Times*, March 10, 1939; for Christy, see the *Salisbury Daily Times,* March 11, 1939; on Powell, see the *Salisbury Daily Times*, March 14, 1939.
6. Keen and Easton are in the *Salisbury Daily Times*, April 24, 1939; Federalsburg, *Salisbury Daily Times*, April 27, 1939.
7. *Sporting News*, May 18 and 25, 1939; *Salisbury Daily Times*, May 9, 1939; *Salisbury Daily Times*, May 18 and 23, 1939; *Salisbury Daily Times*, June 7, 1939.
8. *Salisbury Daily Times*, June 30, 1939; *Salisbury Daily Times*, July 14 and 15, 1939; *Sporting News*, July 20, 1939.
9. Quotes are from the *Salisbury Daily Times*, June 24, 1939; *Salisbury Daily Times,* July 7, 1939; *Salisbury Daily Times*, July 24, 1939.
10. The Cambria contract incident is found in the *Salisbury Times*, June 6, 9, and 27, July 5, and August 21, 1939.
11. On Hutt, see the *Salisbury Daily Times*, May 22 and 27 and July 25, 1939; on Jefferson, *Sporting News*, August 10, 1939.
12. Bill Perry, "Young Players Found Hospitality in Easton, A League of Our Own," part 6, *Easton Star Democrat*, September 4, 1992.
13. *Salisbury Daily Times*, August 1, 1939.
14. *Salisbury Daily Times*, September 5 and 27, 1939; playoffs are found in the *Salisbury Daily Times*, September 7 through 16, 1939; the number of players promoted are in the *Sporting News*, August 31, 1939.
15. The Orioles are in the *Sporting News*, October 19, 1939; Easton is in the *Salisbury Daily Times*, November 2, 1939; Pocomoke City appears in the *Sporting News*, November 2 and 23, 1939, and the *Salisbury Daily Times*, November 14, 1939.
16. *Sporting News*, November 11, 1939; *Salisbury Daily Times*, November 27, 1939; *Sporting News*, December 22, 1939.
17. On attendance, see *Sporting News*, November 9, 1939; *Salisbury Daily Times*, October 23, 1939; *Salisbury Daily Times*, January 5, 1940.

Chapter 17

1. On Rickey, see the *Sporting News*, January 25, 1940; the Tigers are from the *Salisbury Daily Times*, January 15, 1940; McPhail is in the *Salisbury Daily Times*, February 2, 1940; on bondage, *Salisbury Daily Times*, February 14, 1940; the player contract numbers and eventual agreement is from "Compromise Ends Uncertainty Over Minor's Future This Year," *Sporting News*, February 22, 1940.
2. Reference to camp meeting baseball is from the *Salisbury Daily Times*, July 25, 1940.
3. *Salisbury Daily Times*, May 27, 1940; *Sporting News*, May 30, 1940.
4. *Sporting News*, June 27, 1940.
5. *Salisbury Daily Times*, June 4, 1940.
6. For Family Night, *Salisbury Daily Times*, August 3, 1940; the tomato story is in the *Sporting News*, August 29, 1940.
7. *Salisbury Daily Times*, August 6, 1940.
8. *Salisbury Daily Times*, April 2, 1940.
9. Cambria talking in riddles is in the *Sporting News*, September 5, 1940.
10. More on Cambria in the *Sporting News*, November 7 and 14, 1940. Milford had drawn 24,835; Easton 20,731; Centreville 18,500; Cambridge 18,360; Salisbury 16,000; Pocomoke City 14,681; and Federalsburg only 9,731; *Sporting News*, November 21, 1940.
11. *Sporting News*, November 7, 1940, and *Salisbury Daily Times*, November 25, 1940; for Pennock, *Salisbury Daily Times*, September 5, 1940; on Hermanski, *Sporting News*, December 26, 1940.
12. *Salisbury Daily Times,* October 28, 1940, and *Sporting News*, October 31, 1940.
13. *Salisbury Daily Times*, August 21, 1939. The Baltimore entry in the National League at this time was actually the Elite Giants. Since these games were billed as a championship, the correspondent may have been confusing them with the Black Sox who played in the defunct Eastern Colored League a decade earlier.
14. Robert V. Leffler, Jr., "Boom or Bust: The Elite Giants and Black Baseball in Baltimore, 1936–1951," *Maryland Historical Magazine*, Summer 1992; see also *Salisbury Daily Times*, June 27, 1939; for prices, *Salisbury Daily Times*, July 26, 1939; for other promoted Negro League exhibitions, see *Salisbury Daily Times*, June 26 and August 21, 1939; *Salisbury Daily Times*, July 23, 1940; *Salisbury Daily Times*, June 6 and July 16, 1941.

15. Chris Knauss, "Shore Once a Popular Baseball Spot," *Easton Star Democrat*, January 16, 2011.

Chapter 18

1. On Russell, *Sporting News*, January 23, 1941; for Wilmington, Fowler, *Sporting News*, January 30, 1941; Baker, *Sporting News*, February 27, 1941; Ehlers, *Sporting News*, January 9, 1941; Centreville, *Salisbury Daily Times*, January 24, 1941; Levin's quote is in *Salisbury Times*, January 21, 1941.

2. *Salisbury Daily Times*, February 24, 1941; for fans in control, see *Sporting News*, March 13 and 30, 1941; the DelMar League, *Salisbury Daily Times*, March 11, 1941.

3. Easton, *Sporting News*, April 10 and 17, 1941; Chicks, *Sporting News*, April 24, 1941; umpires, *Sporting News*, April 17, 1941; schedule, *Salisbury Daily Times*, April 7, 1941; Rickey quote, *Salisbury Daily Times*, April 8, 1941; Levin quote, *Salisbury Daily Times*, April 18, 1941; Hutt, *Salisbury Daily Times*, April 22, 1941; WBOC, *Salisbury Daily Times*, April 28, 1941.

4. Herring quote, *Salisbury Daily Times*, April 28, 1941; first Russell quote, *Salisbury Daily Times*, May 3, 1941; second Russell quote, *Salisbury Times*, May 5, 1941.

5. On Milford, *Sporting News*, June 12, 1941; Levin's money problems are found in the *Salisbury Daily Times*, June 9 and 28, 1941.

6. All-Stars, *Salisbury Daily Times*, July 3, 1941; Jambeau, *Salisbury Daily Times*, July 18, 1941.

7. Parnell told of this musical duet in an interview with Ed Nichols, *Salisbury Daily Times*, March 31, 1947.

8. Padlock incident is "Rescue the Indians from Sheriff," *Salisbury Daily Times*, July 30, 1941; suits and receivership, *Sporting News*, August 21, 1941.

9. Phantom franchise is in the *Salisbury Daily Times*, August 16, 1941; creditor quote, *Salisbury Daily Times*, August 20, 1941; see also *Salisbury Daily Times*, August 21, 23, and 28, 1941.

10. *Sporting News*, September 11, 18, and 25, 1941; *Salisbury Daily Times*, September 17, 1941.

11. *Salisbury Daily Times*, September 6, 1941.

12. *Sporting News*, November 13, 1941; Rickey proposal is found in the *Sporting News*, December 11, 1941.

13. For players produced, see the *Sporting News*, December 11, 1941. On Gunning, Bill Perry, "Baseball First Took Gunning to Milford, Now It's His Home, A League of Our Own," #20, *Easton Star Democrat*, September 27, 1992; on Elmer Valo, Ed Nichols, "Shore Sports," *Salisbury Daily Times*, April 14, 1949.

Chapter 19

1. "A Hunting Trip Revived Baseball on the Shore: Fred Lucas as Told to Barry Sparks," *Baltimore Sun*, August 24, 1975; see also Bill Mowbray, *Fred Lucas Testimonial Program*, November 16, 1971.

2. On the Macks, *Sporting News*, February 7, 1946; Ball park improvements are found in the *Salisbury Daily Times*, April 17 and 27, 1946; Lien, *Salisbury Daily Times*, February 22, 1946.

3. Chuck Wamsley quote is from the *Salisbury Daily Times*, February 22, 1946. The Eastern Shore fan is found in Ed Nichols, "Shore Sports," *Salisbury Daily Times*, April 9, 1946.

4. "Home Run Worth Milk and Money, Jack Dunn III as Told to Barry Sparks," *Sun Magazine*, July 3, 1977.

5. The story is told in Ed Nichols, *Eastern Shore League Record Book*, 1947; the second Horsey quote is from the *Salisbury Daily Times*, December 20, 1947.

6. Quote is from Ed Nichols, "Shore Sports," *Salisbury Daily Times*, July 25, 1946.

7. Story is found in Ed Nichols, "Shore Sports," *Salisbury Daily Times*, August 2, 1946.

8. *Salisbury Daily Times*, August 14, 1946.

9. Kibler's letter is from the *Salisbury Daily Times*, September 4, 1946; for Honochick, *Salisbury Daily Times*, July 31, 1946.

10. On crowds, see *Salisbury Daily Times*, September 12, 17, 18, and 19, 1946.

11. *Salisbury Daily Times*, September 14, 1946; the Orlando incident is from the *Salisbury Daily Times*, September 27, 1946; Dunn quote is in "A Home Run Worth Milk and Money, Jack Dunn III as Told to Barry Sparks," *Baltimore Sun Magazine*, July 3, 1977.

12. Minor league attendance is in *Sporting News*, October 23, 1946; *Sporting News*, October 30 and November 6, 1946; local attendance, *Salisbury Daily Times*, November 11, 1946; on Centreville, see *Sporting News*, November 20, 1946.

13. For Baker, see *Salisbury Daily Times*, November 20, 1946; the sports boom is from the *Salisbury Daily Times*, December 24, 1946.

14. Conversations with Dr. Kirkland Hall of Oaksville and panel discussion at the Nabb Research Center, Salisbury University, May 16, 2019.

15. See Baseball-Reference.com and Seemheads.com.

Chapter 20

1. *Salisbury Daily Times*, January 3 and 15, 1947; *Salisbury Daily Times*, February 4, 1947.

2. Kibler quote on coming back, *Salisbury Daily Times*, January 13, 1947; on G's, *Salisbury Daily Times*, January 14, 1947; Porter's assessment, *Salisbury Daily Times*, January 9, 1947.

3. *Salisbury Times*, January 30, 1947; on Evangeline, see the *Sporting News*, February 12, 1947; Kibler and Nichols quotes, Ed Nichols, "Shore Sports," *Salisbury Daily Times*, April 7, 1947; Kelchner, *Salisbury Daily Times*, March 12, 1947.

4. The Kibler quote is from Ed Nichols, "Shore Sports," *Salisbury Daily Times*, April 7, 1947.

5. Tournier's lament is in the *Sporting News*, January 8, 1947; Kibler, *Salisbury Daily Times*, February 22, 1947; on paper cups, *Sporting News*, February 19, 1947.

6. *Salisbury Daily Times*, February 8, 1947.

7. Ehlers is from the *Sporting News*, February 5, 1947.

8. For Salisbury, *Salisbury Daily Times*, February 24, 1947, and *Sporting News*, March 12, 1947; Easton, *Salisbury Daily Times*, April 3, 1947; Seaford, *Salisbury Daily Times*, April 1, 1947; Rehoboth, *Salisbury Daily Times*, April 12, 1947.

9. For Easton, see Bill Perry, "Do That Again, I'll Knock You Off the Mound, A League of Our Own," part 5, *Easton Star Democrat*, September 3, 1992; Salisbury meal money is in *Salisbury Daily Times*, April 24, May 12, and September 11, 1947.

10. Bill Torrey is from Bill Perry, "Do That Again, I'll Knock You Off the Mound, A League of Our Own," #5, *Easton Star Democrat*, September 3, 1992; "A Skunk in the Shower and Watermelon for Dinner: Carroll Beringer, as Told to Barry Sparks," *Sun Magazine*, September 10, 1978; Thompson quote, Bill Perry, "Tim Thompson Can Attest to Concern Shown Young Players in Cambridge, A League of Our Own" part 23, *Easton Star Democrat*, October 25, 1992.

11. *Salisbury Daily Times*, March 27, 1947.

12. *Salisbury Daily Times*, May 22, 1947; also Ed Nichols, *Eastern Shore Record Book*, 1948; "Skunk in the Shower and Watermelon for Dinner: Carroll Beringer as Told to Barry Sparks," *Sun Magazine*, September 10, 1947; Bill Ripken, *Salisbury Daily Times*, May 27, 1947.

13. On home team advantage, "A Skunk in the Shower and Watermelon for Dinner: Carroll Beringer as Told to Barry Sparks," *Sun Magazine*, September 10, 1978; Westfall is in the *Salisbury Daily Times*, June 9, 1947; flashlight story is from Bill Perry, "Then There Was the Night the Lights Went Out, A League of Our Own" part 7, *Easton Star Democrat*, September 6, 1992.

14. J. Howard Anthony is in the *Salisbury Daily Times*, June 24, 1947; second quote on new policy, *Sporting News*, July 2, 1947.

15. For Trautman, see the *Salisbury Daily Times*, July 25, 1947; for fines, *Salisbury Daily Times*, August 27, 1947; tomatoes are in "A Skunk in the Shower and Watermelon for Dinner: Carroll Beringer as Told to Barry Sparks," *Sun Magazine*, September 10, 1978.

16. *Sporting News*, August 27, 1947; Berringer's version is in "Skunk in the Shower and Watermelon for Dinner: Carroll Beringer as Told to Barry Sparks," *Sun Magazine*, September 10, 1947.

17. For prices see the *Salisbury Daily Times*, August 26, 1947; fines are in the *Salisbury Daily Times*, September 16, 1947; the large crowd, *Salisbury Daily Times*, September 16, 1947; see also *Sporting News*, September 24, 1947, and "A Skunk in the Shower and Watermelon for Dinner: Carroll Beringer as Told to Barry Sparks," *Sun Magazine*, September 10, 1978; resignation, *Sporting News*, September 17, 1947.

18. Playoffs are in the *Salisbury Daily Times*, September 18, 19, 20, 22, and 24, 1947; play off and split, "A Skunk in the Sower and Watermelon for Dinner: Carroll Bellinger as Told to Barry Sparks," *Sun Magazine*, September 10, 1978; attendance, *Salisbury Daily Times*, September 24, 1947.

19. On minor leagues, *Sporting News*, November 15, 1947, and Ed Nichols, "Shore Sports," *Salisbury Daily Times*, September 15, 1947; on Rehoboth, *Salisbury Daily Times*, October 10, 1947; losses, *Salisbury Daily Times*, November 7, 1947; Seaford and Easton, *Sporting News*, December 17, 1947; Anthony's aspirin, *Salisbury Daily Times*, November 26, 1947.

20. *Salisbury Daily Times*, November 3, 1947; on Culver, *Salisbury Daily Times*, 1947; Ehlers is in the *Salisbury Daily Times*, October 29 and December 4, 1947.

Chapter 21

1. Trautman is from Ed Nichols, "Shore Sports," *Salisbury Daily Times*, January 29, 1948; for Bentz, *Salisbury Daily Times*, March 17, 1948; Horsey on umpires is from *Salisbury Daily Times*, March 24, 1948; for Horsey on pitching, *Salisbury Daily Times*, May 28, 1948.

2. *Salisbury Daily Times*, January 12, 1948.

3. For Culver, see Ed Nichols, "Shore Sports," *Salisbury Daily Times*, January 30, 1948; the Kiwanis dinner, *Sporting News*, May 19, 1948; Ehlers is in the *Salisbury Daily Times*, April 12, 1948.

4. For the clinic, see the *Salisbury Daily Times*, April 30, 1948; Dot and Minnie are in the *Salisbury Daily Times*, April 24 and May 5, 1948; Becky Shockley is found in the *Salisbury Daily Times*, April 5, 1948, and *Salisbury Daily Times*, January 31, 1950.

5. *Salisbury Daily Times*, May 26, 27, and 28, 1948, and June 3, 1948.

6. *Salisbury Daily Times*, June 2, 1948.

7. Anne Corbett tells her story in the *Salisbury Daily Times*, August 13, 1948.

8. The quotes from Widow Garton and the umpires are from Ed Nichols, "Shore Sports," *Salisbury Daily Times*, June 7, 1948.

9. Mickey Micoletta is in the *Salisbury Daily Times*, June 12, 1948.

10. Ed Nichols, "Shore Sports," *Salisbury Daily Times*, June 26, 1948.
11. Ed Nichols, "Shore Sports," *Salisbury Daily Times*, June 28, 1948; *Sporting News*, July 7, 1948.
12. Bill Perry, "Ed Nichols Recorded League Highlights, A League of Our Own" part 18, *Easton Star Democrat*, September 20, 1992. Squirrel added to local lore by telling multiple versions of this incident. The three consistencies were that he wiped the plate, the umpire was the biggest man that ever lived, and he was ejected.
13. On umpires, see the *Salisbury Daily Times*, July 2, 1948.
14. Attendance is in the *Salisbury Daily Times*, July 28, 1948; standings, *Sporting News*, August 11, 1948.
15. The home runs are in the *Salisbury Daily Times*, August 7, 1948; no hitters, *Salisbury Daily Times*, August 17 and 20, 1948, and *Sporting News*, August 25, 1948; fan appreciation, *Salisbury Daily Times*, August 31, 1948.
16. For statistics see Bill Mowbray, *The Eastern Shore League*, pp. 173–189, and Ed Nichols, *Eastern Shore League Record Book*, 1948. Scorekeepers and statisticians of the 1930s and 1940s saw their Eastern Shore League as distinct from the one in the 1920s. That league had folded and forfeited all their franchises back to the National Association. When the league formed in 1937, it was considered an entirely new league with entirely new franchises to be distributed. The league then suspended operations for the war, but when play resumed in 1946, it was considered the same league.
17. *Sporting News*, October 6, 13, and 27, 1948; *Salisbury Daily Times*, October 13, 16, 18, 22, and 28, 1948.
18. *Sporting News*, November 3, 1948.
19. *Salisbury Daily Times*, November 3, 8, 15, 16, 18, and 20, 1948; *Sporting News*, November 21, 1948.
20. *Salisbury Daily Times*, July 25, 1949; on WBOC, *Salisbury Daily Times*, January 18, 1949; camp, *Salisbury Daily Times*, January 21, 1949; gamblers, *Salisbury Daily Times*, April 28, 1949.
21. *Salisbury Daily Times*, December 8, 1948; *Salisbury Daily Times*, April 4, 1949.
22. On the minors, *Sporting News*, May 11, 1949; Farmer is in Ed Nichols, "Shore Sports," *Salisbury Daily Times*, May 13, 1949; for Len Baker, *Salisbury Daily Times*, August 19 and 27, 1949.
23. Standings from the *Sporting News*, June 8, 1949; attendance, Ed Nichols, "Shore Sports," *Salisbury Daily Times*, July 16, 1949; Ocean Downs, *Salisbury Daily Times*, August 5, 1949.
24. Zimmer story and quote cited from Bill Perry, "Baseball Is More Than Just a Game, A League of Our Own" part 8, *Easton Star Democrat*, September 7, 1992.
25. *Salisbury Daily Times*, July 30, 1949; for fines see the *Sporting News*, August 31, 1949; Farmer, *Salisbury Daily Times*, August 25, 1949; Corbett, *Salisbury Daily Times*, September 6, 1949.
26. Walls quote from Ed Nichols, "Shore Sports," *Salisbury Daily Times*, July 16, 1949.
27. Final of 1949 season, *Salisbury Daily Times*, September 21, 1949.
28. *Salisbury Daily Times*, September 6, 1949; *Salisbury Daily Times*, September 30, 1949.
29. Lucas is in the *Salisbury Daily Times*, October 18, 1949; *Sporting News*, November 2, 1949; Rickey-Weiss feud, *Sporting News*, November 2, 1949.
30. Rehoboth is in the *Sporting News*, December 7, 1949; Cambridge and affiliation, *Salisbury Daily Times*, December 9, 1949; Ehlers, *Salisbury Daily Times*, December 13, 1949. See also, *Salisbury Daily Times*, December 17 and 19, 1949; Salisbury and Rehoboth, *Salisbury Daily Times*, January 2 and 16, 1950.
31. Ed Nichols, "Shore Sports," *Salisbury Daily Times*, January 24, 1950; working agreements, *Salisbury Daily Times*, January 39, 1950; on Easton, *Salisbury Daily Times*, December 7 and 13, 1949; pull out and epitaph, *Salisbury Daily Times*, February 1, 1950; Lucas quote, Bud McCarter, *Sporting News*, February 8, 1950.

Appendix A

1. Multiple dates have been given for Johnson's birth to no real conclusion. The date used here is that used by the National Baseball Hall of Fame and Baseball Reference.com. For Johnson's early recollections, see John Holway, "Judy Johnson: A True Hot Corner Hotshot," *Baseball Research Journal*, 1986.
2. For Johnson's early years, see Ellen Rendle, *Judy Johnson; Delaware's Invisible Hero* (Wilmington, DE: Cedar Tree Press, 1994); story of Judy and Anita is from John Holway, "Judy Johnson: A True Hot Corner Hotshot," *Baseball Research Journal*, 1986.
3. The oft-cited quote is from Kevin Kerrane and Rod Beaton, "Judy Johnson: Reminiscences by the Great Baseball Player," *Delaware Today*, May 1977; see also Thomas Kern, "Judy Johnson," SABR Biography Project.
4. For Anita and Judy see undated manuscript by John Holway, Judy Johnson file at the Hall of Fame as cited in Thomas Kern, "Judy Johnson," SABR Biography Project; see also Ellen Rendle, *Judy Johnson, Delaware's Invisible Hero* (Wilmington, DE: Cedar Tree Press, 1994).
5. Baseball-Reference.com.
6. Johnson's relationship with Gibson is from Kerns, "Judy Johnson," SABR Biography Project. See also John Holway, *Blackball Stars; Negro League Pioneers* (Westport, CT: Mercker Books, 1988) and *Josh and Satch: The Life and Times of Josh Gibson and Satchel Paige* (New York: Carroll and Graf, 1992.)

7. On Holway's observation, see Holway, "Judy Johnson," *Baseball Research Journal*, 1986. Cool Papa Bell is from the Judy Johnson article on the National Baseball Hall of Fame website.

8. On Robinson cited from "Baseball Hall of Famer Judy Johnson Dies," *Washington Post*, June 17, 1989; on his quote to Mack, see Ryan Whirty, "If Only Judy…" written for the *Philadelphia Inquirer*, June 14, 2014.

9. Unpublished manuscript by John Holway, pp. 8 and 24, as cited in Kerns, *Judy Johnson*, SABR Biography Project.

10. Johnson's saying is from "Delaware Backstory: Honoring Hall of Famer Judy Johnson," *The News Journal*, April 20, 2015; Knott's recollections are in Richard Pollitt, "Judy Johnson," *Salisbury Daily Times*, February 25, 2019.

11. Major league game account is from the *Chicago Daily Tribune*, June 23, 1894.

12. Descriptions are from the *Chestertown Transcript*, July 8, 1897, and April 14, 1898; the Washington College years were compiled from the *Chestertown Transcript*, May 12, June 9, and July 14, 1892; June 1, 15, and 22, 1893; April 5 and 19 and June 21, 1894; April 18, June 20, and July 25, 1895; April 16, 1896; April 4 and July 8, 1897; April 14, 1898; July 20, 1899; June 9, 1900; April 19, 1902; April 25, 1903; and June 9, 1906. Also see the *Kent News*, June 9 and August 18, 1906.

13. *Dorchester Democrat-News*, July 11, 1908; exploits of the Eastern Shore League of 1904 and Burris' participation are found in the *Dorchester Democrat-News*, August 6, 13, 20, and 27, 1904. See also the *Salisbury Advertiser*, July 30, August 6, 13, 20, and 27, and September 3 and 10, 1904; and the *Wicomoco News*, August 11 and 25, and September 1 and 8, 1904. For information on Burris and the Cambridge championship teams of 1907 and 1908 see the *Cambridge Daily Banner*, June 13 and 27, 1908, and the *Dorchester Democrat and News*, July 13 and August 3 and 10, 1907, and June 11, 1908.

14. *Salisbury Daily Times*, March 24, 1938, and *Salisbury Daily Times*, March 6, 1938.

15. The attempt to form an independent league appeared in the *Cambridge Daily Banner*, June 7, 8, and 10, 1911; details of the Peninsula League of 1915 are included in the *Wicomoco News*, July 22, August 5, and September 23, 1915, and in the *Baltimore Sun* of August 3, 7, 8, and 31, 1915. Burris' involvement with the Salisbury Club and the Championship series of 1921 can be found in the *Wicomoco News*, August 25 and September 1, 1921.

16. *Salisbury Daily Times*, March 24, 1938.

17. *Salisbury Daily Times*, March 6, 1938.

18. Sources for this sketch are from the newspapers *Washington Post*, July 1908 through October 1909; *Chestertown Transcript*, July 15, 1897; *Cambridge Chronicle*, July 1, 1897; and *Dorchester Democrat-News*, July 8, 1905; see also Ira and H. Allen Smith, *Low and Inside* (Garden City, NY: Doubleday, 1949).

19. Quote is from Ira and H. Allen Smith, *Low and Inside*, pp. 78–79.

20. Quotes are from letter from Harry Pulliam to August Herrmann, March 21, 1906, and letter from Ban Johnson to August Herrmann, March 26, 1906.

21. *Sporting Life*, August 25, 1907.

22. Letter from Robert Unglaub to August Herrmann from Hotel Marion, Little Rock, AK, March 14, 1907.

23. Undated clipping from HOF files quoted from *Washington Times*.

24. From "His Many Faults," Hall of Fame Unglaub files, May 14, 1908.

25. *Washington Post*, July 15, 1908.

26. *Washington Post*, April 8, 1909.

27. *Washington Post*, April 17, 1909.

28. *Washington Post*, April 26, 1909.

29. *Baltimore Sun*, December 1, 1916.

Bibliography

Primary Sources

Manuscripts, Documents, Articles and Collections

August Herrmann Files, National Baseball Hall of Fame.
August Herrmann Papers, A. Bartlett Giamatti Research Center, Cooperstown, NY.
Baseball File, 2000.2256, Talbot County Historical Society, Easton, MD.
Baseball Files, Federalsburg Historical Society, Federalsburg, MD.
Bob Unglaub File, A. Bartlett Giamatti Research Center, Cooperstown, NY.
Bob Unglaub Files, National Baseball Hall of Fame.
Census Bulletin, #28; Maryland, January 3, 1901.
"Death of Robert Unglaub." *Sporting News*, December 7, 1916.
Forstall, Richard, *Population of States and Counties of the United States: 1790–1990*. Washington, D.C., Department of Commerce, U.S. Bureau of Census, 1996.
Herrmann, August to Robert Unglaub. Letter, March 13, 1907.
"His Many Faults." unknown source, May 14, 1908.
Johnson, Ban to August Herrmann. Letter, March 26, 1906.
Minor league File, A. Bartlett Giamatti Research Center, Cooperstown, NY.
Pulliam, Harry to August Herrmann. Letter, March 26, 1906.
"Robert H. Unglaub." unknown source, June 1, 1907.
Unglaub, Robert to August Herrmann. Letter, Crisfield, MD, March 15, 1906.
Unglaub, Robert to August Herrmann. Letter, Hotel Marion, Little Rock, AR, March 14, 1907.
"Unglaub Settled." *Sporting Life*, September 15, 1906.
"Unglaub Tells How He Used to Chase Balls for Kelly and Jennings." *Boston American*, undated.
"Unglaub's Latest Roar." *Sporting Life*, August 25, 1907.
"Unglaub's Utterances." *Sporting Life*, April 7, 1906.

Newspapers and Periodicals

Afro-American National Edition, 1902–1949.
American Union, 1867–1879.
Baltimore American (News-American), 1882–1891.
Baltimore Sun, 1863–1869, 1874, 1915–1928.
Cambridge Chronicle, 1875–1897.
Cambridge Daily Banner, 1907–1921.
Cambridge Era, 1878–1879.
Chestertown Transcript, 1866–1917.
Denton Journal, 1867–1874
Dorchester Herald-News (Democrat-News), 1872–1913.
Easton Gazette, 1866–1896.
Easton Journal, 1867–1874.
Easton Star, 1870–1890.
Easton Star Democrat.
Grand Island Times, 1871, 1873, 1881.
Kent News, 1866–1913.
Nebraska Herald, 1872.
Nebraska State Journal, 1873.
Omaha Evening Bee, 1874, 1876, 1877.
St. Michaels Comet, 1878.
Salisbury Advertiser, 1873–1918.
Salisbury Daily Times, 1921–1950.
Sporting Life.
Sporting News, 1921–1950.
Syracuse Courier and Union, 1858
Washington Post, 1909.
Washington Times.
Wicomico News, 1902–1921.
Wilmington Herald, 1878, 1963.
Wilmington Morning News, 1963.

Secondary Sources

Adelman, Melvin. "Academicians and Athletics: Historians' Views of American Sport." *Maryland Historian*, Fall 1973.
Alexander, Charles. *John McGraw*. Lincoln: University of Nebraska Press, 1995.
_____. *Ty Cobb*. New York: Oxford University Press, 1984.

Alvarez, Mark. *The Old Ball Game: Baseball's Beginnings*. Alexandria, VA: Redefinition Books, 1990.
Ardell, Jean Hastings. *Breaking into Baseball: Women and the National Pastime*. Carbondale: Southern Illinois University Press, 2005.
Bailyn, Bernard. *Sometimes an Art*. New York: Knopf, 2015.
Black, Jeremy. *Fighting for America: The Struggle for Mastery of North America*. Bloomington: Indiana University Press, 2011.
Block, David. *Baseball Before We Knew It: A Search for the Roots of the Game*. Lincoln: University of Nebraska Press, 2005.
_____. "Polish Workers Play Ball at Jamestown, Virginia: An Early Hint of Continental Europe's Influence on Baseball." *Base Ball: A Journal of the Early Game*, Spring 2011.
Boorstin, Daniel. *Hidden History*. New York: Vintage, 1987.
Bradford, William. *Of Plymouth Plantation*. Mineola, NY: Dover, 2006.
Bready, James. *Baseball in Baltimore: The First 100 Years*. Baltimore: Johns Hopkins University Press, 1998.
_____. *The Home Team: A Full Century of Baseball in Baltimore, 1859–1959*. Baltimore: James Bready, 1992.
_____. "Play Ball! The Legacy of Nineteenth Century Baltimore Baseball." *Maryland Historical Magazine*, Summer 1992.
Burton, R. Lee, Jr. *Canneries of the Eastern Shore*. Centreville, MD, Tidewater Press, 1986.
Carroll, Brian. "Baseball Coverage in Wichita Before Integration, 1920–1930." *Baseball Journal*, 2008.
Casway, Jerrold. *The Culture and Ethnicity of Nineteenth Century Baseball*. Jefferson, NC: McFarland, 2017.
Chadwick, Henry. "New Rules of 1887." *Outing* 10, no. 77, 1887.
Clark, Dick, and Larry Lester, eds. *The Negro Leagues Book*. Cleveland: Society for American Baseball Research, 1994.
Corbett, Warren. *Pitching, Defense, and Three-Run Homers: The 1970 Baltimore Orioles*. Lincoln: University of Nebraska Press, 2012.
"Country Boys in the Big Leagues." *Literary Digest*, April 18, 1925.
Crepeau, Richard. "Urban and Rural Images in Baseball." *Journal of Popular Culture*, Fall 1975.
Delmarva Eastern Shore Association. *Summer White House*. Salisbury: Executive Office of Salisbury, MD, 1929.
DeSocio, Chuck. "Cecil County Plays Ball." *Bulletin of the Historical Society of Cecil County*, Spring 1995.
East, W. Gordon. *The Geography Behind History*. New York: W.W. Norton, 1965.
Emerson, Ralph Waldo. "Self Reliance." *The World's Great Thinkers* from *Man and Spirit: The Speculative Philosophers*. New York: Random House, 1947.
Finch, Robert L., L.H. Addington, and Ben Morgan. *The Story of Minor League Baseball*. Columbus, OH: Stoneman Press, 1952.
Franks, Joel. "From Honolulu to Brooklyn: The Journeys of the Hawaiian Travelers." *Base Ball: A Journal of the Early Game*, Spring 2008.
Gibson, Campbell. "Simon Nicholls: Gentleman, Farmer, Ballplayer." *Baseball Research Journal*, 1989.
Gilbert, Thomas. *How Baseball Happened*. Boston: David R. Godine, 2020.
_____. "Sons of Liberty: The Meaning of Early Base Ball Club Names." *Base Ball: New Research of the Early Game* vol. 11, 2019.
Goldstein, William. *Playing for Keeps: The History of Early Baseball*. Ithaca: Cornell University Press, 2014.
Gorman, Bob. *Double X: The Story of Jimmie Foxx–Baseball's Forgotten Slugger*. Camden: Diocese of Camden, NJ, 1990.
Green, Guy. *Fun and Frolic with an Indian Ball Team*. Lincoln: Woodruff-Collins, 1907. Reprint, Mattituck, NY: Amereon House, 1992.
Griffith, William Ridgely. *Amateur Baseball in Maryland, 1858–1871*. Baltimore: John Cox's Sons, 1897.
Hall, Dwight. *Memorial History of Syracuse*. New York: H.P. Smith Co., 1891.
Hall, Edward H. *Appletons' Hand-Book of American Travel: The Southern Tour*. New York: D. Appleton, 1866, 1867.
Harle, Rudolph K., Jr. "The Athlete as Moral Leader." *Journal of Popular Culture*, Fall 1975.
Hart, John Fraser. "Small Towns, Railroads, and Ethnicity." *Historical Geography* 3, 2003.
Hayman, John C. *Rails Along the Chesapeake: 1827–1978*. Salisbury, MD: Marvadel Publishers, 1979.
Hershberger, Richard. *Strike Four: The Evolution of Baseball*. Lanham, MD: Rowman & Littlefield, 2019.
Hittner, Arthur D. *Honus Wagner: The Life of Baseball's "Flying Dutchman."* Jefferson, NC: McFarland, 1996.
Holl, James. "Baseball Braggin' Rights: The Five State Series, 1922–1927." *National Pastime*, 2009.
Holtgrieve, Donald G. "The Effects of the Railroads on Small Town Population Changes." *Association of Pacific Geographers Yearbook*, 1973.
Holway, John. *Black Ball Stars: Negro League Pioneers*. Westport, CT: Merker Books, 1998.
_____. *Josh and Satch: The Life and Times of Josh Gibson and Satchel Paige*. New York: Carroll and Graf, 1992.
_____. "Judy Johnson; A True Hot Corner Hot Shot." *Baseball Research Journal*, 1986.
_____. "Untitled Manuscript." Judy Johnson File, National Baseball Hall of Fame.
"Home Run Baker's Rise." *Literary Digest*, April 6, 1912.

Bibliography

Johnson, Lloyd, and Miles Wolf, eds. *Encyclopedia of Minor League Baseball*, 3rd ed. Durham: Baseball America, 2007.

Jopp, Harold, et al., eds. *Rediscovery of the Eastern Shore: Travelogues of the 1870s*. Wye Mills, MD: Chesapeake College Press, 1984.

Keenan, Jimmy. "July 19, 1923: Judge Landis Day in Salisbury, MD." SABR Website.

Kern, Thomas. "Judy Johnson." SABR Biography Project.

Kerrane, Kevin, and Rod Beaton. "Judy Johnson: Reminiscences by the Great Ball Player." *Delaware Today*, May 1977.

Knopp, Japheth. "Negro League Baseball: Black Community and Socio Economic Impact of Integration: Kansas City, Missouri as Case Study." *Baseball Research Journal*, Spring 2016.

Lambert, Mike. *Eastern Shore League*. Charleston, SC: Arcadia, 2010.

Lamoreaux, David. "Baseball in the Nineteenth Century: The Source of Its Appeal." *Journal of Popular Culture*, Winter 1977.

Lancaster, John H. "Baltimore, a Pioneer in Organized Baseball." *Maryland Historical Magazine*, March 1940.

Leffler, Robert V., Jr. "Boom or Bust: The Elite Giants and Black Baseball in Baltimore, 1936–1951." *Maryland Historical Magazine*, Summer 1992.

Mars, Ken. *Baltimore Baseball: First Pitch to Pennant, 1858–1894*. Baltimore: Old Frog Printing, 2018.

Matthews, C. Starr. "Work and Win Is Motto of Clever Charley Herzog." *Baltimore Sunday Sun*, March 12, 1911.

McGraw, John J. "Baseball Has Changed in the Last 30 Years." *Literary Digest*, May 10, 1919.

Millen, Patricia. *From Pastime to Passion: Baseball and the Civil War*. Berwyn Heights, MD: Heritage Books, 2019.

_____. "On the Battlefront: The New York Game Takes Hold, 1861–1865." *Base Ball: A Journal of the Early Game*, Spring 2011.

Millikin, Mark. *Jimmie Foxx: The Pride of Sudlersville*. Lanham, MD: Scarecrow, 1998.

Morris, Peter. *Baseball Fever: Early Baseball in Michigan*. Ann Arbor: University of Michigan Press, 2003.

_____. *But Didn't We Have Fun? An Informal History of Baseball's Pioneer Era, 1843–1870*. Chicago: Ivan R. Dee, 2008.

_____. *Catcher: How the Man Behind the Plate Became an American Folk Hero*. Chicago: Ivan R. Dee, 2009.

_____. *Game of Inches: The Game Behind the Scenes*. Chicago: Ivan R. Dee, 2008.

_____. *Game of Inches: The Game on the Field*. Chicago: Ivan R. Dee, 2008.

_____, et al., eds. *Baseball Pioneers, 1850–1870*. Jefferson, NC: McFarland, 2012.

Mowbray, William W. *The Eastern Shore Baseball League*. Centreville, MD: Tidewater Publishers, 1989.

_____. "History of the Eastern Shore League." *Fred Lucas Testimonial Program*, 1971.

Newton, James E. "William 'Judy' Johnson: Delaware's Folk Hero of the Diamond." *Negro History Bulletin*, Fall 1980.

Nichols, Ed. *Eastern Shore League Record Book, 1937–1947*. Salisbury, MD: Salisbury Times, 1948.

Patten, William, and J. Walker McSpadden, eds. *The Book of Baseball, 1911: Our National Pastime from Its Earliest Days*. Mineola, NY: Dover, 2010.

Patterson, Todd, "May the Best Man Win: The Black Ball Championships, 1866–1923." *Baseball Research Journal*, Spring 2013.

Paxson, Frederick. "Rise of Sport." *Mississippi Valley Historical Review*, September 1917.

Payne, Marty. "Al Burris." SABR Biography Project, 2005.

_____. "Bob Unglaub." SABR Biography Project, 2003.

_____. "Business of Baseball in Small Towns." *Outside the Lines*, 2005.

_____. "Country Ball: Big Teams in Small Towns." *National Pastime*, 2009.

_____. "Country Baseball on the Eastern Shore of Maryland, 1867–1921." *Cooperstown Symposium on Baseball and American Culture*. Jefferson, NC: McFarland, 2002.

_____. "Diffusion of the New York Game in Maryland." *Base Ball: A Journal of the Early Game*, Spring 2011.

_____. "Frank 'Home Run' Baker: Not Just His Name Was Interesting." *Baseball Research Journal*, 2000.

_____. "More Than Ballplayers: Baseball Players and Pursuit of the American Dream in the 1880s." *Baseball Research Journal*, 2017.

_____. "Washington College." *National Pastime*, 1995.

Perry, Thomas. *Textile League Baseball: South Carolina's Mill Teams, 1880–1955*. Jefferson, NC: McFarland, 1993.

Perry, William. "A League of Their Own." *Easton Star Democrat*, Parts 1–23, August 30, 1992–October 25, 1992.

Pierza, Richard. "Engineering Baseball: Branch Rickey's Innovative Approach to Baseball Management." *Cooperstown Symposium on Baseball and American Culture*. Jefferson, NC: McFarland, 2002.

Preston, Dickson. *Newspapers of the Eastern Shore*. Centreville, MD: Tidewater Publishers, 1986.

_____. *Talbot County: A History*. Centreville, MD: Tidewater Publishers, 1983.

_____. *Trappe: The Story of an Old Fashioned Town*. Easton, MD: Economy Printing, 1976.

Pritchett, H.S. "The Evolution of College Baseball." *Scribner's Monthly*, April 1910.

Rapp, David. *Tinkers to Evers to Chance: The Chicago Cubs and the Dawn of Modern America*. Chicago: University of Chicago Press, 2018.

Rendle, Ellen. *Judy Johnson: Delaware's Invisible Hero*. Wilmington, DE: Cedar Tree Press, 1994.

Riess, Steven A. "Professional Baseball and Social Mobility." *Journal of Interdisciplinary History*, Autumn 1980.

_____. "Professional Sunday Baseball: A Study in Social Reform, 1892–1934." *Maryland Historian*, Fall 1973.

_____. "Race and Ethnicity in American Baseball, 1900–1919." *Journal of Ethnic Studies*, Fall 1977.

_____. *Touching Base: Professional Baseball and American Culture in the Progressive Era*. Urbana: University of Illinois Press, 1999.

Ryczek, William. *Baseball's First Inning: A History of the National Pastime Through the Civil War*. Jefferson, NC: McFarland, 2009.

Salisbury Chamber of Commerce. *Survey of Salisbury, 1951*. Salisbury, MD: Messick and Son, 1951.

Seymour, Harold. *Baseball: The People's Game*. New York: Oxford University Press, 1990.

Seymour, Harold, and Dorothy Seymour Mills. *Baseball: The Early Years*. New York: Oxford University Press, 1989.

Shattuck, Debra A. *Bloomer Girls: Women Baseball Pioneers*. Urbana: University of Illinois Press, 2017.

Smith, Ira, and H. Allen. *Low and Inside*. Garden City, NY: Doubleday, 1949.

Solomon, Burt. *Where They Ain't*. New York: Doubleday, 1999.

Sparks, Barry. "Comebacks and Fisticuffs: The Eastern Shore Baseball League, 1922–1949." *National Pastime*, 2009.

_____. "Comebacks and Fisticuffs: The Many Lives of the Eastern Shore League, 1922–1949." *Maryland Historical Magazine*, Summer 1972.

_____. *Frank "Home Run" Baker: Hall of Famer and World Series Hero*. Jefferson, NC: McFarland, 2006.

_____. "Home Run Worth Milk Money: Jack Dunn III as Told to Barry Sparks." *Sun Magazine*, July 3, 1977.

_____. "A Hunting Trip Revived Baseball on the Short: Fred Lucas as Told to Barry Sparks." *Baltimore Sun*, August 24, 1975.

_____. "Skunks in the Shower and Watermelons for Dinner, Carroll Beringer as Told to Barry Sparks." *Sun Magazine*, September 10, 1978.

Stubbs, Lewis St. George. *Shoestring Glory: Semi Pro Ball on the Prairies, 1886–1994*. Manitoba: Turnstone Press, 1996.

Taylor, Bayard. "Down the Eastern Shore." *Harper's New Monthly Magazine*, October 1871.

Thorn, John. *Baseball in the Garden of Eden: The Secret History of the Early Game*. New York: Simon & Schuster, 2011.

"To Rescue Baseball in Small Towns." *Literary Digest*, April 8, 1925.

Townsend, Alfred. "The Chesapeake Peninsula." *Scribner's Monthly*, March 1872.

Tuohey, George V. *A History of the Boston Baseball Club: A Concise and Accurate History of Baseball from Its Inception—Primary Source Edition*. Charleston, SC: Nabu Press, 2013.

_____. *The Story of Baseball: Scrap Book Vol. 1*. 1906.

Turner, Bernard, and Larry McCray. "Pilgrim Stoolball and the Profusion of American Safe-Haven Games." *Base Ball: A Journal of the Early Game*, Spring 2011.

Turner, Frederick Jackson. "The Significance of the Frontier in American History." Wisconsin Historical Society, 1893.

12th Census of the United States Census Bulletin #28: Maryland, January 3, 1901.

Tygiel, Jules. *Baseball's Great Experiment: Jackie Robinson and His Legacy*. New York: Vintage, 1983.

_____. *Past Time: Baseball as History*. New York: Oxford University Press, 2000.

Usilton, Fred. *The History of Kent County*. 1923. (The copy found by the author included a chapter 33, "A Breeding Ground for Sports Stars," not found in all editions.)

Veblen, Thorstein. *The Theory of the Leisure Class*. New York: Viking, 1953.

Vernon, Edward, ed. *American Railroad Manual, 1873*. Philadelphia: American Railroad Manual Co., 1873.

_____. *American Railroad Manual, 1874*. Philadelphia: American Railroad Manual Co., 1874.

_____. *Travelers' Official Railway Guide of the United States and Canada, 1868*. New York: J.W. Pratt, 1868.

_____. *Travelers' Official Railway Guide to the United States and Canada, 1869*. New York: J.W. Pratt, 1869.

_____. *Travelers' Official Railway Guide to the United States and Canada*. Philadelphia: American Railroad Manual Co., 1870.

Walsh, Harry. *The Outlaw Gunner*. Cambridge, MD: Tidewater Publishers, 1971.

Weber, Max. *The Protestant Work Ethic and the Spirit of Capitalism*. Mineola, NY: Dover, 2003.

"Where Are the Baseball Stars of Twenty Years Ago." *Literary Digest*, January 24, 1925.

Whirty, Ryan. "If Only Judy…" *Philadelphia Inquirer*, January 14, 2014.

White, Sol. *History of Colored Base Ball: With Other Documents of the Early Black Game, 1886–1936*. 1907. Introduction by Jerry Malloy. Lincoln: University of Nebraska Press, 1995.

Whitman, T. Stephen. *Challenging Slavery in the Chesapeake: Black and White Resistance to Human Bondage, 1775–1865*. Baltimore: Maryland Historical Society, 2007.

"Why the Athletics were Scrapped." *Literary Digest*, July 24, 1915.

Wilson, Ben. *Heyday: The 1850s and the Dawn of the Global Age*. New York: Basic Books, 2016.

Wilson, Robert. "On the Eastern Shore." *Lippincott's Magazine*, July 1876.

Index

Adams Floating Theater 95
Adleman, Melvin 49
admissions *see* finances
African American baseball 12–13, 28–29, 41–42, 53–54, 73–74, 114–117, 137–139, 188–190; exhibitions 75, 80, 169–170
Afro-American 73, 115, 139
Agrarian Myth 77, 95
alien rule 154–155
American Association 36
Andre, Johnnie 202, 205
Andrews, Raintree 108
Anthony, J. Howard 197
Armstrong, Herb 86, 99, *106*, 120
attendance *see* finances

Bailey, Russell 115
Baines, Linwood 170
Baker, Frank 61, 68–70, *71*, 78–80, 81–82, 85, 107–108, 109, *110*, 112–113, 119, 131, 171, 187, 213
Baltimore American 39
Baltimore Base Ball Convention 9, 14
Baltimore Base Ball Emporium 14; *see also* Gratton, George
Baltimore Bugle Coat, Tie, and Apron Co. 169; *see also* Cambria, Joe
Baltimore Daily News 7
Baltimore Elite Giants 169
Baltimore Orioles 36–37, 39, 50, 55–57, 61, 212
Baltimore Sun 67, 74, 87, 89, 99, 104–105, 114, 124–125, 129, 145, 148, 214, 221
Barnie, Billie 36
barnstorming: black teams 75, 80, 169–170; Cherokee Nationals 49, 71–72, 79; Chinese Nationals 49, 79–80; exhibitions 82–83, 153, 163; Kilduff All Stars 49,
70; Stricker All Stars 49, 70; women's teams 49, 86
Baseball Town USA 182–184, 186–187
Batt's Neck 139, 188
Beam, George 8–9
Bellevue All-Stars *116*
Bender, Chief 198, 205
Bennett, Frank 86
Bentz, Roman 198
Beringer, Carroll 193–196
Berlin 67, 85, 89
Betterton 33–34, 213
bicycle craze 51–52, 54, 73
Big Woods 188
Bi-State Loop 139
Black, Ed 202
Bloomer Girls 49, 86
blue laws 7, 149, 154, 161, 171–172, 193
Blue Ridge League 84–87, 89, 101, 104, 114, 122, 132
Boley, Joe 60
Bolingly Club 30
Bottomley, Jim 140
Boyer, Jim 150
Bradford, William 7
Bradley, Bob 149–150
Braham, William G. 150, 161, 167
Breadon, Sam 98, 140
Brodie, Steve 61
Brooklyn Excelsior 8–9
Bucktown 37
Bugle Field 170
Bulger, Bozeman 78
Burbage, Knowlington "Buddy" 190
Burnette, Wally 204
Burris, Al 45–*47*, 48, 50, 54, 61, 68, 76, 80–81, 87, 110–111, 212–215

Cambria, Charlotte 173
Cambria, Joe: Wonder Club 148–149, 153–155, 157; 162–163, 165, 168–170, 174
Cambridge 13, 19–20, 22–25, 25, 31, 36–39, 40–43, 46–49, 55, 60–62, 64, 66–67, 72–74, 77, 79, 84–86, 89, 98–99; *see also* Muffers
Cambridge Canners 106–108, 111–112, 114–115, 119–120, 122, 125
Cambridge Cardinals 146, 148, 151, 155, 157, 162, 163–164, 168, 171, 173
Cambridge Daily Banner 78, 80
Cambridge Dodgers 192, 194–196, 201–206
Cambridge State Championships 70–71
Cambridge v. Chestertown 56–58
Cambridge v. Salisbury 51–53
Camden Yards 220
camp meetings 34–35
Cantillon, Joe 216, 219–220
Cantwell, Mike 61
Cape Charles, VA 13, 196
Caputo, Johnny 204
Carey, Betty 203
Central Shore League 179, 182, 193, 199
Centreville 13, 30, 58, 87–88, 98, 116, 138, 153, 155–156, 161–162, 164, 169, 171, 174, 180, 182, *183*, 185, 186, 187, 191–192
Centreville Orioles 182, 186–187
Cephas, Goldie 190
Charles, Chappy 44, 46–47, 62, *68*, 213, 216
Charleston, Oscar 169
Cherokee Nationals 49, 71–72, 79
Chestertown 13, 15, 18, 34, 37, 44–45, 51, 54–55, 70, 73, 85, 98, 115, 180, 188, 197
Chicago Defender 210
Chicago Stars 64

Chinese Nationals 49, 79–80
Church Hill 170
Cincinnati Reds 68
Civil War 9–10, 12, 14, 17, 19, 84, 89
Claggett, Walter 202, 206
Claiborne 31, 47, 104–105, 112
Clark, Nig 121, 131
Clark, Robert. M. 146, 148
Clark, Win 145
Clarkson, Dad 56
Cobb, Ty 61, 77
Cochrane, Mickey 106–107, 131, 146
Coleman's Corner 188
Collier's Magazine 9, 75
combination clubs 51, 54
commerce 11–12, 35, 94, 97, 134–135, 179
commercial gunning 35–36
Comellas, Jorge 149, 151–152, 157, 163
Constitution and Bylaws of the Eastern Shore League of Professional Baseball Clubs 154
Contini, Harry 194
Corbett, Gene 199, 201, 205
Corbett, Joe 56
Cramer, Roger 137
Crepeau, Richard 77
Crisfield 13, 32, 46–47, 58, 66–67, 70, 74, 85, 87–89, 139, 145–146, 148, 153, 161, 184, 187, 192–193, 203, 216, 217
Crisfield Crabbers 98, 100, 107, 111, 115–116, 119–120, 125, 127–129, 131
Crotcher's Ferry 37
crowds *see* finances
Crumpton 64, 77
Culver, Dallas 197–198, 203, 205

Dallas Texans 68
Davis, Joe 155, 157
Day, Leon 169
Deaton, Ralph 170
DeFazio, Ernie 199, 201
DeForge, Barney 199
Delaware Railroad 47; *see also* New York Norfolk RR
Delmarva Baseball League 127
Denton and teams 31, 73, 139, 199
Deshong, Jimmie 137
Detroit Tigers 62
Detweiler, Ducky 194, 204–205
diffusion 7–10
Disharoon, Elisha 153

Donahue, Jiggs 111, 120
Donaldson, Rev. Thomas 107
Dorchester Democrat-News 11, 59
Dorchester Railroad 13
Douglas, Charles 28
Douglas, Frederick 12, 28
Dover 31, 56, 80, 98, 104, 106–108, 114–115, 119–121, 124–126
Dover Orioles 146, 148, 154, 156–157, 163, 168, 172
Drawbridge 37
Druids of Baltimore 23
Dunn, Jack 55, 70–71, 86, 99
Dunn, Mrs. Jack 164
Dunn, Jack, III 182, 186, *187*
Dykes, Jimmie 60, 193
Dyott, Squirrel 201, 204

Early, Dick 111–112
Eagles Park 188
East Texas League 187
Eastern Colored League 115, 128
Eastern Shore League 1904 66–67
Easton 13–14, 17, 19, 24, 28–31, 34, 39, 41, 47, 51, 53, 62–64, 66–67, 70, 73, 86, 88, 98–99, 138
Easton Athletic Association 158, 160
Easton Browns 145, 153, 155, 158–160
Easton Farmers 108–*110*, 115, 118, 120, 124
Easton Gazette 14, 42, 44, 53
Easton Star 29, 31
Easton Yankees 172, 174, 180, 191, 193, 199, 202, 204–205
Eddington, J.R. 164, 169, 171
Ehlers, Art 148, 154, 161–162, 164, 171, 192–193, 197–198, 202, 205–206
Ehmke, Howard 154
Ekaitis, George 172
Etchison, Buck 204–205
Evangeline League 191
Excelsior of Baltimore 15

Fair Play 15, 17–18
Farlow, Dave 26
Farmer, Jack 204
Farrell, Howard "Toots" 189
Farrell, J.H. 96–98, 100–102, 125, 134–135, 139
Federal Park, Easton 108, 118, 122, 132, 135, 139, 142, *149*, *156*, 158, *159*
Federalsburg 13, 33, 39–40–44, 46, 51, 58, 70, 98, 137, 140

Federalsburg Athletics 148, 162–163, 169, 171, 174, 180, 192, 194, 205, 194, 199, 204, 216
Ferber, Edna 95
Fields, Maurice 155
finances: Centreville Orioles 186–188; Federalsburg 137–138; funding 49–50, Landis at Easton 112–114; Peninsula League 82; Wonder Team 152–153; 18, 22–24, 33–34, 39, 41, 46–47, 52, 54–55, 57–58, 60, 62–63, 66–67, 85, 86–88, 97, 99, 105, 108, 118–119, 122–123, 125–127, 128–129, 148, 161, 165, 171–174, 180, 182, 184, 187, 191–193, 196, 201–204
Fishing Creek 85
Fitzberger, Freddie 111, 113, 132
Five State Series 84, 101–102, 106–107, 113–114, 121, 125, 127, 129
Florida State League 129, 151
Flowers, Jake 86, 132, 140, 147–148, 150, 153–154, 157, 162
Fong, Lee 72–73, 79–80
Foreman, Frank 62
Foreman, Johnnie 62, *63*
Forest City 57–58
Foster, Rube 80
Fowler, Joe 136–137, 169, 171
Foxx, Dell 64–65
Foxx, Jimmie 62, 64, *109–110*, 112–114, 131, 137, 146; signing 108–110;
Frederick 14, 87–88
Frock, Sam 60, 68–69, 100, 102–103, 105
Furillo, Carl 167–168

gambling 27–28, 30–31, 34, 40–41, 51, 95, 187, 191–192, 199, 203
Gans, Joe 209–210
Garton, Mom 200–201
Garvey, Marcus 80
George, John E. 64–65, *73*
Gettig, Charlie 60
Gibson, Josh 210–211
Gillis, Ned 33
Gordon, Sid 157
Gordy, S.E. 81, 102, 105
Gordy Park 83, 98, 102, 118, 146, 148, 150, 152–153, 167, 169, 171–173
Graham, Col. Samuel A. 31
Gratton, George 14, 18, 21–22
Green, Guy 69–70
Green, Jimmie 64, 81

Index

Greenville, NC 187
Grier, Dr. Walter 180
Griffith, Clark 145, 148, 150, 152–153, 163–164
Griffith, William Ridgely 9
Guerra, Fermin 149, 153, 155
Gunby, L.W. 104
Gunning, Art 174

Haddaway, Arthur 50, 54
Hafey, Chick 140
Hagerstown 14, 114, 122
Halstean, William 31–32
Hanover 46
Harper's Magazine 75
Harrisburg Senators 115
Harvey, Robert 189
Hawke, Dick 45, 212
Hayes, Frankie 137
Hayman, Charles "Bugs" 189
Henry, Daniel 158, 160
Hermann, Augustus 217–218
Hermanski, George 168–169
Herring, Fred 163, 172
Herzog, Buck 60–62, 67–*69*, 75, 79–80, 83, 119, 122, 124, 213
Heydler, John 113
High, Lefty 60, 63–64
Highland Light 19
Hilldale Baseball Club 115, 210
Hinkle, Les 163
History of Base Ball in Maryland, 1858–1871 9
Hoffman, Izzy 99
Honochick, John 182, 185
horse racing 34
Horsey, Hanson 84, 87, 111, 155, 167–168, 182–183, 198–199, 201, 213
Horton, Elmer 58
Huggins, Miller 109
Hughlett 57
Hurley, Officer 111
Hurlock and teams 13, 61, 66, 81, 86
Hutt, Billy 163

Interstate League 169, 171
Irons, Anita 210, 212
Irvin, Monte 169
Ivins, C.P. 182

Jablonski, Ray 202
Jackson, Alan 125–126
Jacobs, George "Doc" 148, 151, 154, 156, *159*, 161–163; see also Secret Deal
Jamison, J. Vincent 87, 89, 104
Jefferson, Laura 163
Jennings, Hughie 44

Johnson, Ban 101, 106, 119–120, 218
Johnson, Harry "Steamboat" 168
Johnson, Judy 74, 209–212
Johnson, William 74, 209

Kansas City Monarchs 210
Keeler, Wee Willie 44
Keen, Vic 86, 148
Kelchner, Pop 192
Kellogg, Bill 67–68
Kibler, J. Thomas 85, 146–147, 150, 153, 173, 180–*181*, 184–186, 191–193, 195–199
Kilduff, Pete and All-Stars 80
King, Garfield 73
Knopp, Japheth 29
Knotts, Dr. W.K. 169, 180, 196, 202, 206
Kohlman, Joe 149, 151–153
Koste, Nick 163
Ku Klux Klan 95, 114

Lajoie, Napoleon 77
Lambert, Pop 194
Landgraf, Ernest "Duke" 148, 158, *159*, 160
Landis, Kenesaw Mountain 95–96, 100, 102–106, 107–108, 112, 121, 126, 132, 135–136, 150, 158, 160, 163, 165, 166
Lattimore, "Virginia Wizard" 58
Laurel, Delaware 50, 89
Laurel Blue Hens 98, 100, 103, 106, 114, 118
Lewis, Adeline 73
Levin, Reubin 169, 171–172, 174
Literary Digest 75, 77
Lloyd, John Henry "Pop" 210–211
Loos, Pete 60, 213
Lord Baltimores 27
Louisville Four 28
Lucas, Fred 148, 151, 161, 171, 180–*181*, 194, 186–197, 203–206
Luque, Dolph 128
Lush, Billie 129
Lynn, Jerry 149, 151

Mace, Dr. 55–56
Mace, W. Irving 55
Mack, Connie 61, 70, 81–83, 99, 109–110, 132, 140–141, 153, 163, 180, 193, 211
Mackey, Biz 169
Maddox, Nick 60, 66–67
Malfara, Nick 185
Malzone, Frank 202

Marcell, Oliver "Ghost" 211
MarDel League 171
Maguire, Ed 24
Martinsburg 102, 106, 114
Maryland Agricultural College *see* University of Maryland
Maryland Club of Towsontowne 37
Maryland Commission 87
Maryland Intercollegiate Athletic Association 44, 212
Maryland State Championship 86–89
Mathison, Jimmie 55, 60, 64
Matthews, C. Starr 67–68, 75, 78
Matthews, Robert 112
Maxa, Don 202
McGann, Dan 58, 64
McLaughlin, Jim 132
McGowan, George 84, 182, 198
McGowan Umpiring School 198
McGraw, John 44, 119
McMahon, Sadie 60
McPhail, Larry 160–161, 167
McQuillan, Cal 204
Migratory Bird Act 134
Milford 84
Milford Giants 104–105
Milford Red Sox 153, 157, 168, 172–174, 180, 185–186, 199, 202
Miller, Stu 204
Miller, Walter 98, 100, 105, 124–125, 127
Millington 46, 57–58, 182, 188, 216
Minor leagues 96–98, 135–136
Modern Baseball Strategy 132
Montero, Juan 149, 151–152, 155
Mount Saint Mary's College 45
Muffers 20, 38–39, 40–41, 49
Murrell, Paul 201
Murtaugh, Danny 150, 156–157

Nakomas 69
National Association 30, 36
National Association of Professional Baseball Leagues 95–97, 125, 129, 145
National Commission 217–218
National League 28, 30, 36, 55, 96
Nebraska Indians 69–70, 79

Ned Hanlon Trophy (cup) 106–107, 122
Negro National League 115
Nelson, Maud 71–72
Neville, Dr. John 22
New England League 68
New Windsor College 45
New York Black Yankees 169–170, 172
New York Eagles 169–170
New York Game 8–9, 14, 16, 20, 77
New York Giants 61
New York Knickerbockers 7, 15
New York-Norfolk RR 13, 19
New York State League 84
New York Yankees 161, 169, 180, 205
Newark Eagles 169
Nichols, Ed 173, 179, 181–184, 191, 199–201, 206
Nichols, Simon 62, 67–68, 213
Nicholson, Bill "Swish" 146
night games 148–149, 157
Norfolk 47
Northampton 126, 129
Northern League 169
Northwest League 96, 132
Nugent, Gerald 148

Oakley, Annie 71
Oaksville 139, 188
Ocean City 31, 33, 48, 55, 67, 166, 214
O'Connelley 168
Ogden, John 145–147
Oliphant, Harry 206
Olsen, John B. 72
Onancock 97
O'Rourke, Joe 148, 155
O'Rourke, Patsy 148, 155
Oval Blues 116
Oxford 35, 42–43, 73, 98
oyster wars 35, 95
Ozenies 15

Pacific Coast League 146
Paige, Satchel 169, 211
Parks, C.T. 40
Parksley Spuds 98, 102, 104, 107, 111, 114, 119–121, 124, 127, 129, 132, 187
Parnell, Mel 173
Pasquella, Dan 127–128, 203
Pastor Fox *see* blue laws
Peninsula League 61, 80–84, 101, 214
Pennock, Herb 169
Pennsylvania RR 46, 220
Perkins, George 58
Perry, Bill 151

Perry, Slim 133
Philadelphia Athletics 17, 61–62, 67, 108, 161
Philadelphia Giants 169, 189
Philadelphia Nationals 46, 50, 212
Philadelphia Stars 169
Phillips, Col. Albanus 136–137
Phillips Packing 136, 189
Piedmont League 171
Pittsburg Courier 210
Pittsburg Pirates 66, 192
player sources 60–62
Playground Association 76
Playground Movement 76
Pocomoke City 11, 66–68, 87, 89, 98, 100, 104–106, 127, 146, 187, 191–193, 213
Pocomoke Red Sox/Chicks 148, 151, 153–154, 156, 161, 164, 166, 168–169, 171–172
Polhemus, Henry B. 8–9
Police Gazette 75
Pondtown 117, 188
Pony League 172
population 11, 13, 31, 32, 35, 41, 47–48, 79, 89, 94, 97
Porter, Dickie 61, 70, 86–87, 136–137, 145, 191
Posey, Cum 210
Powers, Patrick 96
Princess Anne 11, 64, 67, 70, 74, 86–89, 139, 188
Printers Athletic Club 20
Pritchett, Wilbert 115, 190
Progressive Movement 75–78
Pulliam, Henry 218

Queen Anne-Kent RR 13
Queen Anne Sports Authority 161
Queenstown Club 30
Quill, Mike 194, 196

radio 108, 129, 154, 172, 201, 203
Raffensberger, Ken 151
railroads *see* steam transportation
Reach, Al 14
Reed, Jack 74
Rehoboth 192, 196, 202, 204–206
Rensa, Tony 128, 131–132
Rew, J. Harry 107, 110–111, 119–121, 125–126, 147
Rickey, Branch 98, 132, 140, 146, 148, 160, 171–172, 174, 180, 194, 197, 203, 205
Rickey, H. 15
Ridgely 62, 66–68, 119, 160–161, 166

Riess, Steven 77–78; *see also* Progressive Movement
Ring Tail Rovers 40
Ripkin, Bill 194
Rising Sun 27
Roettger, Harold 202
Rommell, Eddie 60, 83
Rooney, Art 61
Ruffing, Red 108, 131, 146
rule and equipment changes 19, 25–26, 38
Rullo, Joe 163
Rupert, Jacob 136
Russell, Harry 153, 155–158, 160, 162–163, 167, 171–172, 174

St. John's of Annapolis 45, 112
St. Louis Browns 158, 191
St. Louis Cardinals 98, 140, 194
St. Michaels 18, 23, 30, 38, 47, 66, 82, 87, 116, 137–138, 170, 189
St. Michaels Comet 30
Salazar, Joe 149, 155
Salisbury 13, 15, 23, 28, 31, 33, 37, 47, 50, 54–56, 62–64, 66–67, 73, 78, 86–89; *see also* White Cloud
Salisbury Advertiser 33
Salisbury Award 215
Salisbury Business League 80
Salisbury Cardinals 179, 185, 187, 192, 195, 199, 202–203, 205, 206
Salisbury Indians: first class D league 97–99, 105, 107, 111–112, 115, 118–122, 124, 127–129; second class D league 146, 149, 151–152, 154–155, 162–163, 168, 171, 174
Salisbury Ministerial Society 154, 161; *see also* blue laws
Salisbury Times 93, 131, 169, 173
Salisbury v. Cambridge 51–53
San 128
Scribner's Magazine 75
Scull, Bill 196
Seabold, Socks 201
Seaford 25, 33, 84, 192, 195–196, 199, 201
Secret Deal 158–160; *see also* Jacobs, George
Selkirk, George 131–132
Sexton, Michael 96, 98, 101–102, 106, 125, 132, 134–135, 139
Sheehan, Tom 202
Shepherd, Dr. J.H. 38
Shockley, Betty 199
Shuttles, Mule 169

Index

Smith, Samuel S. 105
Smoot, Homer 45, *46*, 118, 120
Snow Hill 67, 86, 89, 209
Southern League 101
Spalding, Al 9, 14
Sparrow, C.E. 87, 101, 122, 127, 132, 214
Sporting Life 75, 217–219
Sporting News 75, 77, 93, 99, 102, 104, 106, 108, 119, 128, 131, 187, 193
Stanley, John "Neck" 190
Starlight of Baltimore 55–56
steam transportation 13–15, 19, 23, 31, 34
steamboats *see* steam transportation
Stricker All Stars 49, 80
Sudlersville 38, 40, 58, 73, 109; *see also* George, John E.
Sutton, A.N. 17
Syracuse Club 14
Syracuse University 46, 213

Tabler, Dan 187
Taylor, John 217–218
Taylor, Leon 137, 139
Taylor's Island 20, 37–38, 40
Terry, Bill 153
Texas Colored League 115
Texas League 101
Thayer, Alfred 53
Thompson, M.L. 76
Thompson, Tim 194
Toadvine, E. Stanley 37, 105
Todd, H.S. 105
Tolchester 33, 46–47
Tournier, Leo 192
Townsend, Jack "The Whirlwind" 44, 46, 57, 216
Trappe 17, 18, 23, 31, 42, 113
Trautman, George 191, 195, 198, 203
Treschock, Frank 151, 153
Tri County League 139, 170
Tripartite League 62–63

Tri State League 111, 218
Truitt, C. 131
Turner, J.F. 17
Twining, Doc 81, 84

umpires: incidents 39–40, 50, 52, 58, 66, 84, 100, 107, 113, 120, 125, 128, 148, 150, 155, 157, 167, 168, 182–183, 198, 184, 185, 187, 192; 195–196, 199, 201; uprising 121; *see also* violence
Underground Railroad 12
Unglaub, Bob 44, 46, 61, 215–221
Unique of Chicago 28
University of Maryland 45, 62, 67, 213, 215–216
University of Pennsylvania 46, 50
Usilton, F.G. 56

Valo, Elmer 163, 174
Van Cuyk, Chris 194, 196
Vernon, Mickey 151, 154, 168
Villanova University 46, 154, 158, 213
violence 26–28, 40, 42–43, 100, 111, 120, 184, 195, 196, 199; *see also* umpires
Vereker, Tommy 111, 113
Vogel, Marty 201
Volstead Act 94
Voshell House 56

Waldt, Dick 182
Walker, Fleet 53
Walker, Weldy 53
Wallace, Doc 86
Wallaesa, Jack 163
Waller, R. Felton 87
Wallop, L.D. 87
Walls, Captain Jim 205
Wamsley, Chuck 180
War Memorial Park 186, 188, 193
Washington, Booker T. 80
Washington College 18, 23, 44–45, 54–55, 57, 68, 76, 85, 146–147, 197, 212, 216; professionals 46–50
Washington Nationals 9
Weiss, George 161, 205
Werber, Billie 137
Werner, Jack 196
Western Association 168
Western Bloomer Girls 72
Western Maryland College 45
Western Maryland Railroad 46
Westfall, Bob 194–195, 204–205
Wethered, Dr. John L. 76
Whalen, Poke 99, 108–109, 114, 120, 129, 131, 145, 148, 153, 168, 185
White Cloud *16*, 24, 26, 33, 37, 49, 50–51, 56, 99, 105, 131, 148; Quicksteps 30–31
White Haven 85
White Sol 53, 75
Wicks, Elmer 190
Wicks, M. 115
Williams, Dot 199
Wilmington Blue Rocks 171
Wilmington Quicksteps 30–31
Wilson, Jud 169, 211
Windsor, Minnie 199
Wissahicons *see* Washington College
Women's New York All-Stars 49
Woodberry Mills 9
Worrell Field 115
Wrightson, Mayor 156, 158

Yannigans, Baltimore 58, 60
youth baseball 20–21, 75

Zaharczyk, Ted 201
Zauchin, Norm 202
Zearfoss, Dave 45–*47*, 50, 54, 212–213
Zimmer, Don 204

www.ingramcontent.com/pod-product-compliance
Lightning Source LLC
Chambersburg PA
CBHW060339010526
44117CB00017B/2888